The Emerging Church, Millennials, and Religion

The Emerging Church, Millennials, and Religion

Volume 1: Prospects and Problems

Edited by

RANDALL REED
and
G. MICHAEL ZBARASCHUK

CASCADE *Books* · Eugene, Oregon

THE EMERGING CHURCH, MILLENNIALS AND RELIGION
Volume 1: Prospects and Problems

Copyright © 2018 Wipf and Stock Publishers. All rights reserved. Except for brief quotations in critical publications or reviews, no part of this book may be reproduced in any manner without prior written permission from the publisher. Write: Permissions, Wipf and Stock Publishers, 199 W. 8th Ave., Suite 3, Eugene, OR 97401.

Cascade Books
An Imprint of Wipf and Stock Publishers
199 W. 8th Ave., Suite 3
Eugene, OR 97401

www.wipfandstock.com

PAPERBACK ISBN: 978-1-5326-1762-1
HARDCOVER ISBN: 978-1-4982-4244-8
EBOOK ISBN: 978-1-4982-4243-1

Cataloging-in-Publication data:

Names: Reed, Randall W., editor. | Zbaraschuk, G. Michael, editor.

Title: The emerging church, millennials, and religion, vol. 1, prospects and problems / edited by Randall Reed and G. Michael Zbaraschuk.

Description: Eugene, OR: Cascade Books, 2018. | Includes bibliographical references.

Identifiers: ISBN: 978-1-5326-1762-1 (paperback). | ISBN: 978-1-4982-4244-8 (hardcover). | ISBN: 978-1-4982-4243-1 (ebook).

Subjects: LCSH: Emerging church movement. | Christianity—21st century. | Church renewal—21st century.

Classification: BR121.3 E55 2018 (print). | BR121.3 (epub).

Manufactured in the U.S.A.	10/23/18

For Laura, whose brilliance, wit, and patience
made this work possible;

and

For Lisa, who helps so many to become themselves,
and for Ana and Elizabeth, who are continuously emerging.

"The unripe grape, the ripe bunch, the dried grape, are all changes, not into nothing, but into something which exists not yet."

—Marcus Aurelius, *Meditations*

Contents

List of Contributors | ix
Introduction | xi
    Randall Reed and G. Michael Zbaraschuk

Part 1: Millennials and the Emerging Church —Surveying the Landscape

1 Certain of the Uncertain: Millennials, the Search for Truth in a Technological Age, and the Emerging Church | 3
    Shenandoah Nieuwsma

2 The Southern Strategy | 15
    Randall Reed

3 Playing Offense or Defense? The Theological Playbook of the Emergent/ing Church, with Some Armchair Quarterbacking | 31
    Michael Zbaraschuk

Part 2: What Is the Emerging Church? —Definitions and Constructions

4 A Generous Heterodoxy: Emergent Village and the Emerging Milieu | 45
    Adam Sweatman

5 Deconstructing Westphalia: The Emerging Church, Citizen Pilgrims, and Globalization | 66
    Terry Shoemaker

6 From Monks to Punks: Emerging Christianity in Canada | 84
    Steve Studebaker and Lee Beach

7 Emergent Church as Experimental Program:
   Embodied Hypotheses in Cognition and Value | 108
   BRANDON DANIEL-HUGHES

Part 3: The Emerging Church and Millennials —Challenges and Opportunities

8 Losing My Religion:
   Why Millennials Are Leaving the Church | 141
   STEPHANIE YUHAS

9 The Problem of Anti-Institutionalism in Millennials | 166
   RANDALL REED

10 A Church for the De-Churched and Un-Churched:
   Sunday Assembly as a Response to and Space for the "Nones" | 188
   JOEL D. DANIELS

11 Race and the Emerging Church:
   A View from South Africa | 212
   RACHEL SCHNEIDER

12 Emerging out of Patriarchy?
   The Emerging Church Movement from a Feminist Practical
   Theological Perspective | 236
   XOCHITL ALVIZO AND GERARDO MARTÍ

Afterword: A New Generation, A New Church? | 261
   PHILIP CLAYTON

Index | 271

Contributors

Shenandoah Nieuwsma is an independent scholar from Durham, North Carolina.

Randall Reed is Professor of Religion at Appalachian State University in Boone, North Carolina.

G. Michael Zbaraschuk is Associate Professor of Religion at Pacific Lutheran University in Tacoma, Washington.

Adam Sweatman is an Instructor at Florida State University in Tallahassee, Florida.

Terry Shoemaker is an Lecturer at Arizona State University in Tempe, Arizona.

Steven M. Studebaker is Associate Professor of Systematic and Historical Theology and the Howard and Shirley Bentall Chair in Evangelical Thought at McMaster Divinity College in Hamilton, Ontario, Canada.

Lee Beach is Associate Professor of Christian Ministry and the Garbutt F. Smith Chair of Ministry Formation at McMaster Divinity College in Hamilton, Ontario, Canada.

Brandon Daniel-Hughes is an Instructor at John Abbott College, in Sainte-Anne-de-Bellevue, Quebec, Canada.

Stephanie Yuhas is an Instructor at Naropa University, in Boulder, Colorado and a Lecturer at University of Colorado, Denver.

Joel D. Daniels is a doctoral candidate and a resident chaplain at Georgetown University in Washington, DC.

Rachel C. Schneider is a Visiting Research Associate in the Religion and Public Life Program at Rice University in Houston, Texas.

Xochitl Alvizo is Assistant Professor of Religious Studies and Philosophy at California State University, Northridge, in Northridge, California.

Gerardo Martí is the L. Richardson King Professor of Sociology and the Chair of the Department of Sociology at Davidson College in Davidson, North Carolina.

Philip Clayton is the Ingraham Professor of Theology at the Claremont School of Theology in Claremont, California.

Introduction

RANDALL REED AND G. MICHAEL ZBARASCHUK

HISTORY OF THE RESEARCH SEMINAR

In 2012 the Emerging Church was a movement that had recently entered the popular collective consciousness. Since its origins as a web community in the early 2000s it had developed a bibliography of work from different authors that were also wrestling with a similar set of questions. These questions focused on a rethinking of the philosophical, doctrinal, theological and liturgical basis of modern Christianity. There were, around the country, a number of churches that were experimenting with some of these ideas and practices. It felt as though this movement might be poised to represent a significant change in Anglophone Christianity.

There had been some academic work on this movement. Sociologists of Religion like James S. Beilo, Josh Packard and James Wellman had written on the movement. Theologians like John D. Caputo and N.T. Wright were working on engaging similar issues and were feeding the movement itself. But the work that had been done was largely isolated in sub-disciplines in Religious Studies. What was lacking was a larger interdisciplinary examination of the topic that would put sociologists, historians, theologians, philosophers and anthropologists of religion all in dialogue about the Emerging Church.

Concomitantly, there was another trend in religion particularly in the U.S. that was making headlines. In 2012, the Pew Research Forum published their study "Nones on the Rise." Pew suggested that for the first time in contemporary America there was an unmistakable trend towards individuals disclaiming a religious identification. Likewise, church affiliation in Catholic, Protestant Mainline, and Evangelical denominations was seeing decline. The Pew study noted that this trend was particularly pronounced among the generation known as the "millennials."

It became clear then to a group of scholars at the AAR that the time was ripe to consider these two phenomena together. The Emerging Church and the change in Millennial religiosity both spoke of a potential sea-change in Christian religion in the U.S. The group saw the moment as being particularly momentous, as a moment to track and understand religious change as it was happening from the perspective of scholars with a multiplicity of areas of study. The steering committee that was formed was diverse not just in terms of area of studies but in terms of rank, gender and ethnicity.

In 2014, then, an initial meeting sponsored by Critical Research on Religion was held at the American Academy of Religion (AAR) Annual meeting in San Diego. The focus of the first meeting was to measure the level of interest the academy had for the topic. The session was titled, "Is the Emergent/ing Church Important?" and had a panel of 5 of the steering committee members addressing the question from the perspective of sociology, race and gender theory, theological trends, and American religious history. The room was full, the papers insightful and the discussion interesting. The steering committee became convinced that there was sufficient interest to continue our discussions with the academy. The papers from this session have been expanded and included in this volume.

The AAR accepted our proposal to become a research seminar, and the next year (2015) the group sent out a call for the topic "What Is the Emerging Church? Definitions and Constructions." The call came out of our discussion of the previous year. The question was raised, what was the Emerging Church? Could we find a way of defining our object of study? As a research seminar we were focused on significant explorations, we wanted our participants to engage in thoughtful and sustained work. To that end the papers for the session were distributed in advanced, and presenters gave short 5 minute summaries of their papers, with the bulk of the session committed to the respondents and then discussion.

This approach proved advantageous, and the quality of discussion was high. Attendance was also high, with more than 50 people crowding into a conference room designed for far fewer. The papers addressed the topic from the kind of breadth of perspective that the seminar was committed to, with sociologists, historians of American religion, and cognitive science analysis all in the mix.

For 2016 the steering committee determined that we needed now to shift focus to include the religious proclivities of Millennials more explicitly. We divided the session into two segments, the first focusing of "Millennials, Nones, and Religious Responses." The second focused on "Race and

Gender and the Emerging Church." The two sessions dovetailed quite nicely in that they each focused on the problems with which the "church," even the Emerging Church, was struggling.

After 2016 we had reached a half-way point. The five year course of the research seminar was two years in, and with the initial session we had done with CRR we had three years of papers. We decided that the time had come to make the work of the seminar available to the larger scholarly audience. Adhering to a double review process, members of the steering committee peer-reviewed the papers. Accepted papers were then revised as appropriate and the result is this volume.

ISSUES OF THE SEMINAR

Sociological Issues

It may at some level not be immediately clear why the combination of Millennials and the Emerging Church is a good fit. After all many of the most well-known Emerging Church representatives are from the Boomer generation (Brian McLaren, Doug Padgit) or Generation X (Rob Bell, Mark Driscoll, Nadia Bolz-Weber, Peter Rollins). In fact of the most prominent Emerging Church leaders, not a single Millennial comes to mind.

This however belies the fact that there are strong connections between the religious responses of the Millennial generation and the Emerging Church. The Emerging Church has a strong critique of the traditional church, particularly the Evangelical tradition. The conventional focus particularly in the Evangelical tradition on a strong set of behavioral practices coupled with a clearly defined and required adherence to a set of doctrinal affirmations has been a point of critique used by Emerging Church advocates. Likewise, millennials as well seem to be turned off by this combination. The work of David Kinnaman and Gabe Lyons showed early on that Millennials thought the church was "homophobic," "too judgmental," and "too political." The Public Research on Religion Institutes studies on Nones (who are disproportionately millennial) likewise indicated that rejection of both traditional beliefs and recoiling at the treatment and attitude of the church toward LGBTQ+ people were motivation for a large number of nones.

On the other hand, the Emerging Church often seems to fit Millennial values. The National Youth Study of Religion conducted by Christian Smith showed a Millennial focus on the value of tolerance. While Smith has been critical that such an approach has led to a lack of "moral reasoning," he commends the social impact of greater diversity and acceptance. Likewise Jean Twenge and Strauss and Howe have all focused on the issue of tolerance as a premiere value for Millennials. To this end, the same values can be found in the Emerging Church, as Nadia Bolz-Weber makes clear as she talks about the homosexual and transexual members of her church, or as Jay Bakker makes clear in his passionate defense of Gay Marriage in his book "Fall to Grace" or Rob Bell's YouTube video in which he equates "god before us" with an advocacy for gay marriage. Thus, there seems to be a congruence between the position of the Emerging Church and the values of Millennials on this area of tolerance particularly related to LGBTQ+ issues.

But it is not just on issues of gender and sexuality where the Emerging Church and Millennials coincide. Shane Claiborne and the Red Letter Christian movement has sought to prioritize the poor and focus on serving the needy. Political polls of Millennials show they likewise tend towards the left side of the spectrum and a greater number of them than previous generations have engaged in types of volunteerism and community service. Thus the more liberal political take of the Emerging Church certainly would seem to promise a connection with the Bernie Sanders-loving Millennials.

Likewise, as Gerardo Martí and Gladys Ganiel point out in their work the Emerging Church can be characterized by a disposition toward dialog. This seems to be similar to what we see among Millennials. As Michael Hout notes in an interview, Millennials have a more "'do-it-yourself' attitude toward religion." Such a perspective coincides with the Emerging Church perspective where participants are encourage to be actively involved in the worship service.

Thus from these examples we might suspect that Millennials would be good candidates as participants in the Emerging Church movement. And certainly, our research seminar saw exactly these parallels as we included Millennials as part of our primary topic of research. Several articles in this volume draw this connection in a variety of ways and while a final conclusion has not yet been reached, the exploration of these connections seemed necessary to our understanding of the wider religious change we suspected we were seeing.

But aside from its possible connection with Millennial values, the Emerging Church itself brought a series of issues out that the seminar and this volume seek to address. Obviously the first issue has been one of definition — what is the Emerging Church? Can we give definitional specificity? Several attempts were made at doing this from sociological, historical and theological/philosophical perspectives. While the details will be elucidated in the texts below, what has become clear is two-fold: first, there seems to be a reactive element to much of the Emerging Church movement; what it is, is more about what it isn't. It isn't judgmental, it isn't right-wing, it isn't hung up on atonement, it isn't literalist when it reads the Bible, etc. Second, and largely because of this, the Emerging Church movement is complicated and fluid. Different permutations of the Emerging Church take on a different hues and different perspectives. Martí and Ganiel likewise identify this same problem in their work and settle on the notion of a common "disposition" rather than definition.

Equally important, however, are the kinds of liturgical and theological experimentation of the Emerging Church. While the theological issues will be dealt with at length later in this introduction, one of the advantages of this collection is the detailing of a variety of different Emerging Church experiments ranging over a variety of countries and regions and engaging different types of innovations in terms of communities, worship services and organizations.

What the essays in this volume lead us to is an appreciation of the dynamics, sometimes haphazard, of religious change. The intuition of the steering committee has certainly been right on this point, this is a time of religious change. Emerging Church chronicler Phyllis Tickle and sociologists Strauss and Howe have both characterized this in structural ways. Tickle argued there is a historical pattern of a "great intellectual rummage sale" every 500 years which was taking place now 500 years after the Protestant Reformation, Strauss and Howe argued that there was a generational shift that could be mapped with the advent of the Millennials. In each of these analyses, however, there is a kind of teleological inevitability. Such analyses have yet to be firmly established, and certainly will not be conclusively confirmed by the essays in this volume. But what these explanatory schemas point to, and what this volume does do, is chronicle the moves towards change seen in both the Emerging Church Movement and the Millennial generation. Whether such structural explanations of change will bear out or not, what these analyses and the essays in this volume do is call for a deeper discussion and analysis of what constitutes religious change sociologically, historically, psychologically and theologically, and begin to prompt us towards constructing a theory of religious change. For this endeavor we will begin to build a foundation here, and hope to address this issue more fully in a subsequent volume.

Theological and Philosophical Issues

In terms of the issues relating to the philosophical and theological issues arising from our reflection on the Emerging Church, Millennials, and religion, there are, broadly speaking, two themes that our discussion and the seminar worked with. The first of these is the larger question of postmodernity and the question of an overall stance in terms of how to relate to a coming postmodern Christianity (and perhaps the post-Christianity toward which many Millennials seem to be headed). The second is how this more postmodern sensibility affects how the Emerging Church does or doesn't construct (or, in some cases, deconstruct) specific doctrines and practices.

As pointed out by many observers and participants (Martí and Ganiel, McLaren, Rollins, Jones, to name only a few), the Emerging Church has spent a lot of time self-consciously wrestling with the question of postmodernity. Sweatman's article in this volume notes that even as early as the Emergent Village's first meetings, the participants there were talking about how there was a philosophical and cultural shift that they came to name postmodern. In one sense, much of the theological work that is taking place within the Emerging Church can be conceived as confronting the postmodern in a variety of ways. Much of the intersection between the sociological and philosophical/theological reflection in our seminar has centered around the issue of if Millennials and the postmodern sensibility of the EC are a good fit, and if Millennials themselves will see that fit in their various contexts in the USA.

The second theme, that of constructing and/or deconstructing various doctrines and practices within the more and more Millennial context of the Emerging Church, is, again, one that is well documented in the literature. Much of the Emergent Church literature is a series of dialogues with the tradition, pointing out that a more static, orthodox, traditional (however one might define the tradition) vision is not the only way to conceive of the church, of the Bible, of leadership, of the Eucharist, etc. Two themes dominate much of the discussion in this field. The first of these, perhaps reflecting the evangelical and mainline Protestant roots of many Emerging Church participants, is the question of the Bible—its status, use, and interpretation. Hermeneutics dominates a tremendous amount of Emerging Church time and energy. Many other questions, such as gender roles, or sexuality, or economic justice, get discussed in and through interpretive Biblical treatments. The second theme, perhaps fittingly, is the question of ecclesiology. In addition to more formal treatments like Jones' *The Church is Flat*, much of the experimental, lived theological experimentation that is taking place like the missional communities detailed by Studebaker and McMaster's and Schneider's articles in this volume, with their conscious attention to questions of economic and racial justice, is trying to theologically articulate and live out what the idea of the church for Millennials in their postmodern world might look like. This may be what is emerging from the Millennial generation.

In addition to addressing the questions of postmodernity and what hermeneutics and ecclesiology might look like in an Emergent and Millennial world, there are several theological and philosophical issues that we have touched on in the course of the seminar that beg for more extensive treatment. The first of these is hinted at in the sociological questions—that is, what sense will an Emergent Church make for Millennials who are less and less educated within church institutions and inclined to formal religiosity? This is formally different from the question of atheism or secularity (such questions are, in many senses, dependent on their "other" of theism or religiosity). Several of our contributors discuss the question of the relation of the Emergent Church and what it is emerging *from* (Sweatman, Daniel-Hughes, Zbaraschuk). Largely, it is emerging from evangelical and mainline Protestantism. When those are less culturally prevalent, what might Millennial religiosity be? Daniels' article on the Sunday Assembly starts this discussion, but it could be extended.

Another issue that could use more discussion is the formal question of what sort of postmodernity could best serve or explain the Emerging Church. In my (Michael Zbaraschuk's) judgment, there have been two main uses of postmodern thought in the Emergent Church—it has either served as a loosening of the hyperrational strictures of (mostly evangelical) interpretation and practice, while still allowing folks to keep a mostly evangelical form of worship and structure; or it has been a sort of Caputo-Rollins-influenced form of deconstruction. We have started this conversation, as Alvizo's and Schneider's constributions indicate. Bringing the full range of postmodern discourse into conversation with Millennials and the Emergent Church should continue.

And, finally, it seems that there should be a more extensive and focused discussion of Millennials and the question of the Christian tradition, largely conceived. Both Yuhas and Reed point to anti-institutionalism and individualism as a factor in Millennial attrition from Christian churches, but Daniels points to the Sunday Assembly as evidence that Millennial "Nones" don't necessarily mind the structure. The kind of pastiche of a deconstructive practice does seem to depend upon a more formal tradition for material. Daniel-Hughes has started this discussion with his hypothesis that Millennials move between the Emerging Church and a more traditional church in order to increase intensity. What parts of the tradition do Millennials use? What about the Emergent Church? How are they related? We hope to these and perhaps other issues further in future seminars and volumes.

CONTENTS AND STRUCTURE OF THE VOLUME

The essays in this volume are largely organized around the order of the themes of the seminar, with some movement in order to place an essay with others that deal with similar topics. The first section surveys the landscape of the where Millennials and the Emerging Church come together. Shenandoah Nieuwsma draws on her own experience, both teaching Millennials in the classroom setting and encountering them in a self-styled Emerging Church, to explore what Millennial values like a search for authenticity and meaning look like in one particular setting. Randall Reed draws on his own sociological research at Emergent Church-oriented festivals to show that Millennials, especially in the American South, have some affinity with views that are also held by Emerging Church mileaux. He finds that their distrust of institutions and their orientation to the Bible probably signal some mixed prospects for those hoping for a perfect fit between the two groups. Michael Zbaraschuk outlines some of the theological currents at work (and play) in three theologians of the emergent church—Rob Bell, Tony Jones, and Peter Rollins. He locates them in their larger theological contexts, and finds a surprising depth of engagement in their work.

The second section works towards some preliminary definitions, from a variety of disciplinary perspectives, of the Emerging Church. Adam Sweatman constructs a historical outline of what he calls the milieu of the Emerging Church, providing valuable context and background to those who self-consciously identify as Emerging. Terry Shoemaker uses Richard Falk's concept of a "citizen pilgrim" as a way to read Emerging Church beliefs and practices in a context of globalization. He sees the Emerging Church's suspicion of exploitative economic practices as aligning with larger critiques of globalization and the question of living an ethical life in the increasingly connected world. Steven Studebaker and Lee Beach move us into Canada to consider some Emerging Church ecclesiological and theological experiments that are taking place in urban, secularizing contexts. They maintain that Emerging Church missional churches in the Canadian urban context are incarnational, contextual, and holistic, in contrast to the suburban prosperous churches from which many of those attempting these experiments come. And, finally, Brandon Daniel-Hughes assesses the Emerging Church from the perspective of the cognitive study of religion. He offers a philosophical analysis of some of the religious dynamics of the Emerging Church, and maintains that it can have both parasitic and symbiotic relationships with the larger, more traditional churches out of which it is emerging.

And, finally, the third part of the book moves into the challenges and opportunities for the future of the relationship between the Emerging Church and Millennials (and maybe for this seminar as well!). Stephanie Yuhas points to a possible problem in relating the Emerging Church and Millennials—the fact that Millennials are leaving organized Christianity in far greater numbers than they are joining it. She outlines some of the factors in Millennial life that might be leading them to leave churches in general. Randall Reed, in his second article in the volume, tackles the question of Millennials' anti-institutionalism. He surveys the extant sociological work on the subject, and brings it into conversation with his own research with Millennials, both Emergent and non-Emergent, in the American South. He notes that there may be some opportunities for the Emergent Church to recruit from Millennials, in that they share some anti-institutional views, but that their general lack of interest in institutions may also curb some of the knowledge and animus that the Emergent Church uses. Joel Daniels takes us directly into the question of the religiosity of the Millennial "Nones" in his article on the Sunday Assembly. He concludes that it may not be the form (Sunday morning meetings) that Millennials object to, but the content (theism, dogma, division). He also notes some of the theological consonances that the Sunday Assembly has with the liberal theological tradition of Schleiermacher, Rahner, and Tillich. Rachel C. Schneider moves the discussion on the Emerging Church to the South African context, drawing on her own research as she addresses questions of race and socioeconomic privilege in missional churches in South African townships. She pays attention to how the Emerging Church figures and projects both affirm and challenge some of the racist structures of South African Christianity, and examines the effects on the members of these communities. And, finally, Xochitl Alvizo and Gerardo Martí address the question of patriarchy and its incarnation in the Emerging Church from the perspective of practical feminist theology. They note a tension between the egalitarianism of the Emerging Church's rhetoric and its practices of being mostly led and commented upon by white men. They conclude that more self-consciously feminist work needs to be done in the Emerging Church if it is to become post-patriarchal.

Part 1

Millennials and the Emerging Church
Surveying the Landscape

1

Certain of the Uncertain

Reflections on Millennial Epistemology and the Emerging Church

SHENANDOAH NIEUWSMA

Abstract

This chapter considers the ways in which the Emerging Church may or may not have special currency among hard-won Millennials, ever-reluctant religionists. Included in this investigation is a reflection on Millennial cultural and technological trends, but perhaps more importantly, an observation of how epistemologies among Millennials might be shifting. This paper ponders how such epistemological shifting (which I have delineated as "hyper-subjective") has affected Millennial perceptions of religion and more specifically, how this particular shift might work to make the Emerging Church tradition uniquely attractive to Millennials. The practices and beliefs of an Emerging Church called Emmaus Way, located in downtown Durham, North Carolina, serve as a case study for these considerations. This paper briefly examines on the one hand how this church's attention to the arts, its focus on visceral experience and its practice of the French Situationist technique détournement jive with Millennial practices of hyper-subjectivity, making an argument for the Emerging Church's relevance and potential draw to the younger generation. I also make the case that on the other hand, if the Emerging Church's philosophic underpinnings are reactionary and deconstructive, these might actually be at odds with Millennial thought, many of whom are growing up without a religious tradition with which to react. This point would make the Emerging Church's appeal to Millennials not so clear-cut. Whatever the case, this paper demonstrates that the Emerging Church is worthy of more study particularly because of the unique ways that it engages with postmodern thought and practices, potentially providing unreligious Millennials rare access to a religious tradition.

INTRODUCTION

"What do I stand for? What do I stand for? Most nights, I don't know. . .anymore." Some may recognize this popular song called "Some Nights," belted out by Nate Ruess, the lead singer of the indie pop band Fun.[1] This song could be considered the battle cry of the Millennials: it issues a defiant declaration of uncertainty with nary a warning or apology. It would be wrong to read this as the product of someone who is lost, however. Instead, the song with its electrifying beat offers young people a triumphant strategy for discovering authenticity in a world made increasingly complex and diversified by the iPhone microcosms at our fingertips. Who am I? What do I stand for? Perhaps for many Millennials, the self's existential depths are plumbed not by proclaiming the old creeds but in getting comfortable with feeling uncertain about the answers to life's big questions. If one thing is for certain, it is that things are uncertain.

But "Some Nights" doesn't just leave the world meaningless or vapid. It attempts to recover significance through the visceral experience of synthetic explosions. The insistence that truth might be more likely found in instinctual aesthetic experiences than in intellectual appeals is, I suggest, one compelling response to the ironic uncertainty that the information age has gifted its crown generation, the Millennials.

An immensely important question for scholars of religion today is the question of how Millennials (people aged 18–30) will alter the religious landscape in the next few decades. There are 83 million Millennials in the United States; they make up 26% of the U.S. population, a greater portion than any other generation.[2] They already make up the majority of the rapidly growing religiously unaffiliated, the "nones."[3] Will those unaffiliated Millennials turn to religion once they have children, like previous generations? Will they invent traditions of their own? Or will they primarily continue to

---

1. Reuss/Fun, "Some Nights."
2. Searcey, "Marketers Are Sizing Up the Millennials."
3. Pew Research Center, "Religion among the Millennials."

carve out atheist, agnostic, and freethinker spaces in the American public? It is too early to say now, of course, but in the following pages, I suggest that the Emerging Church is worthy of scholarly attention because of the way that the movement is responding to problems of meaning that young people in particular appear to wrestle with.

MILLENNIALS, KNOWLEDGE, PERSONAL CONTEXTS

First, however, I want to share that this paper was directly influenced by some experiences in the classroom. A few years ago, I began teaching at a university in North Carolina that will remain anonymous. I quickly discovered that the undergraduate cohort there was a bit different from the undergraduates I was used to teaching at the University of North Carolina at Chapel Hill (UNC). Most of the undergraduates in my religion classes at UNC were Protestant Christians from North Carolina, and at least half were evangelical.

In contrast, most of the students at the other school were from New England, and the vast majority of them identified, from what I could tell, as religiously unaffiliated. Many of these students were so unfamiliar with religion that I had to drastically alter the course content to shore up any fundamental misunderstandings. In nearly every way, students from this school exhibited other generational characteristics that squared with research I had seen: they were staggeringly optimistic and polite.[4] They placed a premium on tolerance and valued difference. While they were more reluctant to argue with each other or engage in conflict than any cohort I had ever taught, they felt comfortable pushing back against my authority. They happily acknowledged that life was painted in shades of grey, and seemed perfectly content with relativity and ambiguity.

This group presented me with a few pedagogical challenges, as I had to contend with the fact that their smart phones and laptops seemed more like bodily extensions than learning aids. They also demanded that I taught only what seemed readily applicable, and they insisted on learning through hands-on experience. Many students explained to me that they thought a typical lecture was pointless, and some did not see the value of memorizing facts. They pushed me—in a good way—to consider that young people today require educational strategies that engage the body and the heart, not just the mind.

Although the student demography of this school was similar to those in my UNC classes (the majority of students were middle-class Caucasians),

---

4. Pew Research Center, "Millennials: A Portrait of Generation Next."

some differences between the students seemed sharp. Students at UNC accepted my authority and rarely pushed back against assignments, even if they required rote memorization. Students at the other school often challenged my authority and the legitimacy of what they were learning, always preferring knowledge to be verified through personal experience before accepting it as legitimate or relevant.

Most of all, these students caused me to question how and why some young people might have different demands when it comes to making truth claims, reminding me of a scene described in Bruno Latour's *An Inquiry into Modes of Existence*. Early in the book, Latour recounts a story in which a scientist gave a public lecture and an attending young person vehemently challenged his findings with the rather pointed question, "why should we believe you?"[5] Part of Latour's point was that increasingly we are living in a world in which traditional authorities and methodologies (in this case, scientific propositional statements) are being challenged and sometimes overturned by the weighty force of subjective opinion. It was not enough in this case for science to be intellectually and rationally compelling to be considered true. This individual insisted that the science had to be personally compelling to be true; it had to be "believable."

I realized that I (at 36) am truly of a different generation from my students: I expected rote memorization in the classroom, and I expected to swallow whatever authority figures told me. My non-UNC students, though, seemed to be always asking, "What about what *I* think and feel?" Like in Latour's example, knowledge seemed to have no authority without being "believable," and for something to be believable it had to have the power to move a person—in all of her idiosyncratic complexity—on the inside. No truth could take priority over what one felt with her own hands, saw with her own eyes, and heard with her own ears. For this paper's purposes, I am calling this epistemological stance "hyper-subjective."

If "subjectivity" suggests that a person's perception of an object is mediated through her own unique lens, then "hyper-subjectivity" suggests that a person's experience of an object as real and worthy of mediation to begin with is highly constrained to personal preference. Hyper-subjectivity suggests that the traditional modern rules of digesting an object's veracity no longer hold. Typical subjectivity might come into play when a person, upon hearing a scientist present data, filters the information through her personal points of references. Hyper-subjectivity, on the other hand, would manifest in the refusal to filter the information at all based on the self-constructed premise that the data did not constitute a legitimate object to

---

5. Latour, *An Inquiry into Modes of Existence*, 2.

the self to begin with. In the world that Latour introduces, objects must be made personally compelling as objects before they can be digested as having any veracity or practical use. If post-modern epistemologies do sometimes fall prey to hyper-subjectivity as I have suggested, then it problematizes the possibility of finding common ground, since the equalizing force of rational appeals can no longer be counted on.

The hyper-subjectivity that I witnessed among some of my Millennial students could result in two different outcomes when it came to engaging with different viewpoints. The first outcome, what I call "strong hyper-subjectivity," can allow a person either to immediately dismiss facts that do not support her worldviews or to assert opinions as if they were facts, based on the strength of emotional force. Strong hyper-subjectivity values epistemological autonomy to such an extent that one's feeling takes priority over all other criteria when evaluating truth. Here, upholding an ethic of autonomy can mean that a person's specific stance can take priority over all other stances.

Hyper-subjectivity, however, can also come in a "weak" variety, as demonstrated when an ethical discussion of jihadist-inflicted beheadings came up in the classroom. Students were generally reluctant to condemn the beheadings, reasoning that because each person had a right to read the beheadings in her own way, none of them should cast judgement. The value of epistemological autonomy was still in play, but because it was understood to apply universally (to everyone), my students concluded that no one had a right to judge. Here, every person's specific stance was subjugated in order to uphold an ethic of tolerance.

To recap: subjects employing hyper-subjectivism value epistemological autonomy to such a degree that the veracity of an object as an object is open to idiosyncratic scrutiny. This value of epistemological autonomy sometimes manifests in the strong hyper-subjective assertion of one's ability to either dismiss particular facts presented as objects or to produce objects as facts on the strength of emotional feeling. Sometimes, valuing epistemological autonomy manifests in the proclivity to dismiss all ways of knowing (including one's own), in an act I call weak hyper-subjectivity. Although both forms of hyper-subjectivity rotate around different ethics (strong hyper-subjectivity prioritizes personal feeling while weak hyper-subjectivity prioritizes tolerance and respect), the importance of robust, rational critique is downplayed. In many ways, my students who exhibited these tendencies seemed very post-modern.

Observing these hyper-subjectivities in my students made me wonder what contributed to them favoring visceral experience and devaluing rational or scientific proofs. It seems clear that part of the answer lies in the fact that Millennials exist in a world saturated by media platforms that constantly request opinions about everything, regardless of users' familiarity or knowledge of the subject. Such online polling practices, along with platforms like Facebook that continually elicit users to share "what's on your mind?," give one the impression that one's opinion is all-important.

Although this media-influenced epistemic shift may be experienced by all different ages, Millennial perceptions are likely uniquely affected by virtue of having been the first generation to grow up with computers. 75% of Millennials have created online profiles, and 83% have *slept* with a cell phone.[6] They log hours a day consuming media, and spend an average of 21.7 hours per week on phones alone as of 2015.[7] This consumption has entailed unprecedented explorations, expressions, and redefinitions of aesthetic forms through mediums like Pinterest and Snapchat. It is too early to tell exactly how all of this technology has shaped Millennials' worldviews, but it is plausible that the ever-present stream of visual and auditory information compels Millennials to prioritize aesthetic experience as an authentic and thus veritable way of knowing and being.

Media exposure has likely also contributed to Millennials valuing diversity. In addition to being exposed to visual and auditory experiences via the internet, Millennials are, more than any previous generation, also exposed to social, cultural, and political differences. This exposure to difference likely has been a factor in their tendency to highly value tolerance, most visible recently in Millennials' 71% approval rating of gay marriage.[8] Exposure to difference may also be linked to their low church attendance and increasing doubt in God's existence.[9] Increasing agnosticism or in some cases, apathy, is sometimes a sign of weak hyper-subjectivity, which operates under the assumption that because all opinions are equal, no one stance can be said to be right or more useful than others. It is easier to issue widespread approval, or sweeping skepticism, when every truth claim is suspect.

My non-religious students' epistemology was befuddling to me because it seemed that while they clearly perceived religious teaching and practice as provincial and authoritative, they seemed to demand something akin to a spiritual experience in the classroom. Put differently, these students seemed to prefer ways of knowing based on personal experience to rational appeals, yet saw personal, subjective, "religious" experience as too

---

6. Lenhart et al., "Media and Mobile Internet Use among Teens and Young Adults."

7. Shively, "TNS Study Reveals Millennials Spend Nearly One Day Every Week on Their Phones."

8. Pew Research Center, "Changing Attitudes on Gay Marriage."

9. Lipka, "Religious 'Nones' are Not Only Growing."

enmeshed in power structures to be personally attractive. I began to wonder what sort of religious tradition, if any, might appeal to these students. In the remaining pages, I continue this thought experiment to consider the ways in which the Emerging Church may or may not have special currency among hard-won Millennials, the ever-reluctant religionists.

MILLENNIALS AT EMMAUS WAY

In order to consider this, I examine how an Emerging Church called Emmaus Way, located in downtown Durham, NC, engaged artistic expression as a way of knowing truth and conveying morality. *Emmaus Way* is composed primarily of young, white, middle-class academics, many from Duke Divinity School. This church, unlike some other Emerging Churches in the area, resisted various forms of "preaching" in order to avoid the traditional pedagogical structures that allowed one authoritative figure to dispense knowledge to all the others. When I visited the church in 2012, members sat on plush couches and comfy chairs circled around a stool and a microphone. During a time of reflection, anyone who wanted to share thoughts or questions was welcome come to the center. Several times during the service I attended, congregants milled to the coffee table and back, discretely sipping from paper cups while lounging on the couches. Art, some of which was congregant-produced, hung on the surrounding walls.

Emmaus Way was left-leaning politically and culturally on the spectrum of practice and thought within the Emerging Church tradition. This church adhered more to the theologically open stance of Brian McLaren that made possible the acceptance of other faiths as legitimate, than, for example, the conservatism of Dan Kimball that sought to maintain the supreme authority of Christianity. For those at *Emmaus Way*, artistic engagement was paramount in the discovery of truth in a post-modern world.

When I interviewed the church's art director (at the time, a fellow UNC PhD student) for this paper, he explained to me that art facilitated Emmaus Way's enactment of three core values: humility, agnosticism, and "the search for what is meaningful to the self."[10] The first two prongs of Emmaus Way's philosophy appeared to reflect the cultural value to be "certain of the uncertain" that I suggest is characteristic of many Millennials, and the last prong is suggestive of the hyper-subjectivity that might easily follow agnostic pride.

Although Emmaus Way expressed post-modernist values that were similar to many of my students, unlike many students, the church appeared

10. Interview dated August 28, 2014.

reflexive regarding its own epistemology. An entire page of the church's web site was devoted to explaining the church's artistic philosophy. According to the site, Emmaus Way believed that art was a primary, not secondary, activity of the church, on equal footing with spiritual discipline. Unlike other mediums, art was "uniquely communicative of sacred truths [and] directly related to Jesus' use of parables to communicate seemingly simple ideas in irreducibly poetic packages."[11] In other words, truth would not be found in straight-forward, intellectual propositions or relegated to texts. According to the church, the discernment of truth must be sought through visceral engagements and personal struggle.

By exulting art as a vessel for sacred meaning and engagement with art as a form of spiritual discipline, the church offered a radical recalibration of modern Christian epistemologies that understand truth as Bible-centric and ways of discerning truth as ultimately reliant on socially-approved church hierarchies. By contrast, Emmaus Way's art philosophy places the power of sacred discernment on any individual willing to feel or see or hear. By suggesting that spiritual truth may be found in art, the church opened wide the parameters for what might count as instructive. The suggestion that truth might be found in "irreducibl[e] poetic packages" casts doubt on the possibility of knowing anything for certain, reinforcing the church's agnostic position. These departures from traditional modern Christianity that offer a liberated view of those discerning sacred truth, the methods of discernment, and the outcomes of such discernment reminded me of my students who professed similar liberations with their pedagogical demands. Operating in a mode of hyper-subjectivity, they similarly claimed to have special authority in the classroom by virtue of feeling something strongly, but they also seemed comfortable with uncertainty.

Unlike my students however, artistic expression for *Emmaus Way* did not appear to be a cloistered form of sacred self-therapy, aimed only at getting comfortable with ambiguity or expressing a hyper-subjectivity. It provided an opportunity to find common ground and offered an avenue for social change. Emmaus Way's art philosophy argued that "art embodies a new economy and a new way of being together" by "encourage[ing] collaboration rather than competition, reveal[ing] abundance rather than scarcity, and priz[ing] beauty over efficiency or utility."[12] According to Emmaus Way, the enactment of art offered a theological apology in that its existence illumined God as "mak[ing] room for all our voices in the ongoing

---

11. Emmaus Way Church, "Our Artistic Philosophy."
12. Ibid.

work of redemption in the world."[13] So although artistic expression for the church could be perceived as a hyper-subjective and isolating indulgence, the practice itself was not meant to be solipsistic. Rather, art was meant to foster engagement and collaboration with others. Its practice was meant to bring different people together by resisting authoritative power structures and empowering individuals. At *Emmaus Way*, putting a paintbrush in a person's hand and saying, "create what you like," was a powerful and sacred social act that had the potential to reverberate from the individual to the rest of society.

Furthermore, although Emmaus Way makes clear that truth is often not crystal-clear or easily discernable, the church's artistic philosophy reveals the belief that not everything is relative. By arguing for the merits of art as a tool for collaboration, abundance, and beauty, the church reflects particular value judgements.

These judgements also became clear in the ways that the church worked to recalibrate the messages of pre-existing art. Detournement projects allowed participants to exercise subjectivity while collaborating in a process to reconstruct and reaffirm collective values.

Détournement, a technique taken from philosopher Guy Debord and the French Situationists, is the practice of creatively defacing images and texts in such a way as to produce meanings that are in tension with the original image or text. Emmaus Way has engaged in this practice through détourning images, blackout poetry, and collage as well as through origami. In each case, participants are encouraged to create their own narratives by taking hurtful items and recalibrating the framework to suggest the desired themes of reconciliation and inclusivity. In the picture above, participants

13. Ibid.

begin with a picture or text of their choosing and black out particular words or parts of images in order to redirect—or redeem—the medium's message.

In some way, maybe this is what conversion in a post-modern context looks like: it is a collaborative, creative rearrangement of values. It is not so much the eradication of one side as it is an artistic repurposing that requires sensory engagement. This process of detournement allows participants to feel their way into an articulated value system using images and ink–intellectual appeals and propositional statements are completely unnecessary in this work of redemption.

In the second and third images, congregants black out or otherwise alter cartoons and texts considered to contain hate speech in order to produce a redemptive narrative. Each person, pen in hand, is meant to feel empowered as an arbitrator for social and ethical change. This process can be personally transformative, as each member confronts the messages before her, negotiates a redemptive message privately or with other participants, and then makes the necessary alterations.

Sometimes, messages require more recalibration than the black-out technique affords, like in the below picture of "conversion therapy." Where the original depiction shows a light switch that flips from gay to not gay, "not" has been crossed out and replaced by "still." The cartoon below it also required more moderation, and the caption was changed to be inclusive, reading, "Personally, I find atheists to be just as beloved by God as fundamentalist Christians."

This entire paper was motivated by the question of whether or not the Emerging Church, with its post-modern adaptations, has the potential to attract post-modern, Millennial "nones." The answer is yes and no. My examination of Emmaus Way's practices helped to briefly illustrate how the Emerging Church might empower individuals, eschew text-based claims of truth and favor visceral engagement, and uphold the liberal value of tolerance. All of these things seem to have a straight-forward import in post-modern thought.

But a major characteristic of the Emerging Church suggests that a fraternization between the non-religious Millennials and the Emerging Church might not be so easy. The Emerging Church formed primarily as a reaction to traditional Christendom, making many of the practices and theologies in the church deeply resistant. Unlike Millennial nones who have no religious backgrounds to resist, many of those in the Emerging Church actively engage with theological ghosts of the past. Even the practice of detournement could be thought to reflect the Emerging Church's proclivity to actively and intentionally resist perceived untruths, as sitting down to creatively alter speech or images deemed hateful is an act of thoughtful rebellion.

The kind of thoughtful rebellion or resistance demonstrated by the Emerging Church does not seem to employ the hyper-subjectivity that I saw in my students. My students seemed generally uninterested in accepting objects as objects when they were presented with them, preferring instead either to present their own objects (employing strong hyper-subjectivity) or ignore them completely (employing weak hyper-subjectivity). Put differently, they tended to prefer not to engage with data or opinions enough to make an argument one way or another. Instead of deconstructing an argument or idea they were presented with, they preferred to either present something else altogether or accepted the argument without hesitation in order to be tolerant. Yet the Emerging Church and the practice of detournement take objects seriously because they take the work of deconstruction seriously.

In conclusion, there are several reasons for why the Emerging Church may and may not appeal to post-modern Millennial nones. This paper briefly described how the practices of Emerging Churches like Emmaus Way value the importance of hyper-subjective characteristics like direct sensory experience, autonomy, and agnosticism. Because of this, the church likely has more potential to attract non-religious Millennials like my students than other, more traditional Christian churches. However, if the Emerging Church movement is, at its core, reactionary and deconstructive, then it would seem that this church may not be as relevant to hyper-subjective Millennial nones who do not have a religious background to resist. Whatever the case, the Emerging Church movement deserves more scholarly consideration for a number of reasons, not least of which is that it appears to be a safe place for those certain about the uncertain.

BIBLIOGRAPHY

Emmaus Way Church. "Our Artistic Philosophy." http://emmausway.net/#/who-we-are/our-artistic-philosophy.

Latour, Bruno. *An Inquiry into Modes of Existence: An Anthropology of the Moderns.* Cambridge: Harvard University Press, 2013.

Lenhart, Amanda, Kristen Purcell, Aaron Smith, Kathryn Zickuhr. "Media and Mobile Internet Use Among Teens and Young Adults." *Pew Internet & American Life Project,* February 3, 2010.

Pew Research Center. "Changing Attitudes on Gay Marriage." May 12, 2016. http://www.pewforum.org/2016/05/12/changing-attitudes-on-gay-marriage/.

———. "Millennials: A Portrait of Generation Next." February 2010. http://www.pewsocialtrends.org/files/2010/10/millennials-confident-connected-open-to-change.pdf.

———. "Religion among the Millennials: An Introduction and Overview." February 17, 2010. http://www.pewforum.org/2010/02/17/religion-among-the-millennials/.

———. "Religious 'Nones' Are not Only Growing, They're Becoming More Secular." November 11, 2015. http://www.pewresearch.org/fact-tank/2015/11/11/religious-nones-are-not-only-growing-theyre-becoming-more-secular/

Ruess, Nate/Fun. "Some Nights." In *Some Nights.* Fueled by Ramen/Atlantic, 2012.

Searcey, Dionne. "Marketers Are Sizing Up the Millennials." *New York Times,* August 21, 2014.

Shively, Stephen. "TNS Study Reveals Millennials Spend Nearly One Day Every Week on Their Phones." *Kantar TNS.* http://www.tnsglobal.com/us/press-release/tns-millenials_study_111915.

2

The Southern Strategy

Randall Reed

Abstract

The Emerging Church is one of the most interesting movements in Western Christianity today. A movement that sees itself as specifically attuned to the postmodern world, the Emerging Church has staked out positions that are pro-gay, socially and economically progressive, and religiously inclusive. This might seem a movement tailor-made for Millennials who generally hold these same values. Studies that have looked at the Emerging Church have often commented on the progressive nature of the movement. However, none of these studies have focused on Millennials or have been centered in the American South. This article will address two significant questions: First, is there a trend toward evangelical defection in the South like there is in other regions of the country and what implications can be drawn from the answer to that question? Second, is there a receptivity that can be seen towards the message of the Emerging Church and what are the openings and barriers to its acceptance by southern Millennials? My research will show that while it does appear that there is an opening for the Emerging Church in the South with its progressive message of tolerance, there are likewise significant barriers, most especially related to the Emerging Church perspective on the Biblical Text that will have to be overcome.

Part 1: Millennials and the Emerging Church

INTRODUCTION

The Emerging Church is one of the most interesting movements in Western Christianity today. A movement that sees itself as specifically attuned to the postmodern world, the Emerging Church has staked out positions that are pro-gay, socially and economically progressive, and religiously inclusive. This might seem a movement tailor-made for Millennials who generally hold these same values. Studies that have looked at the Emerging Church have often commented on the progressive nature of the movement.[1] None of these studies, however, have focused on Millennials or have been centered in the American South. This deficiency I hope to begin to correct in this paper.

The Emerging Church is often characterized as a post-evangelical movement.[2] Many of the leading voices in the Emerging Church, such as Brian Mclaren, Rob Bell, Peter Rollins, and Nadia Boltz-Weber have Evangelical backgrounds. Evangelical categories and concerns often are particularly at issue for Emerging Church leaders (e.g., Rob Bell's rethinking of Hell in *Love Wins*[3]) and conservative Evangelical leaders have often targeted Emerging Church thinkers (e.g., Ron Piper's "Farewell Rob Bell" tweet that precipitated much of the controversy around the Love Wins book[4]). At the same time it is the South that remains the bulwark of evangelicalism. Whereas Evangelicals make up 25.4% of the U.S. Population, in the South Evangelicals range from 27% in Louisiana to 52% in Tennessee. The Pew Religious Landscape[5] shows a clear clustering of Evangelicals in the South and while other regions have Evangelical populations, none have a larger percentage than the South. If the Emerging Church, then, is to change Evangelical Protestantism as we know it,[6] then its "mission field" must be the South.

---

1. McKnight et al., *Church in the Present Tense*; Jones, *The Church Is Flat*.
2. Bielo, *Emerging Evangelicals*.
3. Bell, *Love Wins*
4. Wellman, *Rob Bell*, 7.
5. Pew Research Center, "Religious Landscape Study."
6. Scot McKnight, Biblical Scholar and Emerging Church author notes "the vast majority of emerging Christians are evangelical theologically" but then goes on to label them "post-evangelical" particularly in regards to systematic theology (the ECM is suspicious of such) and non-exclusivist. Mcknight, "Five Streams," p. 35. Likewise many of the Emerging Church leaders themselves come out of Evangelical backgrounds (Brian McLaren, Peter Rollins, James Bakker and Nadia Boltz-Weber to name a few). In fact, Brian McLaren's book *A New Kind of Christian* specifically details the mentoring of one evangelical by another (post)evangelical into the ideas of the Emerging Church.

The other issue that is key is the religious orientation of Millennials. The millennial generation has made headlines by its abandonment of the traditional institutional church with the rise of the millennial "Nones."[7] While the implications of the category of "none" has been questioned by some,[8] there is no doubt that there has been a loss of membership in both mainline and Evangelical Churches.[9] Millennials are dropping out of church, and whether they are taking the moniker of "none" or not, their absence in church pews is a real phenomena charted both by national surveys as well as by denominational reports.

This raises two significant questions: First, is there a trend toward evangelical defection in the South like there is in other regions of the country and what implications can be drawn from the answer to that question? Second, is there a receptivity that can be seen towards the message of the Emerging Church and what are the openings and barriers to its acceptance by Southern Millennials?

To answer the first question about church defection in the South, I will look at the data provided by the General Social Survey, which allows the disaggregation of data by region in conjunction with other surveys that have also touched on this issue. To answer the second question about the receptivity of Millennials to the message of the Emerging Church I will draw upon qualitative research that I have been conducting with focus groups of Southern Millennials. This data, I believe, can help determine some answers to these questions.

---

7. Pew Forum, "'Nones on the Rise."

8 Ramey and Miller, "Meaningless Surveys"; Ramey, "What Happens When We Name the Nones."

9 Jones, *The End of White Christian America*.

EVANGELICALS

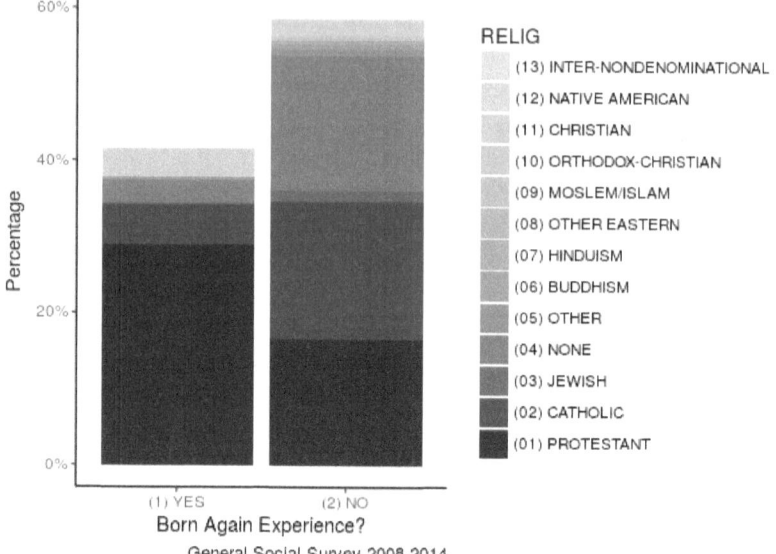

Nat'l % individuals with 'Born Again' Experience
Born Again Experience?
General Social Survey 2008-2014

I will begin with the question of the presence of Evangelicals in the U.S. in both millennial and non-millennial populations. The General Social Survey (GSS) for 2014[10] puts the national percentage of Evangelicals overall at 40% but Evangelical Protestants consist of 27% which is slightly higher than Pew (and probably overstated) but will act as a baseline for comparison. The GSS includes two things here that probably creates a higher number than Pew. First, the question asks whether the respondent has ever had a born-again experience. Individuals, who grew up in Evangelical homes, but are not currently Evangelicals would probably answer "Yes" to this. To that end 1 in 7 "Nones" answer "Yes" though it seems unlikely that this number actually reflect practicing Evangelicals.[11] Second, the GSS includes not just Protestant Evangelicals but also Catholics and (the aforementioned) Nones. Protestants who are currently self-identified as Evangelicals are not differentiated from those who no longer self-identify. Still, the GSS allows for regional and cohort disaggregation which is why I have chosen to use it despite these problems. Thus, among the general population, non-evangelicals outnum-

---

10. Data for the following analysis comes from Smith et al., "General Social Surveys."

11. It is possible that it includes non-denominational Protestants, though there is a separate answer for that. But more likely, the question asks about experience and not current identity and therefore encompasses individuals who have had a born-again experience, but have left the Evangelical fold.

ber Evangelicals by a significant margin. If we consider only Protestant Evangelicals, they are slightly more than 1/4 of the population.

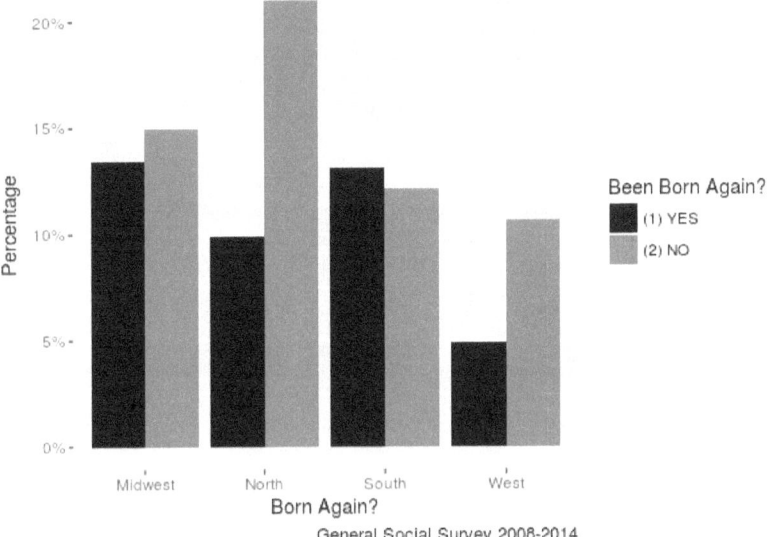

The situation becomes more nuanced when this same data is seen from a regional perspective. The Midwest and the South have the most individuals who have had a born-again experience. But also only in one part of the country do those who have had a born-again experience outnumber those who have not. That region is the American South.

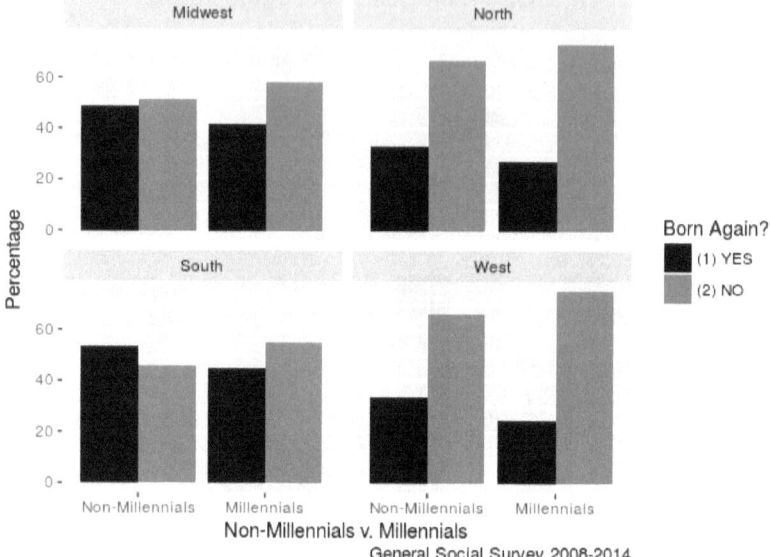

However when we compare non-milennials and Millennials by region, once again the South stands out.

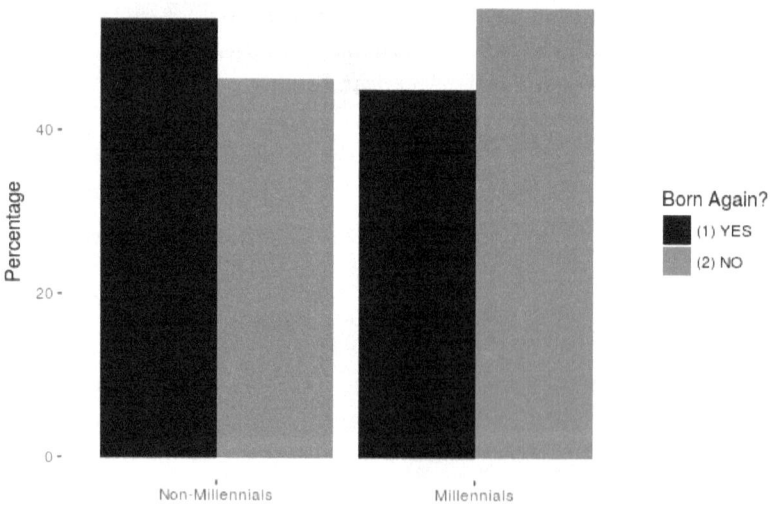

In the South more non-Millennials than not claim to have had a born-again experience. However for Millennials this is reversed, more Millennials claim not to have had a born again experience than those who say they have. While the gap between the "yes's" and the "no's" increases across all regions (more Millennials say "no" than non-Millennials), it is only in the South where there is this kind of reversal.

This leads to the question of the religious "Nones." There has been much made of the advent of the "Nones" and despite initial criticism, it has since become clear that this category is of growing significance particularly for Millennials.[12] As a category it requires context. Some of that context is coming from survey data that continues to be further refined.[13] Still, it is ultimately a variable and as a variable it can tell us whether more or less people are rejecting institutional religious labels, but it cannot tell us why or what it is that these "Nones" actually believe. These questions are left to other variables, more focused surveys and most importantly qualitative work still to be done. Nevertheless it is worth exploring the religious identification variable for what it can tell us.

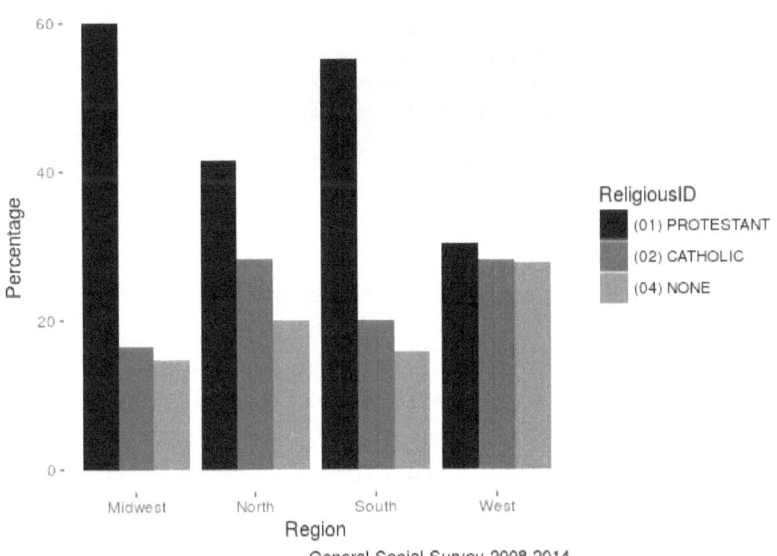

12. Pew Research Center, "Millennials in Adulthood."
13. Cooper et al., "Exodus."

NONES

As mentioned above, the percentage of millennial "Nones" is significantly more than non-millennial "Nones."[14] Correspondingly, using the GSS data again and doing a regional comparison of millennial "Nones" to non-millennial "Nones" one sees that millennial "Nones" significantly outpace non-millennial "Nones" in every region. Millennial "Nones" are a distinctive reality, and a reality that is not bounded by region. Again we may not be able to say what this means, but it is certainly a phenomenon that requires further study.

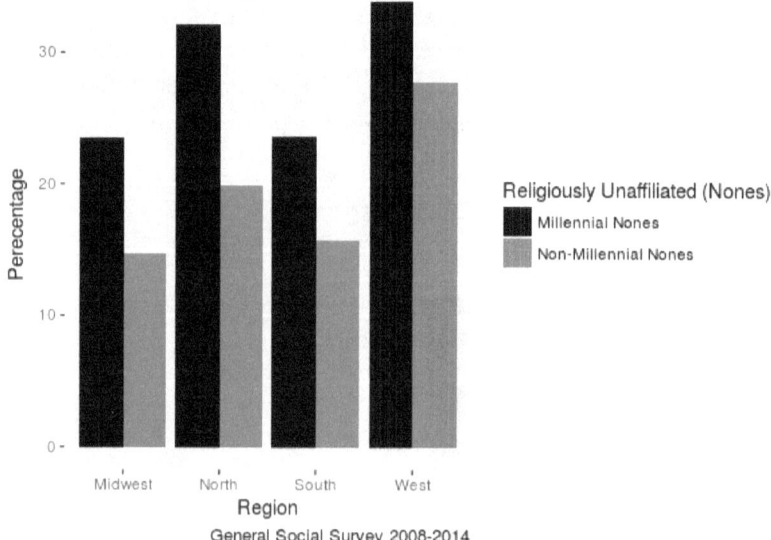

This leads to the question of the religious origin of these Nones? The chart below indicates the current religious identification at the time of the survey in comparison with religious identification at age 16. What is important is that one can chart who is going where. For instance, in the Midwest, the majority of Protestants who are moving, are moving to "None," compared to the few who are moving to Catholicism. This is likewise true of Catholics; about 10% move to Protestantism, but the larger share move to "None." Individuals raised without religious identification ("cradle Nones") are moving (about 18%) to Protestantism and to a lesser degree Catholicism. A couple of observations are appropriate here. First, there is

14. Ibid

movement both ways. Protestants and Catholics are becoming "Nones," but "Nones" are also becoming Protestants and sometimes Catholics. Second, what this chart fails to show is religious retention. All religious identifications are also keeping a majority of their Millennials. Even in the North where over 30% of Protestants are defecting, the reality is that almost 70% are staying put. Third, "Nones" are not strictly the product of movement, there are a significant proportion of "Nones" that are "cradle Nones." Some of the growth of the "Nones" is "second-generation Nones." Among Millennials, "cradle Nones" constitute about upwards of 70% of the "None" population (depending on region).

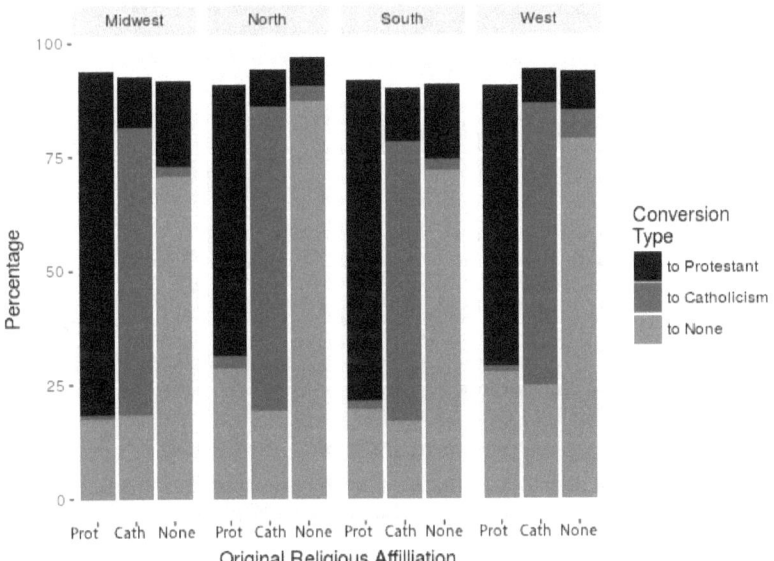

However, one should not be left with the impression that the trade between, say, Protestants and "Nones" is even, both swapping 20%. Thus it is important to recognize that the movement of individuals is significantly disproportionate. Protestant and Catholics are giving up significantly more people to the "Nones" than vice-versa. So the growth of the "Nones" is neither insubstantial nor regionally specific. It spans the nation, with some regional variation, but is present in all regions.

Conversion Rates By Region

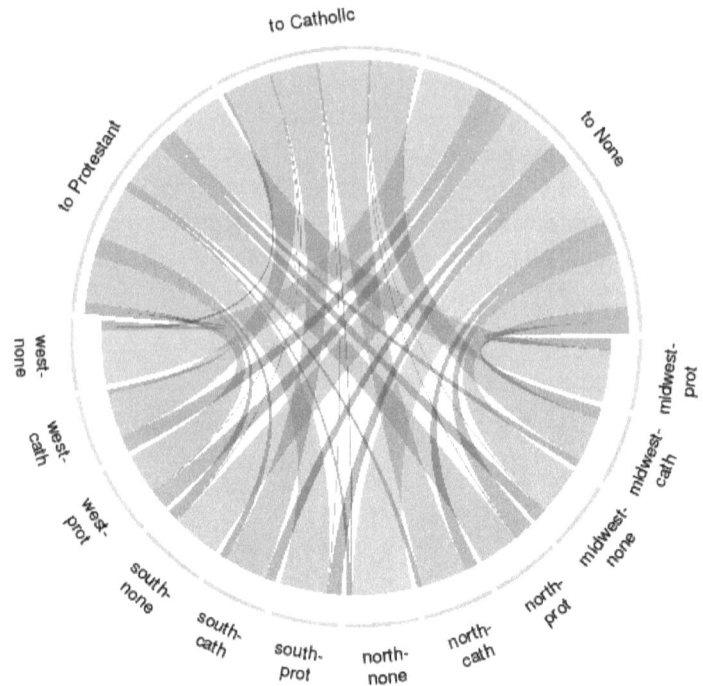

General Social Survey 2008-2014

The above graph attempts to illustrate the number of conversions through the size of the ribbons between each region/affiliation combination that corresponds to the size of the population making the move. What can be seen is that the largest ribbons are from one region/affiliation to the same affiliation. For instance Southern "Nones" largely stay Southern "Nones." The same is true for Southern Protestants. But what is also clear is that a larger band of Southern Protestants ends up as "Nones" than southern "Nones" as Protestants. But neither band is nearly as large as the retention band. The band of Protestants becoming "Nones" however changes based on region, with the western and northern bands of Protestants becoming "Nones" to a larger degree than the Southern and Midwestern bands. But to turn from national trends to focus on a particular region—the South -two conclusions can be summarized that are of relevance: First, fewer Millennials in the South are identifying with Evangelicalism by claiming a born-again experience. Second, Protestant Millennials in the South are shedding their Protestant identification in significant numbers.

Given the reality then of the millennial defection from institutionalized church, the natural next question is—what is driving Millennials away from church? This is a question which has occupied David Kinnaman and the Barna Group. Kinnaman has concluded that there are several factors involved: The church is perceived as judgmental, homophobic and too political. Likewise the concerns of the church are not seen as relevant to the lives of Millennials.[15] The Public Religion Research Institute has additionally shown that part of the millennial negative perception of the Evangelical church stems from its stance against homosexuality.[16]

Into this environment comes the Emerging Church. By all accounts it would seem that the Emerging Church would be ideally suited to appeal to Millennials. Its emphasis on openness, tolerance and focus on discussion over doctrinal purity seems well-suited for the Millennials. My own research has focused particularly on this question but with a regional emphasis precisely because of the aforementioned strength of evangelicals in the South: Are Southern Millennials receptive to the Emerging Church? Using a series of focus groups and interviews of Millennials I have posed this and related questions in an attempt to provide some insights unavailable in survey data. The results begin to speak to some of these issues.

My research indicates that Southern Millennials are potentially receptive to the Emerging Church. During the focus groups, the participants made roughly twice as many statements that were positive versus negative when introduced to statements from leaders of the Emerging Church.[17] When we dig a little deeper into the areas that Southern Millennials saw that were positive about the Emerging Church the picture becomes clearer.

---

15. Kinnaman and Lyons, *Unchristian*.

16. Fetsch, "Are Millennials Leaving Religion over LGBT Issues?"; Jones, et al., "A Shifting Landscape."

17. The participants were shown several videos from Peter Rollin https://vimeo.com/19258866, Brian McLaren https://youtu.be/puBolEen9yQ, and Jay Bakker https://youtu.be/s30ZKjNfRlU which attempted to briefly sample perspectives about the Resurrection, Biblical Authority and Gay Marriage.

Gerardo Martí and Gladys Ganiel's recent study emphasizes that openness is key aspect of the Emerging Church.[18] My research confirms this, as there was a generally positive view of the openness of the Emerging Church. As one participant stated "I would go towards the emerging church [sic] because it's more open-minded and progressive and gives me a little bit of freedom to think." Another person echoed this perspective, contrasting it with her other experiences of church agreeing, " It would definitely give a person more freedom to think for themselves and [from] my personal background, you could not really think for yourself and could not question why you believe what you believe, so that is probably why I would join. . ." Here an openness to questioning is seen as an important attractor and the converse is likewise seen as a failing of the institutional church.

Additionally, focus group members saw a significant need for change in the church. This was reflected on the one hand in a pre-survey which, while not representative of all Millennials, supports other survey research by indicating that the vast majority of participants were "dissatisfied" or "very dissatisfied" with the church, this subset of dissatisfied Millennials includes individuals who indicated they were still attending church regularly. But likewise participants voiced this need for change in the church in the focus group. One participant stated bluntly, "I do think that religion, especially Christianity, will die out if nothing changes." On the other hand the change that the Emerging Church represents caused some excitement, as one participant noticed, "[in] one of the videos, the guy was talking about a change in the church and he said 'I really think this can happen' and he was really confident in it. And when I hear something like that, I get really excited . . ." In each of these cases there is a recognition that from the perspective of these Millennials the church is broken and the Emerging Church offers for these Southern Millennials one avenue for change.

The most contested category for these participants was the Bible. The Emerging Church position on Biblical authority was both the largest asset for southern Millennials and also the biggest liability. Some focus groups were shown a short video of Brian McLaren talking about the difference between viewing the Bible as a library versus a constitution.[19] Libraries have a variety of opinions whereas the constitution is more a place to find answers. Some participants were quite taken in a positive way by this distinction. One participant stated clearly, "As far as my reception to the emerging church [sic]. . . this is kind of a breath of fresh air for [me]. . ." Another

---

18. Martí and Ganiel, *The Deconstructed Church*, 34.

19. McLaren, "Q2 The Authority Question." See also McLaren, *A New Kind of Christianity* and McKnight, *The Blue Parakeet*.

returned to the issue of openness, "I think it gives our generation more freedom to form their own thought with [the Bible]. As more like. . . guidance rather than an end-all to end all." Those participants who were attracted to this way of thinking found the lack of fixity, the lack of a single answer, to be a refreshing change.

On the other hand, different participants found this approach to the Bible problematic, one participant said plainly "it's editing the Bible, in a way, that['s]. . . taking away from what's written in it. . . . you're actually changing Christianity, you're changing the word of God. . ." Another voiced an opinion that asserted a single interpretation, "I feel like. . . at some level there is going to be . . . a correct answer. You just have to figure out what it is." Here we see push back against an Emerging notion of Biblical interpretation.

But more problematic than just the response to McLaren was that many of these participants still saw the evangelical understanding of the Bible with its legacy of Scottish Common Sense Realism as the touchstone for their own ways of sorting out issues. Even when not talking specifically about the Bible, often the reference point was the Bible. For instance in response to a video where Jay Baker talks about his support of Gay Marriage in a interracial congregational setting, one participant said, "I feel like that he should [have] gone into certain passages of the Bible . . . It think that might've been helpful for his argument." Other participants connected the immutability of God with Biblical interpretation. One participant, recoiling against the idea of parts of the Bible being outdated, said, " To say the Bible is outdated but that God isn't [is problematic] because if the Bible is God's word [then] God's word isn't going to be outdated." Another participant was concerned since for them the Bible was the "cornerstone of Christianity." Criticizing McLaren another interlocutor complained, " So he never really answers, like, 'Is the Bible the ultimate authority?' And he says that [all] people [are] interpreting it. . . But then you're opening Christianity to be anything." In each of these cases the Bible is the immovable touchstone to which everything must be subject.

This then seems to be the place where the Emerging Church has its greatest challenge among Southern Millennials. There is a culture of significant reverence for the text. Those Millennials who have this perspective need every position justified from the Bible or they see such positions as unacceptable. For these Millennials, the Emerging Church will need to engage with the text in a way that either can convince these Millennials that there is room for the sort of interpretive freedom the Emerging Church envisions or somehow shake their interpretive commitment to the text.

And yet with this proviso, even the more conservative Millennials indicate that they are dissatisfied with the church. So while their commitment to the text is undiminished their commitment to the institutional church seems waning. Thus the potential to find a way to speak to these Millennials remains. They are not generally happy with the church as it stands.

Nevertheless the data here brings up a more important issue and that is the question of the instantiation of authority. Kosmin and Keysar's American Religious Identification Survey[20] showed a significant division on the question of whether the Bible is an appropriate moral guide. My study confirms this conclusion. And yet the question of what can challenge the Bible as an authority is a larger question about the construction of authority in general and its possible failure. The mixed nature of the data indicates at this point a contestation of authority without a new center. Bruce Lincoln's theory of Authority[21] suggests that multiple factors play into its construction, from audience to environment to message. Yet such a theory only begins to scratch the surface of the problem. What is needed is a theory of religious change.

Some helpful work in this area has been done in the sociology of conversion. As space does not permit a lengthy discussion I will simply make some observations based on the insights of these studies. What seems clear from this literature is that individual religious change is dependent upon a failure of religious identity.[22] The problem with identity is that it is dependent on significant investment in upkeep. Identity requires constant reaffirmation both at the individual and social level. The basic problem with the number of Millennials leaving and being disaffected with the institutional church is that it lessens the potential for religious identity reaffirmation. Such weakening of reinforcers ultimately leads to identity insecurity.

Authority plays an important part in the formation of identity. Authority becomes the center point for identity, whether that authority be a community, a tradition or a text. Appeals to that authority are a strategy for shoring up identity. Challenges to that authority likewise can constitute a challenge to the identity associated with it as well.

However making a text the locus of authority is actually problematic as the text is not self-interpreting. It requires a community to extract authorized meaning and foreclose unacceptable interpretations. What appears

---

20. Kosmin and Keysar, "Religious, Spiritual and Secular."
21. Lincoln, *Authority*.
22. Rambo, *Understanding Religious Conversion*.

then to be the locus of authority grounded in the text in reality is community authority masquerading as textual authority. Such insights go far in explaining why the central point of contestation is the Bible for these millennial Protestants. The Evangelical championing of the Bible, is really a championing of a particular and communally-driven interpretation of the Bible.

Yet with the millennial distrust of institutional religion and consequent disaffillation, there is a weakening of interpretive reinforcement. The allegiance to the Bible still remains and yet the concomitant communal interpretive structure has been abandoned. It is possible that such might precipitate an opening for the Emerging Church and we saw just such an opening in our study.

Thus the issue for Southern Millennials in large measure reduces to the Bible. It would seem that attempts to simply ignore or sideline the text as some mainline denominations have done, will ultimately not be effective for these Millennials. The data presented here indicates that if the Emerging Church were to reclaim the Bible in such a way that they still encourage the openness that Millennials value there may be receptiveness from Southern Millennials. The "Bible as Library" approach of McLaren shows some promise in this regard. Whether the Emerging Church can build on that in the South has yet to be seen.

BIBLIOGRAPHY

Bakker, Jay. "Jay Bakker's Speech on Gay Marriage." https://www.youtube.com/watch?v=s30ZKjNfRlU.

Bell, Rob. *Love Wins: A Book about Heaven, Hell, and the Fate of Every Person Who Ever Lived*. San Francisco: HarperCollins, 2011.

Bielo, James S. *Emerging Evangelicals: Faith, Modernity, and the Desire for Authenticity*. New York: NYU Press, 2011.

Cooper, Betsy, Daniel Cox, Rachel Lienesch, and Robert P. Jones. "Exodus: Why Americans Are Leaving Religion—and Why They're Unlikely to Come Back." Public Religion Research Institute, September 22, 2016. http://www.prri.org/research/prri-rns-2016-religiously-unaffiliated-americans/.

Fetsch, Emily. "Are Millennials Leaving Religion over LGBT Issues?" Public Religion Research Institute, 3–13, 2014. http://www.prri.org/spotlight/leaving-religion-lgbt-issues/.

Jones, Robert P. *The End of White Christian America*. New York: Simon & Schuster, 2016.

Jones, Robert P., Daniel Cox, and Juhem Navarro-Rivera. "A Shifting Landscape: A Decade of Change in American Attitudes about Same-Sex Marriage and LGBT Issues." Public Religion Research Institute, 2–26, 2014. http://publicreligion.org/site/wp-content/uploads/2014/02/2014.LGBT_REPORT.pdf.

Jones, Tony. *The Church Is Flat: The Relational Ecclesiology of the Emerging Church Movement*. Minneapolis: JoPa Group, 2011.

Kinnaman, David, and Gabe Lyons. *Unchristian: What a New Generation Really Thinks about Christianity—and Why It Matters*. Grand Rapids: Baker, 2007.

Kosmin, Barry A., and Ariela Keysar. "Religious, Spiritual and Secular: The Emergence of Three Distance Worldviews among American College Students." Trinity College, October 1, 2013. http://commons.trincoll.edu/aris/files/2013/10/ARIS-2013_Students-Oct-01-final-draft.pdf.

Lincoln, Bruce. *Authority: Construction and Corrosion*. Chicago: University of Chicago Press, 1994.

Martí, Gerardo, and Gladys Ganiel. *The Deconstructed Church: Understanding Emerging Christianity*. New York: Oxford University Press, 2014.

McKnight, Scot. *The Blue Parakeet: Rethinking How You Read the Bible*. Grand Rapids: Zondervan, 2008.

———. "Five Emerging Streams." ChristianityToday.com. http://www.christianitytoday.com/ct/2007/february/11.35.html.

McLaren, Brian. *A New Kind of Christian: A Tale of Two Friends on a Spiritual Journey*. San Francisco: Jossey-Bass, 2008.

———. *A New Kind of Christianity: Ten Questions That Are Transforming the Faith*. San Francisco: HarperCollins, 2010.

———. "Q2 The Authority Question." theOOZE.tv, YouTube Video, 2010. https://www.youtube.com/watch?v=puBolEen9yQ.

Pew Research Center. "Millennials in Adulthood: Detached from Institutions, Networked with Friends." Pew Research Center, March 3–14, 2014. http://www.pewsocialtrends.org/files/2014/03/2014-03-07_generations-report-version-for-web.pdf.

Pew Research Center, Pew Forum On Religion and Public Life. "'None' on the Rise: One-in-Five Adults Have no Religious Affiliation." Pew Research Center, 2012. http://www.pewforum.org/files/2012/10/NonesOnTheRise-full.pdf.

Rambo, Lewis R. *Understanding Religious Conversion*. New Haven: Yale University Press, 1995.

Ramey, Steven. "What Happens When We Name the Nones." Huffington Post, 2–21, 2013. http://www.huffingtonpost.com/steven-ramey/what-happens-when-we-name-the-nones_b_2725169.html.

Ramey, Steven, and Monica R. Miller. "Meaningless Surveys: The Faulty 'Mathematics' of the 'Nones." Huffington Post, 11–7, 2013. http://www.huffingtonpost.com/steven-ramey/meaningless-surveys-the-f_b_4225306.html.

Rollins, Peter. "I Deny the Resurrection." https://vimeo.com/19258866.

Smith, Tom W., Peter Marsden, Michael Hout, and Jibum Kim. "General Social Surveys, 1972–2014 [machine Readable Data File] /Principal Investigator, Tom W. Smith; Co-Principal Investigator, Peter V. Marsden; Co-Principal Investigator, Michael Hout; Sponsored by National Science Foundation. -NORC Ed.- Chicago: NORC at the University of Chicago [producer and Distributor]." NORC at University of Chicago, 2016. gssdataexplorer.norc.org.

Wellman, James K. Jr. *Rob Bell and a New American Christianity*. Nashville: Abingdon, 2012.

3

Playing Offense or Defense?
The Theological Playbook of the Emergent/ing Church, with Some Armchair Quarterbacking

G. Michael Zbaraschuk

Abstract

The Emerging Church has made a name for itself to some degree because of its theological innovation. Much of this theological innovation has been done in an ad hoc and practical way—through sermons, Bible studies, and informal presentations. However, in reviewing carefully the work of Rob Bell, Tony Jones, and Peter Rollins, it is possible to discern some of their theological influences and resonances and locate them in the contemporary scene. Rob Bell can be seen to be in consonance with Pannenberg, radical theology, and some of the process theologians. Tony Jones is influenced by Moltmann and the Fuller Theological Seminary post-foundationalists. Rollins has phases, including a deconstructive phase influenced by Caputo, and a later development due to his interest in Lacan. At the end of the article I pose some questions for them, including the nature of their relation to the churches that they are emerging from, the question of political engagement, and how their work and projects might be dependent upon a certain set of social and economic conditions.

INTRODUCTION, AND *MEA CULPA*

In the first place, before moving into a deeper analysis, I have to offer a *mea culpa*. When I first began studying the emergent church theologians, I very much had in mind a hermeneutic of critique. I'd done some preliminary—not to say cursory—reading in the emergent church leaders, and thought I had an angle—"Justice!" and a metaphor "Football!"—that would get me an academic paper.

As I did more research into the subject, however, I found that the folks I was paying attention to—Tony Jones, Rob Bell, and Peter Rollins—didn't fit my angle or my hook so neatly, so my attempts to place them and their ideas into the boxes I had lined up to show their irrelevance didn't fit. I thought I was going to criticize a shallow phenomenon, and none of these folks fit my initial suspicion of a lack of sophistication or theological interest. So, while I am going to do what I started out to do—an evaluation of some of the theological dynamics operating in the Emergent/ing[1] movement, I'm not going to be standing in judgment in the same way I thought I was going to. To attempt to retrieve my metaphor—I will offer more attempts at thoughtful commentary from someone who really cares about football, and less armchair quarterbacking. I hope to make comments that do justice to the more substantial work I see being done.

THE DYNAMICS OF THE POSTMODERN, WITH APPLICATION TO EMERGENT/ING

It's hard to think about everything that is involved with the term "postmodern," (are we in it still? Were we ever?) which of course applies to this self-consciously postmodern movement in Christianity—that is, Emergence. When I feel like I am thrashing about too much in the postmodern sea, I always look back to my teacher, David Griffin, who held that the only sort of postmodernism that made sense was one that had a clear idea of what modernity is or was—and why it wanted to be or was "post" this idea or practice.[2] So, for example, we don't talk as much about "postmodern politics" as much as "post-colonialism," precisely, I think, because "post-colonial" has a very clear idea of what it wants to be *after*,

---

1. This phenomenon suffers from a nomenclature problem. Various folks want to refer to themselves as Emergent or Emerging or Missional or none of the above. I'm going to use a variety of terms, including Emergent and Emergent/ing, in order to illustrate the slipperiness of the label.

2. Griffin said this in my hearing in a seminar on Whitehead in fall 1997. It's stuck with me as the best way that I can make sense of postmodernity.

although it is still indebted to the same discourses of power, situatedness, ideologies, and so forth. "Post-modern literature" is much more ambiguous, I think, because the kind of post-modernity that is envisioned is less clear. Are we after literature? Modern literature? This is less clear—people are still writing and reading novels with plots. So, what are the Emergents "post?" Denominations? Culture-war evangelicalism? Perhaps. But many of them are not post-tradition.[3] It's a bit more confused, more like literature than politics, in my mind.

This does seem to me to be concerned with how some of the various Emergent thinkers interpret their postmodernity. One of the things that at least some forms of postmodernity claims to be "post" is the idea of progress, of a certain better future.[4] "The Embrace of the New"—simply for its novelty—is an ongoing trope of "modern" life. Several of these Emergent thinkers that I have focused on think that their post-modernism allows them to retrieve some of the measures of the past. It allows them to be more open to tradition. This freedom from the tyranny of the incessantly novel can allow Emergents to appreciate liturgy, tradition, discipline, neo-monasticism, etc.

It can also lead them to have a quite conflicted relationship with some of the less "progressive" elements of the Christian tradition—for example, patriarchy and classism. Also, who really challenges the white status quo in Emergence? Are they post-patriarchal? Engaged in racial justice? Or are they "post" the struggle against some of these things that are, by definition, progressive and modern?[5] Unsurprisingly, Emergent thinkers interpret their own postmodern condition in a variety of ways—including in ways that many could still think of as hyper-modern or even progressive. Let's turn, for a closer look at the first of our thought leaders of the Emergent movement, Rob Bell.

---

3. John Caputo notes in a podcast conversastion with Tripp Fuller that many of the evanglicals that he is in dialogue with are post-absolute Biblical authority, in the same way that he is post-absolute Church authority. Perhaps Emergents are post-absolute authority? See Fuller, "Stargazing."

4. See, for example, Anthony Giddens, in his *Making Sense of Modernity*.

5. Note, for example, the sometime inclusion of Mark Driscoll, one-time pastor of Mars Hill church in Seattle, and ongoing provocateur in the right-leaning authoritarian evangelical movement. Driscoll is postmodern in the reactionary sense—his authoritarianism, rigid gender codes, as well as the cult of personality and power mark his as *not* oriented to democracy, rationality, equality, etc.,—many of those hallmarks of modernity. Tony Jones makes the point over and over that Driscoll was there at the beginning of the Emergence network, and Driscoll works within many of the same dynamics as other Emergenters, but in a radically different way. I think that's telling.

IS ROB BELL A CONSTRUCTIVE POSTMODERNIST? (NOT THAT HE WOULD CARE)

So, first off, in talking about Rob Bell, he wears his seminary intellectual training lightly. His books are not generally scholarly or oriented to making one see the theological ideas that are influencing him. Nevertheless, it is certainly possible to lift some of those same influences out—to see some of his playbook after watching the film, so to speak. In the first place, he spends more time talking about the Bible than he does any other source—as one would expect in the pastor of a big church and now communication guru who had been trained at Fuller Theological Seminary. And it's hard to know if his theological ideas come out of some close Bible reading or from the interpreters that he may have encountered. Nevertheless, it's certainly possible to detect some Pannenbergian realized eschatology in his analysis of "aeons" in *Love Wins*. When he points that Jesus and Paul were concerned about how all things are new and changed and makes an interpretation of Jesus' use of "kingdom of god" or "kingdom of heaven" to the rabbinical "world to come" and relates that to a change in the "aeons" which breaks into the present from the future, he's certainly making that Pannenbergian point.

In the same way, when he makes the point of Jesus' total immanence in the world in *What We Talk about When We Talk about God*, that God's "withness" means that God isn't "up there" but is in all things, it's hard not to hear an echo of the radical theologians and their emphasis on radical immanence and the "death" of the transcendent God. Bell has noted in an episode of his own podcast (the RobCast!) that the most influential work of his early theological education was Bishop Robinson's *Honest to God*. Robinson's Tillichian-influenced primer into radical theology continuously emphasizes the divine immanence in this way.

Besides Pannenberg and the radical theologians, what seems to me to be the greatest influence on (or maybe synergy with?) Bell, in both *Love Wins* and *What We Talk About When We Talk About God*, is a kind of process theological or open theistic approach to God, the Universe, and Everything. In his section on notes and resources, he doesn't mention the process theologians (and, again, these are not formal, but meant to be suggestions for the largely non-scholarly reader), but his categories of God "With" and "For" and "Ahead" of us all are oriented to a processive/open theistic understanding of the world.[6] Additionally, his category of radical freedom in *Love Wins* also presupposes an outlook that is similar to process thought—in that human freedom is ontologically assumed, as part of the way things really are. What I found absolutely telling in his sympathy with process thought, even more than these more formal categories, was the examples he used, especially in WWTAWWTAG. From his discussion of the religion/science aspect of things, talking about cosmology and the relatedness of all matter, to the sort of physical causation that "takes places on a molecular level" when someone knows that someone is cheating on them (he referres to Gywneth Paltrow), he absolutely has what I call a "process sensibility" in his discussions in WWTAWWTAG.[7] In this, I don't know if he is formally influenced by those in the process camp. It looks like he has been reading popularly-oriented cosmology and neuroscience, as well as the Bible, and these sources also orient him towards a VERY similar view—open, connected, and oriented to "progress"—however loosely defined. I think that Bell might take the same tack that some open theists do in saying that their ideas of God are from the Bible, and just happen to accord with process thought—that is, this is just the way the world is, and if it looks like a process world, so be it.[8]

And finally, with regards to his postmodernism—this is a difficult question for me to answer, and, again, it revolves around the idea of what he is "post." In one sense, in his openness to some epistemological issues—how we know things, how God influences us, embodied knowledge that is relative—he is quite postmodern. However, in terms of being postmodern in the sense of giving up grand narratives—I don't think he is at all. He uses the narrative of the Bible, especially of an interpretation of it that places God's activity, both in Jesus and pointed towards by Jesus, as the interpretive key to his understanding of epistemology, cosmology, and relatedness. For example, in interpreting God as "With" us, Bell says that God is with us here, and calling us further, interpreting some of the stories about the treatment of women and "an eye for an eye" in this way. This is a clear orientation to

---

6. Note, for example, similar categories utilized by Marjorie Suchocki as an organizing principle in *God–Christ–Church*.

7. That "feeling things at a molecular level" that we don't or couldn't know about from our senses is something that process people call "causal efficacy," for example. See Whitehead's *Process and Reality*, Part III, for the definitive discussion of this phenomenon.

8. See, for example, Richard Rice's discussion of the use of the Bible by open theists in *The Openness of God*, chapter 4.

progress, towards our interpretations getting better, and at least the possibility of our individual lives getting better too. In this sense he may be the form of postmodernity that is "hyper-modern"—placing a new grand narrative over those of the past—that is of an ongoing redemption in God through Jesus. Maybe he is a "constructive postmodernist" in the way in which David Griffin has defined it[9]—although, I don't know if he's that concerned with these sorts of labels.

One last note—back to my trope of football—I see Rob Bell as almost entirely playing offense—that is, he wants to set his own agenda, and say what he wants to say. It may be that I am not attuned enough to the intricacies of his communities to detect his attempts to deflect criticism (to play defense, as it were), but he seems to want to really set the agenda and make others respond to him. Even in *Love Wins*, which could be read as an attack on more traditional doctrines of Hell, he does a nice job of trying to outline what he feels to be the case, and not make the criticisms central to his presentation. He wants to move the theological football, so to speak, and not let any possible defensive opponents deter him from his theological agenda.

TONY JONES—THE SCHOLAR OF THE GAME

In comparison with Bell, Tony Jones is easier (for at least this academic) to read and categorize. This is in many ways because he is more transparent about his academic theological background and sources. He's also clearer about his claiming of the title "postmodern" means, and about locating his own theological discourse and orientation.

With regards to Jones' views about postmodernity—he relates to what he sees as larger cultural movements that have moved away from certainty, while still wanting to be grounded in tradition, practice, and ethics. He advocates an intellectual humility, radical acceptance, and multiple ways of knowing and experiencing as appropriate resources for theological formulations. He is also clear that theology and practice are in a dialectical relationship, affecting one another in a never-ending feedback loop. It's called, for Jones, the Christian Life, and it's clear that he relishes and is fed by being in the process—being a Christian in this postmodern world. He's an insider, but with a keener sense of what some of the "outsiders" might be saying about his theology *and* "Emergence" as a phenomenon.

In terms of his theological influences, he is again clear that Nancey Murphy, Jim McClendon, and Miroslav Volf at Fuller were foundational

---

9. This is one of Griffin's ongoing interpretive schemes. It is stated in many places, including in the introduction to *Varieties of Postmodern Theology*.

to him, mentioning them in several places. While I'm not familiar enough with Volf to find his influences and I hear less of Murphey's orientation to philosophy and science than McClendon's insider hermeneutics of American Christian culture and practice[10] in Jones' theological formulations, it's clear that Jones picked up both Murphey's and McClendon's anti-foundationalism. This is (in my reading) the way in which he is post-modern. He also leans on Moltmann in his published doctoral dissertation, engaging him on questions of the relation between church, politics, and theological formulations of the Trinity.

What was, for me, the eerie experience of reading Jones was the way in which he was able to anticipate my criticisms, almost as I was coming up with them. For example, as I was making notes to myself to critique him about social justice, the next section of *The New Christians* was about social justice activities of the various emergent churches he studied. When I wondered about theological education and how the emergent church would retain its theological depth without something like the formal training of either education (like seminary) or a more structured tradition, he addressed that very question and pointed to the possibility of communities shaped by rules—the kind of neo-monastic movements beloved and sometimes even practiced by the Emergent/ing church—as a possible resource for theological education. In an overall sense, Jones is relational, traditioned, non-foundational, and oriented to the dialectic of praxis and theology in a balanced way. He does share Rob Bell's orientation to the meta-narrative of redemption of the Bible (maybe slightly more loosely defined), so in that sense he may be less post-modern than in his practices and epistemology.

Jones is, however, much more explicitly attuned than Bell to the criticisms leveled at Emergent churches in general, and maybe himself in particular. He does, in a variety of forms (formal discourse, dialogue, etc), defend his own views of the interpretation of the Bible, the anti-foundationalism of much Emergent church practice, and the engagement of the Emergents with culture, rather than against it. He mentions conservative thought leaders, constructs "types" to engage in dialogue, and historically and conceptually situates the Emergent church in its American, anti-denominational, post-evangelical context, outlining nicely the critiques of some mainline and evangelical folks (it's too trendy! It's immature! It's parasitic!)—and attempting to show that they don't concretely apply to all forms of the Emergent church that he's familiar with. In this sense, he supplements his extensive offensive work—getting to the heart of Emergent types trying to live their

---

10. See, for example, McClendon's discussion of being within the church as the ground and norm of activity in the first volume of his systematic theology, *Ethics*.

understanding of the gospel in their culture—with some equally as good defensive activity. If this football metaphor is still alive, he's got the most balanced playbook, moving between offense and defense rather seamlessly and showing his clear understanding of both activities in his larger context of the game of defining post-authoritarian North American Christian activity.

ROLLINS—PLAYING A DIFFERENT (DECONSTRUCTIVE) GAME

Which brings us to Peter Rollins. While Rollins doesn't always claim "Emergent" status, it's clear from his practical work (where and how he speaks and organizes events) and his own affinities with groups on both sides of the Atlantic that he's in the same camp. Rollins' theological orientation comes from a different tradition from the other two discussed above. Both Jones and Bell were pastors, educated at Fuller, Americans, and generally practically oriented to church life. Rollins is from Northern Ireland, with a background in community organizing and a PhD in Post-Modern Philosophy from Queen's University, Belfast, and more influenced by Derridian deconstruction and the continental hermeneutical heritage than the American post-evangelical anti-foundational tradition of Jones and Bell. He offers Marxist, Nietzschean, and especially Derridian readings of the Bible, culture, and Christian practices, always looking for the openness, the rupture, and forward-ness of the interpretation.

In contrast to both Jones and Bell, who explicitly hold the redemptive narrative of the Bible as their own meta-narrative (and, in that sense are not postmodern, unless perhaps in a constructive sense), Rollins extends his deconstructive reading to the Bible narratives themselves—hence insurrection and not resurrection, the Prodigal Father, etc. He (really in a Caputo-esque sense) reads and finds ruptures in Christian practices, doctrines, and the Bible, always pressing for openness and transformation, the spaces between the doctrines, places, and other reified materiality of Christian culture. This can be seen clearly in the meditations and the examples of the liturgy that he presents in *How (Not) to Speak of God*. Although he is forward-looking in his earlier works, he has abandoned the meta-narrative—speaking of giving up hope and certainty as addictions that oppress us, not reaffirming them as Bell might. To follow our football metaphor to a perhaps absurd length, Rollins is introducing concepts from soccer to American football, showing that the game is played for power and profit, and asking us why we do it. He is criticizing some established beliefs and practices, but in a way that shows their own terms to not be the only or the best way in which to organize human effort. He would like us to play a different game.

One aspect of playing a different game can be seen in how Rollins thinks of social and political engagement. Moving towards a more engaged social and political stance has always been a part of Rollins' work (for example, his work in IKON and in *The Fidelity of Betrayal*). He at times seems to go back and forth between an engagement which is semi-artistic and expressionistic (seen in IKON and in his public presentations), and calling for more radical social and political engagement (some of the examples which are alluded to but not spelled out in the *Orthodox Heretic*). However, he has a consistent incarnational bent in seeing how the word made flesh might act in the world. This is a thread which can be traced out throughout his various trajectories. It is the linking of resurrection with insurrection.

Another aspect of how he might see the game being played differently is as he introduces a sort of Lacanian analysis into his work.[11] This really does feel like an even more radical departure than his earlier material, where he subverts and deconstructs, and moves into a curious sort of neo-dogmatism about the Lacanian dynamics that (might be) present in some forms of Christian belief and practice—e.g., "the prestige," in *The Divine Magician*.[12] Instead of offering us a possibility for a different game, Rollins seems to want to be telling us that Christians are not playing the games they thought they were. He is (at times) almost adapting the trope of the older, nineteenth-century critics of Christianity, especially Freud, but also Marx and Nietzsche, who are trying to explain away Christianity by showing that it is shallower, uglier, and more self-serving than its practitioners think it might be. The lightness of tone and the playfulness of the deconstruction has gone. It's curiously stolid, critical, and pointed. What's happening? Does he not want to accept Lacan? Where are the ruptures, the openness, the events in the Lacanian readings that Rollins offers us? He's moved out of soccer or football at all, to a sort of powerlifting that he doesn't seem to care for very much. Where's the joy of sport, here? This analysis of what is going on doesn't seem like it is freeing the (ex?)-Christian subject for more authentic action in the world, and is instead a retreat from more political and social stances.

---

11. For example in *The Divine Magician*. I say "sort of" because Lacan's views are so highly contested.

12. See his discussion of the prestige in *The Divine Magician*, Section Three.

ARMCHAIR QUARTERBACKING, REVISITED

Although I said at the beginning that I was going to be appreciative of these Emergent church thought leaders, I do think I can't help myself from engaging in at least a little armchair quarterbacking! (I said there would be less, not *none* . . .). I will pose them in terms of questions, with some commentary. I will note, as well, that Tony Jones and Peter Rollins have addressed some of these criticisms and responded to them, at different times and places—that doesn't mean that they still don't apply (some of them are pragmatic as well as theological questions).

First, is the Emergent/ing movement a sort of spiritual consumerism? It's mostly white, urban, and relatively well-off. Is it simply another "spiritual consumer choice?" Put concretely, do pub or coffeehouse churches or meetings depend upon disposable income, an aesthetic orientation, and a consumerist mentality for their very existence? How committed are such practices to economic justice? To "the least of these?" To borrow a concept from an ongoing set of liberation theologians, in what sense to such practices make a preferential option for the poor, as Gustavo Gutiérrez or Ivone Gebara might say? If the members of a coffeehouse meeting were asked, as Leonardo and Clodovis Boff ask of their critics, "what have you done to further the integral liberation of the poor"[13] today—how might they respond?

Additionally, how "grassroots" and "decentralized" is the Emergent Church? Jones addresses this explicitly, bringing Weber's concept of the "routinization of charisma" into conversation with some existing Emergent churches. I don't think the question can really be answered at this point—but I think it still remains to be seen if Emergent is a movement with deep roots, or the result of some really talented and like-minded individuals.

There is, additionally, always the question of whether and how a postmodern or deconstructive stance can turn into a practice of constructive political engagement. The question is mostly directed towards Rollins, as Jones and Bell's continual reference to the meta-narrative of Jesus probably takes them outside the kind of deconstructive work that Rollins is doing. Is a deconstructive politics possible? Or is it that his work is critical, rather than practical? If so, where is the practical work?

And, finally, the question of tradition. Jones, at the end of *The New Christians*, holds that the Emergent movement is one of "Feral Christians"—those who were once domesticated Christians, but have "gone wild"—and there is no getting them back inside their cages. I am captivated by the image of Feral Christianity, and would love to see it explored. Even given Jones'

---

13. In the Boffs' *Introducing Liberation Theology*, chapter 1.

hinting at neo-monasticism as a training ground for seminarians and as a form of traditioning, however, I am unsure that feral Christianity is possible without larger forms of tradition from which to draw, deconstruct, and make into pastiche. Does "Going Wild" need a domesticated space to use as its "other" to even have a reason to be? Is such a movement sustainable in a lasting, multi-generational way?

This larger question of tradition might be illustrated by Tillich's ideas of Protestant and Catholic "types" as ways of organizing religious life—that is, the "Catholic principle" is one of appreciating and trying to maintain the tradition, and the "Protestant principle" is the critical stance towards the tradition. Are all of these Emergent leaders ones who are only Protestant? As a very concrete example, can Rollins ask questions of the Prodigal Father without the story of the Prodigal Son as a backdrop?

There. I'm done armchair quarterbacking. These folks are out on the field playing the game, and I am (in this context) a commentator. I have respect and appreciation for what they are trying to do. I find the Emergent church movement deeper than I had first believed, and enormously suggestive of possibility. My own criticisms notwithstanding, I hope (as a sort of theological virtue) that it is one facet of the world Christian scene for many years to come.

BIBLIOGRAPHY

Bell, Rob. "Episode 111: Pete Rollins on God Part 1." Podcast, July 25, 2016. http://robbell.podbean.com/2016/07/.
———. *Love Wins: A Book about Heaven, Hell, and the Fate of Every Person Who Ever Lived*. San Francisco: HarperOne, 2012.
———. *What We Talk about When We Talk about God*. San Francisco: HarperOne, 2014.
Fuller, Tripp. "Stargazing with Nietzsche and Caputo." Podcast audio, March 31, 2016. https://homebrewedchristianity.com/2016/03/31/stargazing-with-nietzsche-and-caputo/.
Giddens, Anthony, and Christopher Pierson. *Conversations with Anthony Giddens: Making Sense of Modernity*. Stanford: Stanford University Press, 2013.
Griffin, David Ray, William A. Beardslee, and Joe Holland. *Varieties of Postmodern Theology*. SUNY Series in Constructive Postmodern Thought. Albany: State University of New York Press, 1989.
Jones, Tony. *The Church Is Flat: The Relational Ecclesiology of the Emergent Church*. Minneapolis: JoPa, 2011.
———. *The New Christians: Dispatches from the Emergent Frontier*. San Francisco: Jossey-Bass, 2008.
Robinson, John A. T. *Honest to God*. Philadelphia: Westminster, 1963.

Rollins, Peter. *The Divine Magician: The Disappearance of Religion and the Discovery of Faith*. New York: Howard, 2015.

———. *The Fidelity of Betrayal: Towards a Church Beyond Belief*. Brewster, MA: Paraclete, 2008.

———. *How (not) to Speak of God*. Brewster, MA: Paraclete, 2006.

———. *Insurrection: To Believe Is Human, To Doubt, Divine*. New York: Howard, 2011.

———. *The Orthodox Heretic: And Other Impossible Tales*. Brewster, MA: Paraclete, 2016.

Suchocki, Marjorie Hewitt. *God—Christ—Church: A Practical Guide to Process Theology*. New York: Crossroad, 1992.

Whitehead, Alfred North. *Process and Reality: An Essay in Cosmology*. Corrected ed. New York: Free Press, 1979.

PART 2

What Is the Emerging Church?
Definitions and Constructions

4

A Generous Heterodoxy

Emergent Village and the Emerging Milieu

ADAM SWEATMAN

Abstract

How might one define the Emerging Church Movement (ECM)? How does the ECM fit into the history of evangelicalism? This paper seeks to advance towards an answer to these questions by providing a history of the most prominent ECM organization, Emergent Village, and by considering it through the lens of the sociological work of Colin Campbell, whose model of a "cultic milieu" aligns neatly with a description of ECM activities in the late 1990s and early 2000s. Like Campbell's cultic milieu, the ECM functioned as a kind of social environment, rather than a cohesive theological or political movement, that encouraged mysticism, seekership, and forms of internal syncretism. This is evident in the history of Emergent Village, which began as the Young Leadership Network, a generation X outreach group, but evolved into a complex network of churches, websites, books, and conferences under the Emergent Village banner. This reading of Emergent Village facilitates establishing the ECM into the broader history of late twentieth-century evangelicalism through its institutional connections as well as through its theology. Like prior evangelicals, participants in the ECM valued conversation as a practice, ecumenical and interfaith interaction (within carefully scripted boundaries), and praxis over doxis. This conception of the ECM casts its true innovation—the inclusion of the language of postmodernity and deconstruction into existing evangelical discourse—into sharp relief. It also provides a method of critique for existing definitions of the ECM produced by historians and anthropologists like Martí, Ganiel, and Bielo.

On a Sunday evening in 2004, a group of roughly thirty twenty-somethings gathered at the Menagerie Bar in Belfast, North Ireland, in a neighborhood adjacent to Queen's University.[1] The gathering referred to themselves as Ikon, and described their meeting as, "Inhabiting a space on the outer edges of religious life," through, "anarchic experiments in transformance art."[2] After many of the congregants acquired a drink from the bar, a service began with Peter Rollins, the founder of Ikon, delivering a short speech outlining the events to follow. In this speech, Rollins discussed the ways he had come to have certainty in the Christian faith, and how he had learned the importance of self-love. Following Rollins' introduction, there would first be the delivering of a testimony, interspersed with ambient electronic music and poetry. The testimony was delivered by Mervyn McCullagh, a regular Ikon participant, from an armchair in front of rows of tables and seats with maroon velour cushions.[3] Simultaneously, a large television off to the side was projecting video of an American televangelist. During the testimony, in which he spoke about the freedom he felt from pain and the peace he found in Christ, McCullagh smoked a cigarette. Then, McCullagh and Rollins invited those gathered to partake in the true body and blood of Christ by coming forward and receiving a piece of chocolate cake and a glass of champagne.[4] After this invitation to Communion (which few of those gathered accepted), a third speaker, Cary Gibson, came forward and told two stories.[5] Like McCullagh, Gibson was a regular participant in Ikon's transformance art. The first of Gibson's stories was a parable about Jesus feeding his disciples while the poor watched (rather than being fed themselves), and the second was a tale about someone going on trial for their alleged Christianity but being found 'Not Guilty.' Finally, those gathered were encouraged to discuss with those around them their reaction to the things they had just seen, and the remaining cake and champagne were informally distributed.

1. "855: Ikon, Menagerie Bar, Belfast, North Ireland."
2. "About Ikon."
3. Ibid.
4. Rollins, *How (Not) to Speak of God*, Kindle edition.
5. "855: Ikon, Menagerie Bar, Belfast, North Ireland."

Ikon's performance that Sunday evening was intended to be an ironic critique of the existing Christian Church, and is representative, albeit in the extreme, of the type of practice performed by those participating in the Emerging Church Movement (ECM). Though Ikon ceased meeting in 2013, its New York City church plant, begun in 2011, still gathers regularly at bars, coffee shops, and art galleries across Brooklyn.[6] Though participants in Ikon Belfast and Ikon NYC consider themselves artists, ECM Practice has historically included a diversity of practices, including—but not limited to—traditional congregational meetings, pub churches, transformation art performances, online worship services, and new monastic communities. Originating in the mid-1990s, the ECM has been notoriously difficult to define, not least because those operating under its aegis have engaged in myriad community formations and have actively resisted any kind of formal classification. As a result, little scholarly work has been produced dealing directly with either the social structuring or the history or lexicographic delineation of the ECM.

However, two significant works prove exceptions to the trend of avoiding definitional practice, currently exist. The most significant work, and most recent, is Gerardo Martí and Gladys Ganiel's *The Deconstructed Church: Understanding Emerging Christianity*. According to Martí and Ganiel, the ECM is, "a discernible, transnational group who share a *religious orientation* built on a continual practice of deconstruction."[7] The second work is James S. Bielo's *Emerging Evangelicals: Faith, Modernity, and the Desire for Authenticity*. In his text, Bielo defines the ECM as, "a movement organized by cultural critique, a desire for change, and grounded in the conditions of both modernity and late modernity."[8] While these definitions are worthwhile in that they represent a significant step towards better understanding the dynamics and bounds of the ECM, they are both ultimately too limited in scope. In Martí and Ganiel's case, a reliance upon the notion of identity confines the ECM to individual feeling. With Bielo's work, the ECM is restricted to a cultural critique. Viewed as an object of history, the ECM comes sharply into focus: the Emerging Church Movement is a milieu of progressive evangelical organizations engaged in a productively fraught relationship with evangelicalism as a whole. The ECM participates in this discursive tension with the tools received from its predecessors—a commitment to discourse as a spiritual practice, ecumenical and interfaith interaction, and praxis over doxis—and is marked by the innovation of the

---

6. "Ikon NYC: About."
7. Martí and Ganiel. *The Deconstructed Church*, 6.
8. Bielo, *Emerging Evangelicals*, Kindle edition.

inclusion of postmodern philosophical language, particularly regarding the problems of modernity and deconstruction.

EMERGING, EMERGENT, EMERGENCE: A WORD ABOUT TERMS

Any discussion of the ECM necessarily begins with terminology. Much ink has been spilt over the nomenclature of the ECM. Should the movement be labelled the Emerging Church, the Emergent Church/Emergent Christianity, or Emergence Christianity? Some combination of the three? None of the above? Confusion has been the order of the day among those inside the movement and those outside its bounds. In a post dated April 15, 2008 on the blog *Theoblogy*, Tony Jones, then the National Coordinator for Emergent Village, wrote about an experience in which he was asked whether the term 'emergence' or 'emergent' was technically correct.[9] In his post, Jones responded, "I get that this whole thing—emergent vs. emerging—is a meme being repeated by some people who mean well and others who, well, mean less well. But those people are making a huge mistake, methinks, because they are perpetuating the very modern mistake of separation and fragmentation."[10] Jones' attitude of avoiding classification is typical for those participating in ECM activity. Jones himself engages in this kind of "separation and fragmentation," however, in his book *The New Christians: Dispatches from the Emergent Frontier*.[11] In a section of the book entitled, "Some Working Definitions of Terms Used in this Book," Jones uses the term "emergent church," and he defines it as follows: "The specifically new forms of church life rising from the modern, American church of the twentieth century."[12] Jones goes on to distinguish between "the emergents," adherents in the ECM, and "Emergent," the latter meaning, "Specifically referring to the relational network which first formed in 1997; also known as Emergent Village."[13] Jones' definitions, while vague, are informative given his position within the ECM. Jones limits the emergent church to a specific time, place and ideological position—postmodern, late twentieth/early twenty-first century America—and he distinguishes between those generally engaging with the ECM and those associated with Emergent Village.

9. Jones, ""Emerging" v. "Emergent.""
10. Ibid.
11. Ibid.
12. Jones, *The New Christians*, Kindle ed.
13. Ibid.

Jones' definitional distinctions have largely been adopted by those in theological and sociological circles. Ed Stetzer, in his report to Lifeway Research in 2008, cedes authority on nomenclature to Jones, writing, "*The New Christians: Dispatches from the Emergent Frontier* bears the weight of its endorsers as 'the' definitive 'explication and explanation' of emergent."[14] Scot McKnight, a theologian loosely connected to the ECM, uses Jones' definitions as well, with one slight but important divergence. Speaking at Westminster Theological Seminary in October of 2006, McKnight said, "'emerging' is not the same as 'emergent.' . . . 'Emergent' refers to Emergent Village . . . 'Emerging,' on the other hand, is bigger, broader, and deeper."[15] Like Jones, McKnight distinguishes between those connected to Emergent-Village and the broader movement, but, rather than distinguishing via capitalization, McKnight creates a division based upon suffix.

A third, less commonly-used term, is Emergence. Touted primarily by Phyllis Tickle, the former Religion editor at Publisher's Weekly, the term is generally used to suggest the ECM as a new phase in the overall life of the Christian Church. In her book *The Great Emergence: How Christianity is Changing and Why*, Tickle writes, "'The Great Emergence' refers to a monumental phenomenon in our world," one which, "In its totality, . . . interfaces with, and is the context for, everything we do socially, culturally, intellectually, politically, economically."[16] Tickle's argument, essentially, is that the Great Emergence, like the Protestant Reformation and Great Schism before it, marks a turning point in the history of Christendom, one which, though still in its primordial phase, will ultimately reshape the entire landscape of Western Christianity. This providential conception of the ECM, despite being formally supported by Emergent Village, has not gained much traction academically or with the public.

A discussion of terms regarding the ECM is important for understanding the movement for several reasons. First, formal classification as an intellectual practice, and, more importantly, resistance to it, is a critical concept for the ECM. Building on the work of Jacques Derrida, many in the ECM value deconstruction as an individual and collective spiritual practice. John D. Caputo, a Derrida scholar with close ties to Ikon and others active in the ECM, writes, "deconstruction is treated as the hermeneutics of the *kingdom* of God, as an interpretive style that helps get at the prophetic spirit of Jesus."[17] Caputo argues that, rather than being a tool for the dismantling

---

14. Stetzer, "The Emergent/Emerging Church," 66.
15. McKnight, "What Is the Emerging Church?," 4.
16. Tickle, *The Great Emergence*, 13–14.
17. Caputo, *What Would Jesus Deconstruct?*, 26.

of Christianity, deconstruction can be a way of getting at the very heart of the Christian message. ECM practitioners model this through the common process of deconverting, an often painful release of former religious beliefs and affiliations. As a result, many within the ECM are resistant to any form of labelling as it results, in their view, from an unnecessary and most likely destructive systematizing impulse. Though this concern may well be legitimate, because deconstruction is an intellectual practice rooted in the analysis of terms, terms themselves become significant.

A second reason this discussion is important is it points to the way many within the ECM understand the movement in its broader context. Tony Jones, Brian McLaren, and others have alluded to the origin story behind the word 'emerge.' McLaren, in his book *A Generous Orthodoxy* (a text, coincidentally, Tickle refers to in the foreword as "our 95 theses"), writes briefly about the term, describing it originally as a word borrowed from environmental science that refers to the "small saplings that grow up in the shadow of the mature forest canopy."[18] For McLaren, Jones, Tickle and others, the ECM is the sapling which is growing up beneath the shadow of a dense Christian forest. From this perspective, the ECM is an outsider group, an Other defining itself as Other against the Christian hegemony. This perspective generates an attitude of distinction and opposition and, thus, specificity about terms becomes paramount.

A third reason this discussion of nomenclature is important is purely practical. If this religious movement is to be discussed historically, sociologically, or otherwise, it is necessary to have a standardized name for it. Emergent, as a term, hews too closely to an association with Emergent Village, an important but by no means all-encompassing organization within the scope of the movement. Emergence, on the other hand, seems far too grandiose, inaccurate, and lacking in consistent usage. Because of its adherence to the original meaning of the word as used by McLaren and the rest of the Young Leadership Network, because of its breadth in relating to the movement as a whole by McKnight and others, and because it is listed as such in the *Encyclopedia of Religion in America*, it will be referred to here as the Emerging Church Movement, or ECM.

EMERGENT VILLAGE: A HISTORY

In 1991 Douglas Coupland published *Generation X: Tales for an Accelerated Culture*. A frame story about the trials and tribulations of young Americans in their twenties, the book went on to become a sleeper hit, and the

---

18. McLaren, *A Generous Orthodoxy*, ePub Reader Format.

term "Generation X" became the de facto term used to define those born between 1961 and 1981.[19] Members of Generation X were considered the first postmodern generation, a group of Americans born into a culture of rampant materialism and, as a result, a group of Americans disenfranchised from mainstream cultural, economic and religious systems. Though studies have since dispelled this perception as a stereotype (most notably Jon D. Miller's 2011 report titled, "Active, Balanced, and Happy"), Christian ministers in the 1990s were distressed over their inability to connect with this new crop of twenty-somethings.[20] In the cover story of the September 1994 issue of *Christianity Today*, Andres Tapia writes of Generation X, "whatever one calls these 38 million young men and women . . . what makes them unique is that they are the first generation to grow up in a post-Christian America."[21] In an effort to address this problem, the Leadership Network, a nonprofit organization focused on helping "foster innovation movements that Activate the Church to greater impact," held a forum in 1996 to discuss new methods of bringing members of Generation X into the church.[22] This forum was followed by a conference in 1997 in Mount Hermon, California, and the instatement of Doug Pagitt as the coordinator of the Leadership Network's Young Leadership Network (YLN).[23] Pagitt had most recently been a youth minister at Wooddale Church in Edina, Minnesota, a suburb of Minneapolis, and is currently on staff at Solomon's Porch, one of the most prominent ECM congregations in the U.S. Pagitt was tasked by the Leadership Network with finding a Christian leader who could effectively communicate with members of Generation X in a way other megachurch pastors in the 1990s were reaching Baby Boomers.

One of Pagitt's initials actions as YLN Coordinator was to host a series of retreats for a small group of pastors that would come to be known informally as the "group of 20."[24] This group of ministers met all across the country in small groups, and included Chris Seay, Mark Driscoll, and Brian McLaren, among others.[25] The title of these retreats was "Gen X 1.0."[26] One of these retreats, held in Glen Eyrie, Colorado, became a turning point for YLN. During the multi-day meeting, Brad Cecil, then of Pantego Bible

19. Coupland, *Bookclub*.
20. Miller, "Active, Happy, and Balanced."
21. Tapia, "Reaching the First Post-Christian Generation."
22. "About Us."
23. Stetzer, "The Emergent/Emerging Church," 68.
24. Ibid.
25. Jones, *The New Christians*.
26. Jones, *The New Christians*.

Church in Fort Worth, Texas, was asked to give his assessment of the North American church's ideological situation. Cecil responded, "OK, I think you have it all wrong."[27]

Prior to his involvement with YLN, Cecil had undergone an intellectual and spiritual crisis which had led him to begin reading twentieth century philosophers like Jacque Derrida and Gilles Deleuze. Drawing on this experience, Cecil proceeded to deliver an overview of Western philosophical thought, beginning with the early church fathers and St. Augustine and ending with Richard Rorty.[28] Cecil argued that during the medieval period, truth was mediated by mystical experience, and that the originator of truth was the divine. During the Enlightenment and Modern periods, truth was mediated by texts, and humanity was seen as the originator of truth. Western civilization was now in a postmodern period in which truth was mediated by a synthesis of mystical experience and enlightenment empiricism. Cecil located the origination of this period with Wittgenstein and the publication of the *Tractatus Logico-Philosophicus* in 1921, and called this the "Age of Enlightened Mysticism."[29] For Cecil, the church's problem reaching Generation X went beyond just a communication disconnect, as many at the conference has previously suggested; the church's problem stemmed from its being a product of an outdated epistemological mode.

Cecil's talk changed the dynamic of the conversation happening among the group of 20, and it changed the dynamic of the YLN's efforts going forward. Practices common to future ECM congregations began to take shape, most notably a heightened emphasis on conversation and dialogue as a means to not only understanding truth, but experiencing it. Describing YLN practice in 2001, Brad Smith, then the president of Leadership Network, said that they use, "a "forum-style" process that doesn't force a particular agenda. The process allows the selection of a group of leaders around a common affinity, the right environment to learn from each other, and the ability for LN to understand the implications of the discussion so other groups can be 'spurred' to greater innovation."[30] The process of generating forum-style discussions became central to the work done by Pagitt and the rest of the YLN during this time as they wrestled with the collision of postmodern thought and traditional church practice. Brad Cecil adapted his impromptu talk at Glen Eyrie into a lecture and powerpoint (referred

---

27. Ibid.
28. Knight, "Ministry in the Emerging Postmodern World."
29. Ibid.
30. Smith, "What's Next with Terra Nova Project."

to by some ECM practitioners as the "legendary powerpoint") that he took across the country, delivering to churches, youth groups, and conferences.[31]

Breaking New Ground

In 1998, Pagitt organized a conference in Glorieta, New Mexico called the "National Re-Evaluation Forum" in order to bring more church leaders into contact with the ideas generated at the Glen Eyrie retreat. More than just talk at pastors and ministers, Pagitt hoped to demonstrate the kinds of practices YLN was beginning to develop. Having met earlier when both were serving as youth ministers in Minnesota, Pagitt invited Tony Jones to work at the conference as the leader of a youth ministry cohort.[32] Jones instantly connected with the other leaders, and became an integral part of subsequent YLN activities. After leading the YLN for 3 years, Pagitt stepped down in 1999 in order to found Solomon's Porch, and was replaced by Jason Mitchell, a well-known church planter.[33] Though Pagitt was no longer formally leading YLN, he remained involved in many of its activities, speaking at conferences and engaging in forums with other speakers. In early 2000, a new network under the provenance of YLN was formed for the purpose of encouraging experimentation with church practice. This network, named "The Terra Nova Project," involved many of the same ministers involved with YLN's early group of 20, including Brian McLaren and Brad Cecil.[34] Describing Terra Nova's mission and its participants, Brad Smith states, "These Groundbreakers are a new breed with a new calling, new tone and new priorities. They spend more time experimenting with new creations than critiquing past assumptions."[35] Terra Nova held a series of national conferences from 2000 to 2002 in Texas, California, Missouri, New Mexico, and Wisconsin.

A conference call occurred in May of 2001 between six YLN and Terra Nova leaders: Doug Pagitt, Brian McLaren, Tim Keel, Chris Seay, Tim Condor, and Brad Cecil.[36] In this teleconference, these six men discussed their takes on the importance of theology, their critiques of the churches within which they served, and their growing differences with Leadership Network.

31. Knight, "Ministry in the Emerging Postmodern World."
32. Jones, *The New Christians*.
33. Ibid.
34. Smith, "What's Next with Terra Nova Project."
35. Ibid.
36. "The Emergent Church: An Evaluation from the Theological Perspective of the Lutheran Church-Missouri Synod."

Despite supporting much of their early activity, Leadership Network's executive level staff had grown increasingly uncomfortable with the distance some YLN participants were putting between themselves and orthodox evangelicalism. Of particular concern to many involved with YLN were ecclesial structures. Everything from the types of denominational hierarchies in place in various institutions to the types of music and orders of worship came under scrutiny by YLN participants. This questioning of method from a theological perspective put the leadership of Leadership Network ill at ease because of their stated goal of focusing pragmatically on church practice. In the conference call, the six YLN leaders wanted to create a more formal structure within which to explore theological questions, and they wanted to develop a term to label this structure. The word 'emergent' was settled upon, based on the phrase 'the Church Emergent' popularized several years prior by the progressive Christian blogger Andrew Jones.[37] YLN was then officially disbanded, and Emergent Village formed.

The formation of Emergent Village, and the concurrent dissolution of YLN and Terra Nova, marked a cessation in funding and official support from Leadership Network.[38] In its earliest formation, Emergent Village existed as a mostly egalitarian organization consisting of volunteers under the direction of an unpaid Coordinating Council.[39] The group also selected Tony Jones to function as their National Coordinator. The first event organized by Emergent Village was "The Emergent Gathering" held in Glorieta, New Mexico in 2003. Though relatively small, the Emergent Gathering continued annually until 2007, increasing in attendance each successive year.

Boom and Bust

Until 2003, the history of the ECM and the history of Emergent Village are one and the same. The birth of Emergent Village, however, spawned the birth of a myriad of other ECM services, churches, conferences, and conversations. Over the course of the next six years, new organizations, such as Presbymergent for Emerging Presbyterians, were formed. New congregations such as Jacob's Well in Kansas City or Ecclesia in Houston took shape. Conferences, like the Wild Goose Festival held annually in Hot Springs, North Carolina, began taking place. Growth in the ECM has been difficult to measure formally, but one data set, collected in 2005 by Eddie Gibbs and Ryan K. Bolger, identified about 200 networks that could be

37. McLaren, phone conversation with author.
38. Jones, *The New Christians*.
39. Stetzer, "The Emergent/Emerging Church," 73.

labelled emerging.[40] These networks include large multi-site networks like Emergent Village, individual congregations like House of All Sinners and Saints in Denver, Colorado, and internet-only groups like Darkwood Brew or TheOOZE.com.

Emergent Village remained active during this time, hosting conferences, supplying congregations with speakers, and maintaining their internet presence at emergentvillage.com. The website particularly became an important gathering place for ECM participants. At the Emergent Village site, numerous writers, both those formally associated with Emergent Village, like Brian McLaren, and those not, like Micky Jones, were able to write blog posts and host discussions. Resources for those curious about theology or philosophy were made available on the Emergent Village site, and information about congregations sympathetic to ECM points of view could be obtained. Emergent Village also contracted with Baker Publishing Group to produce a line of officially sanctioned emergent texts, with titles such as *Thy Kingdom Connected* by Dwight J. Friesen and *An Emergent Manifesto of Hope* by Doug Pagitt and Tony Jones.[41] During this time, Emergent Village worked with other Christian organizations as well, most notably Mike Yaconelli's group Youth Specialities and the National Pastor's Convention.[42]

Momentum in the ECM began to slow, however, in 2008. On October 31, 2008, the Emergent Village board of directors voted to eliminate the National Coordinator position, removing Tony Jones from his leadership position with the group.[43] The stated purpose of this shift was to, "reclaim the Village's founding purpose as an 'egalitarian social-networking organization.'"[44] Other sources indicate, however, that the move may have been motivated by financial concerns and internal disagreements over the nature of Jones' leadership.[45] After this, in January of 2010, an exchange between blogger Andrew Jones and Tony Jones erupted across both of their blogs and on Twitter. The initial exchange centered on the continuing influence of the ECM for Christianity as a whole, and the use of the term "radical."[46] As a part of this discussion, Tony Jones communicated a distinction he made between a legal marriage and a covenantal marriage. These

---

40. Gibbs and Bolger, *Emerging Churches*, Kindle edition.
41. "Emergent Village Resources for Communities of Faith Series."
42. Stetzer, "The Emergent/Emerging Church," 73.
43. O'Brien, "Emergent's Divergence."
44. Ibid.
45. "The Emergent Church: An Evaluation from the Theological Perspective of the Lutheran Church-Missouri Synod."
46. Jones, "A Response to Tony Jones."

comments coincided with Tony Jones' divorce, remarriage, and accusations of having had an affair during his first marriage. In the comment section of Andrew Jones' blog, "TallSkinnyKiwi," and in the comment sections of other ECM-affiliated blogs, Tony Jones' ex-wife, Julie McMahon, made claims about negative treatment she had received from her ex-husband and from other ECM leaders. Her most pointed criticisms were leveled at Doug Pagitt, who she claimed tried to have her committed to a mental institution in order to make it easier for Tony Jones to quietly divorce her and preserve the good press associated with the release of his newest book.

Though these allegations remain unverified and highly contested by all involved parties, the effect they had on the ECM as a whole was profoundly negative. John Piper, a Minnesota-based pastor and frequent critic of the ECM, decried Jones and the ECM in a much-circulated YouTube video. Released March 24, 2010, Piper declares the ECM, "a fading reality," and goes on to say, "its leadership is in shambles, and I could give you horrible specifics from personal lives."[47] Piper's criticism was in keeping with other sentiments about the state of the ECM. Andrew Jones, previously a vocal supporter of and participant in the ECM, published a post entitled "Goodbyes to Emergent Village," in which he writes, "I will not be using the emerging church vocabulary . . . also over is any official relationship I have left with one of those emerging church groups called Emergent Village."[48] Other ECM participants chimed in as well during this time, including Brian McLaren in a post entitled "Is the Emerging Church Movement Fizzling Out?," and Tony Jones in a post entitled, "Is the Emergent Church Dead?," both written in 2012.[49]

In 2013, Emergent Village sold its website and reduced itself to a blog channel on Patheos, a web portal geared towards hosting blogs from a variety of religious points of view. Emergent Village also ceased producing content on either its Facebook page or Twitter feed, and it discontinued its publishing contract with Baker Publishing. Though blog posts do regularly appear, the channel was renamed "Emerging Voices" after a post by Mike Clawson declared in its title, "Emergent Village is NOT Dead. It's Just Different Now. . ."[50] According to Clawson, "Emergent Village seems to be a victim of its own success. As emergent ideals filter throughout the broader church, EV itself sometimes appears to lack a distinctive identity or

---

47. Piper, "The Emergent Church."
48. Jones, "Goodbyes to Emergent Village."
49. Jones, "Is the Emergent Church Dead?"
50. Clawson, "Emergent Village is NOT Dead. Its Just Different Now . . ."

purpose."[51] Clawson alludes in his post to the decline of Emergent Village, and of the ECM as a whole. Emergent Village/Emerging Voices exists now as a shadow of its former self, and none of its former Board of Directors participate in its management.

EMERGING PRACTICE

Numerous individuals have attempted to define the different strands of ECM practice since the formation of Emergent Village in 2001, at times in order to critique the ECM and at times to support. Mark Driscoll, for example, wrote in 2006 that there were three types of ECM practitioners: Relevants, Reconstructionists, and Revisionists. Driscoll, an early leader in YLN, discontinued participating in ECM activities in 2003 after developing significant theological differences with Emergent Village, and it is not difficult to discern based upon his classificatory language that he is leveling criticism at certain individuals active in the ECM. Relevants, the more generously titled sub-group, are described as "theologically conservative evangelicals," while Revisionists are pronounced, "theologically liberal."[52] Scot McKnight, on the other hand, defines the ECM much more generously in an attempt to support it. McKnight calls the ECM a "lake" with "four rivers" flowing into it.[53] The four rivers streaming into "Lake Emerging," for McKnight, are "postmodern, praxis, postevangelical, and politics."[54] McKnight describes the ECM essentially as a politically left-leaning, anti-institutional group of people focused upon a reorientation towards practice over belief for the sake of critiquing meta-narratives in keeping with postmodern tradition. McKnight vocally identifies particularly with the postmodern aspect of the ECM, as well as its generally progressive political perspective, and thus paints a glowing picture of the movement as a whole.

The question remains, then, as to how ECM practice can be defined and categorized without folding in latent praise or critique. The most efficient method is to examine commonalities between numerous ECM activities, and to then describe consistent patterns of thought and behavior. In doing this with the ECM, several key trends emerge that can serve to demarcate the ECM and its various sub-groups.

The first significant aspect of ECM practice is the notion of faith as dialogue or conversation. According to Martí and Ganiel, "People in the

51. Ibid.
52. Driscoll, "A Pastoral Perspective on the Emergent Church," 89–90.
53. McKnight, "What is the Emerging Church?," 9.
54. Ibid.

Part 2: What Is the Emerging Church?

Emerging Church Movement (ECM) can't stop talking. They talk and write continually both face to face and through social media."[55] This emphasis on dialogue is intended to be a critique of the traditional church practice of mediating truth through lectures or sermons. For many engaging in ECM activities, the traditional means of receiving truth, ideas, or doctrine is too linear, and, as a result, discourages genuine spiritual engagement. A better way, the ECM contends, to encourage people to connect with belief statements and theological concepts is to foster spaces in which numerous voices can be heard. Describing a typical meeting at Solomon's Porch in 2005, Kim Lawton says for *Religion and Ethics Newsweekly*, "Every member has a say in what happens. They don't call it a Sunday worship service; it's a worship gathering, and it happens on Sunday evenings. Pagitt doesn't preach sermons, he leads discussions. No question is off limits."[56] An important component of this method of spiritual practice is the breaking down of power structures. By not preaching sermons, and by communicating freely with those in the congregation, Pagitt intends to de-position himself as an authority figure. This move to eschew hierarchy informs much of the activity in the ECM.

Another important component of ECM practice is the notion of plurality. Central to the ECM's critique of traditional evangelicalism is that adherence to orthodoxy necessarily means the exclusion of a vast swath of humanity. In *A Generous Orthodoxy*, McLaren writes:

> To add insult to injury, nearly all orthodoxies of Christian history have shown a disdain for other religions of the world: Buddhism, Hinduism, Judaism, atheism, etc. A generous orthodoxy of the kind explored in this book, while never pitching its tent in the valley of relativism, nevertheless seeks to see members of other religions and nonreligions not as enemies but as beloved neighbors, and, whenever possible, as dialogue partners and even collaborators.[57]

Throughout *A Generous Orthodoxy*, and in other works like *Why Did Jesus, Moses, the Buddha, and Mohammed Cross the Road?*, McLaren attempts to walk a fine line between a universalistic approach to religious pluralism and a more exclusivist take on Christian dogma. This tension informs much ECM activity, and it plays a part in the emphasis on conversation as opposed to preaching. In a conversation, there is significant room for divergent belief and opinion that is absent, ECM participants would

---

55. Martí and Ganiel, *The Deconstructed Church*, 78.
56. Lawton, "The Emerging Church, Part One."
57. McLaren, *A Generous Orthodoxy*.

contend, from the traditional Christian practice of delivering or hearing a sermon. An example of this is a practice begun at Ikon, but now being performed in various ECM groups across the country, called "Atheism for Lent."[58] As a part of Atheism for Lent, Emerging Christians renounce their belief in God for forty days, choosing, instead of reading the Bible or praying, to complete a series of readings from atheist historians, psychologists, and philosophers. The purpose of this exercise is not to actually become an atheist at the end of forty days, but to inculcate in the participant's faith a higher degree of flexibility and tolerance.

A third significant ECM concept is that of praxis. Because of the existence of a plurality of beliefs and opinions (even under the umbrella of Christianity), and because heterodoxic grouping is encouraged, religious performance takes precedent over religious belief in ECM communities. Peter Rollins writes:

> I picture the emerging community as a significant part of a wider religious movement which rejects both absolutism and relativism which hide their human origins in the modern myth of pure reason. Instead of following the Greek-influenced idea of orthodoxy as right belief . . . the emerging community is helping us to rediscover the more Hebraic and mystical notion of the orthodox Christian who believes in the right way.[59]

Rollins makes a distinction here between holding to a rigid doctrinal system and participating in a ritual system regardless of doctrine. This attitude is prevalent in ECM activities, as evidenced by the fusion of contemporary Protestant behaviors, such as worship led by a rock ensemble, and pre-Enlightenment Christian behaviors, such as the lighting of candles or the practice of *lectio divina*. The purpose of this ancient-modern, or, as Episcopalian priest Robert E. Webber terms it, "ancient-future," ritual practice is to involve both the body and the emotions into a Christian practice many felt had been reduced to a purely intellectual exercise.[60]

There are numerous other distinctions that could be made regarding the ECM, but that are ultimately less significant. The emphasis on technological interaction, for example, or the emphasis upon political action, stand out. These traits, while prevalent, are not universal across the ECM spectrum, however. Neo-monastic communities, like Shane Claiborne's The Simple Way in Philadelphia, PA, do not stress the importance of blog-writing for example, and *Anglimergent*, a blog for emerging Anglicans and

58. "Giving up God for Lent."
59. Rollins, *How (not) to Speak of God.*
60. Webber, *Ancient-Future Worship*, 19.

Episcopalians, does not emphasize political involvement. Regardless of these lesser distinctives, at the root of all ECM activity is an awareness of Christianity as a Western meta-narrative, and an effort to deconstruct it. By shifting to conversation over sermon, ECM participants hope to break down denominational hierarchies and the authority structure inherent in a typical Protestant service. By attempting to generate nuanced conceptions of plurality, ECM groups try to critique dogmatic certainty. By favoring orthopraxis over orthodoxy, the ECM works to integrate the body, the heart, and the mind into ritual practice in response to a perception of the absence of the body or the heart in contemporary Protestantism. Taken together, ECM practice can be seen as a deliberate move against the elements of modernity perceived to be at the heart of twentieth-century evangelicalism, and an embrace of self-identified postmodern concepts.

MORE THAN A MOVEMENT

In light of the history and practice of the ECM, a classificatory problem emerges. How aptly can the ECM be limited, as Martí and Ganiel argue, to those who take on a particular religious orientation? Is the ECM, as Bielo suggests, strictly a cultural critique? Using the term 'movement' insinuates organizational coherence and unity of belief. Though much of the ECM world centered in the early 2000's around Emergent Village, it had no formal creed nor any theological monopoly. This allowed groups with ECM characteristics to exist across the United States in a variety of guises and with connections to a variety of preexistent organizational structures. Critique was certainly a fundamental element of all of these groups, but some retained connection to existing denominational structures, while others removed themselves entirely. Additionally, while deconstruction is an important concept for the ECM, it more readily describes the intent of ritual or organizational activity as opposed to the identity of a given individual. Definition strictly along the lines of orientation or resistance proves ultimately inadequate in the face of the full breadth of the ECM.

In order to better define the ECM, two things must be considered. First, the historical moment of the ECM's creation places it on a cultural crossroads. Stephen Ellingson, building off of the work of Jackson Carroll, argues that tradition consists of two components, "archive and activity."[61] As an archive, Ellingson writes, "tradition is a repository of symbolic forms."[62] As an activity, tradition informs contemporary religious behavior.

61. Ellingson, *Megachurch and the Mainline*, 23.
62. Ibid.

In the 1990's, many American Protestants experienced a schism between the archival and activist functions of tradition. While these practitioners continued to connect with the activist component, the archival component became segmented and separate, and many of them experienced a moment of crisis. The second consideration is the influence of postmodernity upon identity construction. As evidenced by the concern over Generation X, by the mid-1990's postmodernity was very much on the American church's radar. This signaled, more than anything else, a shift in the way Christian identities were being formed. According to sociologist David Lyon, "Religious identities today are being reconstructed to overcome the felt disjuncture between the legacy of conventional identities, with their traditional, linear progression, and the diverse experiences cobbled together under the sign of mobility."[63] Lyon points out the importance of the tension between traditional forms of identity construction in the Church through instruction and legacy, and newer forms of identity construction through a pastiche of perhaps incongruous experiences. This tension had a destabilizing effect for many. Taken together, both considerations reveal a situation ripe for the birth of something new.

What emerged from this instance of friction was less a movement, however, and more, drawing on the work of Colin Campbell, a milieu. Campbell describes, in his 1972 article, "The Cult, the Cultic Milieu, and Secularization," the existence of a "cultural underground" in which a whole host of New Religious Movements (NRMs) jostle against one another, rising and falling in a heterodox landscape set against the dominant orthodoxy.[64] Campbell's cultic milieu incorporates a whole host of religious identities, and is structured around the unifying concepts of seekership, syncretism, and mysticism. The ECM looks and acts remarkably like Cambell's cultic milieu. First and foremost, the ECM functions as a kind of underground against the backdrop of orthodox Christian structures. Martí and Ganiel point out that ECM participants are often caricatured as being "reactionary" in relation to established evangelical groups, but they argue this is the case only because ECM participants possess a religious identity of deconstruction and not necessarily of reconstruction.[65] In reality, the ECM is caricatured as reactionary because it is exactly that. Bielo points this out repeatedly in his work. "Emerging Evangelicalism," he writes, "is a movement defined by a deeply felt disenchantment toward America's conservative Christian

---

63. Lyon, *Jesus in Disneyland*, 91.
64. Campbell, "The Cult, the Cultic Milieu, and Secularization," 122.
65. Martí and Ganiel, *The Deconstructed Church*, 58.

subculture."[66] Without a hegemonic orthodoxy to push against, the ECM would have been boundless and unable to sustain its existence.

Campbell's cultic milieu, in addition, allows for a broad range of fluctuating groups and identities. This is the case because the cultic milieu is structured around seekership and syncretism. Describing the culture of the milieu, Campbell writes, "individuals who 'enter' the cultic milieu at any one point frequently travel rapidly through a wide variety of movements and beliefs."[67] Participants in the ECM behave similarly: a common narrative in the ECM is an introduction through the reading of a book, occasional visits to a local cohort or conversation group, and the eventual development of a unique, individualistic spiritual identity that may or may not align with an existing creed or denomination, and may or may not continue to evolve over time. Just as in Campbell's milieu, media, such as books and magazines (or, for ECM participants, blogs and podcasts), serve as entry points and points of continued connection. A push for syncretism exists in the ECM, too, as groups combine and dissolve over time. Hyphenate emerging groups exist across the board, from Presbymergents to Baptimergents, in which orthodox denominational theology is combined with ECM language and structure. Some ECM groups have experimented as well with short term church projects that arise for a set amount of time in order to deal with a specific issue, then disband. In both of these contexts, the ECM displays a highly flexible belief structure capable of sustaining recombination, restructuring, and radically altered organizational paradigms.

Lastly, as with Campbell's cultic milieu, the ECM displays a distinct tendency towards mysticism. According to Campbell, the mystical component of the cultic milieu, "emphasizes that the single ideal of unity with the divine can be attained by a diversity of paths," and that, "no matter how diverse or how many versions of the truth there are, all can lead to the same all-encompassing truth."[68] Many within the bounds of the ECM would be hesitant to use the language of mysticism to describe their religious point of view. Yet the mysticism Campbell describes fits succinctly into much of the rhetoric concerning pluralism in the ECM. For example, Tony Jones writes, "the emergent response to pluralism is always ad hoc, always contextual, always situational. It does not lend itself to tidy books or simple blog posts."[69] Jones goes on to describe the ECM as "pluriform and multivocal."[70]

66. Bielo, *Emerging Evangelicals*, Kindle edition.
67. Campbell, "Cultic Milieu," 123.
68. Campbell, "Cultic Milieu," 123, 125.
69. Jones, "Emergent Frontier," 39.
70. Ibid.

Though Jones does not go so far as to suggest that all religious paths lead to one divine truth, he does hint at the concept of a recognizable truth buried amidst the complexity of multi-faith interaction. Speaking more explicitly, Rob Bell, a popular religious writer with connections to the ECM, says, "If it is true, if it is beautiful, if it is honorable, if it is right, then claim it. Because it is from God. And you belong to God."[71] Bell neatly enmeshes New Testament language here with a call to seek out truth wherever one might find it. This mystical notion of truth facilitates the fluctuations of the milieu and the inclusion of diverse religious elements across its breadth.

WHAT'S BEHIND CHANNEL NUMBER THREE?

In August of 2013, the Values Voters Summit was held in Washington, D.C. Hosted by the Family Research Council, and highlighted by keynote addresses from Paul Ryan, Rand Paul, and Marco Rubio, the conference focused upon what it claimed were the three, "channels the adversary is using to bring America down."[72] According to the developers of the Summit, these three adversaries were Communism, Islam, and, much to the surprise of many, the ECM. Though the ECM's inclusion on this list of adversaries was not taken seriously by most outside of the conference, its inclusions as a dominant threat indicates the level of popular awareness the ECM has garnered since its development in the late 1990s and early 2000s. The ECM remains a relatively under-studied entity, and, despite the recent efforts of Gerardo Martí, Gladys Ganiel, and James Bielo, a relatively misunderstood one as well. An examination of the ECM reveals it to be a progressive Christian movement that centers on the practice of deconstruction as a form of resistance, particularly through its approaches to discussion, the plurality of belief, and the centrality of ritual performance. A broader heuristic provides a more complete picture, however. The ECM exists as a religious milieu in the tradition of Campbell's cultic milieu. Like Campbell's milieu, the ECM is a heterodox network of fluctuating groups and actors that is positioned against the backdrop of evangelical Christianity, and is united by threads of mysticism, seekership, and syncretism that run throughout.

BIBLIOGRAPHY

Atheism for Lent. "Giving up God for Lent." http://www.atheismforlent.net.

71. Bell, *Velvet Elvis*, Kindle edition.
72. Bailey, "Top Three Adversaries of Christian Conservatives: Communism, Islam... and the Emergent Church?"

Bailey, Sarah Pulliam. "Top Three Adversaries of Christian Conservatives: Communism, Islam . . . and the Emergent Church?" *Christianity Today*, August 27, 2013. http://www.christianitytoday.com/gleanings/2013/august/values-voter-summit-emergent-church-america-adversary.html?paging=off.

Baker Publishing. "Emergent Village Resources for Communities of Faith Series." Last modified 2014. http://bakerpublishinggroup.com/series/emersion-emergent-village-resources-for-communities-of-faith.

Bell, Rob. *Velvet Elvis: Repainting the Christian Faith*. Grand Rapids: Zondervan, 2005. Kindle edition.

Bielo, James S. *Emerging Evangelicals: Faith, Modernity, and the Desire for Authenticity*. New York: New York University Press, 2011. Kindle edition.

Campbell, Colin. "The Cult, the Cultic Milieu, and Secularization." In *A Sociological Yearbook of Religion in Britain* 5.1 (1972) 119–36.

Caputo, John D. *What Would Jesus Deconstruct?* Grand Rapids: Baker Academic, 2007.

Clawson, Mike. "Emergent Village is NOT Dead: Its Just Different Now . . ." Last modified February 23, 2014. http://www.patheos.com/blogs/emergentvillage/2014/02/emergent-village-is-not-dead-its-just-different-now/.

Coupland, Douglas. Interview with James Naughtie. *Bookclub*. BBC4, 11 March 2010.

Driscoll, Mark. "A Pastoral Perspective on the Emergent Church." *Criswell Theological Review* 3 (2006) 87–93.

Ellingson, Stephen. *Megachurch and the Mainline: Remaking Religious Tradition in the Twenty-First Century*. Chicago: University of Chicago Press, 2007.

Gibbs, Eddie and Ryan K. Bolger. *Emerging Churches: Creating Christian Communities in Postmodern Cultures*. Grand Rapids: Baker Academic, 2005. Kindle edition.

Ikon Belfast. "About Ikon." Last modified September 22, 2013, http://ikonbelfast.wordpress.com/about/.

Jones, Andrew. "A Response to Tony Jones." Last modified January 6, 2010. http://tallskinnykiwi.typepad.com/tallskinnykiwi/2010/01/a-response-to-tony-jones.html

———. "Goodbyes to Emergent Village." Last modified January 7, 2010. http://tallskinnykiwi.typepad.com/tallskinnykiwi/2010/01/goodbyes-to-emergent-village.html

Jones, Tony. ""Emerging" v. "Emergent."" Last modified April 15, 2008. http://www.patheos.com/blogs/tonyjones/2008/04/15/emerging-vs-emergent/.

———. "Is the Emergent Church Dead?" Last modified April 14, 2012. http://www.patheos.com/blogs/tonyjones/2012/04/14/is-the-emergent-church-dead/.

———. *The New Christians: Dispatches from the Emergent Frontier*. San Francisco: Jossey-Bass, 2008. Kindle edition.

Knight, Steve. "Ministry in the Emerging Postmodern World." Last modified April 14, 2008. http://www.slideshare.net/knightopia/ministry-in-the-emerging-postmodern-world.

Lawton, Kim. "The Emerging Church, Part One." July 8, 2005. http://www.pbs.org/wnet/religionandethics/2005/07/08/july-8-2005-the-emerging-church-part-one/11744/.

Leadership Network. "About Us." http://leadnet.org/about-us/.

Lutheran Church, Missouri-Synod. "The Emergent Church: An Evaluation from the Theological Perspective of the Lutheran Church-Missouri Synod." Last updated March 2014. http://www.lcms.org/page.aspx?pid=695.

Lyon, David. *Jesus in Disneyland: Religion in Postmodern Times.* Cambridge, UK: Polity, 2000.

Martí, Gerardo and Gladys Ganiel. *The Deconstructed Church: Understanding Emerging Christianity.* Oxford: Oxford University Press, 2014.

McLaren, Brian. Interview with Adam Sweatman, September 15, 2015. Transcript.

———. *A Generous Orthodoxy.* Grand Rapids: Zondervan, 2004. ePub Reader Format.

McKnight, Scot. "What Is the Emerging Church?" Lecture given at the Fall Contemporary Issues Conference at Westminster Theological Seminary, Philadelphia, PA, October 26–27, 2006.

Miller, Jon D. "Active, Happy, and Balanced: These Young Americans Are not Bowling Alone." *The Generation X Report: A Quarterly Research Report from the Longitudinal Study of American Youth* 1.1 (2011).

O'Brien, Brandon. "Emergent's Divergence." *Christianity Today.* December 2008.

Piper, John. "The Emergent Church." Youtube video, posted by, "Desiring God," March 24, 2010. https://www.youtube.com/watch?v=MkGq5A4QEjg.

Rollins, Peter. *How (Not) to Speak of God.* Brewster, MA: Paraclete, 2006.

Smith, Brad. "What's Next with Terra Nova Project: The Emergence of Terra Nova." *Terra Nova Network.* http://web.archive.org/web/20010419192307/http://www.youngleader.org/WhatsNext.htm

Stetzer, Ed. "The Emergent/Emerging Church: A Missiological Perspective." *Journal for Baptist Theology and Ministry* 5.2 (2008) 63–97.

Ship of Fools. "855: Ikon, Menagerie Bar, Belfast, North Ireland." http://www.shipoffools.com/mystery/2004/855.html.

Tapia, Andres. "Reaching the First Post-Christian Generation." *Christianity Today,* Sept. 1994.

Tickle, Phyllis. *The Great Emergence: How Christianity Is Changing and Why.* Grand Rapids: Baker, 2008.

5

Deconstructing Westphalia

The Emerging Church, Citizen Pilgrims, and Globalization

Terry Shoemaker

"Either religion will disappear due to the challenge [of globalization] or it will re-emerge as a force for renewal that offers resistance to globalization and provides alternative readings of reality."[1]

"The world has indeed gone flat again, the Reformation's nation-state having given way to the Emergence's globalization."[2]

Abstract

This project contributes to an understanding of the Emerging Church movement by conceptualizing the political activities and engagements of those within the movement. As a means of understanding these political engagements, this paper situates the Emerging Church in relation to the external forces of globalization to provide a "stipulative" definition of the Emerging Church as a geopolitical movement religiously activated. In other words, the Emerging Church movement utilizes religious resources and understandings to engage with aspects of globalization that

1. Falk, "The Monotheistic Religions," 140.
2. Tickle, *The Great Emergence*, 106

are perceived as corrupt or unjust. Specifically, this paper utilizes Richard Falk's call for "citizen pilgrims" to engage and challenge prevailing neoliberal enterprises at the global level. Falk argues that religiosity and spirituality are essential in interrogating dominant neoliberal systems that prioritize economy over human life and environmental concerns. The praxes of the Emerging Church align with Falk's citizen pilgrim model by engaging in critical patriotism and constructing an ethos of solidarity. Furthermore, the religious understandings of the Emerging Church movement transcend the nation-state model in recognizing the universal worth of human life while working to ameliorate perceived unjust economic conditions exploiting fellow humans around the globe by enacting charity practices and direct engagement with systemic criticism. As a result Emerging Church adherents are both engaging with the current nation-state system while also posturing and preparing for future forms of globalized life. In the end, I argue that the Emerging Church offers space for scholars to (re)consider the potentialities and possibilities of religious expansions and transformations of faith traditions vis-à-vis globalization.

INTRODUCTION

The very premise of definitions as exact meanings supplies a troublesome framework by which human movement is captured. By nature, human movement is fluid, dynamic, and circulating. Accordingly, I feel obligated to begin this project by detailing my working hesitance toward definitions, for I understand that definitions construct fences around entities of focus. These definitive fences constitute limits and bounds—temporary frameworks, which stultify future potentialities and possibilities by regulating ethics, practices, rituals, motions, signals, shifts, reformations and so forth. As scholarship amply demonstrates, historical attempts to define "religion" are broadly actualized in unidirectional comparisons (Christianity as the standard by which other "religion" stands in contrast); putative internalizations (unquestioned, tacit assumptions); and biased permanencies (once-adopted definitions maintain a life and strength) that instrumentalize hegemonic power structures.[3]

In this particular case, any attempt to define a human endeavor that self-describes, self-recognizes, and self-constructs its motion as "emerging"

3. Dubuisson, *The Western Construction of Religion*; and Masuzawa, *The Invention of World Religions.*

is fraught with challenges and irony. Particularly how do analyses define the motion, structures, and lived experiences of participants within the Emerging Church who industriously work to avoid singular categorizations but instead seek to reconfigure multidimensionality? As such, the Emerging Church (aka Emergent church)[4] continues to elude definition. For example, the structural fluidity, which "flattens" hierarchical leadership formations and rejects traditional institutional configurations, results in challenges of utilizing previous methods to analyze the forms and shapes of Emerging Churches.[5] Quite possibly the best that one can hope to accomplish is not an exact definition, but an adventurous attempt to capture a fleeting moment—a capturing that generates refined questions to continue the processes of capturing.

My first premise is based on the inabilities and historical deficiencies of definitions and refuses attempts to interrogate the Emerging Church from a singular plane of existence. Alternatively, I fully admit that this project only supplies one angle by which to capture a dynamic property or characteristic of the Emerging Church through a "stipulative" definition as Thomas Tweed suggests that "cannot be true or false . . . only more or less useful."[6] Ideally, definitions of the Emerging Church include a corpus of disciplinary approaches (i.e. theological, sociological, anthropological, psychological, historical), which is why the current collaborative research approach is functionally useful. The second assumption works from the notion that the Emerging Church is truly emerging—taking shape or materializing from multiple contexts because human motion extends from multiple vectors. Therefore this project intentionally strives to provide both a framework of juxtaposition while also acknowledging the unique constructs of the Emerging Church that allows the Emerging Church to stand by itself as unique as well as simultaneously contingent upon others.

With these considerations on definitions and assumptions in mind, let me get on with the business of explaining my research objectives in this paper. I want to argue that by situating the Emerging Church within Richard Falk's "citizen pilgrim" framework, a stipulative definition of the Emerging Church materializes. To achieve this objective, I briefly engage with current literature imagining citizenship at a transnational level in light of globalization advancements. The literature review contextualizes an outline of the "citizen pilgrim" paradigm as proposed by Richard Falk. Subsequently, I

---

4. Emerging and Emergent are two distinct labels, but the distinctions can be quite unclear. For simplicity, henceforth, I utilize Emerging Church.

5. Discussing the idealized structures of Emerging Churches, Tony Jones utilizes "flat" to conceptualize the limited hierarchy. See Jones, *The Church is Flat*.

6. Tweed, "Marking," 262.

situate the Emerging Church within these frameworks by demonstrating that Emerging Church adherents exemplify the Falkian ethos of solidarity both philosophically and through praxis. All of this leads to a "stipulative" definition of Emerging Church participants as geopolitical agents implicitly and explicitly practicing the concepts of citizen pilgrim through a "postmodern" posture.

CITIZEN PILGRIMS

The processes of globalization continue to proliferate through increasing transnational advancements in economics, communication, and migration. These proliferations include global market realities actualizing in the severing of labor forces and consumers. Beyond market realities, globalization involves the narrowing of geographical and cultural distances. The present connectivity of humans exists at an altered state allowing ideas to spread at an increasingly quick rate. In addition, due to these advancements, today's borders are more porous. Although many decry the enhanced mobility of persons through nation-state boundaries, transnational movement is enhanced through globalization.

The advancements engender conversations regarding the reconceptualization of citizenship to encompass a global civil society.[7] And the shared realities of human beings across the globe as it relates to ecological, economic, and humanitarian issues catalyze the discussions. Nigel Dower and John Williams' conceptualization of global citizenship exemplifies contemporary attempts at defining global citizenship:

> a member of the wider community of all humanity, the world or a similar whole that is wider than that of a nation-state or other political community of which we are normally thought to be citizens. This membership is important in the sense that it involves (or would involve if people accept that they are global citizens) a significant identity, loyalty or commitment beyond the nation-state.[8]

Structurally and institutionally, however, there remain debates regarding the possibilities of an emerging global citizenship. For instance, some have questioned the ability of a globalized citizenship to displace

---

7. K. Anthony Appiah is one scholar who demonstrates the long history of the concept of global citizenship or cosmopolitanism. Thus herein, global citizenship and citizen pilgrim are understood as modern *re*conceptualizations. See Appiah, "Global Citizenship."

8. Dower and Williams, "Introduction," 1.

the Westphalian model of citizenship tied to statehood.[9] Others argue that global issues transcend nation-states requiring an expanded model of citizenship to be reconceptualized and reconfigured to meet these global demands.[10] In this regard, Luis Cabrera goes so far as to argue for an institutionalized suprastate to properly define and regulate global citizenship.[11] Yet others suggest an abstract conceptualization of global citizenship, recognizing the interconnectedness and necessity of adequately addressing global issues, but through the nation-state model.[12] In sum, no consensus regarding global citizenship, whether in potentiality or in form, currently exists; however, acknowledgements that a movement toward materializing forms of global citizenship exist.

Within the discursive practice of conceptualizing citizenship within a global civil society there is a broad assumption, both implicitly and explicitly, that religion competes with national and global structuring identities. The processes of globalization, mediated and catalyzed through advancements, also engender new ontologies and identity formations for religious persons around the world. Historically speaking, religion played a central function in preserving, maintaining, and forming particular cultural identities; thus often religion is understood as competing with globalization. This competition induces theorists to exclude religion from the globalization discussion, usually based on a secularization theory.[13]

If religion enters into the discourse of globalization, it is typically framed as a foil of globalizing enterprises in a particular agenda of religious antiglobalism or "mobilizing public religions."[14] Antiglobalizing religious persons actively resist many of the characteristics of globalization while envisioning the formation of new religious states based from specific doctrines, dogma of religion, or prioritizing religious identity formations. These religious persons tend to be of the fundamentalist or radical religious nature (although, admittedly, the categorizations of fundamentalist and radical are problematic) with narratives that compete with national narratives. Thus positioned to resist the impacts of globalization into a transnational world order, the antiglobalizing religions perpetrate doctrines which are "regressive and carr[y] with it a genuine danger of a new cycle of religious warfare

9. Liu, "Why There's no Such Thing"; and Paraekh, "Cosmopolitanism."
10. Ignatieff, "The Myth"; and Appardurai, "Broken Promises."
11. Cabrera, *The Practice of Global Citizenship.*
12. Appiah, "Global Citizenship."
13. Bush, "Measuring Religion."
14. Beyer, *Religion and Globalization*; Kinnvall, "Globalization and Religious Nationalism"; Juergensmeyer, "Religious Antiglobalism"; Casanova, *Public Religions in the Modern World.*

carried out on a civilizational scale."[15] Many of the antiglobalizing religions outside of the United States are in response to American neo-colonialism, the challenge of globalization to nationalism, and a distrust of Western secular society. Possibly the most well known prediction of antiglobalizing religion is Huntington's "clash of civilization" theory.[16] To be sure, antiglobalizing religions accept many of the forms of globalization—communications, technologies, and economics as examples—but the insistence in resisting uniformity with the creation of religiously based nation-states are what make this type *anti*globalizing.

Yet there exist conceptualizations that integrate religious persons into the manifesting forms and structures of globalization, while not necessarily seeking to make religion a legally controlling form at either the nation-state or global level. A leading voice of this perspective is Richard Falk. In fact Richard Falk proposes that the processes of globalization *require* religiosity or spirituality to integrate empathy, action, and relational aspects into the globalization discourse and praxes.[17] Ethical input from religious persons is warranted within this understanding due to the dominant economic prioritizations. The globalized neoliberal economic philosophy, according to Falk, subverts the authority of nation-states. He describes the current states of globalization:

> To the extent that the state has been instrumentalized by a combination of global market forces and a general antipathy toward bureaucracies and regulation, the sphere of governmental autonomy with respect to promoting the well being of the territorial citizenry is diminished.[18]

Consequently, nation-states are at the mercy of economic agendas. With limited external accountability measures, nation-states become complicit in the neoliberal agenda of protecting economic rights over and against human rights. And Falk perceives the dominance of world economic philosophy and unbridled neoliberalism as inherently destructive.

To conceptualize the role of religion in opposition to the current, dominant forms of neoliberal globalization, Falk introduces a hierarchical paradigm. He defines a "globalization-from-above" predicated on the unjust ways in which transnational market forces influence state polices ignoring

---

15. Falk, "Religion and Global Governance," 7.
16. Huntington, "The Clash of Civilizations."
17. Falk, "Religion and Global Governance."
18. Ibid., 16.

negative humanitarian consequences.[19] The unjust actions of market forces include disproportionate wealth distributions, alarmingly dangerous and extended labor conditions for workers, and policies prioritizing economic gains over and against human life. "Globalization-from-above" describes the current processes of globalization, which need to be mitigated according to Falk.

Oppositional to "globalization-from-above," Falk proposes a framework of "globalization-from-below" working against unjust and dominant transnational market forces. This "globalization-from-below" is dependent upon religious and spiritually minded "citizen pilgrims" who embrace their roles and responsibilities within the globalizing civil society. On this topic, Falk submits, "religious response itself constitutes a form of globalization that seeks to challenge capital-driven globalization on the basis of a more spiritual and ethical understanding of the human condition."[20] For Falk, religious actors will ameliorate and mediate the current unjust realities of globalization because the "citizen pilgrim" model is built upon an "ethos of solidarity," which includes (1) "the unity of all creation, and, with it, the sense of both wholeness of human experiences and the dignity of the individual" and (2) "a sign of religious inclusiveness and celebration of religious diversity."[21] Both of the required ethical components allow space for religious persons to maintain particularities while simultaneously embracing universalities. Falk's proposed ethos also recognizes an inherent wholeness or a connectedness to "creation." I interpret Falk here as attempting an inclusionary way of extending the ethos of solidarity beyond the human—establishing an ethos that considers plant, animal, and environments.[22] Others, like Robert Wright, call for the monotheistic religions "to create tolerant scriptures or to find tolerance in existing scriptures" while also developing universal soteriology, but few integrate religious persons into the manifesting globalized society like Falk.[23] And as far as I can find, Falk never spotlights particular models of the citizen pilgrims operative in the world today.

---

19. Falk, "Resisting 'Globalisation-from-Above' Through 'Globalisation-from-Below.'"

20. Falk, "The Monotheistic Religions," 144.

21. Falk, "Religion and Global Governance," 29.

22. Current conversations regarding biocentrism and the extension of rights to animals vis-à-vis religion expand well beyond Richard Falk, Christianity and the Emerging Church. For more information on this topic see Attfield, "Biocentrism, Religion, and Synthetic Biology."

23. Wright, *The Evolution of God*, 426.

THE EMERGING CHURCH AS CITIZEN PILGRIMS[24]

Religious expression serves as a way of conceptualizing episodes of human movement. In the Western world premised on modernity, a plethora of religious options are available to religious persons and nonreligious persons alike.[25] One of the religious options available to those within the United States is referred to as the Emerging Church. Materializing out of American evangelicalism, definitive categorization of the Emerging Church proves challenging. The movement is not a traditional denomination connected through common beliefs or physical structures; rather, it is a phenomenon across the theological and doctrinal spectrum that maintains shared values. And although the movement started from within the evangelical branch of Christianity, it now includes participants from Mainline Protestantism, charismatics, and Catholicism, as well as those outside of the Christian tradition altogether.

One approach to capturing the Emerging Church movement seeks to map its surfacing. Determining an exact time and location when the Emerging Church began proves challenging because devotees envision the phenomenon as organic and as a progression of myriad religious narratives and cultural shifts (thus "emerging.") But scholars position the Emerging Church as starting in the 1990s as a reaction and response to various cultural shifts in the United States and around the globe.[26] The Emerging Church as a movement within the United States is situated as initially a reactionary movement over and against American Evangelicalism. Perceiving American Evangelicalism as deficient in social engagement, spiritual discipline, ecclesiological structure, and reactions to a diversifying society, early devotees (not then known as the Emerging Church) sought to reconfigure and reform existing components of American Evangelicalism in order to recalibrate a new way of "being" the church.

The recalibration of the Emerging Church works in formulating new praxis within the increasingly pluralistic religious environment by understanding their motion as an anthropological moment based in a specific context and time. Doug Pagitt, an organizer within the Emerging Church and a pastor of a church called Solomon's Porch, echoes these sentiments

---

24. Because of the novelty of the Emerging Church movement, only minimal research has attempted elucidation. As such, much of the following thick description relies on Emerging Church elites' writing and practices. I utilize research where available to substantiate the objectives stated by said Emerging Church elites.

25. Taylor, *A Secular Age*.

26. Bielo, *Emerging Evangelicals*; and Burge and Djupe, "Truly Inclusive or Uniformly Liberal?"

by describing his faith as, ". . . a faith of creation, participation, movement and change."[27] The acknowledged and embraced fluidity produces an emphasis on creating social contexts that foster freedom of thought resulting in a wide-variety of political and theological perspectives. This emphasis results in a self-description as a conversation, a network, or a friendship. Moreover, the Emergent Village website, an information center that allowed members to connect, describes the movement as "a growing, generative friendship." Brian McLaren, a leading figure and writer within the Emerging Church movement, states, "[Emerging Christians] stand wide-eyed, trying to take in what's going on . . . understanding [life] as an unfolding story, an emergent family drama, with birth, growth, struggle, maturity, death, and resurrection."[28] And the network is not exclusive. Anyone of any religious or nonreligious tradition is invited into the conversation to discuss his or her religious/nonreligious narrative.

The open dialogue practices decenter rigid doctrinal stances, which cultivates a freedom of religious expression. Structurally, there are no official leaders, offices, or institutional guidelines within the Emerging Church. In essence there is no standard model. Dan Kimball, an Emerging Church pastor in Santa Cruz, California, posits, "Instead of one emerging-church model, there are hundreds and thousands of models of emerging churches."[29] Others have noticed that the less corporatized version of religiosity fashioned by the Emerging Church communities "results in a new kind of organizational arrangement—one that continually and consistently re-formulates itself in order to avoid becoming static and predictable."[30] And Stephen Hunt notes, "in principle, at least, heated theological debates are not on the agenda for the Emerging Church since Christians should present the faith through loving attitudes rather than logical arguments."[31]

The dynamism in organizational structures and the attempt to foster dialogues are well highlighted by current scholarship. James Bielo describes these characteristics as "emerging genealogies" focusing on "five intersecting points of dialogue . . . theology, missiology, ecclesiology, liturgy, and politics."[32] To be sure, the characteristics, politics, and theologies of the Emerging Church should be understood partially as a response to American

---

27. Pagitt, *A Christianity Worth Believing*, 7.

28. McLaren, *A Generous Orthodoxy*, 321.

29. Kimball, *The Emerging Church*, 4.

30. Packard and Sanders, "The Emerging Church as Corporatization's Line of Flight," 441.

31. Hunt, "The Emerging Church," 291.

32. Bielo, *Emerging Evangelicals*, 10.

Evangelicalism and other forms of religiosity within the United States. My overall argument is that Emerging Church devotees are not simply responsive and reactionary to American evangelicalism but are also responding to new globalizing social conditions resulting in new national and global identity constructs. Beyond the scope of this work, other projects seek to fully describe the emergence of the movement—its resistance to structures and hierarchy—and the main actors supplying voices to the critiques and postulations.[33] Thus, instead of providing a full explication of the movement, I will focus henceforth primarily on the geopolitical praxis of the Emerging Church vis-à-vis the Falkian citizen pilgrim paradigm.

As previously mentioned, the first responsibility of a Falkian citizen pilgrim is to engage unjust global practices based from neoliberal economics and policies. My reading of this portion of Falk's model extends beyond uncritical charity models and procedures. Admittedly, there exist myriad examples of religious organizations facilitating good work to ameliorate inadequate access to resources (e.g., food banks, soup kitchens, financial assistance programs, etc.). Many religious communities and agencies provide resources with the tacit intention of assisting an individual or family for it is at the locale of the individual or family where assistance is perceived as warranted. To be sure, many of the practices of the Emerging Church include endeavors like volunteering at soup kitchens and food banks. Yet there is a distinction here to be made. Beyond the charity model, Emerging Churches engage in a critically reflective discourse with the prevailing systems that cause poverty, inequality, etc. seeking to recognize and react to unjust economic conditions around the globe.

Let me provide one example of this critical charity model. Rick McKinley, pastor of Imago Dei Community in Portland, Oregon, organizes his church to work against powerful consumerist forces in American society by organizing a national campaign called "Advent Conspiracy." This campaign asks everyone who celebrates Advent to consider purchasing fewer gifts during the Advent season and, instead, reallocate the funding toward providing clean water to those in need around the globe.[34] Inherent in this program is a simultaneous charity for those in need of clean water and a critique of consumerist values. This moral criticism that, "American churches have over accommodated to a superficial consumer culture and a complacent middle-class lifestyle that disregards social justice and concern for the

---

33. Kimball, *The Emerging Church*; Tickle, *The Great Emergence*; Jones, *The New Christians*; Martí and Ganiel, *The Deconstructed Church*.

34. For more information visit http://www.adventconspiracy.org.

poor" accentuates the engagement with current economic realities and the subsequent attempts at improving the lives of those around the globe.[35]

In short, the Emerging Church, like Falk's model, criticizes the consequences of unfettered capitalism and imperialism. In fact, Emerging Church authors engage in full structural analyses including ecological and environmental considerations. Brian McLaren's book *Everything Must Change: Jesus, Global Crises, and a Revolution of Hope* offers the most trenchant critique of major systems operating in the world, which he categorizes as the prosperity system, the equity system, and the security system. According to McLaren, all of these systems are interdependent and contain negative consequences for the global ecology, economy, and humanity. He suggests that the prosperity system is based from natural resources. These resources are harvested at an alarming rate and result in engendering economic and political inequality. The prosperity system forces the equity system to be unjust because those that are wealthy are working from the oppression of the less fortunate. The unjust disparity between the wealthy and the poor is the impetus for the security system due to the wealthy endeavoring to ensure their continued wealth. For McLaren, these three systems have created the current environmental catastrophes, perpetuated war, and generated a class system around the globe.[36] In response to the injustice systems operating in the world, McLaren imagines, almost echoing Falk's citizen pilgrim framework, "the development of faith-inspired movements for social justice around the world" as the solution.[37] These practices are postulated as a direct challenge to global systems of injustice and "serve to create a religious challenge to US imperialism and, in some cases, to market capitalism."[38] Furthermore, Shayne Lee and Phillip Sinitiere note, "The Emerging Church gives evangelicalism a liberationist facelift by demonstrating what the gospel has to say about the global economy, the growing economic divide between the rich and the poor, and the mounting danger of violence from both terrorists and antiterrorists."[39]

Emerging Church devotees exemplify the second characteristic of the Falkian paradigm—the ethos of solidarity, expressed philosophically and actualized through praxis. Many organizers and authors of Emerging Churches refuse to avow the primacy of Christianity in relation to other

---

35. Harrold, "Deconversion," 82.
36. McLaren, *Everything Must Change*, 151–52.
37. Ibid, 253.
38. Reed, "Emerging Treason," 67.
39. Lee and Sinitiere, *Holy Mavericks*, 105.

religions.[40] In fact, Emerging Church devotees are creating multi-faith sites for dialogue and worship.[41] For instance, one Emerging Church practitioner, Samir Selmanovic organizes a worship center that welcomes Jews, Christians, and Muslims to worship together. Selmanovic is a proponent of the potentiality of "finding god in the other."[42] Or as Tony Jones, an Emerging Church organizer and theologian states, this is "an attempt to both maintain one's distinctive identity while also being truly open to the identity of the other."[43] In this regard, I posit that the Emerging Church works to expand and embrace multidimensional understandings of identity—both as universal and particular. This is not to devalue other forms of identity. Instead this is an inclusive move toward joining in sexuality, gender, and racial discursive practices.

The Emerging Church acknowledgement of a universal human value also manifests again with critical engagement of systemic structures. Consider another example from Brian McLaren, who *Time* called one of "The 25 Most Influential Evangelicals in America." McLaren wrote a letter to then President George W. Bush requesting him to include the number of Iraqi deaths into the total death toll numbers released to the public during the Iraq War. Also, McLaren has spoken out against what he perceived as irresponsible use of power by the Western world:

> Here in the United States we see large sectors of the Christian community associated with American hyperconfidence, white privilege, institutional racism, civil religion, neocolonialism, and nationalistic militarism—often fortified by a privatized faith in a privatized nationalistic/tribal god . . . We find ourselves awakening to a pervasive mindset that feels capable of self-doubt and is quick to judge "the other," slow to admit its own faults.[44]

Accordingly, McLaren and many Emerging Church devotees refuse to maintain an uncritical patriotism contrasting sharply with the nationalistic tendencies of other American religious persons (i.e. Evangelicals). Critical patriotism requires one to be "both devoted to American political values *and* possess a critical understanding" of how these values actually operate within the nation and beyond.[45] The critical patriotism embraced by the Emerging

40. Hunt, "The Emerging Church."
41. Chia, "Emerging Faith Boundaries."
42. Selmanovic, "The Sweet Problem," 189.
43. Jones, *The New Christians*, 39.
44. McLaren, *Everything Must Change*, 148.
45. Parker, "Symbolic versus Blind Patriotism," 98. Within the context of the United

Church expands their sense and scope of political and moral obligations. This is similar to Bhikhu Parekh's philosophical understanding of globalization narrowing the disparity between general and specific responsibilities.[46] Within this framework, Parekh suggests micro and macro levels of responsibility maintained by individuals. The general duties (macro) consist of those responsibilities to all humans, and the specific duties (micro) consist of those responsibilities to one's close network (family, friends, etc.). Due to increasing global awareness, the two levels of responsibilities are in the process of converging. This framework aids in situating the Emerging Church's approach to understanding themselves less as American citizens and more as transnational agents. The critical patriotism corresponds to Falk's notion of the citizen pilgrim's political identity:

> This distinctively religious understanding of essential political identity by reference to a spiritual journey that is unseen and unlikely to be completed within the span of a lifetime but the value of which is an object of intense faith and dedication that extends beyond prescribed and instinctive loyalties to nation and state.[47]

The Emerging Church, antithetical to antiglobalizing religion, embraces many aspects of globalization while working to ameliorate perceived unjust economic conditions exploiting fellow humans around the globe by enacting charity practices *and* direct engagement with systemic criticism. This is based from an ethos and praxis similarly aligning with the Falkian responsibilities of citizen pilgrims of constructing universal soteriologies and acceptance; criticizing of unjust practices outside of nation-state membership; while also embracing cultural diversity. But it extends further as well. The Emerging Church formulates and constructs new ways of knowing and being vis-à-vis both the current Westphalian nation-state system and transnational potentialities with the employment of unique resources.

Like other religious persons, the Emerging Church employs particular resources at its disposal to assist in the articulation and work of critical engagement.[48] A resource that Emerging Church devotees utilize is the

---

States there exists a rich history of critical patriotism. For more information, see Berns, *Making Patriots*.

46. Parekh, "Cosmopolitanism."

47. Falk, "Religion," 30.

48. As an example of another resource, liberation theology, particularly in the South American context, proved quite useful in mobilizing and organizing adherents into action.

philosophical concept of deconstruction.[49] Martí and Ganiel posit that deconstruction for Emerging Church participants incorporates "a form of micropolitics in which actors establish competitive arenas in response to pressures for conformity."[50] Dan Kimball, pastor of Vintage Faith Church, suggests that the Emerging Church is predicated on first deconstructing and then reconstructing.[51] Often this tool of deconstruction is situated as primarily theological or ecclesiological, but I want to posit that deconstruction is a political resource that applies to the current nation state system. Deconstruction does not simply mean elimination. Rather it is a process by which one disassembles an entity, evaluates the components for usefulness, and then reconstructs, refashions, or reforms the useful components often with the addition of new components. Emerging Church praxis and ethos tend to acknowledge some retainable elements of the current nation-state system. Thus the Emerging Church is not simply anarchist with intentions of destroying the long-standing Westphalian system. Rather the current movement works both from within the current system and beyond it allowing for critiques and movement.

Here is quite possibly where an additional understanding of the Emerging Church's infatuation with postmodernism manifests. Like Paul Rabinow, many Emerging Church participants recognize that modernity is an ethos, not simply an epoch.[52] The ethics of the modern valorize the new over the old. "Post" in this context of modern signifies a posture vis-à-vis this ethos. This posture is constituted by both an acknowledgement of past and present realities and future-looking potentialities. Again this is typically applied to theology, but in this context, the future-looking potentialities include new forms of citizenships, cosmopolitanism, and new motions of being human. To be sure, these postures are dynamic and unstable allowing participants to navigate and negotiate their positions.

CONCLUSION

Religious movements tend to spawn reformed or modified versions of the initial movement especially when social contexts transform. One such example accentuated by historians and anthropologists is the Axial Age period

---

49. Although some Emerging Church voices link directly to Derrida's philosophical notion of deconstruction most utilize an adaptive version of deconstruction like indicated by Martí and Ganiel.

50. Martí and Ganiel, *The Deconstructed Church*, 26.

51. Kimball, *The Emerging Church*.

52. Rabinow, *Marking Time*.

of human history. During this period, a nascent version of globalization manifested due primarily to advances in technology and new economic practices. Consequently, David Graeber strongly posits a fundamental reason for new religious expressions (i.e. Buddhism, Christianity, and Islam) emerging during this time period as a counter to unjust economic philosophies, which increased poverty while reducing human value.[53] Likewise the current period of globalization is envisioned as corresponding to the Axial Age.[54] Falk would concur that the current globalization trends are due to transnational and unjust economic philosophies resulting in negative consequences for people across the globe. The ability of the nation-state system to address the unfair practices, posits Falk, is diminishing as the nation's authority decreases. The result is a necessitated space for religious and spiritually motivated actors to address these injustices by developing moral ontologies and epistemologies, which counter the prevailing market philosophies.

All this considered, religion could be categorized as either resisting or contributing to current globalization. As demonstrated within this paper, the Emerging Church with critical patriotism, inclusivity, and contestation of modern neoliberal economics is indicative of the Falkian citizen pilgrim paradigm, which under the Falkian model is essential for an ethical response to current globalization trends. By focusing on the practices and ideals of Emerging Church voices, numerous examples validate this categorization with several more examples available.

Also recognized within the study is the dynamic nature of religion, especially of loosely organized human movements like the Emerging Church. These movements provide a loose structure allowing religious expressions more flexibility in adjusting to social and economic shifts. Therefore, human movements are not static, largely due, as I have argued to the continual discourses proliferating within these Christian movements. Hence the descriptions contribute to the understanding of religion in the United States as globalization continues to challenge American hegemony both at the global and national level.

Equally important, the Emerging Church provides one potentiality regarding the conceptualizing of global identity by religious persons. Whereas many within the globalization discourse marginalize or eliminate religion from positively contributing to the processes of globalization, the Emerging Church could conceivably furnish a way of conceptually producing new responsibilities through religious frameworks. This process depends more

---

53. Graeber, *Debt*.
54. Szakolczai, "The Concept."

on values, which recognize a universal worth to humans and just economic practices, and less on doctrinal and belief systems. It is too early at the present time to speculate on the future of global citizenship, but, to be sure, current and future contributions of religious persons should not be overlooked or minimized.

To conclude this research I want to return to the notion of providing a stipulative definition of the Emerging Church. For this particular angle of research, the research provided in this paper situates Emerging Church participants as creative geopolitical agents engaging with unjust global systems through localized practices and critiques of the current nation-state system in a form paralleling Richard Falk's "citizen pilgrim" model. At the disposal of Emerging Church adherents are resources—theological, philosophical, and political—that permit current engagement with current systems while also posturing and preparing for manifesting systems. And Falk's citizen pilgrim model instantiates the fluidity of the process as a moving journey, a pilgrimage. But this research also yields more refined questions beyond the inquiry of "what is the Emerging Church?" For instance, guiding future questions should focus more on the human motion of the movement. How does the Emerging Church continue to shape and reform? What are the other arenas in which the Emerging Church is moving that are ignored by analyses? Can the Emerging Church resist the Weberian routinization model? If so, what practices facilitate this resistance? How do the commitments of the adherents highlighted in this paper react and respond to other religious persons' resistance to globalization and in support of national identity? If citizenship is conceivably a pilgrimage, then what other pilgrimages are performed and constructed?

BIBLIOGRAPHY

Appardurai, Arjun. "Broken Promises." *Foreign Policy* 132 (2002) 42–44.
Appiah, K. Anthony. "Global Citizenship." *Fordham Law Review* 75 (2007) 2375–91
Attfield, Robin. "Biocentrism, Religion, and Synthetic Biology." *Worldviews* 17 (2013) 26–35.
Beyer, Peter. *Religion and Globalization*. London: Sage, 1994.
Bielo, James. *Emerging Evangelicals: Faith, Modernity, and the Desire for Authenticity*. New York: New York University Press, 2011.
Burge, Ryan and Paul Djupe. "Truly Inclusive or Uniformly Liberal? An Analysis of the Politics of the Emerging Church." *Journal for the Scientific Study of Religion* 53 (2014) 636–51.
Bush, Evelyn. "Measuring Religion in a Global Society." *Social Forces* 85 (2007) 1645–65.

Cabrera, Luis. *The Practice of Global Citizenship*. New York: Cambridge University Press, 2010.
Casanova, Jose. *Public Religions in the Modern World*. Chicago: University of Chicago Press, 1994.
Chia, Lloyd. "Emerging Faith Boundaries: Bridge–Building, Inclusion, and the Emerging Church Movement in America." PhD diss., University of Missouri–Columbia, 2010.
Dower, Nigel and John Williams. "Introduction." In *Global Citizenship: A Critical Introduction*, edited by Nigel Dower and John Williams, 1–10. New York: Routledge, 2002.
Dubuisson, Daniel. *The Western Construction of Religion: Myths, Knowledge, and Ideology*. Translated by William Sayers. Baltimore: John Hopkins University Press, 2003.
Falk, Richard. "An Emergent Matrix of Citizenship: Complex, Uneven, and Fluid." In *Global Citizenship: A Critical Introduction*, edited by Nigel Dower and John Williams, 15–29. Edinburgh: Edinburgh University Press, 2002.
———. "Citizenship and Globalism: Markets, Empires, and Terrorism." In *People Out of Place: Globalization, Human Rights, and the Citizenship Gap*, edited by Alison Brysk and Gershon Shafir, 177–190. New York: Routledge, 2004.
———. "The Monotheistic Religions in the Era of Globalisation." *Global Dialogue* (1999) 139–48.
———. "Religion and Global Governance: Harmony or Clash?" *International Journal of World Peace* 19 (2002) 3–37.
———. "Resisting 'Globalisation-from-above' Through 'Globalisation-from-below.'" *New Political Economy* 2 (1997) 17–24.
Graeber, David. *Debt: The First 5,000 Years*. Brooklyn: Melville House, 2011.
Harrold, Philip. "Deconversion in the Emerging Church." *International Journal for the Study of the Christian Church* 6 (2006) 79–90.
Hunt, Stephen. "The Emerging Church and Its Discontents" *Journal of Beliefs & Values* 29 (2008) 287–96.
Huntington, Samuel. "The Clash of Civilizations." *Foreign Affairs* (1993) 22–49.
Ignatieff, Michael. "The Myth of Citizenship." *Queens Law Journal* 12 (1987) 399–420.
Jones, Tony. *The New Christians*. San Francisco: Jossey–Bass, 2008.
Juergensmeyer, Mark. "Religious Antiglobalism." In *Religion in Global Civil Society*, edited by Mark Juergensmeyer, 135–48. Oxford: Oxford University Press, 2005.
Kimball, Dan. *The Emerging Church*. Grand Rapids: Zondervan, 2003.
Kinnvall, Catarina. "Globalization and Religious Nationalism: Self, Identity, and the Search for Ontological Security." *Political Psychology* 25 (2004) 741–67.
Labanow, Cory. *Evangelicalism and the Emerging Church: A Congregational Study of a Vineyard Church*. Burlington, VT: Ashgate, 2009.
Lee, Shayne and Phillip Luke Sinitiere. *Holy Mavericks: Evangelical Innovators and the Spiritual Marketplace*. New York: New York University Press, 2009.
Liu, Eric. "Why There's no Such Thing as Global Citizenship." *The Atlantic*, August, 2012. http://www.theatlantic.com/national/archive/2012/08/why-theres-no-such-thing-as-global-citizenship/261128/.
Masuzawa, Tomoko. *The Invention of World Religions: Or, How European Universalism Was Preserved in the Language of Pluralism*. Chicago: University of Chicago Press, 2005.

Martí, Gerardo, and Gladys Ganiel. *The Deconstructed Church: Understanding Emerging Christianity*. Oxford: Oxford University Press, 2014.

McLaren, Brian. "Brian D. McLaren Blog." http://www.brianmclaren.net/emc/archives/imported/a-sermon-for-president-bush.html.

———. "Church Emerging: Or Why I Still Use the Word Postmodern but with Mixed Feelings." In *An Emergent Manifesto of Hope*, edited by Doug Pagitt and Tony Jones, 141–52. Grand Rapids: Baker Books, 2007.

———. *Everything Must Change: Jesus, Global Crises, and a Revolution of Hope*. Nashville: Nelson, 2007.

———. *A Generous Orthodoxy: Why I am missional + evangelical + post/protestant + liberal/conservative + mystical/poetic + biblical + charismatic/contemplative + fundamentalist/calvinist + anabaptist/anglican + methodist + catholic + green + incarnational + depressed-yet-hopeful + emergent + unfinished Christian*. Grand Rapids: Zondervan, 2004.

———. *Why Did Jesus, Moses, the Buddha, and Mohammed Cross the Road? Christian Identity in a Multi-Faith World*. New York: Jericho, 2012.

Packard, Josh, and George Sanders. "The Emerging Church as Corporatization's Line of Flight." *Journal of Contemporary Religion* 28 (2013) 437–55.

Pagitt, Doug. *A Christianity Worth Believing: Hope-Filled, Open-Armed, Alive-and-Well Faith*. San Francisco: Jossey-Bass, 2008.

Parekh, Bhikhu. "Cosmopolitanism and Global Citizenship." *Review of International Studies* 29 (2003) 3–17.

Parker, Christopher. "Symbolic versus Blind Patriotism: Distinction without Difference?" *Political Research Quarterly* 63 (2010) 97–114.

Putnam, Robert, Lim, Chaeyoon, and Carol Ann MacGregor. "Secular and Liminal: Discovering Heterogeneity Among Religious Nones." *Journal for the Scientific Study of Religion* 49 (2010) 596–618.

Rabinow, Paul. *Marking Time: On the Anthropology of the Contemporary*. Princeton: Princeton University Press, 2007.

Reed, Randall. "Emerging Treason? Politics and Identity in the Emerging Church Movement." *Critical Research on Religion* 2 (2014) 66–85.

Selmanovic, Samir. "The Sweet Problem of Inclusiveness: Finding Our God in the Other." In *An Emergent Manifesto of Hope*, edited by Doug Pagitt and Tony Jones, 189–200. Grand Rapids: Baker, 2007.

Szakolczai, Arpad. "The Concept of 'Axial Age' or New Light on the Question of Globalization." *Szociologiai Szemle* 1 (2004) 36–65.

Taylor, Charles. *A Secular Age*. Cambridge, MA: Belnap, 2007.

Tickle, Phyllis. *The Great Emergence: How Christianity Is Changing and Why*. Grand Rapids: Baker, 2008.

Turner, Victor. "Liminality and Communitas." In *The Ritual Process: Structure and Anti-Structure*, 94–113. Chicago: Aldine, 1969.

Tweed, Thomas. "Marking Religion's Boundaries: Constitutive Terms, Orienting Tropes, and Exegetical Fussiness." *History of Religions* 44 (2005) 252–76.

Wright, Robert. *The Evolution of God*. New York: Back Bay, 2009.

6

From Monks to Punks
Emerging Christianity in Canada

Steven M. Studebaker and Lee Beach

Abstract

This chapter is based on research done across Canada in 2011—14 thanks to a grant received from the Lilly foundation. The authors visited and interviewed numerous people and groups that were seeking to develop creative and contextually relevant approaches to church ministry. This chapter brings to light the innovations to church practice that are taking root in the increasingly secular, multicultural, pluralistic, and post-Christian culture of North America and specifically Canada. This essay, however, is not simply a survey of new practices in Christian ministry. Rather, this research showcases that the motivation for this kind of contemporary ministry comes from core biblical and theological convictions that direct these innovative churches and ministry leaders. As a result, their theological sensibilities give these initiatives cross-contextual applications. This chapter considers three key theological ideas that shape emerging churches in Canada. First, these churches reflect a move from Christendom to post-Christendom and offer a model for thinking about how the Christian faith relates to a culture that is increasingly post-Christian. Second, incarnational ministry offers an approach to ministry that has urban and rural ramifications. Third, holistic spirituality affirms the goodness of God's creation and all areas of life are the arena of discipleship. These theological convictions promote a vision for Christian life and ministry that offers a counter narrative to the secularization and privatization of religion that is the overriding narrative of current Canadian life in popular discourse on religion in Canada (and North America) today.

Until just a few decades ago Canada was predominantly a Christian nation. Today it is one of the West's most post-Christian nations. In post-Christian Canada, declining involvement in traditional churches continues unabated. Attendance at evangelical churches remains static, due mostly to the assimilation of new immigrants and the rise of churches that are populated by these new Canadians. Without this injection of new life, the traditional evangelical churches would also be in serious decline. The prognosis for Christianity in Canada appears grim. But that is not the whole story. During this period of decline, new and vital forms of church arose. Often called "emerging churches," they are fresh responses to the new cultural location of the Canadian churches and to what they perceive as the problematic remnants of the Christendom churches.

This investigation derives from a two-member collaborative and interdisciplinary project, "From Monks to Punks: Emerging Christianity in Canada."[1] The researchers teach at McMaster Divinity College in Hamilton, ON. Studebaker teaches in Theological Studies and Beach in Ministry Studies. We teamed together for this project because we believe our distinct areas bring important interdisciplinary perspectives to the project—theological, sociological, and ministry studies. This essay presents the results of this research project on innovative and alternative forms of the church in Canada. A Lilly Collaborative Research Grant provided funding for this project. The majority of our research took place from 2012 to 2014. The Lilly Grant enabled us to investigate emerging churches across Canada in British Columbia, the Prairie Provinces, Ontario, Quebec, and the Maritimes.[2] This

---

1. This project has three objectives. First, describe the Canadian church's cultural context. Contemporary Canadian culture includes 1) a move toward a post-Christian culture, leading to an overall decline in church participation and the church's cultural influence and 2) a growing disaffection with the traditional church among many who identify as Christians. Second, showcase innovative ways that Christians have adapted to the dynamic cultural (and spiritual) landscape of contemporary Canadian culture—e.g., the house church movement, new monastic/intentional communities, and urban revitalization church communities. Third, identify core theological themes that inspire these new expressions of the church in their effort to live an authentic spiritual life and to engage people in a post-Christian culture.

2. The primary source of data for identifying the theological themes and motivations at the heart of these churches is direct participation and interaction with

essay first outlines the post-Christian cultural context and types of emerging churches in Canada.³ The second and primary part details three of the key theological characteristics of these churches.

FROM CHRISTENDOM TO POST-CHRISTIAN AND POST-SECULAR CULTURE

The context of emerging Christians is the broader erosion of religious involvement in Canada over the past several decades (similar statistics also characterize religious trends in the United States).⁴ From the beginning of its European and English colonization through the 1960s, Canada was a Christendom culture.⁵ Decline of faith and religious activity is most sig-

---

emerging churches and their leaders and congregants. The project uses the analytic-inductive sociological method of grounded theory, wherein theoretical propositions and conceptual formulations are developed, informed, assessed, and adjusted by making direct comparisons of the data obtained (i.e., interviews, observations, and participant-observation) from the sites of inquiry. The adaptive nature and interest in the role that meaning making has in human behavior and associations makes grounded theory suitable for this project. The objective is to develop an account of emergent expressions of Christianity based on direct data and not on text-based expert theories and/or a priori academic interpretations. Our use of grounded theory focuses primarily on issues of theology and practice. Our primary data derives from interviews with, and observations of, leaders and practitioners during site visits to emerging churches. These visits also provide us an opportunity to immerse ourselves as much as possible in the everyday life of these churches so that we are able to gain an intersubjective understanding and appreciation of the social meanings and experiences of our participants. For grounded theory, see Blumer, *Symbolic Interactionism*, 1–60, Bryant and Charmaz, *The SAGE Handbook*, Charmaz, *Constructing Grounded Theory*, Lorenz Dietz, Prus, and Shaffir, ed., *Doing Everyday Life*, 7–54, 373–412, and Glaser and Strauss, *The Discovery of Grounded Theory*.

3. Also, reviewing innovations in church ministry in Canada is Bowen, ed., *Green Shoots out of Dry Ground*. The key difference between Bowen's project and our research is that Bowen focuses primarily on new practices and ministry initiatives, whereas we emphasize the theological convictions that inspire the new visions of Christian life and ministry.

4. Kevin N. Flatt, focusing on the United Church, attributes decline to the dissipating effects of liberal theology—*After Evangelicalism*. Joel Thiessen, considering religious activity more broadly, attributes religious decline to falling demand for religion among Canadians—*The Meaning of Sunday*. Flatt, along with David Millard Haskell and Stephanie Burgoyne argue that slumping religious activity is not a problem of dropping demand for religion, but the supply of theologically conservative religion that people want ("Theology Matters" 515–41). Although recognizing that Christianity, measured by adherents and participation, is in overall numerical decline in Canada, Sam Reimer and Michael Wilkinson show that among evangelical Christians religious activity remains relatively high and vigorous—*A Culture of Faith*.

5. For the history of Christianity in Canada, see Bramadat and Seljak, "Charting

nificant among emerging adults (ages 18–29). Through most of the 1960s more than half of Canadians reported they had attended religious services in the past seven days.[6] Not so today. Nearly half of pre-boomers (born before 1946) report monthly attendance at a religious event. Less than one in five post-boomers (born after 1965) attend religious services on a monthly basis. But the downturn also affects older generations. Attendance figures among boomers (born between 1946 and 1965) show significant drop-offs. Where 45% of pre-boomers indicated monthly religious attendance, only 30% of boomers did so in 2000.[7] Since the 1970s the percentage of people who never attend religious services doubled (from 20% to 40%).

Even bleaker is the statistic that only 13% of the post-boomer generation attends religious services on a weekly basis.[8] As David E. Eagle points out, "Canada has transitioned from a country where less than one-fifth of the population would not set foot in the door of a church or other religious venue in a given year to one where this is the norm for almost half of the population. This change occurred over a mere 22 years . . . these changes signal major societal shifts." Eagle believes this transition reflects the process of secularization. He does not see secularization as the inevitable result of the rise of modern culture, but as an undeniable historical phenomenon taking place in Canada.[9] Sociologist Reginald Bibby's interpretation of the decline and whether or not a renaissance of involvement with organized religion or polarization of religious and non-religious groups is underway has come under scrutiny. Significantly, however, the scholarly debate is one of degree and not kind. They all agree that religious participation among Canadians is in decline and the only categories that show any meaningful growth are non-attendance and no religious affiliation.[10]

Yet, the outlook is not entirely gloomy. The overall decline of participation in Christian religious activities seemed to reach a bottom at just under one in three Canadians in the late 1990s.[11] Statistics from 2010 show that while only 28% of Canadians attend religious services on a monthly basis, 65% say that spirituality and religious issues are important to their

---

the New Terrain," 6–11.

6. Bowen, *Christians in a Secular World*, table 2.3, p. 28

7. For statistics in this paragraph, see Bibby, *The Emerging Millennials*, table 9.1, p. 165.

8. Bowen, *Christians in a Secular World*, 31.

9. Eagle, "The Loosening Bond of Religion," 838–39.

10. Bibby, "Continuing the Conversation"; and Bibby, *Beyond the Gods and Back*, 133–35; Eagle, "Changing Patterns of Attendance"; and "The Loosening Bond of Religion"; and Thiessen and Dawson, "Is There a 'Renaissance' of Religion?"

11. Bibby, "Continuing the Conversation on Canada," table 2, p. 835.

everyday life.[12] Michael Wilkinson and Sam Reimer, moreover, document that Canadian evangelical Protestant churches, if not mainline Protestant and Catholic churches, have retained institutional vitality.[13] This vitality is often most clearly seen in new initiatives, often called "emerging" churches.

EMERGING CHURCHES

Though these emerging Christians share a common commitment to the Christian faith, they are not monolithic. They range from retired people, to mid-career upper-middle class professionals, young hipsters, refugees from traditional forms of Christianity, street people, and more. "Emerging" is not limited to the "emergent church" movement, though many of them began in, and may still fit within, that movement. The term refers to new alternatives to traditional forms of the church. The term is as fluid and difficult to define as "alternative" music. Emerging Christians represent a diversity of backgrounds, interests, social lifestyles, and age groups. They have a vibrant faith and a desire to develop their spiritual lives and theological perspectives.

Like the diversity found among emerging Christians, the emerging churches have numerous forms. These new forms of the church include intentional communities, colonizing churches, social enterprise churches, and third space churches. They encompass a diverse spectrum of churches from small urban communities like "Little Flowers" in Winnipeg that practice monastic vows together to "Look to the Cross for Victory" a group of Christians in Edmonton that are committed to ministry among the anarchist and "punk" community. Though these churches are diverse, they reveal common theological values and patterns of practice.

Intentional communities or new monastic communities are an important form of the emerging church. Matthew 25 House is an intentional community in Hamilton, a struggling industrial city in Southern Ontario. A group of seminary and university students, with the financial support of a couple from the Maritimes, started Matthew 25 House. The group consists of single young adults and a married couple. They live according to a covenant of community life. They pool and share their resources. Their vision of community life also includes serving and connecting with their neighbors through undertakings such as organizing activity days for neighborhood children.

Colonizing churches enter once thriving middle class communities and Christendom churches. Another Hamilton church, Eucharist,

12. Bibby, "Continuing the Conversation on Canada," table 2, p. 835.
13. Reimer and Wilkinson, *A Culture of Faith*.

represents this form of emerging church. Central to the vision of Eucharist is living and working in the neighborhood of the church. Suburban evangelical churches are often commuter churches. Parishioners travel from various middle and upper middle class suburbs to attend them. In contrast, the members of Eucharist believe that being a part of the local community is essential. Many of the members have relocated to the immediate vicinity of the church. Some have started small businesses in the community. This active participation in the revitalization of the neighborhood helps them to build relationships with people in the community.

Social enterprise churches endeavor to enhance community life. The Crossings church combines a coffee shop, community center, and affordable housing for people on public assistance in the downtown area of Acton, a small town on northwest outskirts of Toronto. The Story, an innovative church in Sarnia, Ontario, is one such church. The Story inhabits two storefront spaces in the old downtown center. Based on the petro chemical industry, Sarnia boomed in the middle decades of the twentieth century, but has ever since steadily declined. Like many former and dying industrial towns in the Great Lakes Rust Belt, Sarnia faces a shrinking population, poor air quality, and economic atrophy. The Story is part of the town's effort to revitalize its urban core. The Story promotes micro-businesses, local artists, and community initiatives.

Third space churches meet in non-church venues such as community centers, coffee shops, and youth centers. Their goal is to reach people who are unlikely to enter a traditional church. Café Church in Kingston (Ontario) is a third space church. Kingston is a professional and university town. The church meets in a coffee shop in the business district of Kingston. Their goal is to provide a church for unchurched professionals.

While diverse in practice all of these churches embody certain theological values that guide them. The three characteristics described in detail below help to define the theological foundations and motivations of the emerging churches that we visited. They include 1) a movement from Christendom to community churches, 2) a focus on the Incarnation and contextual theology, and 3) holistic spirituality.

FROM CHRISTENDOM TO COMMUNITY CHURCHES

During the era of Christendom, the churches enjoyed a dominant social role. They expected to, and often did, guide the moral mind of Western culture. That day has passed. Canada's political, educational, and public social institutions promote secular identities. The lingering legacy, or perhaps the last gasp, of Christendom is the culture wars. That is, trying to maintain a "Christian" culture through political means. Pursuing political influence is the churches' desperate attempt to retain and regain its role as the moral soul of society. Emerging churches, however, have a different orientation to culture than Christendom churches. Where some churches run to defend the last ramparts of Christian cultural influence, emerging Christians regard Christendom as a lost cause and have no interest in fighting the culture wars. They are not without, however, an interest in social engagement. But their social vision is local rather than national. Moreover, their issues differ from those that characterized the culture wars. They are more interested in finding ways to build relationships with gay people than boycotting a corporation for its policies toward gay people. Their vision of social engagement differs theologically from what animated, and still does in some cases, the Christendom churches. Christendom churches want to see their view of Christian morality implemented through political and judicial processes. The emerging churches, however, focus on bringing justice, often understood in terms of the biblical concept of shalom, to the lives of people. The emerging Christians' rejection of Christendom and adaptation to post-Christian Canada is pragmatic, theological, and local.

Pragmatic

Emerging churches are pragmatic because they recognize that Christian churches no longer occupy a privileged place in Canadian culture and the church's effort to regain widespread social influence is fruitless. Emerging Christianity is a realistic adaptation to the reality of post-Christendom. They are not, however, indifferent to their culture. They believe churches should turn to areas where they can make a difference. For example, they want to build relationships with the lesbian, gay, bisexual, and transgender (LGBT) community rather than boycott a corporation for its policies toward them or try and overturn marriage equality laws.

Darrell Muth has been a pastor for many years and, coming from a conservative tradition, never thought that his ministry would include dancing with a drag queen on one of Edmonton's main streets, but that is what it meant for him to tangibly express Jesus' presence among the people he serves and loves. Being pragmatic about ministry to his community included marching in the annual HIV parade as a result of his churches involvement with HIV Edmonton. It was a moment of solidarity with a group of people who are often devalued and ostracized but are loved by the church that Muth pastors; "the Urban Bridge." One of the members of the "Urban

Bridge" commented that she knew she was in the right church when she witnessed Muth dancing with the drag queen because she thought that is what Jesus would do given the same set of circumstances. She intuitively sensed that Darrell's spontaneous action was a reflection of a practical willingness to go in uncomfortable directions in order to show Jesus' love to people. For her, dancing with a drag queen seemed more appropriate than marching in a protest against such people.

Theological

The rejection of Christendom is also theological. Emerging Christians not only see efforts to shore up the crumbling walls of Christendom as pointless, but also problematic. Where Albert Mohler laments that the "Christian church" is no longer at "the center of Western civilization," emerging Christians join with Stuart Murray and Stanley Hauerwas and celebrate "the end of Christendom and the distorting influence of power, wealth and status quo on the Christian story."[14] Leaving behind the institutional Christendom churches, authentic Christianity emerges as a new movement on the margins of Western society.

Emerging Christianity rejects not only the collusion of the church with culture that characterized the Christendom churches, but identification with and participation in mainstream culture as well. The problem is not simply Canadian, and more broadly North American, culture and its decadence. The marginalization of the church in the increasingly post-Christian West is not just a historical circumstance. It is the ecclesiological ideal. Marginal identity is essential for faithful Christian identity and witness. Whether in ancient Rome or modern North America, authentic Christianity can only emerge on the edge of empire and not in collusion and collaboration with it. Faithful Christian witness requires relocating to the margins of the empire. Just as Jesus came to the world on the outskirts of the imperial order and ministered among the discarded detritus of the imperial order, so Christians today must abandon the comforts of power and privilege and go to the "wilderness outside" the empire.[15]

Rejecting the Christendom project means that their theology of social engagement differs from that of the Christendom churches. Christendom

---

14. Mohler, "Keeping the Faith"; Murray, *Post-Christendom*, 21; and Hauerwas and Willimon, *Resident Aliens*, 18.

15. Claiborne and Haw, *Jesus for President*, 79. Claiborne is American but frequently speaks to Canadian audiences and was, moreover, frequently mentioned as a formative model by emerging Christians in Canada.

churches sought to implement their vision of Christian morality through political, judicial, and social policies. Emerging churches, however, want to bring justice, often understood in terms of the biblical concept of shalom, to people's lives. They want the gospel and God's grace to transform people in personal relationships.

When asked about the idea of the church using political influence to bring about more "Christian" social policies, one Ontario church leader responded directly, "that's a load of crap." He went on to articulate a theology of the church in culture that anticipates that God is deeply at work in the world and the role of the church is to develop relationships with people in authentic ways that allow a natural influence to take place. Fighting culture-war battles lost long ago is pointless. In post-Christendom, the focus must be on local incarnation of the gospel so that its wisdom and attractiveness are embodied in the life of the church as an alternative community rather than as a political force.

Thus, these churches have no interest in mandating and imposing Christian morality through legal fiat. The church is about ministry on the margins and not manipulating the levers of social power. Indeed, they believe the church's collusion with political power corrupts the church's mission. Jesus met and touched the lives of people on the margins of society, not by issuing edicts from the corridors of political power.

Local

Engaging the world for emerging Christians has a local orientation. They believe churches should attend to social justice issues in their local communities. Less concerned with the national moral crusades of Christendom churches, alternative churches want to bring tangible grace to the forgotten people on the margins of empire. The margins they have in mind, however, are more often the post-industrial economic dead zones of cities like Hamilton and Sarnia than the slums of Calcutta. Local orientation is a product of accepting the post-Christian condition of Canadian society. Mission is not primarily something that happens overseas, but across the street. Local also means living in the neighborhood of the church and building relationships with their neighbors. They reject the commuter church. Commitment to the place and people of their Church is central to their ecclesiology.

For Mosaic church in Vancouver commitment to place meant making the "most marginal, the center" in their poor, urban neighbourhood. They structure congregational life around those who are mentally and physically challenged, living with addictions, or are socially marginalized because of their lifestyles. Because large portions of the population in their community reflect one or more of these realities, Mosaic has endeavored to reflect the demographic make-up of their neighborhood in their church congregation and leadership. They could be a church of middle-class, suburban, white people who parachute into the urban core and run a ministry for a poor, disadvantaged neighborhood, in which case the church would primarily be led by people who do not resemble the population of their immediate surroundings. Instead, they have taken seriously the place where they are planted and sought to include their community in a way that reflects the make-up, lifestyles, habits, and ideas of their community. Their embeddedness in their local community is apparent to anyone who shows up at one of their gatherings.

For some people in the churches that we visited being embedded means actually moving in to the communities where their church is located. Eschewing the possibility of being a "church commuter" members of the "Commons" in Hamilton, Ontario moved into one of downtown Hamilton's poorest and most challenging neighbourhoods in order to be among the people that they seek to serve. They shop at the same stores, they frequent the same coffee shops, their kids play in the same parks, they bump into one another on the street. Their vision is fueled by the simple question, "how can we really know our neighborhood and get to know the people we are seeking to serve without being present with them and living life together?" This kind of commitment to locality is characteristic of the churches that we studied and derives from a theology shaped by the incarnational ministry of Jesus himself.

INCARNATIONAL AND CONTEXTUAL CHURCHES

Among innovative and self-described "missional churches" the word "incarnational" is pervasive. Ignoring incarnational theology and ministry as just another faddish way for making Christianity culturally relevant, however, is a mistake. For these missional churches, being incarnational defines the essence of Christian life and ministry for emerging Christians and their churches. Why? Because the fundamental work of salvation was the Incarnation of God in Jesus Christ. The following discusses three facets of the vision for the Christian life and ministry practice that flow from this theology of the Incarnation.

From Theological Mystery to Tangible Ministry

In the world of theology, the Incarnation is the Christian doctrine that describes the union of the divine Son of God with human nature in Jesus Christ. Probing the mystery of how the divine and human natures were united in Jesus Christ is important. But more is at stake in the Incarnation than the subtleties of Christian doctrine. The Incarnation speaks to the very nature of God's redemptive activity in history. Among emerging Christians, the Incarnation has become more a theology for concrete Christian life and ministry and less a doctrine of mystery. Darrell Guder expresses the view common among emerging Christians, "We must ask, are our missional institutions, our churches and organizations, incarnational?"[16]

What does it mean to be "incarnational"? Incarnational ministry means doing what Jesus did. Not in a moralistic way, as emphasized in the once popular WWJD (what would Jesus do?) movement. Emerging Christians want to follow the pattern of the Incarnation itself, understood as the way God entered into the reality of life in this world. In Christ, God stepped into the midst of human life. A member of Matthew 25 House, an intentional community in Hamilton, Ontario, says that incarnational ministry requires a new way of seeing Jesus. The "wavy hair" and "golden locks" Jesus that hung on the wall in grandma's house gives way to an earthy and sweaty Jesus that walks the broken backstreets of Hamilton. Incarnational ministry means leaving the soft and secure cloister of the church. It means venturing out into the world with Jesus to bring the Gospel to the "sinners and the tax collectors."

The Incarnation is also understood as a contextual event. In Christ, God spoke human languages, ate local food, and experienced the travails and joys of the human condition. God became "Emmanuel," "God with us" (Matt 1:23). He lived and shared life with a particular group of people. Jesus' cultural context shaped his ministry and the manifestation of the grace he brought to the world. Context matters. Following Jesus means imitating his entry into the realities of place and culture. Incarnational ministry is grace embodied in and for a particular cultural context. Deep engagement with their neighborhoods is the tangible consequence of this theology of the Incarnation. Incarnational ministry practices are theological because they follow the activity of God in the Incarnation of Jesus Christ. In short, being incarnational means finding tangible ways to enact the grace of Christ in the world. Emerging Christians and their churches do not want to run church

---

16. Guder, *The Continuing Conversion*, 192.

programs for Christian club members. They want to see the kingdom of God come to their neighborhoods.

Embedded Churches

All of life, not just church-related activities, becomes the arena for incarnational life and ministry. Most of the people we encountered in alternative churches were reluctant to claim that their ministry practice is superior to that found in traditional suburban middle and upper middle class churches. Emerging church practice, born in a theology of the Incarnation, nevertheless, implicitly critiques more traditional seeker and attractional approaches to ministry. Why? These latter approaches ask people to leave their context and make the church the primary platform for the practice of their faith rather than the rest of their lives. Incarnational ministry does exactly the opposite. It goes to people. Being incarnational shapes emerging Christian life and ministry in two vital ways: 1) living with and loving people and 2) adapting ministry to the lives of people in their local context.

First, being incarnational shapes the way emerging Christians live and love. Eugene Peterson's translation of John 1:14 in The Message captures the essence of the Incarnation: "the word became flesh and blood and moved into the neighbourhood" (emphasis added). John 3:16, "For God so loved the world," declares the reason for the Incarnation. Certainly, God cares for all of creation, but "world" in John 3:16 means people. God loves people. Not just the mass of the human race, but specific people in particular places, people with particular names, dreams, fears, and passions. "God loves context," writes Scott Frederickson, and churches that are incarnational (and missional) are an expression of this love.[17] They love their context and the people who live there. God became incarnate, dwelled with people, because God loved them. Emerging churches believe that the church is called to love and live with people. Being incarnational, therefore, means moving into and living in the neighborhood. Love motivates moving into the neighborhood.

Incarnational ministry puts a premium on people, not programs. Emerging Christians want people to come to Christ, but do not regard them as targets of evangelism and human resources to staff church programs, which they believe too often characterizes seeker and attractional churches. They want to bring the gospel to people like Jesus did. He lived with them and shared life with them. Jordan, a twenty-something who is part of the Urban Bridge in Edmonton talked about living incarnationally and how his view on what that means has developed. Before, he saw people around him

---

17. Frederickson, "The Missional Congregation," 49.

as "projects" or people who needed his help to get right with God. Now, he sees them as people he loves. His relationships with people are genuine and without an agenda beyond demonstrating the reality of the Gospel by living an authentic life among people he rubs shoulders with on a regular basis.

Identifying with the community where they live also characterizes incarnational ministry. Incarnational ministry does not fit the traditional notion of ministry to people. "Ministry to" assumes an "us to them" attitude. Jordan's experience at Urban Bridge reflects this transition in outlook. Initially he regarded the people in his community as others. He was the Christian full of grace who would minister to them. At some point, however, he identified with the people in his community. They were no longer the other. He was, moreover, no longer the other to them. He ceased to be a church guy coming to help. He became one of them. Incarnational ministry emerged and took root in that transition from being the other to one of them. Emerging Christians believe that as they live among and love their neighbours, they identify with them. Incarnational ministry involves solidarity with people because it is the essence of the Incarnation—the Son of God became one of us in the humanity of Jesus Christ.

Second, incarnational ministry adapts to the local circumstances. It, therefore, rejects the franchise ministry methods that became popular in seeker and attractional churches. Emerging Christians believe these approaches mirror the mass production techniques of modernism. Ministry is a standardized, one size fits all, affair with processing the maximal number of people being the key, if not only, benchmark of success. Emerging Christians believe that Jesus Christ, the incarnate Son of God, connected with people and adapted his ministry to their circumstances. He fed the hungry; forgave the guilty; comforted the broken-hearted; healed the sick; and rebuked the self-righteous. The people we encountered and their churches possess a deep commitment to live out their faith in their specific contexts. They are glad, even excited, to adapt culturally relevant language and practices into their church life. Jesus calls the church to follow him. He came and took up residence in a particular time and place, adapting to the language, ideas and customs of his particular place. The church is to do the same. Emerging churches endeavor to incarnate God's grace in their local context.

The Crossings Community Church in Acton, Ontario illustrates the practice of incarnational ministry. The church began with five families meeting as a home church. They wanted to become a visible and tangible avenue of grace for their community. Acton is a small rural and vintage town within commuting distance of Toronto, the largest metropolitan area in Canada. Starting with their community, they asked where do people get together in Acton? Answer: at the hockey arena and the Tim Hortons coffee shop. They knew they could not build a better hockey arena, but the idea of starting a coffee shop seemed reasonable to them. But where and how to do it in a way that not only served coffee, but also nurtured the life of the community? The answer came in the opportunity to purchase Manny's Road House. Manny's was a notorious drinking establishment, hangout for biker gangs, and place for drug and sex trafficking. The small group purchased Manny's and converted a bar into a coffee shop and a house of prostitution into affordable living space for people with mental disabilities. Moreover, they remodeled the building to accommodate community activities—from weddings to union local meetings—and church gatherings. The Crossings is way of being the church, incarnating the grace of Christ, that arose organically from its local context.

Incarnational ministry is unavoidably contextual ministry. This perspective holds that God sent his Son to live with and bring grace to the lives of people. Christ sends his followers to do the same. Incarnational ministry is walking in the way of Jesus. Like Jesus, emerging churches connect with people and adapt ministry to the circumstances on the ground. They craft their ministry to their context. Contextual ministry rejects standardized ministry models. It is organic. The cultural habitat shapes ministry. It grows out of what is there. The church is a living organism, always ready and able to change, evolve, and respond to new people and ideas. Emerging churches agree with Michael Frost that "[t]hey take the idea of place seriously."[18] Church practices embody Christ's grace in ways that make sense in the local community. Incarnational and contextual ministry is ecclesial adaptation to the local context. Emerging church structures and habits of ministry do not always fit with traditional models or lead to enduring and settled methods of ministry. Emerging churches tend to be fluid, open, and malleable on the particular ways of practicing incarnational life and ministry. Ministries and church activities most often arise from relationships and the specific circumstances of their communities. Consequently, incarnational ministry is dynamic and seldom static.

This aspect of the church's identity, however, has not always been recognized or appreciated. For many, the idea that the Incarnation has relevance beyond being a doctrine of Christian faith is a new idea. Some people even find it troubling. Suggesting that the sacred doctrine of God becoming human has implications for the rather earthly business of the church engaging its culture sounds blasphemous. Even worse, it may even infer some kind of pseudo-divinity for the church itself.[19] At times and in

18. Frost, *The Road to Missional*, 136.
19. Frost, *Missional*, 122. The way incarnation is used here, and understood in the

places when the church enjoyed a powerful place in culture and the culture even reflected Christian ideals, perhaps the concept of Incarnation and the kind of radical identification with cultural context that it presents seemed unnecessary. The post-Christian context of North America, however, is helping the church recapture this core piece of its identity. Living in significantly different circumstances may be leading the church to discover (or re-discover) aspects of its incarnational identity. Although recognizing that it might be difficult to navigate the new cultural terrain, the emerging church can provide pilot projects for understanding the implications of Jesus' Incarnation for the practice of faithful Christian life and ministry in post-Christian North America.

"This World" Churches

The Story, in Sarnia, Ontario, provides venues for the local arts community, band concerts, and affordable incubator space for start-up micro businesses. A two-display window storefront in the old downtown is home for the church. Most of the activities that take place in the church share little in common with traditional church ministries. The church's primary activities touch the lives of non-church people and are not religious per se. They promote the local arts community, musicians, and the economic development and cultural revitalization of downtown Sarnia.

But why? What does the gospel have to do with economic development plans? Emerging churches, like The Story, embrace a 'this world' vision of God's grace and kingdom.[20] They are churches for their communities. Their ministries reflect their vision of preaching the gospel and enacting the kingdom of God. Rather than pining for heaven, they believe the church should be "a pilot project for the New Jerusalem."[21] The gospel is about new life, hope, and transformation for people in this world. Embodying the gospel means engaging in activities that nurture these realities in the concrete circumstances of peoples' lives. The church, the local community of believers, should incarnate the abundant life of God's kingdom *in* and *for* the people of this world. The "this world" orientation of emerging churches means they live in and for their culture.

---

churches we visited, in no way infers some kind of divine equivalence between Jesus and the church.

20. What we call 'this world' orientation among Canadian emerging Christians matches several of the characteristics of Kinnaman's Christian Exiles in the United States. See Kinnaman, *You Lost Me*, 77–78.

21. Joe Manofo, interview, The Story.

First, emerging Christians believe that the church must be engaged in their cultural context. Third Space initiated Word Up at "The Spill," a local café and concert venue on Main Street in Peterborough, Ontario. Once a month church members gather with other people from the community to share poetry, music, and short stories. The pastor and a group from the church wanted to connect with other people in Peterborough who share their love for the arts. Not wanting to create another church event or a covert evangelistic mission, but to share their passion for the arts with other people in their community, they created Word Up. Bringing together diverse people, Word Up has become a popular cultural enrichment event for the community. But what does reading poetry at a local coffee shop say about incarnational theology and ministry?

A positive view toward culture was almost unanimous among the emerging Christians we visited.[22] They regard the world as neither something to be avoided, nor to be engaged only reluctantly. Traditional evangelical churches tend to have a dim or, at best, ambivalent view of world outside the church. They engage the world hesitantly. The world is a place for evangelistic missions. The faithful sally forth only as long as necessary before hustling back to the relative safety of the proverbial holy huddle of the church. One pastor, for example, suggested from the pulpit, that going bass fishing is OK, but be sure to take a friend along and share the gospel. Christians can go bass fishing with a clear conscience as long as they can convert the casting platform into a place for evangelism. New expressions of the church, in contrast, embrace a "this world" Christianity. They reject the binary sacred-secular worldview of traditional evangelical churches. Rather than fearing, they take part in the life of this world and even enjoy it. Little Flowers Community, an intentional community in downtown Winnipeg, defines the heartbeat of their ministry as "participating in the fabric of the neighborhood." Participating in the neighbourhood translates and embodies the incarnational theology that animates Little Flowers. Rather than retreating, emerging Christians and their churches whole-heartedly participate in the realities of life in contemporary North American culture.

One practical outcome is that emerging Christians emphasize the synergies between the church and its context, rather than the discontinuities. Where traditional churches accentuate differences, like views on abortion and same sex marriage, emerging congregations highlight common concerns, such as revitalizing neighborhoods, working for just communities,

---

22. Defining the term "culture" is difficult; however, our use of the term here, and throughout this chapter is broad and refers to the range of things that characterize a society such as its customs, modes of behavior, beliefs, social practices, social structures and the arts. See Vance, *A History of Canadian Culture*, vii–viii.

and taking care of the environment. As noted before, previous generations may have regarded relationships with "non-Christians" as okay as long as they were primarily understood as "evangelistic" in nature (e.g., relational evangelism, which makes evangelism, not friendship, the goal of the relationship). Emerging Christians and churches understand themselves to be cut from a different cloth. They see their relationships with the people that they live among as simply "friendships" with other human beings who are a lot like they are, except that they do not follow Jesus in the same way that they do. This means that there is a lot more emphasis on shared affinities and a lot less emphasis on the things that divide them. The unique features of the Christian faith do emerge, and certainly influence choices Christians make and the way they live in the world. But they become a point of dialogue and sharing the grace of Christ, rather than a barrier to relationships with people. Christian values do not lead the Christian away from the world, but to living in a particular way within it.

"We are not trying to connect with the culture, we are the culture," declared one member of St. Croix Vineyard Church in St. Stephen, New Brunswick. Not an arrogant assertion of power and influence, but an expression that reflects their place and participation in the wider culture of North American society and their town in particular. They share in the life of their specific place and they contribute to the culture of the place. They are not outsiders who need to "connect." They are part of the town and its people. As Christians, they may bring certain ideas and ways of living to their culture, but they do as insiders, who are part of the whole, not as outsiders who really do not belong. On this cultural connection, Frederickson remarks that the church "is the context in the same way that the context *includes* the missional congregation."[23] Consequently, they are more concerned with being present and building authentic and meaningful relationships with people in their communities than participating in traditional church and "religious" activities.

This vision invites an ongoing dialogue between the church and its cultural context. It assumes that they are in relationship with each other, sharing a mutuality that benefits both parties.[24] This dialogue is mutual. Each one, church and culture, can learn from one another. Although a widely-held belief among the churches that we visited, the church has not always embraced a dialogical posture with the broader culture. Always believing that it had something to teach its culture, the church has not always believed that the culture had much to teach it. The church was the herald of

---

23. Frederickson, "Missional Congregation in Context," 49 (emphasis original).
24. Frederickson, "Missional Congregation," 49.

God's Word and its job was to dispense the Word of God to those around it. Many of the churches and Christians we visited disagree with such a narrow view of where God's wisdom can be found. A member of the St. Croix Vineyard church suggested that, "God speaks more into culture than the church sometimes." This view expresses a common belief among emerging Christians that God can be found "in the world." These incarnational communities believe that the Spirit of God is active in the world and in the lives of their irreligious friends, even if their friends were unaware of it. God breaks down barriers just as he did in the church described in the New Testament.[25] The early church grew in its understanding of the gospel as it endeavored to follow Jesus in interaction with its first-century culture. Emerging congregations likewise believe that their context, the people they live among, will shape their way of incarnating the gospel.[26]

Second, emerging Christians believe that the church must be for the people in its cultural context. Members of Urban Bridge volunteer with HIV Edmonton (Alberta) and at the local HIV hospice. They put their faith in action by bringing comfort to people trapped in despair and lingering on the margins of life. Another group from Urban Bridge relocated to the arts district of Edmonton to participate in the life of this niche community. The whole church has taken on the task of breathing new life into an annual music concert that was on verge of dying. The event is a venue for local musicians to showcase their music. It is not overtly religious. But the church decided that providing the leadership to organize this musical festival was an opportunity to serve its community and to be present with its people. In these ways, Urban Bridge hopes to create a "redemptive presence" for the people of Edmonton.

Being for the world is understood as arising from God's mission in the Incarnation. "For God did not send his Son into the world to condemn the world, but to save the world through him" (John 3:17). Love led God to enter into the reality of human life. God's love heals and transforms people so they can flourish and know abundant life (John 10:10). The Incarnation of God in Jesus Christ means that God is with and for people. The Incarnation, therefore, is not an abstract theological doctrine for emerging churches. It is a theological category that inspires ministry practices rooted in practical engagement with the concrete realities of local communities. Not satisfied only offering the hope of heaven, "this world vision" means embodying that hope through tangible acts of service and love for people in this world.

25. Stone, *Evangelism after Christendom*, 238. See the New Testament book of Acts, chapters 10–11, that narrates the story of the apostle Peter and the Roman Centurion Cornelius for a biblical text that illustrates this idea.

26. Van Gelder, *The Ministry of the Missional Church*, 64.

The positive orientation to culture is not without tension and nuance. Emerging Christians read poetry in the downtown coffee shop and participate in the local art festival, but they also critique the dominant culture. Like Shane Claiborne, they regard mainstream culture as the oppressive empire.[27] They claim that true Christianity lives on the margins of empire. Along with participating in the church's cultural context, the Incarnation also promotes counter-cultural postures. Incarnational life and ministry, therefore, involves both dwelling comfortably and freely within a particular place and time and critiquing it. The Bible describes this tension as being "in," but not "of" the world. Christians are both at home in and at odds with the world. The churches we visited inevitably struggle with this tension. Their critique of the world, however, is not against the world per se. They bear witness to the brokenness of the world and testify to the promise of grace to transform the world. They want to see the kingdom of God come to their communities.

A member of "Spirituality Unedited," a church in Calgary, Alberta, expressed this vision: "What our people want is different from the culture." Although rooted in and involved with the life of their local communities, they want to embody for each other and their communities a vision of an alternative way of life in this world.[28] They hope for a way of life rooted in love and personal relationships that promotes meaning, authenticity, equality, and justice—a way of life informed by the gospel of Jesus Christ. While sometimes messy and challenging, these churches are determined to navigate their way through their dual calling—a calling that means engaging the world in which they live and offering an alternative way of life to that world.

HOLISTIC SPIRITUALITY

Emerging Christians believe that a grace reaches every corner of life. Their spirituality is comprehensive, not compartmental. Many emerging Christians come from more or less traditional evangelical church backgrounds, but regard its view of the gospel as too individualized and spiritualized. For them, the gospel is not a superadditum to a life that is otherwise secular. They are not satisfied with tacking on a set of spiritual disciplines and church activities. Following Jesus, Christian spirituality, shapes every area and activity of life. It entails where and how Christians live, where they work, and the type and amount of food and consumer items they buy. Experiencing

---

27. Claiborne and Haw, *Jesus for President*.

28. The congregations we visited shared a vision similar to the one described by Darrell Guder in *The Continuing Conversion*, 159.

the justice and renewal of God's kingdom in all the dimensions of life, not piously waiting for transport to heaven, is Christian spirituality. Emerging spirituality offers a counter narrative to the popular secularization thesis and rejects a sacred-secular worldview. Understanding the quest for a holistic spirituality among emerging Christians can only be understood in light of their view and rejection of the traditional evangelical church.

Rejecting Traditional Evangelical Church Spirituality

Emerging Christians are dissatisfied with the established evangelical church. Most of the people we encounter, leadership and parishioners, have backgrounds in more traditional evangelical and (to a lesser degree) mainline Protestant churches. For most of them that experience was negative. Whether or not their perspectives on the church are accurate is in many respects irrelevant. The salient fact is that these experiences cause emerging Christians to leave traditional churches in favor of alternative forms of church life. Their rejection of the traditional church is not a rejection of the church per se, but only of the late twentieth-century North American versions of the church.

The traditional church is not monolithic. Its diversity is apparent to anyone who takes the time to observe it. Although important differences abound among evangelical, mainline, and Catholic (not to mention Orthodox) expressions of the Church, the following categories offer a broad description of the congregations that many emerging Christians and seminary students leave. Characteristics of these churches include:

1) Consumer and commodified Christianity. Emphasis on programs tailored to meet the religious needs and wants of middle and upper middle class Christians. They embrace a consumer methodology.

2) Church and messaging programs crafted to a target demographic. Churches specialize in offering a menu of ministries to service personal spirituality.

3) Focus on winning converts and assimilating them to church programs and activities. Church growth and expanding programs become the goal and measure of the ministry success.

4) Oppositional mentality. An "us versus them" attitude to culture that carries with it a general suspicion toward culture and in some instances an outright indictment of the world outside the church. A binary worldview that draws clear lines between the sacred and the secular.

5) A patriarchal and hierarchical culture that often marginalizes those who do not conform to the accepted traditional standards of the established church. These attitudes can cause people to become conformists to the accepted standards as opposed to living authentically and honestly as they truly are.

6) A dependence upon attractional methods of evangelism as opposed to methods that encourage the church to go into the world and to engage people in their own contexts.

7) Finally, and perhaps most significantly, modernist and corporate values shaped their prime metric for success—growth.

In certain fundamental ways, emerging churches are not radically different from the traditional evangelical churches they reject. The traditional church is a sell-out to modern consumer culture, according to the emerging Christians. Emerging Christians believe that the first three characteristics of the traditional evangelical church indicate that modernist and corporate values shaped their prime metric for success and not the gospel. Emerging churches, however, can be understood as adaptations to postmodern and post-Christian culture. The quest for authenticity and desire for religious and spiritual diversity among emerging Christians, for example, is common to the Millennial and emerging adult demographic.[29] The unique characteristics of emerging Christianity, consequently, can be understood as the influence of their postmodern cultural habit than as them having acquired a more "biblical" Christianity. In other words, both Rick Warren's Saddleback Church (Los Angeles, CA) and Bruxy Cavey's The Meeting House (Oakville, ON) can be interpreted as cultural Christianity's adapted respectively to modern and postmodern cultures. Whether or not emerging churches will be as successful as the modernist churches they reject is an open question.

Embracing a Holistic and Worldly Spirituality

Having established the type of spirituality that emerging Christians reject, what are they for? First, emerging Christians regard all creation as sacred space. They want all areas of life renewed and transformed by God's grace. They reject the sacred-secular dualism of modern culture and contemporary evangelical Christianity. For them, everything is spiritual. Desacralizing life is not the emerging Christians' intent. Describing all life as spiritual, moreover, does not reduce everything to the mundane. It also does not reject the

---

29. For these characteristics, see Smith and Snell, *Souls in Transition*, 48–50, 56, 78–79, and 81; and Twenge and Campbell, *The Narcissism Epidemic*.

importance of spiritual disciplines and church life. It frames, however, the totality of human life in terms of a relationship with God.

Evangelicals formally believe in divine omnipresence. Functionally they believe God dwells in the church and the space of individual spirituality. The world outside the church and spiritual disciplines is ambiguous at best and nefarious at worst. It is secular. Emerging Christians deny this dualism. The world outside the church is not void of God. God is no more in the church than anywhere else. A secular world does not exist. The world is not a godless wasteland. God dwells with the world, both the natural environment and human society. Missional endeavors do not bring God where erstwhile God was not. God's presence precedes Christian ministry. Finding people discussing themes that resonate with the gospel does not surprise emerging Christians. They expect to see the fruit of God's work in the lives of the people they encounter.

Second, although regarding the evangelical tradition's view of the gospel as overly individualized and spiritualized, they retain the notion that grace transforms the individual and calls for a life of discipleship. They see this transformation, however, as something that encompasses their whole lives. Christian spirituality is not only adding on a set of spiritual disciplines and church activities but entails where and how Christians live, where they work, and the type and amount of food and consumer items they buy. The experience of grace and following Christ is about realizing the justice and renewal of God's kingdom in this world and not waiting for transport to a celestial heaven. The gospel is not a superadditum to, but inseparable from, the rest of their lives.

Third, the holistic spirituality of emerging Christians connects with the larger narrative of Christianity in particular and religion in general in contemporary North America. Emerging Christian spirituality challenges the secularization thesis. According to the secularization thesis, modern society privatizes religion. Religion loses its public role. Religion has little consequence for people's lives outside of their personal spirituality and morality. Emerging Christians do not fit this widespread perspective. Their spirituality impacts every area of their lives. Their faith is vibrant and informs not only personal spirituality, but also the public areas of life such as where to live and work. Rather than secular and post-Christian Canadian society reducing, it has raised the influence of religion in their lives. Emerging Christian spirituality, moreover, corroborates the spiritual not religious thesis. The story of emerging Christians in Canada dovetails with this larger story of declining participation in institutional religion in Canada (see data presented in the first section). It shows that although many people (primarily emerging adults but also older generations) leave the traditional institutional church, they do not leave their Christian faith, but turn to alternative forms of Christianity and church experiences.

CONCLUSION

This essay brings to light the innovations to church practice that are taking root in the increasingly secular, multicultural, pluralistic, and post-Christian culture of North America and specifically Canada. This research showcases the core biblical and theological convictions that motivate these innovative churches and ministry leaders. Their theological sensibilities give these initiatives cross-contextual applications. Incarnational ministry, for example, has urban and rural ramifications. Holistic spirituality, for instance, affirms the goodness of God's creation and all areas of life are the arena of discipleship. These theological convictions promote Christian life and ministry that offer a counter narrative to the secularization and privatization of religion theses that dominate popular discourse on religion in Canada today.

BIBLIOGRAPHY

Bibby, Reginald W. *The Emerging Millennials: How Canada's Newest Generation Is Responding to Change and Choice*. Lethbridge, AB: Project Canada, 2009.

———. "Continuing the Conversation on Canada: Changing Patterns of Religious Service Attendance." *Journal for the Scientific Study of Religion* 50 (2011) 831–39.

———. *Beyond the Gods and Back: Religions Demise and Rise and Why It Matters*. Lethbridge, AB: Project Canada, 2011.

Blumer, Herbert. *Symbolic Interactionism: Perspective and Method*. Englewood Cliffs, NJ: Prentice-Hall, 1969.

Bowen, John P., ed. *Green Shoots out of Dry Ground: A New Future for the Church in Canada*. Eugene, OR: Wipf & Stock, 2013.

Bowen, Kurt. *Christians in a Secular World: The Canadian Experience*. Montreal: McGill-Queen's University Press, 2004.

Bramadat, Paul, and Seljak, David. "Charting the New Terrain: Christianity and Ethnicity in Canada," in *Christianity and Ethnicity in Canada*, edited by Paul Bramadat and David Seljak, 3–48. Toronto: University of Toronto Press, 2008.

Bryant, Antony, and Kathy Charmaz. *The SAGE Handbook on Grounded Theory*. Los Angeles: Sage, 2010.

Charmaz, Kathy. *Constructing Grounded Theory: A Practical Guide through Qualitative Analysis*. London: Sage, 2006.

Claiborne, Shane, and Chris Haw. *Jesus for President: Politics for Ordinary Radicals*. Grand Rapids: Zondervan, 2008.

Eagle, David. "The Loosening Bond of Religion in Canadian Society: Reply to Bibby." *Journal for the Scientific Study of Religion* 50 (2011) 838–39.

———. "Changing Patterns of Attendance at Religious Services in Canada, 1986–2008." *Journal for the Scientific Study of Religion* 50 (2011) 187–200.

Flatt, Kevin. *After Evangelicalism: The Sixties and the United Church of Canada*. Montreal: McGill-Queen's University Press, 2013.

———. Haskell, David M., and Burgoyne, Stephanie. "Theology Matters: Comparing the Traits of Growing and Declining Mainline Protestant Church Attendees and Clergy." *Review of Religious Research* 58 (2016) 515–41.

Frederickson, Scott. "The Missional Congregation in Context." In *The Missional Church in Context: Helping Congregations Develop Contextual Ministry*, edited by Craig Van Gelder, 44–64. Grand Rapids: Eerdmans, 2007.

Frost, Michael. *The Road to Missional: Journey to the Center of the Church*. Grand Rapids: Baker, 2011.

Guder, Darrell. *The Continuing Conversion of the Church*. Grand Rapids: Eerdmans, 2000.

Hauerwas, Stanley, and William H. Willamon. *Resident Aliens: Life in the Christian Colony*. Expanded 25th Anniversary Edition. Nashville: Abingdon, 2014.

Glaser, Barney G., and Anselm L. Strauss. *The Discovery of Grounded Theory: Strategies for Qualitative Research*. Chicago: Aldine, 1967.

Kinnaman, David. *You Lost Me: Why Young Christians are Leaving the Church . . . and Rethinking Faith*. Grand Rapids: Baker, 2011.

Lorenz Dietz, Mary, Robert Prus, and William Shaffir, eds. *Doing Everyday Life: Ethnography as Human Lived Experience*. Mississauga, ON: Copp Clark Longman, 1994.

Mohler, Albert. "Keeping the Faith in a Faithless Age: The Church as the Moral Minority." AlbertMohler.com, July 16, 2009. http://www.albertmohler.com/2009/07/16/keeping-the-faith-in-a-faithless-age-the-church-as-the-moral-minority-2/.

Murray, Stuart. *Post-Christendom*. Waynesboro, GA: Paternoster, 2004.

Reimer, Sam, and Michael Wilkinson. *A Culture of Faith: Evangelical Congregations in Canada*. Montreal: McGill-Queen's University Press, 2015.

Smith, Christian and Snell, Patricia. *Souls in Transition: The Religious and Spiritual Lives of Emerging Adults*. New York: Oxford University Press, 2009.

Stone, Bryan. *Evangelism After Christendom: The Theology and Practice of Christian Witness*. Grand Rapids: Brazos, 2007.

Thiessen, Joel. *The Meaning of Sunday: The Practice of Belief in a Secular Age*. Montreal: McGill-Queen's University Press, 2015.

———, and Dawson, Lorne L. "Is There a 'Renaissance' of Religion in Canada? A Critical Look at Bibby and Beyond." *Studies in Religion/Sciences Religieuses* 37 (2008) 389–415.

Twenge, Jean, and W. Keith Campbell. *The Narcissism Epidemic: Living in the Age of Entitlement*. New York: Free Press, 2009.

Vance, Jonathan F. *A History of Canadian Culture*. New York: Oxford University Press, 2011.

Van Gelder, Craig. *The Ministry of the Missional Church: A Community Led by the Spirit*. Grand Rapids: Baker, 2007.

7

Emergent Church as Experimental Program

Embodied Hypotheses in Cognition and Value

BRANDON DANIEL-HUGHES

Abstract

This paper analyzes the "emerging church movement" as a large-scale experimental program with the aid of three hypothetical lenses, two core hypotheses in the cognitive science of religion and a naturalist axiological hypothesis. Each section outlines a core hypothesis and suggests ways in which emergent church (EC) phenomena may support that hypothesis. This approach is less concerned with stabilizing the identity of the EC and more interested in construing acts of emergence as explorations of unique cognitive and axiological possibilities. From the perspective of an interested outsider, the paper first considers the EC, in contrast with established Christian churches and denominations, as a preference for smaller, more closely knit and less tightly policed in-groups. The ad hoc character of most EC gatherings allows such groups to forgo the need to build lasting coalitions through the extended trust building exercises and loyalty displays that characterize larger religious institutions. Second, it examines the EC rejection of maximally counter-intuitive notions of divinity in favor of minimally counter-intuitive, more 'authentic' divinity conceptions as an adaptive strategy that is intimately linked to the EC's characteristic social forms. Third, it examines the EC as a unique exploration of the value of high-contrast social harmonies. This is exemplified in the EC's maximization of the contrast between the social forms of established

Christian institutions and its own minimally organized gatherings. The core contention of the paper is that the EC is a late modern experiment in social adaptation and experimentation, albeit an experimental religious social form that is intimately and symbiotically tied to the establishment churches that serve as an enabling context and constant foil.

As a naturalist philosopher of religion with an abiding interest in the relationships between human bio-cultural evolution, the emerging field of the cognitive science of religion, and the contemporary practice of religion, I am keenly interested in the phenomenon of the Emergent Church (EC). There are, I argue below, several reasons that scholars of religion should take heed of the EC. However, before bringing some of the insights of the abovementioned subfields to bear upon the subject and reflecting upon the ways in which the EC may alternatively upend or reinforce particular core hypotheses, I must briefly introduce the working assumptions of my pragmatic and naturalist approach to the study of religious communities. This will allow the reader to appreciate my reasons for focusing so sharply on the EC and its symbiotic relationship to the mainline churches. Section one introduces my naturalist and pragmatic assumptions. Two subsequent sections offer core hypotheses in the cognitive science of religion and argue that the EC appears to validate these core hypotheses. The cognitive science of religion is a relatively new field of study that is still in the early stages of defining itself and its methods. Therefore, both sections two and three offer very general descriptions of broadly shared working hypotheses. The fourth section presents several working hypotheses in naturalist axiology and argues that some of the initial successes of the EC may stem from its engendering valuable high-contrast experiences in its participants. This leads to a concluding section in which I suggest that the EC is best understood as a symbiotic phenomenon in which the EC emerges as a partner to the struggling mainline churches primarily in relatively secular late-modern contexts. The characteristic of EC phenomena that I highlight throughout is their self-consciously experimental orientation, a counter-intuitive orientation that runs against cognitive and social defaults and, therefore, one that we should expect to prove quite fragile. For this reason alone, if for no other, the EC is worthy of serious scholarly attention.

PRAGMATIC NATURALISM

Pragmatism and Naturalism are contested terms, but some characterization of both is necessary to explain why EC phenomena might interest scholars who claim these appellations. Naturalism is best characterized by the claim "that nature is all that there is."[1] This seemingly innocent governing assumption has surprising consequences, especially when examining human consciousness, normative claims, and religiosity. Pragmatism can be circumscribed historically as a set of philosophical ideas growing out of the work of Charles S. Peirce, William James, and John Dewey, but the title is now claimed by a wide array of thinkers in and outside of academic philosophy. Most generally and generously I characterize pragmatism as a primary focus on actions and habits of action along with a tendency to interpret beliefs and statements of beliefs as concomitant phenomena of secondary importance. Together, these two philosophical commitments argue for examining religion primarily as a form of behavior, both individual and communal, and only secondarily as an epistemic discourse. Naturalists do not expect religious doctrines and scriptures accurately to picture the world, but naturalist pragmatists do expect religious ideas and beliefs to act both as manifestations and as signs of human social, emotional, and cognitive habits.

In perhaps his most famous essay, *The Fixation of Belief*, Charles S. Peirce characterized the relationship between belief and action in several ways:

> Our beliefs guide our desires and shape our actions.[2]
>
> The feeling of believing is a more or less sure indication of there being established in our nature some habit which will determine our actions.[3]
>
> Belief does not make us act at once, but puts us into such a condition that we shall behave in some certain way, when the occasion arises.[4]

Beliefs are only secondarily propositions about the world or characterizations of mental states. Their primary significance is indexical. A belief is less often a platform from which actions are launched and more importantly an attestation of some predisposition or habit of action. Following Peirce,

---

1. Corrington, *"Ecstatic Naturalism,"* 9.
2. Peirce, *Essential Peirce Vol. 1*, 114.
3. Ibid., 114.
4. Ibid., 114.

the pragmatist is often interested in religious beliefs as signifiers of such actions. The pragmatic meaning of any doctrine or belief (X) is the behaviors it reinforces and out of which it grows, the conduct it presages, and the general effects we conceive X to have.[5] Neither the belief "in the mind," nor the doctrine on the page, nor the confession on the lips is equivalent to the lived reality that makes use of these signs to navigate a precarious cosmos.[6]

While pragmatism leads one to approach beliefs as signs of much richer living phenomena, naturalism highlights the exploratory character of all such phenomena. To state the matter bluntly, naturalism contends that all propositional truth claims and articulated religious beliefs are fallible hypotheses. There is no supernatural foundation or source of certainty to vouchsafe beliefs. Pragmatic naturalism goes a step further, arguing that, therefore, all actions and ways of life are in turn fallible hypotheses. All species and subspecies, social forms and social groups, ways of living and individual lives are habits of action in and interaction with an environing world that affords many opportunities but offers no certainties. If the naturalist impulse is correct and there are no certainties to be had and the pragmatist impulse is correct and beliefs are best understood as signifiers of habits of action, then it is not just beliefs that are fallible hypotheses, but the believers and communities of believers themselves.

Following Peirce, I argue that inquiry is ubiquitous and continuous. Admittedly, this philosophical orientation can be disorienting, in part, because it asks that we discard some of the usual connotations of "experiment" and treat experimental inquiry as a ubiquitous phenomenon. So, while it is true to say that our lives occasionally involve consciously having and testing hypotheses, it is also true that each organism and community of organisms is itself a collection of hypotheses, perpetually engaged in testing and refining itself. From the first-person point of view, we feel ourselves to be stable actors who occasionally entertain novel hypotheses and experimentally explore new ideas. However, from the third-person philosopher's point of view, a person is less a discrete inquirer testing a determinate set of hypotheses and more a vast continuum of embodied and entangled hypotheses.[7] Some beliefs are held lightly and their associated habits are easily modified, but other beliefs/habits are so intertwined with personal and communal identity that one's very life is best understood as a large scale experiment

---

5. Ibid., 132. All such conceptions are fallible hypotheses, so it is incorrect to suggest, as is commonly done, that the meaning of a sign is its effects. The meaning of a sign is what those effects are conceived to be.

6. Though the pragmatist is cognizant, alongside Wittgensteinians and Austinians, that the speaking and writing of signs are themselves actions in the world.

7. Cooke, *Peirce's Pragmatic Theory of Inquiry*, 77–80.

as to their workability. Thus a pragmatic naturalist understanding of our existential condition includes the claim that, while we consciously entertain only a few select hypotheses at any given moment, unconscious experimental inquiry precedes apace on a much broader scale. We are woven into innumerable experiments and cannot opt out. To choose to ignore one's status as a continuum of fallible hypotheses, is not to avoid inquiry, but rather to choose to inquire poorly. To become conscious of inquiry by choosing to inquire reasonably and efficiently is to make the decision in favor of conscious, perhaps even scientific, experimentation.

Questioning our most closely held beliefs is not solely an intellectual operation, but an exercise in upending habits of action that are constitutive of our very selves. For these reasons Peirce often entertained a stark line of demarcation between the disinterested inquiries of "laboratory-men" and the interested and invested inquiries of everyday practical affairs.[8] Scientists need not and often should not believe the hypotheses they entertain. They need only adopt them provisionally in controlled settings.[9] But in practical matters, beliefs signify general habits of action, what one might call "character." Thus, while the disinterested scientist may subject a hypothesis to testing and wager nothing of personal import upon the procedure, when invested inquirers place beliefs in jeopardy, not only do they maintain an interest in the outcome of the experiment, but the result becomes for them a matter of vital importance. To put the matter starkly, in matters of vital importance an inquirer does not so much put its beliefs to the test as it tests itself and its own character against the real world.[10] Thus Peirce recommended two different strategies for inquiry: 1) bold scientific experimentation in matters academic and theoretical and 2) conservative caution in matters practical and vital.[11]

While not all inquiry is vital, there is no avoiding vital inquiry that tests one's character. But while practical, moral and religious experimentation is unavoidable in the long run, individual inquirers are well advised to follow the time tested habits of previous generations and to adopt their sign systems, religious traditions and moral commonsense as wise hedges against uncertainty. Such a strategy, Peirce argued, promises to maximize

8. Peirce, *Essential Peirce Vol. 2*, 332.

9. In such circumstances belief is wholly inappropriate and perhaps intrusive.

10. My use of the pronoun "it" is intentional in this context and stresses the idea that not all living inquirers are individual persons. I offer an extended treatment of religious communities as inhabited experiments in Daniel-Hughes, *Pragmatic Inquiry and Religious Communities*.

11. See Daniel-Hughes, "Peirce's Conservatism and Critical Commonsense" for clarification of these two Peircean strategies.

the efficiency of inquiry by preserving and protecting the community of inquiry itself. Peirce announced, "*Do not block the road of inquiry*,"[12] as the first rule of reason that should be painted on every wall of the city of philosophy. But while this rule has as its obvious targets authoritative prohibitions and foundationalisms, it has an additional conservative implication. It recommends free and open inquiry in all matters non-vital, but cautions against experimental trials when continuation of the community of inquiry is itself at stake.

If one accepts the broad contours of Peirce's pragmatic and naturalist philosophy of inquiry, then his conservative prescriptions do seem to follow. It makes perfect sense to avoid rash experimentation in matters that concern the existential and religious core of the community of inquiry, as such experimentation would necessarily involve *placing the entire community at risk*, endangering its character, and threatening the continuation of inquiry itself. If the aim of scientific experimentation is self-controlled inquiry, then Peirce's conservative position vis-à-vis vital matters amounts to a recommendation that one exercise a second-order self-control, follow one's cultural instincts, and resist the impulse toward free experimentation.[13] For the Peircean pragmatist, religious actors and communities are natural experiments as to the viability of their beliefs in a particular context and Peirce's conservative recommendation is, in the absence of unambiguous disconfirming evidence or a radical change in context, to continue the present experiment. In short, not all experiments are equally wise.

Evaluating the role of intentional experimentation in religious matters is particularly challenging. Following a tradition of theological analysis that goes back at least as far as Schleiermacher and his characterization of religion as a feeling of "absolute dependence" and includes Tillich's description of religion as one's "ultimate concern," religious communities of inquiry can be provisionally characterized as those that intentionally work to signify their objects of ultimate concern and those objects upon which they feel absolutely dependent. To be clear, if we follow Peirce's theory of ubiquitous inquiry, then all communities have ultimate concerns and are radically dependent in the sense that their continued existence is contingent, but religious communities are unique insofar as they self-consciously strive to signify ultimacy and clarify the meanings of those signs. The interpretation of scriptures and traditions, the performance of rituals, the education of acolytes, and any number of religious acts are all habits of action that

---

12. Peirce, *Reasoning and the Logic of Things*, 178.

13. This is a contested reading of Peirce's mature philosophy of science and vital matters. See Daniel-Hughes, "Defanging Peirce's Hopeful Monster."

embody and enact the beliefs of the religious community, and indexically signify a particular idea of ultimacy.[14] Through actions, perhaps more than through explicitly theological or explanatory texts, religious communities offer an implicit answer to the question, "What is ultimacy?" Ultimacy is that to whom one ought to pray in a particular direction with particular words, or sing at a particular time, or upon which one should meditate in a particular position. Most major world religions insist that ultimacy cannot be accurately depicted or exhaustively described without hedging such depictions and descriptions about with numerous apophatic disclaimers, but then most religious actions are not attempts to represent iconically; they are habitual gestures of response and evocation that strike religious participants as natural reactions to feelings of dependence and ultimate concern. These are the culturally mediated beliefs, signs and customs that are so habitual that they have become "second nature" and characterize the community's sense of self and identity.

Traditional religious sign systems are, like all fallible human endeavors, large scale experimental programs, but their continued survival through the centuries suggests that they are wise bets, and religious inquirers should stick to their well grooved paths. Thus with Peirce we can 1) understand a religious tradition as a series of inductively supported hypotheses, embodied in signs and habits of action that have withstood generations of experimentation, and 2) understand religious communities as communities of inquirers who have adopted and embody these traditional hypotheses, habits and signs, thereby continuing the experimental process. As a naturalist pragmatist I am in general agreement with a Peircean portrayal of the existential status and experimental character of religious communities with one important exception. The key thread in the larger web of arguments that led Peirce in this conservative direction is empirically falsifiable. Experimentation, even in vital, existential and religious matters, need not threaten an entire community of inquiry unless one defines religious communities strictly in terms of highly organized groups with strong hierarchies, centralized control and strictly policed boundaries; and the historical record abounds with religious traditions that throve with minimal centralization and organizational hierarchy and minimally policed boundaries. If all religious communities were organized like the magisterial churches of European origin then Peirce's conservatism would be wise. Free experimentation at the most general levels of communal organization is unwise, especially when options exist at less general levels where exposure to collective risk

---

14. For an in depth analysis and application of Peirce semiotic theories to religious symbols see Neville, *The Truth of Broken Symbols*, ix–75.

is mitigated. But Peirce overlooked the latent potential in dissenting, decentralized and occasionally self-consciously experimental religious communities and his overly conservative attitude toward religion in general is a product of this oversight.

Admittedly, this has been a long path to tread in order to appreciate why the EC might prove so interesting to pragmatist naturalists. If we shed Peirce's relatively narrow construal of religious communities and embrace the conception that emerges from his larger philosophy of inquiry, then we can consider the possibility that decentralized religious communities are well positioned to act as natural experiments, living experimental communities that actively test religious hypotheses even as they embody them. The second Great Awakening gave birth to many such experimental communities including the Shakers, the Oneida community, the Mormons, Christian Science, and even the Holiness antecedents of Pentecostalism, all of which emerged during this time of tremendous decentralization and innovation. To be sure, the members and leaders of these communities would likely not have described themselves as engaged in religious experimentation, but would have thought of themselves as retrieving or returning to earlier Christian practices or embracing new supernaturally bestowed revelations. However, one need not recognize oneself as experimentally innovative in order to be so. From the first-person perspective of the religious actor, the actions that accompany beliefs are the proper, natural and habitual responses of a creature to ultimacy. But from a third-person perspective we can simultaneously understand such actions as living experiments struggling to engage the world and its ultimate dimensions though innumerable fallible hypotheses.

With this characterization of religious communities as living lines of experimental research, I turn now to an examine the loosely affiliated coalition of ideas and communities growing out of mainsteam Christian Evangelicalism that goes by the name of the Emergent Church. My aim is not to circumscribe the EC but to examine the underlying potential of its open structure and to explore several of its characteristic hypotheses, hypotheses that I argue the EC experimentally embodies, even if they remain unarticulated. I approach each of the following three sections by first outlining a set of core hypotheses from the cognitive science of religion (sections two and three) or naturalist axiology (section four). I then outline several ways in which EC phenomena seem to challenge or support those core hypotheses. Following this method, the picture of the EC that emerges in each section will allow for the formulation of several provocative hypotheses regarding the future and limits of the EC. The brief summations of the relevant core hypotheses in the cognitive science of religion and value theory will necessarily be cursory and the portrayal of the relevant EC strategies will be open to empirical disconfirmation and supplementation. While I assume the basic truth of many of the core hypotheses I outline, the tremendous upside of this approach is that it emphasizes the vulnerability of each step in the analysis and each characterization of the phenomena in question.

EMERGENT CHURCH EXPERIMENTS IN "BELONGING BEFORE BELIEVING"

One of the core working hypotheses in the cognitive science of religion is that supernatural agent conceptions help to build and reinforce non-kin coalitions.[15] Group selection may be sufficient to explain both cooperation within bands of closely related individuals and the tendency of individuals occasionally to sacrifice their own good to the good of the larger kin group, but individual sacrifice and group cooperation is much more difficult to explain among non-kin groups. Why, from the perspective of the individual or the gene, would any organism place the good of the community (everyone eats a little) ahead of its own good (I eat a lot)? The cognitive science of religion proposes that the basic Darwinian process of natural selection has selected for individuals who are better able to cooperate in group projects and subordinate immediate individual goods so as to protect and promote the larger social unit, yielding an answer to the previous question: in the long run, the diffuse survival and reproductive advantages of belonging to a cooperative group outweigh the short term gains of selfish behavior. Thus human beings evolved, over the millennia, the cognitive and emotional capacity for complex social coordination and cooperation in which both costs and benefits are shared. The theory of the emergence of cooperative, "prosocial" cognitive capacities is much more complex than I have drawn it and scholarly disagreements flourish within the boundaries I have sketched, but there is additional broad scholarly consensus that the very capacities that allow human beings to cooperate in non-kin groups are 1) ripe for exploitation and 2) often lead to decidedly violent competitive encounters with non in-group members and coalitions.

Within non-kin groups, in which costs and benefits are shared, there is a natural incentive to follow parasitical strategies that extract maximum benefits while paying minimal costs. Such "free riders," if they are not quickly

---

15. The phrase "core working hypothesis" is meant to signify broad agreement within the field on general working principles and should not be taken to mean that scholars in the field agree in detail on the particulars. Lively debates persist at nearly every turn whenever one investigates beyond the most general core hypotheses.

detected and eliminated, would destroy the host group and the dynamics that make non-kin cooperation advantageous. Thus humans evolved additional tools for detecting free riders and reinforcing group identity so as to protect against exploitation and defection. Supernatural agent conceptions serve two important functions in this regard. First, these conceptions work as interested supernatural monitors, ostensibly watching both public and private behavior of group members and threatening both detection of and punishment for selfish or disloyal behavior. Second, since belief in these agents is easy to fake, religion provides occasions for displays of belief and loyalty. From a purely materialist perspective religious rituals and institutions are wasteful and their costs are difficult to explain in terms of survival advantage. But from the perspective of a group that needs to police group loyalties and boundaries, the costliness of religious rituals may be their *raison d'être*. In such contexts costly religious displays (fasting, sacrifice, bodily mutilation) may work as markers of authentic belief, what scholars call "costly signaling" or "credibility enhancing displays" (CREDs) and may earn the signaler social status and trust that outweigh material costs.[16] The implicit logic of these displays is as follows: you can trust that I am a reliable cooperator and loyal to the group because I believe that our gods/God are watching me, and you know that I believe in the supernatural agent(s) because you can see the ritual price I am willing to pay in order to please the gods/God. Additionally, if religious communities are cooperative and loyal communities, then such tightly knit communities are better equipped to compete against outsiders. So not only do supernatural agent conceptions enable intergroup trust and cooperation among non-kin, but they also help such groups win out over less cooperative and committed coalitions. When resources are limited, groups cooperate so as better to compete, meaning that, "[t]he other side of in-group cohesion is out-group hostility."[17]

First Hypothesis: *The EC is composed largely of small, decentralized, minimally organized groups that do not require the costly displays of loyalty and identity routinely exhibited by other groups. Though EC phenomena seem to run against the grain of several core hypotheses in the cognitive science of religion, when closely examined in context, the EC corroborates these hypotheses. Three identifying characteristics bear examination in turn: minimal costly signaling, fluid membership, and minimal identity policing.*

Richard Sosis, perhaps the chief proponent of the role of costly signaling in the evolution of religion, has argued that one of religion's primary functions, specifically the ritual dimensions of religion, is to serve as

16. Norenzayan, *Big Gods*, 60–61.
17. Shults, *Theology after the Birth of God*, 29.

a guarantor of sincerity, an indication of an agent's total commitment to the larger group project.[18] As markers of sincere commitment, costly signs of membership and belonging promise social goods to those who display them and would, if shared across a community, strengthen the community and enhance its longevity.[19] What then are we to make of the almost complete absence of costly signaling inside EC communities, if the absence of such signals is indeed an identifying characteristic of the EC movement? Several non-mutually exclusive explanations are worth considering. First, EC communities are designed less like standing committees and more like *ad hoc* committees, created to perform a specific task or reach a determinate goal and to dissolve upon the attainment of that end. *Ad hoc* communities need not invest in the kind of trust building exercises that only pay off in the long run, but can focus their energies on the immediate rewards of cooperation and communion with minimal regard for potential free riders. If EC communities are organized around proximate finite ends, then we might expect that they would expend minimal energy on boundary policing and allow individuals to forgo initiation rituals and costly signals—to "belong before believing." Second, while EC communities are not liturgical in the manner of the magisterial churches, they do evince an interest in High-Church rituals and spiritual practices that establishment Evangelicals have tended to dismiss as variations of vestigial medievalism or "works-righteousness." These ritual commitments may be minimal and not rise to the level of "costly signaling" but they may also be sufficient to the diminished cooperation and trust building needs of EC communities. To be clear, costly signaling may be one of the most important functions of religious rituals, but it need not be their only function, so ritual may be sporadically present even in cases, like the EC, where it is not necessary as a costly index of loyalty and authentic belief.[20]

A second marker of EC communities is fluid membership. Individuals may belong to several overlapping groups and easily pass between different communities. Were these communities organized as competing coalitions, such fluidity would be unthinkable. In such cases loyalty markers would be key and, as was the case during the heyday of mainline Protestantism, members moving from one city to another might need to carry with them

---

18. See Sosis, "Why Aren't We All Hutterites?," 91–12;, Sosis, "Religious Behaviors, Badges and Bans," 61–86; and Sosis and Alcorta, "Signaling, Solidarity, and the Sacred," 264–74.

19. Sosis and Bressler, "Cooperation and Commune Longevity," 211–39; and Sosis and Ruffle, "Religious Ritual and Cooperation," 713–22.

20. For a sophisticated discussion of this issue see Wildman, *Science and Religious Anthropology*, 75–83.

a letter of good standing from their previous church community as a mark of communal loyalty. How are such fluid membership practices sustainable? One explanation is that while EC communities demonstrate remarkable fluidity when membership is defined in traditional ways (creedal affirmation, financial support, formal initiation or membership), they are much less fluid than one may at first appreciate when other criteria are examined. As denominational loyalty among Protestants has decreased, congregational loyalty among Evangelicals has also declined. Denomination hopping, even among clergy, is no longer a cause for notice and "church shopping" has become common enough to spawn "seeker sensitive" churches that cater to fickle "consumers." If we interpret decreasing denominational and congregational loyalty as a straightforward increase in membership fluidity then the EC seems merely to be the logical extension of the trend. However, it is not necessarily the case that increased fluidity as defined by traditional markers of identity is the most relevant indicator. Research conducted by the Pew Forum suggests that, while denominational loyalties and religious service attendance have decreased, there is remarkable stability across the generations when it comes to a wide range of theistic beliefs.[21] This suggests that membership fluidity as defined by traditional markers may not correlate with the most important markers of membership among EC participants. What most EC participants share is a set of vaguely theistic beliefs, and this set may function as a marker of membership, sufficient to generate trust within a cohort.[22] Ara Norenzayan has argued that some of the same dynamics that lead to the proliferation of religious rituals and CREDs may function across traditional religious boundaries.[23] If humans tend to default to trusting those who display belief in a supernatural agent, then such trust may be reciprocal among theists generally. From the perspective of the individual, the implicit logic is as follows: I am most trusting of those in my own group who show signs of believing in our shared disembodied supervising agent(s), but I am more willing to trust someone who shows signs of believing in any disembodied supervising agent(s) than someone who displays no such signs. In short, any credible marker of religious belief is a sign of relative trustworthiness, especially when compared to markers of nonbelief such as atheism.[24] If these cognitive and emotional defaults regarding trust are broadly shared across the species then the shared vague theistic assump-

---

21. See http://www.pewforum.org/2010/02/17/religion-among-the-millennials/.

22. Martí and Ganiel, *The Deconstructed Church*, 26–32.

23. See Norenzayan, *Big Gods*, 55–75.

24. See Norenzayan, *Big Gods*, 66–75; and Sosis, "Does Religion Promote Trust?," 1–30. This phenomenon may be particularly pronounced in EC congregations. See Martí and Ganiel, *The Deconstructed Church*, 142–144.

tions of most EC participants may be sufficient to hold together religious coalitions, especially if they are small *ad hoc* groups. It is also important not to confuse the fluid membership of small *ad hoc* groups and gatherings that take place in cafés, homes and pubs with more stable markers of identity (a vague set of theistic beliefs) that persist across these smaller groups and may characterize the EC as a whole.

While the number of participants in EC gatherings and groups may be quite large, a final marker of EC communities is their size. There are, almost by definition, no EC mega-churches, though there may be considerable overlap in membership.[25] The basic organizational unit of the EC is the small group. How small? The question is difficult to answer because the units are often informally organized groups that do not keep membership rolls or show up in surveys. However, working on the assumption that the basic units of the EC movement are small groups in which most members would know most other members, we can speculate as to several possible effects of EC ecclesiology. Norenzayan argues that "Big God" conceptions evolved from mere disembodied agent conceptions (gods) as a way to facilitate "the rise of cooperation in large groups of anonymous strangers."[26] Big Gods are thought to be 1) active agents who are 2) concerned with human morality and 3) located in the sky so as to have a "God's-eye view" of all people, not merely those who enter their territory.[27] Thus Big Gods act as social facilitators among strangers, and researchers have found that cooperation among strangers is enhanced when experimental participants are primed with Big God reminders.[28] If Norenzayan is correct, then we can hypothesize that EC small groups, in which most participants are personally acquainted, would not need to reinforce cooperation through Big God conceptions. Trust and cooperation might instead grow out of personal familiarity and exchange. Further, we might consider the possibility that EC groups, freed from the need to maintain Big God conceptions, might explore other theistic conceptions that would better serve their emotional, social and existential needs. This line of speculation leads to a more focused consideration of EC theology and the intimate connection between social organization, human cognition and theological conceptions.

---

25. Ibid., 67–69.
26. Norenzayan, *Big Gods*, 140–54.
27. Ibid., 23–29.
28. See Norenzayan and Shariff, "The origin and evolution of religious prosociality," 58–62, Berring, "The folk psychology of souls," 453–98.

EMERGENT CHURCH EXPERIMENTS IN SMALL GROUPS AND SMALL GODS

As in the last section, I begin my analysis with a cursory presentation of a widely shared working hypothesis in the cognitive science of religion regarding the emergence of disembodied agents, Big Gods and rationalist theisms. In early hominid ancestral environments it would have been important to be able to detect and predict the actions of other agents. Agents are likely to be either enemies (predators and competitors), allies (cooperators), or prey and there would have been strong survival and reproductive advantages to detecting and predicting their behavior. This can be accomplished most effectively by conceiving of other agents as having minds of their own. The cognitive capacity for imagining other minds is both an adaptation and a heuristic mechanism that can be fruitfully applied to agents (other humans), non-agents (rocks), and pseudo-agents (plants and insects) so as to predict future behaviors (My enemies want to hurt me, the rock wants to sink in the water, the tree wants sunlight and the moth wants to fly to the fire). Thus human ancestors took to imagining agency where there was none, and some of these imagined agents developed into god conceptions.[29] With disembodied agent conceptions present in the human cognitive tool kit, social evolution took over and the gods became Big Gods as larger and larger groups of *homo sapiens* formed coalitions for both mutual protection against other coalitions and more efficient exploitation of natural resources. Most god conceptions share a repertoire of traits. They tend to be anthropomorphic intentional agents with supernatural or counterintuitive powers that violate some, but not all, expectations about how agents behave.[30] Such "minimally counterintuitive" conceptions are both memorable and easily transmittable so that they persist over time and become the common possession of communities.[31] Larger communities need larger god conceptions. Thus Axial age religions pushed the notion of a Big God to eternity and the conception of a single creator God was born.[32]

---

29. This phenomenon is often referred to as "hyper-active agency detection" or HAAD. The stock example involves running away from rustling bushes. The rustling may come from the wind, but it may also be a tiger. Thus humans develop a habit of hyperactive agency detection as a hedge against danger. Better falsely to detect an agent and run from the wind than fail to run from a tiger.

30. Nicholson, "Social Identity Processes in the Development of Maximally Counterintuitive Theological Concepts," 737.

31. See Nicholson, "Social Identity Processes in the Development of Maximally Counterintuitive Theological Concepts," 737–42; and Wildman, *Science and Religious Anthropology*, 91–93.

32. See Shults, *Theology after the Birth of God*, 41. This argument is also remarkably

In its most rationalist instantiations the God conception is stripped of its minimally counterintuitive trappings and becomes a maximally counterintuitive conception of divinity. Justin L. Barrett has explored this theme at length, arguing that human minds have evolved to prefer minimally counterintuitive notions of divinity that are similar enough to human agents so as to be both intuitive and relevant to human actions and intentions and dissimilar enough so as to be memorable and religiously potent.[33] These minimally counterintuitive conceptions of divinity may be gods or Big Gods, but they have little in common with the rationalist, maximally counterintuitive, "theologically correct" conceptions of divinity proffered in the official teachings of religious institutions. "Precisely because they conform to our natural default inference systems, "theologically incorrect," anthropomorphic concepts of supernatural beings persist in spite of theological efforts to modify, contain, or repress them."[34] Put simply, *homo sapiens* are natural theists (monotheists, polytheists, henotheists) and it requires considerable institutional and social energy to create and maintain more "rational," and less "natural" theological conceptions. Why would any group expend so much energy promoting maximally counterintuitive conceptions of divinity? Hugh Nicholson has recently argued that maximally counterintuitive religious conceptions in both Christianity (consubstantiality) and Buddhism (no-self) might serve to reinforce communal identity by maximizing the contrast between in-group and out-group members.[35] However, while "theologically correct" conceptions of divinity may work to stabilize group identity, we should also expect that less counterintuitive "theologically incorrect" conceptions (folk theology) would reemerge whenever institutional pressure to conform is relaxed.

Second Hypothesis: *The EC appears to confirm several core hypotheses of the cognitive science of religion regarding the production of divinity conceptions and the relationship between those conceptions and the construction and maintenance of group boundaries. The EC movement is characterized by its explicit rejection of jargon laden doctrinal formulations and evidences*

---

similar to Hume's speculations on the origins of monotheism in Book VIII of Hume, *The Natural History of Religion*, 36–38.

33. See Barrett and Keil, "Conceptualizing a Non-natural Entity: Anthropomorphism in God Concepts," 219–47; Barrett, "Theological Correctness," 325–39; Barrett, "Exploring the Natural Foundations of Religion," 29–34; and Barrett and Nyhof, "Spreading Non-natural Concepts," 69–100.

34. Nicholson, "Social Identity Processes in the Development of Maximally Counterintuitive Theological Concepts," 738.

35. Ibid., 736–70. See also Nicholson, *The Spirit of Contradiction in Christianity and Buddhism*.

a return to "theologically incorrect" minimally counterintuitive conceptions of divinity. These theological formulations are reciprocally linked to the EC movement's rejection of central organization and hierarchy. Three additional distinguishing marks of the EC are worth exploring: the self-conscious recognition of the close relationship between political power and theological formulations, the embrace of open and relational theologies, and the construction of local and authentic testimonial theologies.

Within the EC, the phenomenon of "Christendom," the conflation of state and Church interests, is a cause of concern and an object of self-criticism and reflection. This concern is addressed in a host of different ways. First, EC writers are less enthusiastically supportive than their establishment Evangelical colleagues of the early Protestant project. The Protestant Reformation, they argue, offered cogent critiques, but while it splintered Christendom, it failed to address its logic, repeating instead of dismantling the alliance of church and state. This critique is visibly manifest in the relative comfort the EC evinces in borrowing devotional practices from the Roman Catholic Church, a comfort not shared by many mainline Protestants and establishment Evangelicals. Second, the EC has worked to understand and embrace the best of postmodernism, specifically the postmodern critique of modernist ideologies that consolidate power and silence dissent by promulgating "neutral and objective" visions of reality that support the *status quo*. Many EC authors acknowledge that postmodernism is more a critical mood than a coherent worldview, but are equally eager to embrace postmodernism's "hermeneutics of suspicion." Worldviews and sacred canopies should not be trusted, for they are less reflections of objective reality and more subjective constructions of realities that camouflage and legitimate the workings of political power. The EC's flirtation with postmodern criticism has led to a deep concern to expose the hidden power dynamics of Anglo-Evangelical worldviews, including but not limited to those occasions where Evangelical theology and politics unambiguously overlap. Third, the self-conscious recognition of the connection between political power and theological formulations is manifest in the EC movement's interest in shedding the vestiges of Western colonialism. Mainline Evangelical missions work has too often uncritically and perhaps unintentionally promoted a determinately Western worldview as it worked to share the Christian Gospel. The EC movement maintains a focus on missions work, but strives to free those undertakings from colonialist assumptions about race, class, education, consumerism and liturgical propriety. These three criticisms demonstrate the EC impulse to combat the Christendom ideal by identifying the linkages between political power and theological formulations. More importantly, EC conceptions of divinity are evolving to support less magisterial forms of ecclesiology as EC authors recognize a necessary connection between upending hierarchical "top-down" ecclesiologies and rethinking hierarchical "top-down" theological conceptions.

The notion that human minds have been designed by millennia of evolution to create and host divinity conceptions can be met with a wide range of emotions and has given birth to a broad spectrum of projects both secular and theological. If the core hypothesis of the cognitive science of religion is correct, 1) that humans share an evolved cognitive preference for divinity conceptions that are minimally counterintuitive and support prosocial in-group behavior, and 2) that the relationship between these two preferences is reciprocal, then we should expect the modification of one to effect the other. Indeed, early research in the field supports the general hypothesis that bigger in-groups and Big Gods are mutually reinforcing. However, cognitive preferences or what are sometimes called "cognitive defaults" are general tendencies, not deterministic laws of behavior. Just as some social groups have expanded their notions of in-group identity to include large groups like nation states or transnational ethnic or religious coalitions, human groups have found ways of resisting the cognitive default preference for minimally counterintuitive divine agents. Not only atheists, but also rationalist theists with maximally counterintuitive theological conceptions may resist the tendency to conceive of divine disembodied agents in minimally counterintuitive ways. The cognitive science of religion does not suggest that human cognitive defaults cannot be resisted, only that such resistance is socially or intellectually costly. For some atheists, the price of resisting religious cognitive defaults may be worth paying for intellectual or axiological reasons.[36] Classical theists or deists may be willing to perform the systematic theological or creedal acrobatics necessary to reconcile intellectual and moral coherence with the revealed symbols and narratives of their particular tradition, but they must do so at the cost of intuitive plausibility. To state the matter bluntly, there is nothing intuitively plausible about transubstantiation, eternal election, salvation by grace through faith, or the metaphysics behind the *filioque* controversy. Sustaining these conceptions requires a tremendous outlay of energy and attention. By contrast, a cursory survey of the theological language of the EC suggests that, unlike much of the Protestant mainline and Evangelical establishment, the EC is less worried about resisting religious cognitive defaults and enforcing doctrinal conformity by means of theologically correct, maximally counterintuitive theological conceptions. Put simply, within the EC, the audience for rationalist, theologically correct, systematic exposition (maximally counter-

---

36. This is the central moral claim of Shults, *Theology after the Birth of God*.

intuitive conceptions of divinity) seems to have dwindled, to be replaced by an audience that is not willing to pay the considerable price in intuitive plausibility.[37] The general theological impulse of the EC is toward intuitively plausible divinity conceptions. Such conceptions can flourish within the EC context because they need not bear the considerable burden of policing community identity, restricting inter-group migration, and enforcing group loyalty.

The late twentieth and early twenty-first centuries have seen a proliferation of theological schools that might best be characterized as sharing a concern for intuitive plausibility and the EC movement is drawn in this direction. The narrative theologies of Stanley Hauerwas and James William McClendon, the post-Liberal theology of George Lindbeck and Hans Frei, the avowedly postmodern theology of Stanley Grenz, and the open and relational theologies of John Sanders and Greg Boyd all speak to the EC concern for intuitive plausibility. Each of these theological movements is less concerned with traditional standards of creedal conformity, doctrinal purity and rational systematic coherence and more interested in fidelity to the traditions, symbols, stories and practices that contemporary Christians find compelling. Theologians and EC leaders may "go behind" the intuitively plausible narratives and traditions and articulate a postmodern epistemology that aims to justify or contextualize EC practices as something other than fideism or pragmatism, but the cognitive science of religion suggests that the causal influence works predominantly in the opposite direction. Intuitively plausible, minimally counterintuitive conceptions of divinity flourish in human minds and groups with minimal social and intellectual support. Theologies that go beyond describing these conceptions serve primarily to defend such conceptions and their utilization within churches to outsiders and provide an apologetic framework for intellectually curious insiders. Therefore, the working theologies of the EC should not be understood as the intellectual achievement of educated elites, but rather as a return—perhaps even a self-conscious return—to folk conceptions of divinity that are so intuitively plausible as to require minimal intellectual maintenance or institutional support.

As a watchword of EC theological discourse, "authenticity" captures something of the movement's concern to avoid jargon laden, "theologically correct" religious language on the one hand and manufactured, focus-grouped, "seeker sensitive" formulations on the other. This suggests an additional hypothesis about the character of the EC movement: the EC is

---

37. This claim is empirically vulnerable, perhaps even risible given that doctrinal police abound even within the EC movement, but I am after a general non-exhaustive characterization.

characterized by an emphasis on "local" theological portrayals and narrative testimony that highlight a contrast between "authentic experience" and the dominant enveloping corporate environment that offers only "manufactured experience." Two points emerge from this thesis that bear further examination. First, EC theology evinces a mood of protest or dissatisfaction with the homogenized products of popular culture, both religious and secular, preferring "local" theologies that speak to local concerns, and contexts. Terms like "local," "artisanal," "craft," "homemade," and "terroir" may seem more pertinent to discussions of farmer's markets and restaurants, but are appropriate to discussions of EC theological styles insofar as both the local food and the EC movements understand themselves as offering more authentic alternatives to mass-market products. Additionally, the EC movement's self-conscious emphasis on the local context of theological language allows for both a wider range of expression and deeper context-appropriate theological formulations that do not have to meet the standards of mass appeal or universal applicability. Second, insofar as EC theology reveals a mood of protest against manufactured and homogenized theological signs and religious experiences it actually relies on popular culture, both secular and religious, to provide the relevant terms of contrast. Personal testimony in cafés, bars and blogs conveys special authenticity, small groups and *ad hoc* gatherings seem particularly intimate, and humble even folksy religious practices are experienced as especially significant when held up against shopping mall sized mega-churches, pop-music praise choruses and perfectly coiffed, cookie-cutter pastoral teams. If the present hypothesis is accurate, and one of the marks of EC theology is its rejection of maximally counterintuitive "theologically correct" formulations in favor of more intuitively appealing minimally counterintuitive conceptions, and if it is the case that the EC preference for intuitively plausible theological conceptions is causally linked to EC social forms, then I would further hypothesize that the plausibility of EC theological formulations and the appeal of EC social forms is heightened by the contrast between EC habits of action and thought and those of the environing culture. Put simply, the appeal of EC theology and ecclesiology is not only rooted in human cognitive, social and emotional defaults, but their appeal is also a product of the stark juxtaposition between "authentic" EC phenomena and late-modern, consumer driven, mass culture that provides the backdrop against which the EC defines itself. For individual participants in the EC movement, the constant tension between EC and environing culture may actually yield a creative tension that evokes a religious response. The next section takes up this theme at length as it examines a particular theory of value that emphasizes the axiological import of contrast.

EMERGENT CHURCH EXPERIMENTS IN MAXIMIZING VALUE THROUGH HIGH CONTRAST HARMONIES

This section explores a particular hypothesis in naturalist axiology, rather than a core hypothesis from the bio-cultural study of religion. Specifically, it uses the work of Robert Cummings Neville and his theory of harmony and value. Naturalist axiology and the bio-cultural study of religion may turn out to be closely allied and might serve as intellectual partners in the study of religion, aesthetics and cognition.[38] At present, however, I treat Neville's axiology independently of the cognitive science of religion, and offer only a brief synopsis. In numerous books and articles Neville offers variations of the characterization of value as harmony.[39] Naturalist axiology is a rare phenomenon in contemporary philosophy in part because many philosophers see no way of perceiving and knowing value, much less analyzing value, that does not merely attempt to justify personal or cultural preferences. Thus modern philosophy tends to run aground on epistemological questions surrounding value and reifies the fact/value distinction. However, the analysis of value and the perception of value are related but distinguishable, and Neville follows Peirce's notion that "our grasp of the values achieved . . . is *fallible and corrigible*."[40] Though we intuit the value of harmonies, and intuition is the fallible product of determinate lines of evolution and inquiry, the values it indicates are real insofar as we may be wrong about them. Thus our formulations of value are hypothetical, and our transactions with value experimental. When Neville analyzes value with Plato, Leibniz, Kant, Peirce and Whitehead as primary discussion partners, he defines the value of a harmony as "a function of its degrees of complexity and simplicity together."[41] He writes:

> In a harmony, the various features are integrated in patterns that cohere in one definite overall pattern. A pattern's harmony exhibits both complexity and simplicity. . .Complexity refers to the different things involved as components, including the patterns of components. Simplicity refers to the economy with which the components are harmonized, such that higher levels contain relatively little complexity but encompass great variety

---

38. Nathaniel F. Barrett's work is an effort in this synthetic direction. See Barrett, "Skillful Engagement and the 'Effort after Value,'" 92–108; and Barrett, "Toward an Alternative Evolutionary Theory of Religion," 583–621.

39. See Neville, *Recovery of the Measure*, 129–46; Neville, *Cosmology of Freedom*, 174–206; and Neville, "Sketch of a System," 253–274.

40. Neville, *Recovery of the Measure*, 160; emphasis added.

41. Ibid., 137.

in the components of components, etc. Every harmony thus has both complexity and simplicity, and the degree of harmony is dependent on maximizing both complexity and simplicity. It is easy to gain simplicity by sacrificing complexity; this happens as one approaches homogeneity. Equally, one can maximize complexity at the expense of simplicity by leveling off the harmony and having the components related by mere conjunctions. Harmony is increased in value as both complexity and simplicity are increased. Since these are two variables, both of which might be subject to increase, there are many possible ways in which a harmony might be increased in value.[42]

Neville's axiology is deeply embedded in a philosophical system and numerous questions are likely to occur to the reader when it is first encountered. His larger *Axiology of Thinking* aims to provide answers and context.[43] For our purposes, however, we can utilize his description of value as a character of harmonies that can be increased and decreased by raising and lowering the simplicity and complexity of the harmony. A collection of books, for instance, has the collective value of all of the individual titles. As more titles are added, the entire value of the collection increases as the complexity of the collection increases. A maximally complex collection would be quite valuable, but as Jorge Luis Borges illustrates in "The Library of Babel" a complete library with every possible title would be of comparatively little value if it had no simplicity, no organizing principle that turned a mere collection of conjunct titles into a navigable library.[44] So too, a simple library is valuable. The complete works of Robert Cummings Neville, for instance, would be such a simple collection, but its value is severely curtailed by its lack of complexity. Where are the countervailing voices, the referenced works, the spectra of contrasting and conflicting opinions? Value is minimized at the limit cases of mere togetherness (minimal simplicity) and uniformity (minimal complexity). But we can seek to maximize value as well, by working not just to maximize simplicity and complexity independently of one another, but by striving to maximize the harmony between the two. The most valuable collections of books are both complex (full of many kinds of texts on many different topics) and simple (offering a navigable system of organization). Indeed, we would hesitate to call any collection a library that did not display both meaningful complexity and simplicity. Neville's theory of value allows

---

42. Neville, "Sketch of a System," 259–60.

43. Neville's *Axiology of Thinking* is a five-part work, published as three volumes: *Reconstruction of Thinking* (1981), *The Recovery of the Measure* (1989), and *Normative Cultures* (1995).

44. Borges, "The Library of Babel," 51–58.

us to analyze the value of harmonies even when (unlike libraries and books) the components harmonized are not obviously discrete units that one can merely collect. A meal, a career, an artistic creation, a religious tradition, a political system, even a human life are all harmonies with distinct values that might be analyzed in terms of simplicity and complexity.[45] The remainder of this section looks at the EC movement as an achievement of value, an ongoing attempt to harmonize high contrast social forms and theologies so as to generate a maximally valuable religious identity.

Third Hypothesis: *As a late modern experiment in social adaptation, the EC is a unique achievement of value. It can be characterized axiologically as a harmonious integration of several phenomena of contemporary western religious life, phenomena that are often seen as incommensurable or mere contrasts. Thus the EC is a high-contrast harmony, meaning that it achieves considerable complexity by integrating dissimilar phenomena. These diverse phenomena may even be imagined as so dissimilar as to be entirely incompatible. Nevertheless, the characteristic EC strategy (conscious or not) is to embrace and accentuate the fact of contrast, and thereby highlight its own complexity. Put simply, the EC harmonizes very different social forms, theologies and religious identities but it achieves this harmony not through minimizing difference and working toward homogeneity, but by cultivating an experimental attitude that favors difference, tolerance and experimentation as religious goods. Three characteristic high-contrasts of the EC are worth consideration: high-contrast social forms, high-contrast theologies, and high-contrast religious identities. In each case the EC achieves a synthetic harmony that coordinates rather than resolves difference.*

Previous sections have prepared us to recognize the characteristic shape of EC social groups. They tend to be small, minimally organized and transitory. Each of these descriptive terms might, in particular contexts, carry negative connotations, but in the EC such groups are understood as agile, evanescent, responsive, and adaptive. EC writers and participants do in fact muster arguments in defense of small, transient, responsive groups, but it is equally important to note the ways in which these arguments are often constructed to highlight the merits of EC groups in contradistinction to larger, more highly organized, established churches and denominations. These establishment churches provide the larger religious and cultural context over against which the EC defines itself.[46] If we put aside the overblown

---

45. For an excellent theological exploration of this theory see the conclusion of Slater, *C. S. Peirce and the Nested Continua Model of Religious Interpretation*, 202–28.

46. Here I abandon the distinction between mainline Protestantism and establishment Evangelicalism and use "mainline" and "establishment" as synonyms.

rhetoric that often occurs in online forums and intentionally provocative tracts and treatises, the EC seems to function less as a complete rejection of establishment churches and works more as a high-contrast complement. Individual participants in the EC may entirely reject mainstream forms of organization, but EC membership is drawn largely from the establishment, and EC social organization and worship are designed to work in contrast with more traditional forms.[47] Thus, I argue that the EC is best understood not a competing alternative but as a value enhancing foil. To be clear, there is nothing particularly unique about small, minimally organized, transitory groups. However, when such groups are organized around practices and symbols that are traditionally the purview of large, hierarchical institutions, the contrast between the two forms can become the focus. The EC is unique insofar as it forms a complex harmony in which the contrast between establishment and EC social forms is not resolved, ignored or overcome. Complexity is not sacrificed to simplicity. Rather, complexity is maintained whenever EC participants live in and move between mainline or evangelical and EC contexts even as they refuse to resolve the contrast.

Just as the EC emphasizes rather than resolves the contrast between mainstream and EC social forms, the EC is most successful when it develops the high contrast between "authentic" and "theologically correct" theological conceptions and symbols. Such contrastive harmonies can yield religiously provocative, creative tensions. EC theology fixes attention on at least three axes of contrast: a strict/generous axis, a permanent/evolving axis and an adequate/inadequate axis. EC authors (Brain McLaren most famously) characterize their own work as generously orthodox and aim at inclusion; the implication being that mainline theology tends to be strictly or rigidly orthodox and directed toward exclusion.[48] Additionally, as argued above, EC theologies tend to emphasize context-sensitive theological expressions that evolve to meet changing needs and realities over against theologies that work toward final or definitive formulations and pretend to offer a *regula fidei*. All three axes are related as is evidenced in the contrast between the EC emphasis on the fallible and inadequate nature of all theological formulations. While no informed critic would suggest that mainline or evangelical churches have ignored the issue of the inadequacy of language to capture ultimacy, the EC makes the softer case that in practice mainline churches often overlook the need for apophatic speech and theological humility. EC participants may, of course, be guilty of the same. However, the EC evinces a concerted effort along all three axis to contrast

---

47. Martí and Ganiel, *The Deconstructed Church*, 23.
48. See McLaren, *A Generous Orthodoxy*.

strict, final, and adequate theological formulations with open, evolving and fallible formulations without resolving the contrast. The resulting high contrast theological harmonies are valuable insofar as they resist homogeneity and force an encounter with contrasting theological formulations. EC participants inhabit contrasting social worlds and hold on to contrasting theological formulations and this opens up a space of creative tension that is a product of a harmony. Returning to Neville's axiological language, the EC maintains the values of both ends of the high contrast social and theological forms and the achieved value inherent in the new synthetic harmony.[49] In other words, the EC's value is both the combined value of the sustained contrasts and the newly emergent value of the synthesis that preserves rather than resolves those contrasts.

The beginning of this treatment outlined Peirce's theory of ubiquitous inquiry and proposed that we understand all endeavors as experimental. Further I argued that we should understand religious communities as living lines of experimental research. Additionally, I suggested that the EC is a particularly interesting phenomenon, in part, because it is a self-consciously experimental religious orientation. This, I argue, is the unique core of the EC, what sets it off from most other forms of Christian practice. There is a high contrast inherent in the juxtaposition of religion and experimentation. Peirce, despite the fact that he understood all human endeavors as experimental on some level, warned against free experimentation in religion and other vital matters, arguing for a more conservative "commonsense" approach. Most traditional churches also work against preserving the contrast between experimentation and religion, preferring to resolve or hide from the contrast by building institutions and constructing theologies that give the appearance of permanence, stability and certainty. The self-conscious recognition of the experimental quality of all human endeavors obliges one to acknowledge with Schleiermacher that humanity is absolutely dependent i.e. that one's being is wholly contingent. Our fundamental contingency should be a matter of ultimate concern. However, continuing along the lines of Tillich's existential analysis, many religious traditions work to domesticate and disguise contingency with comforting theological certainties and imposing traditions and hierarchies. If my characterization of the EC movement is correct, then the EC thrives by cultivating an experimental religious identity in contrast to the settled or resolved identities of its mainstream counterparts. In so doing the EC ventures out from the safety of established and respected social forms and theological formulations in order to cultivate engagements with the ragged edge of contingency.

49. Neville, *Recovery of the Measure*, 136.

To be clear, the EC develops two relevant high contrast harmonies. The first contrast is the ontological contrast, engaged at least tangentially by all religions, between determinate being and indeterminacy. In theistic language this is the ultimate contrast between creation and Creator; in naturalist terms this is the ultimate contrast between nature natured and Nature naturing. The second contrast is between differing strategies for managing and signifying the first. The characteristic worry of the EC is that its symbols and strategies for engaging ultimacy might be inauthentic, too tame and domesticated, too entangled with political interests, power, historical precedents and orthodox theological forms. No religious movement can live perpetually in the apophatic mode, but it can sustain an apophatic mood by insisting on its own experimental identity and the experimental character of all of its forms and formulations. What is more, the EC works to sustain this mood by repeatedly reconstituting itself and constantly contrasting itself to the mainline churches.[50] Put simply, the experimental identity of the EC is reinforced and made more evident by constant comparisons to the more settled identities of mainline groups. All religions are experimental, but the EC movement acknowledges its experimental character to a unique degree and places it squarely at the center of its identity.

EMERGENT CHURCH PROSPECTS: PARASITES OR SYMBIOTES?

Following Peirce, the governing pragmatist and naturalist hypothesis of this essay is that all human endeavors, including religion, are experimental. Thus, to live religiously is to embody particular hypotheses about how best to orient oneself toward ultimacy. If all religions are embodied, large-scale experiments, then the EC is not unique in this regard. However, insofar as the EC recognizes and develops its own experimental character to a unique degree, even emphasizing it in contrast to its mainline alternatives that provide its relevant context, the EC seems to merit special attention. Whether or not such self-awareness on the part of the EC will prove adaptive in the long run, it is worth considering the axiological implications of such a movement. Not only can we analyze the achieved value of the EC as a high contrast harmony as in the previous section, but we can also focus attention on a single promising feature of that harmony: tolerance. In recognizing its own experimental character and acknowledging the hypothetical status of all of its social forms and theological formulations, the EC eschews claims to certainty, finality, and adequacy—or at least it should. Personalities and

50. Martí and Ganiel, *The Deconstructed Church*, 58–60.

prejudices will always obscure the ideal, but the EC appears to be working toward developing a culture of humility that reinforces itself even as it breeds an attitude of tolerance toward competing and contrasting religious practices and symbols. As the EC matures into its third decade, it is tempting to use the metaphor of the big tent to describe its experimental, humble and tolerant ethos, but that metaphor misses the mark. We do better to think of the EC as a diverse collection of small tents springing up (and sometimes folding up) across a wide field of possibilities with individual participants moving easily among them. The variety of tents, the free movement among them, and the evident transience of the tents themselves reinforce the apophatic mood of experimentation.

At the risk of carrying the metaphor too far, it is worth considering the fact that the field of small tents lies on the outskirts of a city full of imposing buildings erected on stone foundations. Individuals may also move freely between the buildings of the city and the tents of the field and gain something valuable in the contrast. The buildings from the metaphor are of course the established denominations and social institutions that provide stability, structure and context in W.E.I.R.D. societies.[51] But these institutions provide more than mere background and context for the EC movement. As argued in the previous section, part of the value of the EC harmony is as a high contrast alternative to the dominant forms of mainline religion. The EC is therefore reliant on the mainstream as a foil. However, despite the fact that the EC is an international movement, it seems to be inextricably linked to the relative social security and stability found in W.E.I.R.D. societies.[52] What Peirce, researchers in the cognitive science of religion, and perhaps most religious practitioners share is a belief in the importance of religion for shaping communal and individual habits of action and existential orientations. Therefore, in most cases, religion is far too important to the continued functioning of the society and the individual to risk haphazard experimentation. The cognitive science of religion suggests that religion has played a crucial role in human history allowing for close cooperation among non-kin in-group members and strengthening the communal boundaries that allow for successful cooperative defense against out-group members. Unless and until these important roles are taken up and fulfilled by some non-religious entity such as the modern secular state, religion is not free to experiment on a wide scale. The stakes are too high.

51. W.E.I.R.D. is an acronym for Western, Educated, Industrialized, Rich and Democratic. See Henrich, Heine and Norenzayan, "The Weirdest People in the World?," 61–133.

52. Steven Pinker makes a similar case in Pinker, *The Better Angels of Our Natures*, 59–128. There Pinker makes the case that the "W" in W.E.I.R.D. may soon need to go.

As an experimental form of religion, the EC may be elegantly designed to thrive in the late-modern western world, but the W.E.I.R.D. world is a peculiar niche, a genuine novelty in human history. We should not, therefore, expect an entity that flourishes in the W.E.I.R.D. world to adapt readily to other environments. Thus I offer a concluding hypothesis: the prospects for the EC are closely tied to the spread of Liberal democratic institutions.

In closing I suggest that the EC movement is not only reliant on the success of secular liberal democratic institutions—much the same can be said for many forms of contemporary religious practice—but it is also intimately linked to the continued vitality of establishment churches. In short, they are symbiotic. I argued above that much of the value of the EC stems from its generating and sustaining a high contrast harmony with mainstream religious institutions. But in addition to my cursory axiological analysis of the contrast, it seems likely that that further sociological analysis might prove fruitful. The work of Wesley Wildman points in this promising direction and is worth quoting at some length:

> liberal religious groups depend on conservative religious groups for their sheer institutional buoyancy, for the steady stream of frustrated immigrants fleeing the hostile shores of conservatism, and for conservatism's ability to win the new converts that make an entire religion socially viable and culturally relevant. Liberal theology also depends on semi-mythic statements of conservative doctrine that function both as easy targets for liberal theological deconstruction and as decoys to deflect attention from the intellectual inadequacies of liberal theological constructions.[53]

While Wildman is describing the relationship between Liberal Protestants (liberal religion) and the Evangelical Protestants (conservative religion) I contend that the relationship between the established churches and the EC is similar in many ways. Most EC participants come from mainline or evangelical churches and many maintain ties even as they participate in the EC movement in various ways. Anecdotal evidence also suggests that the critical energies of the EC are often directed, not against the environing secular culture, as is the case with more fundamentalist forms of Evangelicalism, but squarely at establishment churches themselves. Thus the more traditional churches serve the EC as both fodder and foil. Finally, an additional dynamic may also be at play in which the EC serves the mainstream as a kind of pressure valve, enabling dissatisfied and precocious participants to

---

53. Wildman, "The Ambiguous Heritage and Perpetual Promise of Liberal Theology," 59.

look elsewhere for creative and critical outlets thus ensuring the continued smooth functioning of the mainline.[54] Obversely, the EC is empowered to pursue its more radically experimental program, to act in ways that outsiders and some insiders might consider hasty or reckless, with the knowledge that the mainstream provides a kind of institutional backstop. Thus the conservative traditional churchs unwittingly support and shepherd the more freewheeling experimental program of the EC even as the EC pushes forward with its more radical religious experiments.

BIBLIOGRAPHY

Barrett, Justin L., and Frank C. Keil. "Conceptualizing a Non-natural Entity: Anthropomorphism in God Concepts." *Cognitive Psychology* 31 (1996) 219–47.
Barrett, Justin L., and Melanie A. Nyhof. "Spreading Non-natural Concepts: The Role of Intuitive Conceptual Structures in Memory and Transmission of Cultural Materials." *Journal of Cognition and Culture* 1 (2001) 69–100.
———. "Exploring the Natural Foundations of Religion." *Trends in Cognitive Science* 4/1 (2000) 29–34.
———. "Theological Correctness: Cognitive Constraint and the Study of Religion." *Method and Theory in the Study of Religion* 11 (1999) 325–39.
Barrett, Nathaniel F. "Skillful Engagement and the 'Effort after Value': An Axiological Theory of the Origins of Religion." In *Evolution, Religion, and Cognitive Science: Critical and Constructive Essays*, edited by Fraser Watts and Léon Turner, 92–108. Oxford: Oxford University Press, 2014.
———. "Toward an Alternative Evolutionary Theory of Religion: Looking Past Computational Evolutionary Psychology to a Wider Field of Possibilities." *Journal of the American Academy of Religion* 78 (2010) 583–621.
Berring, Jesse M. "The Folk Psychology of Souls." *Behavioral and Brain Sciences* 29 (2006) 453–98.
Borges, Jorge Luis. "The Library of Babel." In *Labyrinths*, edited by Donal A. Yates and James E. Irby, 51–58. New York: New Directions, 2007.
Cooke, Elizabeth F. *Peirce's Pragmatic Theory of Inquiry: Fallibilism and Indeterminacy*. New York: Continuum, 2006.
Corrington, Robert. "Ecstatic Naturalism." In *A Philosophy of Sacred Nature: Prospects for Ecstatic Naturalism*, edited by Leon Niemoczynski and Nam T. Nguyen, 9–16. Lanham, MD: Lexington, 2015.
Daniel-Hughes, Brandon. "Defanging Peirce's Hopeful Monster: Community, Continuity and the Risks and Rewards of Inquiry." *American Journal of Theology and Philosophy* 37 (2016) 123–36.
———. "Peirce's Conservatism and Critical Commonsense: Insights Toward a more Nuanced Theory of Inquiry." *Southwest Philosophy Review* 33 (2017) 205–14.
———. *Pragmatic Inquiry and Religious Communities: Charles Peirce, Signs and Inhabited Experiments*, New York: Palgrave Macmillan, 2018.

54. Ibid., 57–58.

Henrich, Joseph, Steven J. Heine and Ara Norenzayan, "The Weirdest People in the World?" *Behavioral and Brain Sciences* 33 (2010) 61–133.

Hume, David. *The Natural History of Religion*. New York: Macmillan 1992 (orig. 1757).

Martí, Gerardo, and Gladys Ganiel. *The Deconstructed Church: Understanding Emerging Christianity*. Oxford: Oxford University Press, 2014.

McLaren, Brian D. *A Generous Orthodoxy: Why I am a missional, evangelical, post/protestant, liberal/conservative, mystical/poetic, biblical, charismatic/contemplative, fundamentalist/Calvinist, Anabaptist/Anglican, Methodist, catholic, green, incarnational, depressed-yet hopeful, emergent, unfinished Christian*. Grand Rapids: Zondervan, 2004.

Neville, Robert Cummings. *Cosmology of Freedom*. New ed. Albany: SUNY Press, 1995.

———. *Normative Cultures*. Axiology of Thinking 3. Albany: SUNY Press, 1995.

———. *Reconstruction of Thinking*. Axiology of Thinking 1. Albany: SUNY Press, 1981.

———. *Recovery of the Measure: Interpretation and Nature*. Axiology of Thinking 2. Albany: SUNY Press, 1989.

———. "Sketch of a System." In *New Essays in Metaphysics*, 253–74. Albany: SUNY Press, 1986.

———. *The Truth of Broken Symbols*. Albany: SUNY Press, 1996.

Nicholson, Hugh. "Social Identity Processes in the Development of Maximally Counterintuitive Theological Concepts: Consubstantiality and No-Self." *Journal of the American Academy of Religion* 82 (2014) 737.

———. *The Spirit of Contradiction in Christianity and Buddhism*. New York: Oxford University Press, 2016.

Norenzayan, Ara, and Azim R. Shariff. "The Origin and Evolution of Religious Prosociality." *Science* 322 (2008) 58–62.

———. *Big Gods: How Religion Transformed Cooperation and Conflict*. Princeton: Princeton University Press, 2013.

Peirce, Charles S. *The Essential Peirce: Selected Philosophical Writings Volume 1 (1867–1893)*. Edited by Nathan Houser and Christian Kloesel. Indianapolis: Indiana University Press, 1992.

———. *The Essential Peirce: Selected Philosophical Writings Volume 2 (1893–1913)*. Edited by The Peirce Edition Project. Indianapolis: Indiana University Press, 1998.

———. *Reasoning and the Logic of Things: The Cambridge Conferences Lectures of 1898*. Edited by Kenneth Laine Ketner. Cambridge: Harvard University Press, 1993.

Pew Forum on Religion and Public Life. "Religion Among the Millennials: Less Religiously Active Than Older Americans, but Fairly Traditional in Other Ways." (February, 2010). http://www.pewforum.org/2010/02/17/religion-among-the-millennials/

Pinker, Steven. *The Better Angels of Our Natures: Why Violence Has Declined*. New York: Penguin Group, 2011.

Shults, F. LeRon. *Theology after the Birth of God: Atheist Conceptions in Cognition and Culture*. New York: Palgrave Macmillan, 2014.

Slater, Gary. *C.S. Peirce and the Nested Continua Model of Religious Interpretation*. Oxford: Oxford University Press, 2015.

Sosis, Richard, and Candace Alcorta. "Signaling, Solidarity, and the Sacred: The Evolution of Religious Behavior." *Evolutionary Anthropology* 12 (2003) 264–74.

Sosis, Richard, and Eric R. Bressler. "Cooperation and Commune Longevity: A Test of the Costly Signaling Theory of Religion." *Cross-Cultural Research* 37 (2003) 211–39.

Sosis, Richard, and Bradley J. Ruffle,. "Religious Ritual and Cooperation: Testing for a Relationship on Israeli Religious and Secular Kibbutzim." *Current Anthropology* 44 (2003) 713–22.

Sosis, Richard. "Does Religion Promote Trust? The Role of Signaling, Reputation, and Punishment." *Interdisciplinary Journal of Research on Religion* 1 (2005) 1–30.

———. "Religious Behaviors, Badges and Bans: Signaling Theory and the Evolution of Religion." In *Where God and Science Meet: How Brain and Evolutionary Studies Alter our Understanding of Religion, Vol. 1,* edited by Patrick McNamara, 61–86. London: Praeger, 2006.

———. "Why Aren't We All Hutterites? Costly Signaling Theory and Religious Behavior." *Human Nature* 14 (2002) 91–127.

Wildman, Wesley. "The Ambiguous Heritage and Perpetual Promise of Liberal Theology." *American Journal of Theology and Philosophy* 32 (2011) 43–61.

———. *Science and Religious Anthropology: A Spiritually Evocative Naturalist Interpretation of Human Life*. Burlington, VT: Ashgate, 2009.

Part 3

The Emerging Church and Millennials
Challenges and Opportunities

8

Losing My Religion
Why Millennials Are Leaving the Church

STEPHANIE YUHAS

Abstract

Exposure to globalization and cultural hybridity has influenced younger generations who bring a greater openness to various religious traditions, belief systems and acceptance of difference. According to Pew Research, over 35% of adult Millennials (Americans born between 1981 and 1996) are religiously unaffiliated. These statistics alarm mainline and evangelical religious leaders who find their congregations dwindling. Many factors have contributed to this trend including a focus on rational, pragmatic, and scientific approaches in higher education, geographic nomadism, financial uncertainty, technology, and an anti-institutional outlook. This chapter provides a sketch of the worldview that informs how this generation approaches religion and spirituality. It proposes reasons why this group tends not to identify with religious institutions, even those that utilize progressive doctrine and new technology to entice them. Although many identify as multiple religious belongers, secularists, or even atheists, others struggle to find meaning in the church. Some belong without believing, others are shocked by church scandals they learn about through media exposure and many are cynical about the future. There are places of cross-fertilization with "Nones," seekers, and secularists in the Emerging Church movement. The conclusion will identify several areas that the Emerging Church appeals to Millennials including ritual, technology, experience instead of doctrine and community-building. An open, welcoming and inclusive approach appeals to this younger generation that views the world with a skeptical gaze, while inwardly longing for a deep spiritual experience.

INTRODUCTION

The Millennial generation is often described as entitled, idealistic, unfulfilled, lacking a work ethic, demanding, impatient, and addicted to technology.[1] The cover of *Time* magazine on May 20, 2013, characterized this generation as "lazy entitled narcissists who still live with their parents." But as Sarah Kendzior related on Quartz, a digitally native news outlet,

> But if anything holds this tenuously defined generation together, it is a lack of options. Americans who have lived much of their adult lives in the aftermath of the Great Recession have lower incomes, less mobility, and greater financial dependence on older relatives than any other generation in modern history. Many millennials do not have a lot of choice. They are merely reacting to lost opportunity.[2]

All of the ennui associated with Millennials appears to correlate to a lack of religious affiliation. In 2012, Pew Research published a study titled "'Nones' on the Rise." The survey found that 46 million Americans or one-fifth of the U.S. public are unaffiliated with traditional religion. Of those, 37% identify as "spiritual but not religious."[3] This is particularly true for Millennials.

Defining "Nones" is a difficult proposition as the category attempts to encompass a broad sweeping generality of people who have a wide range of relationships to spirituality. One way to consider "Nones" is as a category that "describes people who do not identify as belonging to a specific group, who are not affiliated with one institutional religion or another."[4] The majority of statistical analysis on the growth of non-affiliated "Nones" is conducted by Pew Research. A September 2016 report on their website considered factors that contribute to the burgeoning number of "Nones" and found that this identification on surveys may not mean individuals are not religious,

---

1. Identifiers gathered from personal conversations and a variety of articles in popular periodicals
2. Kendzior, "The Myth of Millennial Entitlement."
3. Pew Research Center, "Nones on the Rise: Religion and the Unaffiliated."
4. Drescher, *Choosing Our Religion*, 5.

but it may be more socially acceptable now to claim no affiliation with an organized group. Generational change is cited as another factor with the explanation that even middle-aged respondents who once identified with a particular tradition may have dropped that affiliation. Nearly eight-in-ten Millennials with low levels of religious commitment describe themselves as atheists, agnostics or "nothing in particular." Data used in defining "religious commitment" included self-assessment of the importance of religion in one's life, attendance at religious services, frequency of prayer, and belief in God. The anecdotal comments at the end of the article provide more clues about the "Nones" including the influence of science in determining personal and national policy decisions, those who belong without believing, and awareness of church scandals due to media exposure.

A recent update on the Pew Website in 2015 noted that:

> Overall, 35% of adult Millennials (Americans born between 1981 and 1996) are religiously unaffiliated. Far more Millennials say they have no religious affiliation compared with those who identify as evangelical Protestants (21%), Catholics (16%) or mainline Protestants (11%). Although older generations also have grown somewhat more religiously unaffiliated in recent years, Millennials remain far more likely to identify as religious "nones." The 35% of Millennials who do not identify with a religion is double the share of unaffiliated Baby Boomers (17%) and more than three times the share of members of the Silent generation (11%).[5]

These statistics alarm mainline and evangelical religious leaders who find their congregations dwindling. This chapter will summarize the research that attempts to define the beliefs and practices of the Millennial generation, paying particular attention to the "Nones," multiple religious belonging and the advance of secularization. It will propose reasons why this group tends not to identify with religious institutions, even those that utilize progressive doctrine and new technology to entice them. It will then address how progressive Christians and leaders in the Emerging Church movement are breaking down barriers and creating new ways of including Millennials. This chapter will suggest some of the structures, or lack thereof that Millennials identify with and provide a sketch of the worldview that informs how this generation approaches religion and spirituality.

Attempts to definitively identify a position that Millennials hold with regard to religion and spirituality are inconclusive. One reason may be the effects of what Zygmunt Bauman called liquid modernity as a way of

---

5. Lipka, "Millennials Increasingly Are Driving Growth of Nones"

trying to capture the fluidity of structures and boundaries in an increasingly complex world.[6] Most of the literature that seeks to describe the Millennial worldview is found in surveys and statistical analysis, business publications focused on marketing to this demographic or in the popular press. In order to gain a sense of the contributing factors that have effected how Millennials relate to spirituality and religion, I will examine some of these varied sources and consider anecdotal evidence from my own numerous interactions teaching undergraduates in religious studies.

FACTORS INFLUENCING MILLENNIAL RELIGIOUS VIEWS

As discussed at the beginning of this paper, the Millennials are a generation that is more educated as a whole, but with fewer job prospects than Gen X or the Boomers before them. Historians William Strauss and Neil Howe coined the term "Millennial," describing a recurring cycle of four distinct types of peer personalities, arriving in the same repeating sequence" in their book *Generations: The History of America's Future*. Published in 1991, the authors noted that this generation was facing "splintered families, downwardly mobile 20-year-olds, razor-thin savings rates, threats to the global environment, an eroding sense of national mission and pyramiding entitlements for older generations."[7] Strauss and Howe identified seven traits they assigned to the Millennials including:

> special, sheltered, confident, team-oriented, conventional, achieving, and pressured. In contemporary discourse, millennials have been described as tech savvy, open to change, compassionate, inclusive, and politically active, but also self-centered and lacking attachment or direction.[8]

Young people themselves do not always believe the rhetoric and in their own words take a somewhat cynical view of the labels that pundits assign to them.

> Do we use Zipcar because we are ideologically committed to sharing, or because car ownership is still out of reach for a lot of people and renting piecemeal is the next best thing? Does a married couple decide to live with roommates because of our generational "openness to communal living" or because people

---

6. Lassander, *Post-Secular Society*, 239–62.
7. Strauss and Howe, *Generations*, 39.
8. Yazykova and McLeigh. "Millennial Children of Immigrant Parents," S38–S44.

in New York face impossible rents? Do people stop using napkins because of unshakeable cultural convictions, or because they're a waste of money? If the new generation were really waging war on their forebears' way of life, I doubt they'd start with the disposable table settings.[9]

In past generations, religious institutions often provided a social safety net to parishioners who lost a job, had a serious illness, or found themselves unable to cope with life's difficulties. For the Millennials, this does not appear to be an option, as they rely on family and friends for support and develop new technological networks that rarely include religious organizations. In the following section, we will examine several areas of influence that are affecting the worldviews of Millennials including hybridity, education, geographic nomadism, late bloomers, anti- institutional perspectives, and digital natives.

Hybridity and Multiple Religious Belonging

Millennials cross boundaries as a matter of course. Due to the availability of diverse cultures, opinions, and ideas through the Internet, they are naturally interdisciplinary—seeking answers to the large questions that challenge the world they have inherited. Globalization and multi-cultural understandings with waves of immigration and refugees have brought new cultural and ethnic hybridities into reality. Exposure to diverse customs, traditions, and ways of being has influenced younger generations, who bring a greater openness to incorporating various traditions into their belief systems and greater acceptance of difference. Of course, this has also elicited a protectionist response, particularly from traditions and countries who perceive their own worldviews as threatened.

Millennials have a greater exposure to distant cultures and traditions than ever in the history of human habitation on the planet due to global communication networks and instant access to information. The internet provides worldwide access to information and cultural difference. Rather than focusing on local problems, this vast knowledge brings Millennials to an awareness of a larger sphere of injustice which leads them in part, to the global nomadism discussed below. Global outreach for causes that might range from famine in Africa to migrants displaced from the Middle East to slavery in Asia is not only possible, it is looked on favorably by colleges that use service learning or volunteering overseas in the admissions process.

9. Marsh, "The Myth of the Millennial as Cultural Rebel."

Sociologists Roland Robertson and Peter Beyer refer to a process of globalization that they call relativization, in which particular societies are nested within or overtaken by others that results in the relativization of individuals and cultures including religions.[10] This process has led to an eclectic approach to religions that encourages experiences in a variety of traditions.

This eclecticism also in some sense makes the boundaries between different religions more vague. The difference between religions has, for the individual, become increasingly unimportant. In some contexts, elements from different religions are mixed, without awareness even that there is a mixture.[11]

Since the counter-cultural ethos of the 1960's, young people have investigated yoga, Buddhist meditation, Jewish notions of eco-kosher, Sufi rituals, Native American ceremonies and many other forms of practice across multiple traditions. Since the 1990's, the culture wars have pitted liberals against conservatives, cultural identities have clashed as race, gender, class and sexual orientation, to name a few, have become rallying cries for oppression and discrimination and divisions have splintered what appeared to be a solid social fabric in America. Millennials have little allegiance to particular categories. The U.S. Census Bureau reported that, in 2013, about 9 million Americans chose two or more racial categories when asked about their race and the number of multiracial babies has risen from 1% in 1970 to 10% in 2013.[12] A recent report from the Public Religion Research Institute found that "seven percent of Millennials identify either as lesbian, gay, bisexual or transgender." Many of these statistics may be under reported, as people are still cautious about sharing personal characteristics that may increase bias in the workplace or social situations.

Similarly, persons who identify with more than one religious worldview may be hesitant to express that outside of close friends and allies to avoid conflict and discrimination. Linda Mercadante, who interviewed a large number of those who identify as "Spiritual but not Religious" mentions, most unaffiliated types have an essentialist or universalistic perspective that all religions are the same at their core. She noted that they "rejected any 'constructivist' view that considered mystical experience culture-bound and produced. However, underlying their 'perennialism' was the assumption that no one religion gets it completely right."[13] She pointed to a shift in the locus of authority that allows the individual to feel they can make

---

10. Beyer, *Religion and Globalization*, 26–27.
11. Nynas et al., eds., *Post-Secular Society*, 52–53.
12. Pew Research Study, "Multiracial in America."
13. Mercadante, *Belief without Borders*, 81.

their own decisions and interpretations about their experiences. A sense of shallow individualism is one of the critiques of multiple-religious belonging and another is the potential for cultural appropriation. However, terms like ecumenical and interreligious dialogue are gaining in popularity and there are numerous interfaith groups promoting shared worldviews.

Michelle Voss Roberts offered several new metaphors to access these cross-cultural modes of understanding.

> Hybrids, rhizomes, and fluids are the kinds of metaphors needed to theorize the complexities of multiple religious involvements. They circumvent vexing problems of essentialism, theological exclusivity, and institutional elitism. Hybrids reflect the contingency and dynamism of all religious identity. Rhizomes subvert the effort to find a single center (institutional, doctrinal or liturgical) that defines identity. Fluidity offers the permeability of boundaries previously thought to reinforce the incommensurability of religions.[14]

Although syncretism was not widely accepted over the past century, the Millennials may reinforce our need to reconsider how traditions borrow from one another, consciously or unconsciously. The global media, technology and travel have brought cultures and traditions into conversation and young people are not reticent about adopting ideas that work for them.

Education

Students leaving home for the first time encounter a vast world of possibilities and external influences that are challenging and exhilarating. Religious practice may not be at the forefront of an eighteen-year-old's mind. The faculty and course content that young people are exposed to often have a lasting effect on student's views on everything from social cultural and economic values to philosophy and ethics. Students are engaged with big questions around the meaning of life, how to relate to sexual identities or how to navigate issues of privilege. Recreational activities like sports, yoga, or hiking may consume large amounts of extracurricular time. As they near graduation, employment may be their primary focus. The college years are times of experimentation for young adults and an opportunity for seeking an identity, often in opposition to their parents. Studies have shown that while millennials may return to some traditional practices after initially severing ties with religion, they may not return to the same affiliation as their

---

14. Voss Roberts, "Religious Belonging and the Multiple," 59.

parents.[15] Psychologist Jeffrey Arnett confirms that, "a college education leads to exposure to a variety of different worldviews, and in the course of this exposure college students often find themselves questioning the worldviews they brought in."[16]

The results of the study detailed in "Spirituality in Higher Education: Students' Search for Meaning and Purpose" study echo Arnett's statements, especially with regard to religious students questioning their beliefs. A large group of students initially surveyed in 2004, and then again in 2007, showed an overall increase of "Religious Struggle" (from 9% to 13%). Five of the seven items on the scale in this category accounted for the increase, including, notably, "question[ing] religious/spiritual beliefs," which increased from 56% to 61%, "feeling disillusioned with [one's] religious upbringing," which increased from 7% to 10%, "feeling unsettled about spiritual and religious matters," which increased from 14% to 17%, and "[feeling] distant from God," which increased from 64% to 66%.[17]

In a recent book, *Emerging Adults' Religiousness and Spirituality: Meaning-Making in an Age of Transition*, Carolyn McNamara Barry and Mona M. Abo-Zena have moved beyond the adolescent years of development and examine whether adults in their third decade of life may reconsider issues of religion and spirituality. One of the crucial aspects they point to is the role of higher education in minimizing the value of religion or in creating an ethos for meaning-making that reframes an interest in the spiritual dimensions of life.

> The university context can shape emerging adults' religious and spiritual lives through a variety of mechanisms (Calhoun, Aronczyk, Maryl, & VanAntwerpen, 2007). In Chapter 9, Glanzer, Hill, and Ream note that four changes in higher education are likely to contribute to emerging adults' religious and spiritual development: the increasing secularization in higher education; cocurricular offerings of religion on secular campuses; the diminishment of religion in secular institutions' curriculum; and the distinctive role of faith-based colleges and universities. Lastly, they discuss how higher education is likely to influence its students' religious and spiritual beliefs.[18]

---

15. Martinson, "Spiritual but not Religious," 329.
16. Arnett, "Emerging Adulthood," 474.
17. Spiritual Life of College Students: A National Study of College Students' Search for Meaning and Purpose.
18. Barry and Abo-Zena, eds., *Emerging Adults' Religiousness and Spirituality*, 12.

College is often a time for exploration and inquiry among a variety of subjects and the current emphasis on STEM disciplines along with a focus on career goals may leave little time for inner reflection. "A majority of emerging adults are simply following a script that tells them religion has very little to do with this phase of their life and can be safely set aside for a few years" (163).

In *Cultivating the Spirit*, the Astins and Lindholm claim that the origins of the disconnect between spirituality and the college experience can be traced to the nineteenth century's Enlightenment ideals, positivistic models of thinking, emphasis on individualism, and scientific worldviews.[19] Pressure to find a good paying job after graduation, promotes a rational, pragmatic approach to the college years with less spaciousness to explore meaning-making endeavors. The Astins and Lindholm note that there is an increased "emphasis on individual achievement, competitiveness, materialism, and objective knowing."[20]

Geographic Nomadism

Settling down is not a concept in most Millennial's vocabulary. Numerous students I have spoken with over the past few years indicate they prefer to keep their options open and consider distance learning as an alternative to a traditional four year degree. Rather than collecting material goods, they prefer to travel light and collect experiences often with a dozen countries on their bucket list. Rather than stability, they seek novelty and frequently opt for freelancing and remote work instead of a 9 to 5 job. Valuing freedom and spontaneity, they avoid encumbrances. Some will admit they adopted this lifestyle because the economic opportunities were poor in their chosen field or they were tired of accepting unpaid internships that never resulted in a permanent position. Regardless of why Millennials are making these choices, it is important to recognize that this sense of impermanence is common among young adults.

A commitment to social media is normative among today's youth and many create their own blogs, along with extensive posting on Facebook, Instagram and Snapchat. A few entries from sites found surfing the Web illustrate this trend toward global nomadism. Britney Robinson describes that renting is less claustrophobic than being tied down to a lengthy mortgage and a particular location. She notes that she and her peers witnessed the collapse of the housing market and prefer not to incur large debts.

19. Astin et al., *Cultivating the Spirit*, 139.
20. Ibid., 140.

> After extensively interviewing over 60 millennials, Mic contributor James Wolfensbirger notes that our generation is, "quick to openly imagine themselves living and working in not just different parts of the country throughout phases of their lives, but in other nations as well." Every Millennial Wolfensbirger surveyed answered "yes" when asked if they would move to another country for a job opportunity.[21]

Jessica Kumar puts more faith in relationships than in material possessions, but still wonders if the Baby Boomers' commitment to traditions should be re-evaluated by her generation.

> Our generation is a mobile one. I know people who don't even have a vacuum, but just set their Roomba loose while they are at work. We buy condos to sell them and make a profit. We buy IKEA stuff knowing that we will replace it in 3 years when our job moves us across the country. We use Netflix instead of buying the collectors set of "Friends" on DVD. We value digital content over hard copies. We are global nomads, spending money on experiences rather than stuff.[22]

Without putting down roots for any length of time, it is apparent that Millennials would not be easily convinced to join a religious congregation or make any long-term commitment.

Late Bloomers

Statistics regarding Millennials show that as a whole, the group is starting families later than in the past, not settling down buying cars and houses and other material ties to security, and compared to previous generations in the same age range overall they have a lack of disposable income.[23]

According to Gallup statistics from 2014, 59% of millennials are single and have never been married and 60% of millennials do not have any children under 18 in their household. This generation is waiting later to marry, with only 56% reporting tying the knot by age 34. A recent Gallup analysis noted:

> More millennials currently live in multi-adult households than is true for other generations, and the data suggest that unlike those older generations, these multi-adult households consist

21. Robinson, "The Millennial Nomad, "
22. Kumar, "The Ikea Generation"
23. For data references see, Scardamalia, *Millennials in America*.

primarily of single millennials living collectively. Domestic partnerships—not common in general—are much more common among millennials, and millennials are more than twice as likely as older Americans to identify as LGBT.[24]

A recent Washington Post article notes that nearly a third of Millennials still live at home with their parents. The article explains that home ownership for Americans under age 35 is just below 35 percent and suggests that the reason may be a lack of disposable income. "Relative to earlier generations, today's cohort of young people is making less money, given their levels of education; more indebted with student loans; more likely to be underemployed; struggling harder to sock away savings; and facing shallower income-growth trajectories."[25]

An alternate view considers that Millennials are choosing to live with fewer encumbrances, work remotely in coffee shops and live simply in order to maintain a fluid lifestyle. Regardless of which theory one believes, Robert Wuthnow concluded nearly a decade ago that marital status and having children are key indicators for church attendance and affiliation. He noted that "Young adults who are not married are less likely to attend religious services, indeed, many are religiously unaffiliated."[26]

Anti-Institutional Perspectives

Recent events like the Occupy Movement may create a sense that Millennials are anti-establishment in a mode similar to their Baby Boomer predecessors in the Sixties. However, a desire for economic and political change is likely to be the result of mounting student loan debt, dire predictions for long-range earnings potential and the transparent wealth gap between the 1 percent and the 99 percent. When it comes to religion, Linda Mercadante interviewed a number of people she called "Dissenters" who had been "hurt, offended or become angry about some experience of organized religion."[27] This perspective was more apparent in her interviews with Baby Boomers or the Silent Generation, with a sense of hypocrisy or actions not meeting the expressed sentiments of textual doctrine as an example of behaviors that drove some people away from religious traditions. Outright rebellion may be less of a factor, although the lack of acceptance of GLBTQ rights, and

---

24. Gallup Analysis: Millennials, Marriage and Family, May 19, 2016.
25. Rampell, "Millennials Aren't Buying Homes."
26. Wuthnow, *After the Baby Boomers*, 137.
27. Mercadante, *Belief Without Borders*, 53.

a view of women as inferior to their male counterparts are reasons some twenty-somethings are driven away from traditional religious congregations. Although initial research focused on this lack of joining churches and political parties, more recent studies indicate an attitude of "what's in it for me?" Rather than a completely selfish view, this may be more of a cautionary approach of not wanting to select a particular affiliation, but instead keep their options open.

Digital Natives

The U.S. Census Bureau says there are 83.1 million people between the ages of 18 to 34 in the nation. Studies show the average Millennial spends 18 hours per day using some type of digital media. And, 90 percent of young adults use social media, which is up from 12 percent in 2005, the Pew Research Center reports.[28]

The Millennial generation grew up with technology. Often they learned how to surf the Internet on their parents' mobile phone and graduated to their own tablet or computer. As education began to include technology as a mandatory aspect of student learning, elementary students did homework on computers and some schools provided laptops for everyone enrolled.

"Through our formative years, however, digital technology began to make quantum leaps almost daily in the variety and extent of applications and functions, as well as user access and mobility." Burstein (2013) believes that "the power for the young to influence and create new technology has grown tremendously in the last decade."[29] He illustrates this point by saying that the founders of the following companies have all been millennials: YouTube, Facebook, Twitter, Groupon, Foursquare, Instagram, and Tumblr.

> For example, a survey of 4374 students across 13 institutions in the United States (Kvavik, Caruso & Morgan, 2004) found that the majority of respondents owned personal computers (93.4%) and mobile phones (82%) but a much smaller proportion owned handheld computers (11.9%). The most common technology uses were word processing (99.5%), e-mailing (99.5%) and surfing the Net for pleasure (99.5%). These results do demonstrate high levels of ownership of some technologies by the respondents and high levels of some academic and recreational activities, and their associated skills. The researchers found, however, that only a minority of the students (around 21%) were engaged

---

28. Zachos, "Technology Is Changing the Millennial Brain."
29. Burstein, David D. *Fast Future*, 53–54.

in creating their own content and multimedia for the Web, and that a significant proportion of students had lower level skills than might be expected of digital natives.[30]

While there are some on-line religious services and blogs, this is not a sector that is well represented in the app culture. Although Emerging church and megachurch congregations make use of technology in their services, it is not evident that this alone draws in new members. Use of a big screen and flashy videos will appeal to Millennials who would stop attending if worship did not seem current and up to date, but it is one factor among many.

Along with statistical analysis, social science researchers employing qualitative interviews and targeting specific demographics is another avenue that scholars used in an attempt to understand unaffiliated Millennials. In the next section, an overview of the findings of some key monographs from the past 20 years will aid in weaving together the underlying worldviews of this generation that is reluctant to declare allegiance or commit to a singular path.

Spiritual but not Religious

Over the past decade, scholars and researchers have begun to mine the data and draw conclusions about what is perceived as a tendency for younger adults to drift away from organized religion. One of the earliest studies was documented by Wade Clark Roof in his 1993 publication, *A Generation of Seekers: The Spiritual Journeys of the Baby Boom Generation*. Roof updated his research in 1999 with *Spiritual Marketplace: Baby Boomers and the Remaking of American Religion*. He identified five sub-cultural categories as a way of understanding religious trends: the Born Agains, Mainstream Believers, Metaphysical Believers and Seekers, Dogmatists and Secularists. Born Agains, comprised mostly of Evangelicals, Charismatics and Pentecostals are "connected to one another in a shared adherence to a traditional Christian theology, the experience of a very "personal God" or relationship with Jesus, and a redemptive experience of salvation."[31] Mainstream Believers were characterized as "providing for their families, helping and caring for others, doing good deeds, being friendly and civic-minded and living a good life"[32] and who perceived religious institutions as inadequate

---

30. Bennett et al., "The 'digital natives' debate: a critical review of the evidence," 775–86.

31. Markuly, Book Review, "Wade Clark Roof. *Spiritual Marketplace: Baby Boomers and* the *Remaking of American Religion*, 2.

32. Markuly, Book Review, 2.

to support these values. Metaphysical Believers and Seekers were identified as those who may have been wounded by previous experience with religious institutions and sought personal embodied spiritual experiences. These individuals tended to have hyphenated spiritual identities often exploring multiple traditions including "neo-pagans, wiccans, goddess worshippers, Zen Buddhists, Theosophists, nature-lovers, and New Agers."[33] Dogmatists were described as fundamentalist and neo-traditionalists that adhered to literal interpretations of scripture, while Secularists were those who distanced themselves from any relationship with faith and spirituality.

The potential for these spiritual explorations to lead to a deepening of faith and ultimately a return to religious institutions was apparent in the research at the turn of the century. Another important contribution was Robert Fuller's *Spiritual but not Religious: Understanding Unchurched America* published in 2001. As the descriptive summary of the Oxford monograph states, Fuller recognized that alternative spiritualties have been prevalent in American history since the colonial period. He traced unconventional practices from an interest in astrology, magic and witchcraft to Transcendentalism, leading to the current interest in meditation, and channeling. Fuller explained that, those who identify as Spiritual but not Religious, "focus on inner sources of spirituality and on this world rather than the afterlife; they believe in the accessibility of God and in the mind's untapped powers; they see a fundamental unity between science and religion and an equality between genders and races; and they are more willing to test their beliefs and change them when they prove untenable."[34]

Fuller goes on to note that

> Few seekers believe that there is any one single truth that will address all of their emotional and intellectual needs. But most are sure about at least three things. First, they believe it has come time for religions to abandon "old age" dogmatism and incorporate contemporary knowledge. For a religion to be viable in our era it must draw eclectically from science, modern psychology, and the best insights of all world religions. Second, religion must have practical applications in our everyday lives. It must be more psychological than theological. That is, it should be primarily concerned with helping us find fulfillment in the here and now of this life (rather than devoting its attention to some speculative afterlife). And third, metaphysical seekers

---

33. Markuly, Book Review, 2

34. Retrieved from the Internet, Sept. 25, 2016, Oxford University Press, (https://global.oup.com/academic/product/spiritual-but-not-religious-9780195146806?cc=us&lang=en&#).

yearn for an experiential spirituality; they are bored with what they perceive to be the lifeless rituals of established churches and feel the need for some kind of mystical connection with God.[35]

In his book *Restless Souls*, first published in 2005 and updated in 2012, Leigh Eric Schmidt asks the question "How did the spiritual come to be privileged over the religious by so many Americans, and what were the cultural implications of sanctifying that division?"[36] Schmidt tracks the dissent against "organized religion" back to the writings of Emerson, Thoreau and other Transcendentalists who argued that religion was primarily about the sacredness of individual seeking and direct experience rather than acquiescing to the strict guidelines of the institutional church. Along with Transcendentalists, he notes that Unitarians, Quakers, followers of Whitman and other nineteenth-century religious liberals began a sense of openness and searching that has "flowed into any number of new rivulets—from AA to Burning Man to channeling to Druidic nature worship to Esalen." Schmidt argues that many of the ongoing debates such as the need for solitary seeking in contrast with community development, the desire for a universal religion critiqued by those who focused on the particularities of each sect arose not long after the founding of this country. He recognizes that the Americans redefined the term "spirituality" in a "search for a religious world larger than the British Protestant inheritance." What began as an alternative to the rational abstraction of deism morphed into a full blown exploration of alternatives in the Victorian era including yoga and Asian meditation techniques and philosophies. The World's Parliament of Religions held in Chicago in 1893 introduced Americans to the teachings of Swami Vivekananda on Vedanta and yoga, as well as the Buddhist Theravadin tradition of Anagarika Dharmapala. Twentieth-century Americans embraced the new metaphysical options provided by these alternative worldviews and the popularity of non-dual approaches to consciousness blossomed.

Defining this growing population of spiritual but not religious adherents is as tricky as capturing the essence of a cloud as it morphs and dissolves from moment to moment. Courtney Bender applied sociological methods to examine what she terms *The New Metaphysicals*, evoking the alternative spiritualities documented by William James and others to demonstrate the deep roots of an American fascination with mysticism and embodied transcendence. She points to the elusive diversity of shifting allegiances that cannot easily be quantified from shamanistic drumming to Reiki practitioners and yoga aficionados. Simultaneously, Bender explores

35. Fuller, *Spiritual but not Religious*, 98–99.
36. Schmidt, *Restless Souls*, xii.

how spirituality is present in social institutions and practices one might consider secular, for example art, medicine or psychology, and recommends that "the future path lies in cultivating analytical approaches that recognize the processes of secularization as historically embedded, complex and unfinalized traditions."[37]

In her book, *Belief without Borders*, Linda Mercadante describes a rejection of tradition and external authority, an increase in individualism, a view of humans as universally good, a desire for experiences from meditation to yoga and the freedom to explore multiple religious traditions without commitment. She concludes that the SBNR separation of spirituality from religion is more about theology than some political statement. The primary factors Mercadante believes underlie the move to spirituality from religion include: "a prioritizing of personal growth over group identity, a relocation of authority from external to internal, a belief that all religions teach the same things, and an abhorrence of the triple religious sins of judgmentalism, dogmatism and exclusivism."[38]

One of the contested categories of alternative spiritualities is what is called the "New Age movement" which Steven Sutcliffe in *Children of the New Age* (2003) dismisses as simply a precursor to what is now observed as popular religion.

> Sutcliffe speaks of the emergent spiritual discourse as being dissident, striving at finding something other, more and better than institutionalized religion; being lay, having a domestic setting which undermines traditional boundaries between public and private space; being populist, recognizing the supremacy of the will of the people; and being functional, emphasizing short-term achievements of goals and the active creation of meaning in everyday life. [39]

Although the term "spirituality" is problematic, numerous authors have wrestled with the concept and find it is presented as more personal and individual than "religion, "more anthropological than theological, syncretistic and pluralistic, anti-hierarchical and innerworldly."[40]

In Kelly Besecke's *You Can't Put God in a Box*, she describes that for many Americans, religion is an either/or proposition: "on one side, a dogmatic, arrogant, exclusive, and unbelievable religious traditionalism, and on the other, a spiritually vacant secular society obsessed with material gain

---

37. Bender, *The New Metaphysicals*, 183.
38. Mercadante, *Belief Without Borders*, 192.
39. Nynas et al., eds., *Post-Secular Society*, 49.
40. Ibid., 50.

and content to go through the motions of life without asking the deeper questions."[41] Now that we have observed the move to reject religion for freedom to seek alternative spiritualities, in the next section we will consider those for whom religion and spirituality may not even be a consideration.

Secular or Spiritual?

This initial research becomes important as a point of reference for identifying trends and normative behaviors in the following decades. Several important books published in 2007 illustrate the continual grappling with issues of non-belief and withdrawal from institutional religion. Robert Wuthnow's *After the Baby Boomers* remains one of the most thorough studies of the religious tendencies of young adults. He mentioned seven key trends that are still relevant: delayed marriage, fewer children, uncertain economies and job prospects, an educated populace, globalization, technology, and the changing nature of social relationships.[42] These factors influence the next generation's relationship to religion and the church.

In *A Secular Age*, Charles Taylor proposed that the process of secularization has been theorized as the removal of references to God or ultimate reality from public spaces, the decline of religious belief and practice and "a move from a society where belief in God is unchallenged and indeed, unproblematic, to one in which it is understood to be one option among others, and frequently not the easiest to embrace."[43] Although the tendency toward secularization has been more pronounced in Europe, a concern that led Peter Berger to write *A Sacred Canopy* and Grace Davie to explore "Believing without Belonging" in the context of Great Britain, many authors have countered that this is not a global phenomenon. The influence of modernization is often contested, as is the theory that religious violence in Europe led to a secularization in which religion was more of a social phenomenon that centered around weddings and funerals without weekly attendance at a church. Berger and Davie co-authored *Religious America, Secular Europe* in which they outline seven factors that may contribute to the distinctions on each continent including "differences in church-state relationships, questions of pluralism, different understandings of the Enlightenment, different types of intellectuals, variations in culture and how this is understood, institutional contrasts and differences in the ways that

---

41. Besecke, *You Can't Put God in a Box*, 8.
42. Putnam, *After the Baby Boomers*.
43. Taylor, *A Secular Age*, 3.

religious organizations relate to indices of social difference."[44] Any of these possibilities could be the subject of a full-length paper itself, but suffice it to say that while religion as a public good may appear on the decline, private religion is flourishing.

Without jumping into the debate around definitions of religion, which for some might even be sports, music, or economics,[45] the rising tide of atheists and agnostics must be noted. Sam Harris (*End of Faith*, *The Moral Landscape*, *Waking Up*), Christopher Hitchens (*God is Not Great*), and Richard Dawkins (*The God Delusion*) have all contributed to the popularity of rational spirituality that disdains religion as superstition and denies any links between science and religion.

The influence of science and technology may be one key factor in the development of an empirical, objective worldview that denies the existence of God or anything remotely spiritual. The rising tide of ISIS, Al-Qaeda, and the threat of extremist violence overseas and in America in the wake of 9/11 is another important consideration. As society becomes increasingly polarized, there is a tendency for people to go to emotional extremes, either through a fundamentalist view or its opposite, complete denial, and even fear of religion.

In the process of investigating the landscape and context that Millennials are embedded in, we have uncovered numerous factors that influence this generation in their relation to spirituality and culture in general. While they appear to have many choices in the religious marketplace leading to hybridity, identification as Spiritual But Not Religious and exposure to higher education, travel and the resources available on the Internet, Millennials feel confined by economic circumstances. On one hand, they are continuing the metaphysical exploration that seems inherent in American culture; on the other hand, they are exploring uncharted terrain by resisting institutions, labels and expectations. In the next section, we will address how the Emerging Church movement fits into this landscape.

EMERGING CHURCH AND CHRISTIAN RESPONSES TO THE NONES

Leaders in the Emerging Church would likely refer to it as a network rather than a movement. Comprised of evangelical and mainline Protestant pastors and congregations that embrace contemporary culture, this new mode

---

44. Berger et al., *Religious America, Secular Europe?*, 3.

45. Stark, and Iannaccone, "A Supply-Side Reinterpretation of the 'Secularization' of Europe,'" 230–52.

of religious practice was featured in a PBS special in 2005 that highlighted some of the organizers including one of the "founders," Brian McLaren, pastor of Cedar Ridge Community Church in Maryland. McLaren was at the forefront of the network called Emergent that hosted blogs and discussion groups on the Internet that provided a dialogue around the casual and experiential worship style that is gaining traction in America. Congregants want a participatory experience including everything from discussions questioning the afterlife to walking the labyrinth to rock and roll services. Services include elements from Catholicism and Eastern Orthodoxy such as candles, icons and incense and charismatic preaching styles reminiscent of Pentecostal worship.[46] There is a focus on community building and outreach and an inclusive, embodied flavor to the approach of these churches. In many ways, the Emerging Church echoes the characteristics of the Millennials. The movement avoids definition or categorization on purpose, taking a postmodern approach to religion. The authors of the 2015 monograph *The Deconstructed Church*, "argue that Emerging Christians are discernable, transnational group who share a religious orientation built on a continual practice of deconstruction."[47]

After observing young people alienated from the church, an impassioned Lutheran minister Roland Martinson determined to learn about what he calls 'the Invisible Generation' (1962–81) that preceded the Millennials. Referencing George Barna's *GenerationNEXT*, he observed that this group is self-reliant, skeptical without faith in people or institutions and that "their spiritualities are mystical, diverse and often syncretistic."[48] In conversations with youth between the ages of 10 and 35, he found three prevalent approaches to spirituality. One group referred to as skeptics or cynics found common ground with the message of singer Tori Amos feeling that "God is distant, disengaged or impotent; the church is out of touch, unengaging, self-serving, even destructive."[49] Another group he termed spiritual seekers seemed aligned with U2's song "I Still Haven't Found What I'm Looking For." A small portion, 10 to 15 percent identified as evangelical, sectarian, Roman Catholic or mainline disciples and leaders frequently engaged in age-level focused "niche" ministries.

Diana Butler Bass has tracked the evolution of American Christianity for nearly two decades. Her latest book, *Grounded: Finding God in the World* describes an immanent approach to religion that views God as a force in our

---

46. Lawton, "The Emerging Church, Part 1."
47. Martí and Ganiel, *The Deconstructed Church*.
48. Martinson, "Spiritual but not Religious," 329.
49. Martinson, "Spiritual but not Religious," 334.

everyday lives rather than a deity in the sky filled with fire and brimstone. In a recent interview, Butler Bass explained that the vertical structure of what she calls the "three-tiered universe" of God in heaven, hell beneath, and people in the middle no longer makes sense.

> That's not how we conceive of the universe anymore," she said. In the vertical structure, she said, the church functioned as a sort of elevator to bring the sacraments or the word of God to the people. "And if people responded to those things appropriately, they could ride the elevator up to heaven when they died," she said. That vision, she said, is outdated. Citing mankind's understanding of science, technology and politics, she said, people now see God as part of the web or ecosystem humans inhabit rather than as part of a vertical structure. In this view, God is not in some faraway place but much closer to us. "The way we understand the universe now is a much more connected reality. So religious institutions have to learn to function completely differently because it's an entirely different physical and spiritual environment.[50]

Among the mainline groups, some Lutheran synods have started to encourage new approaches to worship. A non-judgmental open-door policy is a cornerstone of Nadia Bolz-Weber's Denver church, The House of All Sinners and Saints. In an interview with Fresh Air's Terry Gross, she remembers finding her calling while giving the eulogy for a friend who committed suicide. Bolz-Weber was a stand-up comic with a drinking problem, who turned to Lutheran theology and was given her own church after attending seminary. Her congregation includes drug addicts and drag queens and everything in between. She asserts, "My job is to point to Christ and to preach the Gospel and to remind people that they're absolutely loved . . . and all of their mess-ups are not more powerful than God's mercy and God's ability to sort of redeem us and to bring good out of bad."[51] Although older mainline Christians have joined the services, for Bolz-Weber and other Emerging Churches, there is nothing conservative about the Denver church. Asked about the difference between her brand of Christianity and the conservative view, she explained, "To them it's about living a very particular, constrained, defined, moral life—which includes never using swear words, or associating with certain types of people, or being gay or gender queer, or a bossy woman, or any number of things that don't fit a narrowly defined lifestyle

---

50. Cornelius, "The Changing Spiritual Movement."
51. *Fresh Air* with Terry Gross, (9/17/2015) interview transcript,

that conservative Christianity has pawned off on us as being what this is all about."[52]

In his 2012 article "Off the Map? Locating the Emerging Church: A Comparative Case Study of Congregations in the Pacific Northwest," Jason Wollschleger sums up the character of the emerging church: "The core allegiance of the emerging church is to radical authenticity; they seek to overcome the 'modern' divisions (of liberal and conservative) they see as causing incompleteness on either side, while incorporating certain aspects of both."[53] In the examples of congregations he observes and many around the country, it is evident that most attendees are under 30 years old, participate through pop culture and digital media, as well as adopting worship styles from a variety of denominations and refuse to be categorized. These familiar characteristics are a version of the findings previously reviewed in factors relating to Millennial spirituality.

CONCLUDING REMARKS

Any attempt to encapsulate the findings of research on Millennials and their attitudes toward religion and spirituality can be deconstructed as soon as the words appear on the page. If there is anything most Millennials share, it is a fierce independence and a refusal to be categorized. There is a kaleidoscopic quality about the practices, values and beliefs of Millennials, always shifting and morphing, ready to experiment and adopt the latest trend or invention. Whether we view a majority of Millennials as "Nones" or "Spiritual But Not Religious" or members of an Emerging Church congregation, they are likely to defy any definition we try to pin on them. Perhaps it is easier to adopt a view like the remarks offered in *Post-Secular Society*.

> Essentialized categories of "religion" and different kinds of religion, whether New Age or Christian, make less and less sense in the global world. All borders blur and elements migrate freely with individual choice as the only limit. Elements of the historical field of alternative religion mix more and more with other elements of religion in the popular mode and have become part of the current mainstream.[54]

In the *Journal for the Scientific Study of Religion*, Nancy Ammerman noted that her research pointed to "spiritual but not religious" as a moral

---

52. O'Connor, "On Sinners and Saints."
53. Wollschleger, "Off the Map?," 77.
54. Frisk and Nynas, *Post-Secular Society*, 63.

and political category rather than an empirical one. She observed the term defined by conservative Protestants as a way of distinguishing themselves from the merely religious and used participation in religious communities as a measure of their spirituality. A more secular view of the term disparaged the hypocrisy and empty ritual in conservative religion. Ammerman noted, "the secularists and disaffiliated among our participants often see organized religion as an oppressive power, depriving individuals of personal and political freedom; and like Enlightenment philosophers for multiple centuries, they pit religious belief against reason."[55]

Ammerman's research problematizes the typical sociological binaries used to pit spiritual understandings against religion. In summarizing her findings, she noted: "The sociological study of religion is not neatly contained in binary categories of organized v. individual, religious v. spiritual, theistic and transcendent v. nontheistic and immanent. All these things are contained within the discourses about spirituality we heard; and all of them exist within religious institutions, as well as outside those institutions."[56]

Religion and spirituality are in a process of splitting, morphing, and reintegrating into new forms that align with a postmodern reality that Millennials have grown up with and learned to navigate. The Emerging Church is one of those forms. Rather than constricting the movement of change, a better strategy might be to appreciate the unfolding of multiple dimensions of spiritual understanding that take global perspectives into account.

Postcolonial and feminist scholar Kwok Pui-Lan expressed concern for Christian churches that do not recognize the need to integrate New Age seekers and multiple religious belongers. "The crux of the matter is that the church's religious language, liturgy, structures and spiritual practices originating in a different age, have not been modified to catch up with the times. Although we have seen the revival of Gregorian chants and interests in the mystical traditions and centering prayers, the churches need to develop practices that are culturally relevant for our time, especially for the younger generation."[57] Like other progressive leaders, she is calling for a more cosmopolitan worldview and an integration of spirituality and sexuality that respects rather than denigrates the body.

Not only has religion proven empirically resilient in the face of modernization, it has also refused to yield ground in the face of its presumed replacement by diffuse individualized spiritualities. At least in the United States, the most pervasive spirituality is the Theistic one defined

---

55. Ammerman, "Spiritual but Not Religious?," 275
56. Ibid., 276
57. Kwok. "Porous Boundaries," 84

and practiced by participants in religious institutions. Yet all but the most conservative of them are also willing to occupy Extra-Theistic and Ethical spiritual discursive territory alongside their secular neighbors.[58]

As we enter the twenty-first century, the challenges of climate change, shrinking economies, waves of immigration and divisive politics threaten to overwhelm the human capacity for innovation and adaptation. Each generation should be encouraged to use the vitality and fresh outlook that the first few decades of life provide. The Millennials have an opportunity to bring new life to old structures and reinvent or rediscover epistemologies that break down barriers and find common ground among perceived disparate peoples and traditions. Taking a cue from systems science, we might consider that new patterns emerge when systems face increasing levels of complexity. The period before an emergent property appears might seem chaotic and unsettled; much like our world does today. Young people are seeking answers to problems that look unsolvable. They will not be satisfied with a static response to questions about meaning-making. Instead, they will seek an embodied, experiential, egalitarian relationship with each other and the spiritual and religious worldview that provides support for their endeavors.

BIBLIOGRAPHY

Ammerman, Nancy T. "Spiritual But Not Religious? Beyond Binary Choices in the Study of Religion." *Journal for the Scientific Study of Religion* 52 (2013) 258–78.

Arnett, Jeffery Jenson. "Emerging Adulthood: A Theory of Development from the Late Teens through the Twenties." *American Psychologist* 55 (2000) 469–80.

Astin, Alexander, et al. *Cultivating the Spirit: How College Can Enhance Students' Inner Lives*. San Francisco: Jossey-Bass, 2011.

Barry, Carolyn McNamara, and Mona M. Abo-Zena, eds. *Emerging Adults' Religiousness and Spirituality: Meaning-Making in an Age of Transition*. New York: Oxford University Press, 2014.

Bauman, Zygmunt. *Liquid Modernity*. Malden, MA: Cambridge, 2000.

Bender, Courtney. *The New Metaphysicals*. Chicago: University of Chicago Press, 2010.

Bennett, S. J., K. A. Maton, and L. K. Kervin. "The 'Digital Natives' Debate: A Critical Review of the Evidence." *British Journal of Educational Technology* 39.5 (2008) 775–86.

Berger, Peter, Grace Davie, and Effie Fokas. *Religious America, Secular Europe*. Burlington, VT: Ashgate, 2008.

Besecke, Kelly. *You Can't Put God in a Box: Thoughtful Spirituality in a Rational Age*. New York: Oxford University Press, 2013. Oxford Scholarship Online, 2014. doi: 10.1093/acprof:oso/9780199930920.001.0001.

Beyer, Peter. *Religion and Globalization*. London: Sage, 1994.

---

58. Ammerman, "Spiritual but not Religious?," 276.

Burstein, David D. *Fast Future: How the Millennial Generation is Shaping Our World.* Boston: Beacon, 2013.

Cornelius, Earle. "The Changing Spiritual Movement: Author Diana Butler Bass Challenges Religion's Hierarchical Structure." LNP, Lancaster, PA, Oct 31, 2015 https://colorado.idm.oclc.org/login?url=http://search.proquest.com.colorado.idm.oclc.org/docview/1823967910?accountid=14503.

Dean, William. *The American Spiritual Culture: And the Invention of Jazz, Football, and the Movies.* New York: Bloomsbury, 2004.

Drescher, Elizabeth. *Choosing Our Religion: The Spiritual Lives of America's Nones.* New York: Oxford University Press, 2016.

Frisk, Liselotte, and Nynas, Peter. "Characteristics of Contemporary Religious Change." In *Post-Secular Society*. New Brunswick, NJ: Transaction, 2010.

Fuller, Robert. *Spiritual But Not Religious.* New York: Oxford University Press, 2001.

Gallup Analysis: Millennials, Marriage and Family. May 19, 2016. http://www.gallup.com/poll/191462/gallup-analysis-millennials-marriage-family.aspx

Gross, Terry. Fresh Air (9/17/2015) interview transcript. http://www.npr.org/templates/transcript/transcript.php?storyId=441139500

Kendzior, Sarah. June 30, 2016. http://qz.com/720456/the-myth-of-millennial-entitlement-was-created-to-hide-their-parents-mistakes/.

Kumar, Jessica. "The Ikea Generation." https://globalnomadism.com/2016/09/13/the-ikea-generation/.

Lawton, Kim. "The Emerging Church, Part 1." July 8, 2005. http://www.pbs.org/wnet/religionandethics/2005/07/08/july-8-2005-the-emerging-church-part-one/11744/.

Lipka, Michael. "Millennials Increasingly Are Driving Growth of Nones." May 12, 2015. http://www.pewresearch.org/fact-tank/2015/05/12/millennials-increasingly-are-driving-growth-of-nones/.

Marsh, Laura. "The Myth of the Millennial as Cultural Rebel." August 30, 2016. https://newrepublic.com/article/136415/myth-millennial-cultural-rebel.

Martí, Gerardo, and Gladys Ganiel. *The Deconstructed Church.* New York: Oxford University Press, 2014.

Martinson, Roland. "Spiritual but not Religious: Reaching an Invisible Generation." *Currents in Theology and Mission* 29.5 (2002) 326–40.

Mercadante, Linda. *Belief Without Borders.* New York: Oxford University Press, 2014.

Nynas, Peter, Mika Lassander, and Terhi Utrianinen, eds. *Post-Secular Society*. New Brunswick, NJ: Transaction, 2012,

O'Connor, Colleen. "On Sinners and Saints." *Denver Post*, September 10, 2015: C.3.

Pew Research Center. "Nones on the Rise: Religion and the Unaffiliated." http://www.pewforum.org/2012/10/09/nones-on-the-rise-religion/.

Pew Research Study. "Multiracial in America." http://www.pewsocialtrends.org/2015/06/11/multiracial-in-america.

Pui-Lan, Kwok. "Porous Boundaries: Eclecticism in Emerging Spiritual Practices." *Spiritus* 7–1. Baltimore: Johns Hopkins University Press, 2007.

Putnam, Robert. *After the Baby Boomers.* Princeton: Princeton University Press, 2007.

Rampell, Catherine. "Millennials Aren't Buying Homes." *Washington Post*, Opinion, August 22, 2016.

Robinson, Britney. "The Millennial Nomad." http://www.thecultureist.com/2014/08/18/millennials-characteristics-becoming-nomadic/.

Roof, Wade Clark. *Spiritual Marketplace: Baby Boomers and the Remaking of American Religion*, by Mark S. Markuly. *Journal of Religion and Society* 4 (2002).

Scardamalia, Robert L. *Millennials in America*. Lanham, MD: Bernan, 2015.

Schmidt, Leigh Eric. *Restless Souls: The Making of American Spirituality*. San Francisco: Harper, 2005.

Spiritual Life of College Students: A National Study of College Students' Search for Meaning and Purpose: Spirituality in Higher Education, University of California at Los Angeles: Graduate School of Education and Information Studies, 2004. http://spirituality.ucla.edu/.

Stark, Rodney, and Laurence R. Iannaccone. "A Supply-Side Reinterpretation of the "Secularization" of Europe." *Journal for the Scientific Study of Religion* 33 (1994) 230–52.

Strauss, William, and Neil Howe. *Generations*. New York: Morrow, 1991.

Taylor, Charles. *A Secular Age*. Cambridge: Belnap, 2007.

Voss Roberts, Michelle. "Religious Belonging and the Multiple." *Journal of Feminist Studies in Religion* 26 (2010) 43–61.

Wollschleger, Jason. "Off the Map? Locating the Emerging Church: A Comparative Case Study of Congregations in the Pacific Northwest." *Review of Religious Research* (2012).

Yazykova, Ekaterina, and Jill D. McLeigh. "Millennial Children of Immigrant Parents: Transnationalism, Disparities, Policy, and Potential." *American Journal of Orthopsychiatry* 85.5 (2015) S38–S44. https://colorado.idm.oclc.org/login?url=http://search.proquest.com.colorado.idm.oclc.org/docview/1721922008?accountid=14503.

Zachos, Elaina. "Technology is Changing the Millennial Brain." http://publicsource.org/investigations/technology-changing-millennial-brain#.WAwPUoozXIU.

9

The Problem of Anti-Institutionalism in Millennials

Randall Reed

Abstract

Millennials have been portrayed in the media as significantly anti-institutional. If this is true it is bad news for a number of elements of society including the church. Certainly the church is, if nothing else, a religious institution. If Millennials are turning off to the very notion of institutions then this threatens the ability of denominations and larger congregations to attract Millennials and perhaps makes any hope of membership replacement from this demographic which is seeing a precipitous decline an impossible dream. On the other hand, if Millennials are as anti-institutional as is often portrayed, perhaps this is a real opportunity for membership expansion for the Emerging Church movement that likewise seems to register a complaint against institutionalization as well. From the IKON movement with its performance art theatrics, to the kind of local and transient congregations seen in "pub churches" and festivals, much of the Emerging Church likewise seems to reflect anti-institutional impulse at its very core. This paper will seek to bring some definition to the issue of anti-institutionalism through a review of some of the data about Millennials and institutions. I will then contribute to the conversation with some of my own research. For the past two years (2014–2015) I have engaged in semi-structured interviews with individuals and focus groups at the "Wild Goose" festival in Hot Springs, North Carolina. During these years at "the Goose" I have interviewed Millennials particularly about their issues regarding the Church as an institution. I have likewise interviewed non-emergent Millennials in the South and I will bring to bear on this discussion of Millennials and anti-institutionalism the data uncovered in those interviews. In the end, I hope to provide a larger view of Millennials' notions, complaints, and analyses of institutionalism as well as explore the challenges this poses to the institutional church and the Emerging Church movement.

INTRODUCTION

Millennials have been portrayed in the media as significantly anti-institutional. If this is true it is bad news for a number of elements of society including the church. Certainly the church is, if nothing else, a religious institution. If Millennials are turning off to the very notion of institutions then this threatens the ability of denominations and larger congregations to attract Millennials and perhaps makes any hope of membership replacement from this demographic which is seeing a precipitous decline[1] an impossible dream. On the other hand, if Millennials are as anti-institutional as is often portrayed, perhaps this is a real opportunity for membership expansion for the Emerging Church movement that likewise seems to register a complaint against institutionalization as well. From the IKON movement with its performance art theatrics, to the kind of local and transient congregations seen in "pub churches" and festivals,[2] much of the Emerging Church seems to reflect an anti-institutional impulse at its very core.

This paper will seek to bring some definition to the issue of anti-institutionalism through a review of some of the data about Millennials and institutions. I will then contribute to the conversation with some of my own research. For the past two years (2014–2015) I have engaged in semi-structured interviews with individuals and focus groups at the "Wild Goose" festival in Hot Springs, North Carolina. Wild Goose is a festival that reflects an Emerging Church perspective with a board that includes Brian

---

1. Jones et al., "Exodus."

2. The Emerging Church movement is often forwarded in conferences and festivals. This paper will deal with the annual "Wild Goose" festival in Hot Springs, North Carolina. But there have been others as well: A western version of the Wild Goose conference outside of Corvallis Oregon (though that has been discontinued), a more recently established (2014) "Moving and Meaning" festival in Albuquerque, New Mexico, and in the UK there is the annual Greenbelt festival. Additionally, many one-off conferences featuring leaders of the Emerging Church like Doug Padgitt, Nadia Boltz-Weber, Shane Claiborne and others are happening multiple times a year.

McLaren and has featured Emerging Church leaders like Doug Pagitt and Shane Claiborne, among others. During these years at "the Goose" I have interviewed Millennials particularly about their issues regarding the Church as an institution. I have likewise interviewed non-emergent Millennials in the South[3] and I will bring to bear on this discussion of Millennials and anti-institutionalism the data uncovered in those interviews. In the end I hope to provide a larger view of Millennials' notions, complaints, and analyses of institutionalism as well as explore the challenges this poses to the institutional church and the Emerging Church Movement.

MILLENNIALS AND INSTITUTIONS

In the landmark study of Strauss and Howe, *Millennials Rising: The Next Great Generation*, the authors are sanguine about how Millennials will view existing institutions: "Their life mission will not be to tear down old institutions that don't work, but to build new ones that do."[4] Later in an exaltation of youth power they state "This will be less the familiar youth power to stop institutions than a newfound power to *energize* them."[5] Their analysis is ultimately a generational understanding that starts with the Boomer generation who sought to diminish institutions that seemed overly strong. In light of the Vietnam War, Watergate, the critiques of the civil rights movement, and feminism, institutions were seen as the problem not the solution. The Boomers then spent their generation weakening institutions. But from the millennial perspective, this ratcheting down of the power of institutions has gone too far. Strauss and Howe's reading of Millennials is that the tearing down of the social safety-net and the demonizing of government left their generation with "weak institutions that seemed to offer their own struggling parents too little help."[6]

Strauss and Howe couple this with a common theme in Millennial studies, the millennial inclination toward volunteer work. They note "A new Millennial service ethic is emerging, built around notions of collegial (rather than individual) action, support for (rather than resistance against) civic institutions, and the tangible doing of good deeds."[7] For Strauss and

---

3. These interviews were conducted between 2012–2015 in focus groups and semi-structured interviews with more than 40 participants. The participants were Millennials who were students at a public university in the South.

4. Howe and Strauss, *Millennials Rising*, 7.

5. Ibid., 28; emphasis original.

6. Ibid., 141.

7. Ibid., 216.

Howe, then, this impulse towards volunteerism is ultimately dependent on institutions for its implementation. Millennials will not work to destroy institutions but build them up in new ways. At one point they note the example of marriage, they will not destroy the institution of marriage but reinforce it with "new forms of certification" (perhaps anticipating the millennial support for same sex marriage which preceded the more general shift in support).

Strauss and Howe's positive perspective on Millennials and institutions however seems toned down by the time they wrote "Millennials Go to College" in 2007. In that book there is scarcely a mention of institutions except by implication. This is most explicitly seen in their chapter on the "Conventional" nature of Millennials. They contend: "Millennials begin with a high level of respect for institutions, but with respect comes high expectations."[8] Life then has not been kind to Millennials' institutional allegiances for they have been witness to "a period in which adults in position of authority (in government, business, academe, the church and elsewhere) were held far less accountable for any misbehavior of their own."[9] While not drawing out the implications of this, the conclusion is clear: from the war in Iraq, to the Global Meltdown, to the Catholic pedophilia scandal—the earlier millennial confidence in institutions has soured.

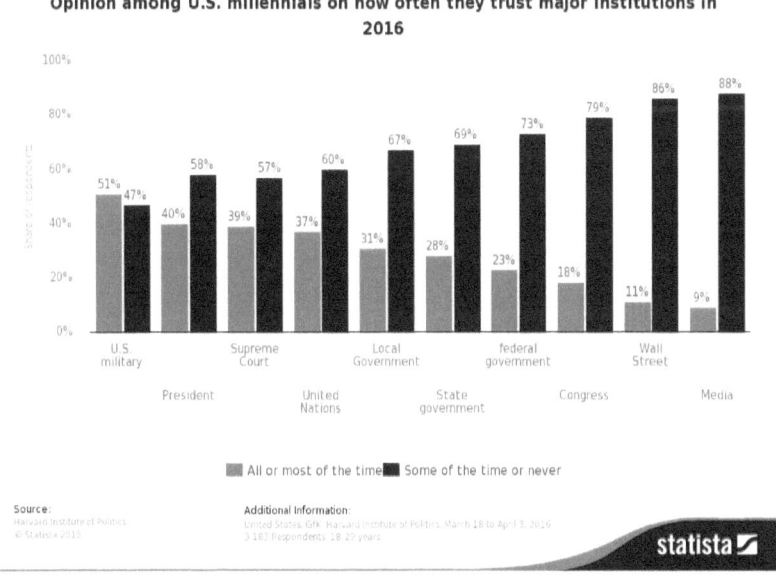

8. Howe, *Millennials Go to College*, 107.
9. Ibid., 109.

Fast-forward to the 2010's and millennial views of institutions have changed significantly from where Strauss and Howe saw them originally. Today, according to a Harvard Institute of Politics survey, the only institution that Millennials say they "trust most or all of the time" is the U.S. Military and that by the barest of 51%.[10] From there the slide is downhill. Only 40% trust the president, 31% trust local government, 28% trust state government, less than a quarter trust the federal government as a whole (23%), less than a fifth trust congress (18%) and just over 1 in 10 trust Wall Street (11%) and the media brings up the rear at 9%. To say the Millennials are distrustful of institutions seems an understatement. What is missing from this chart however, is an indication of how Millennials see the institution of the church.

In January 2016, Hannah Fingerhut analyzed the results of a Pew Poll from Fall 2015. There she traces a significant fall of Millennials "who say churches and religious organizations have a positive effect on the way things are going in this country."[11] In 2010 this number stood at 73% percent. This was the highest of all generational cohorts. By 2015 this had fall almost 20 points to 55% which was the lowest of any generational cohort. All other generational cohorts had seen a rise in the percentage who thought there was a positive effect (though only in single digits). However none had seen decline, and certainly not the kind of significant decline seen among the Millennials.

What is perhaps even more interesting is that the church is unique among non-governmental institutions. "Banks and other financial institutions," "Large Corporations," "Labor Unions" and "Small businesses" had all seen an increase in perceived positive effect among Millennials. Surprisingly, (given the Harvard data), Millennials had a more positive view of Banks and other financial institutions than any other generational cohort. This is likewise true of Large corporations (though by a small margin—4 points) and Labor unions (by a significant margin—15 points). Thus churches are really an outlier among Millennials. While the media too saw significant decline among Millennials, it served to put millennial perspectives largely in line with other generations. It is only on the topic of the church that we see a change from the generationally highest positive view to the generationally lowest and by a non-trivial amount.

---

10. Harvard Institute of Politics, "Opinion."

11. Fingerhut, "Millennials' Views of News Media, Religious Organizations Grow More Negative," *Pew Research Center*, January 4, 2016, http://www.pewresearch.org/fact-tank/2016/01/04/millennials-views-of-news-media-religious-organizations-grow-more-negative/.

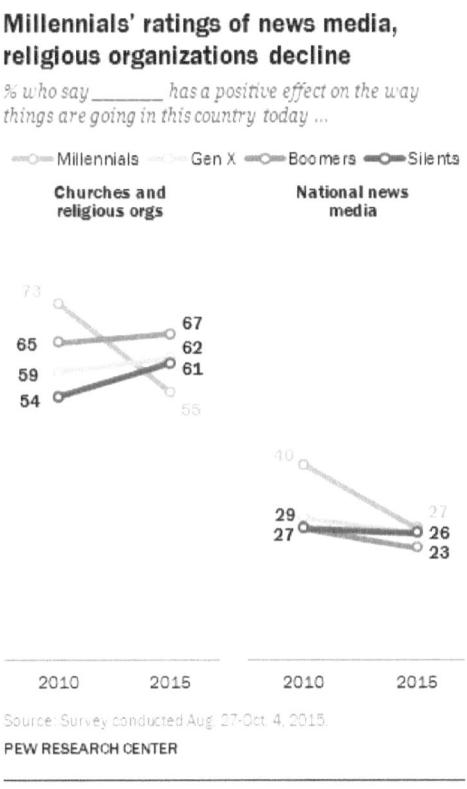

This of course leads us to a discussion of religious disaffiliation among Millennials. It is no exaggeration to say that the issue of millennial disaffiliation is one of the most important issues facing the church today. The warning bell was first rung with Christian Smith's National Study of Youth and Religion study which showed that there was a significant decline in participation in religious institutions among adolescents in the two phases of the study between 2003 and 2005.[12] Some scholars who were studying this were hopeful that this the trend might be a fluke, merely some rearranging of religious constituents. Pearce and Denton suggested that the movement between their various categories of Abiders, Adapters, Assentors, Avoiders and Atheists (the 5 A's) were really only movements of single categories.[13] It was rare for an Abider to become an Atheist. Instead it was Avoiders who ended up being Atheists, and Assentors who became Avoiders and so forth. However, by the third phase of the study (Pearce and Denton only dealt with

12. Smith and Snell, *Souls in Transition*.
13. Pearce and Denton, *A Faith of Their Own*.

the first two phases), it became clear that the downward trend they seemed inclined to downplay was continuing unabated.[14]

By 2012 the Pew Research published "'Nones' on the Rise" indicating the rise of the religiously unaffiliated in the US and noting that in particular Millennials were a significant portion of this group.[15] In 2014 Pew followed up on this with its study "Millennials in Adulthood" which indicated that in fact disaffiliation among Millennials was verging on one-third.[16] The Public Religion Research Institute's (PRRI) *Atlas of American Values* from 2014 puts that number above one-third and indicates an expectation for continued growth.[17] In September PRRI published a study putting the number of millennial unaffiliateds at 39%. The CEO of PRRI, demographer Robert P. Jones, also published a book titled *The End of White Christian America* exploring this data in depth. This study is an interesting contextualization of the phenomenon because it is clear that this is a phenomena that seems mostly relegated to white protestants/catholics. Black and Hispanic churches seem to be struggling far less to hold on to their Millennials. This is seen clearly in the median age of America's Religious groups: Hispanic Catholics and Protestants have the youngest median age in their late 30's, Black Protestants are near the median age for all Americans at 47 (the US median is 46), but White Christians have the oldest median at 53/54 while unaffiliateds are near the bottom at 36. Thus, what Jones clearly indicates is that White Christian America is in its final death throes and it is the Millennials who are digging its grave.

Still, part of the reason Strauss and Howe were so optimistic about Millennials' view of institutions was because of an unprecedented level of volunteerism among their generation. As one of my colleagues put it, they are "do gooders." Evidence for this can be found in the 2006 Cone Millennial Case Study.[18] A quantitative study of Millennials, the Cone study showed that 20% of Millennials volunteered at least once a week. But even for those Millennials not engaged in volunteering, they are highly sensitive to corporate social responsibility. The majority of Millennials reported that they would switch brands if the new brand is associated with a good cause. Additionally Millennials consider a company's reputation for social responsibility when they decide where to shop and they desire to find employment with companies that take social responsibility seriously. McGlone

---

14. Smith, "National Study of Youth and Religion."
15. Pew Forum, "'None' on the Rise."
16. Pew Research, "Millennials in Adulthood."
17. Cited in Jones, *End of White Christian America*, 48.
18. Cone, "2006 Cone Millennial."

et. al. confirmed these findings,[19] concluding "Millennials have internalized the need to make the world a better place and support that attitude by volunteering more."[20] Further, a Deloitte study of its millennial employees found that Millennials see success as more than profit and see the purpose of business as including societal development and changing the world for the better.[21]

MILLENNIALS: GENERATION WE V. GENERATION ME

Yet this issue actually opens up an arena of heated academic debate regarding how civically minded Millennials really are. When Strauss and Howe published *Millennials Rising* in 2000 they argued that the millennial generation would be the most civically minded generation since the World War II generation. "Already Millennial teens are hard at work on a grassroot reconstruction of community, teamwork, and civic spirit. They're doing it in the realms of community service, race, gender relations, politics and faith."[22] One might worry about that last category "faith," but Howe doubled down on this concept of millennial civic mindedness in 2003 where he asserts, "twenty years ago 'community service' was unheard of in most high schools. Today it is the norm."[23] According to a 1999 Roper Survey, more teenagers blamed 'selfishness' than anything else when asked about 'the major cause of problems in this country.'"[24] Strauss and Howe have not been alone in this position, Eric Greenberg and Karl Weber have likewise supported this reading of the Millennials in their book, *Generation We: How Millennial Youth are Taking Over America And Changing Our World Forever*. The so-called "Generation We" perspective argued, in line with Strauss and Howe, that Millennials could be characterized by "selflessness and devotion to the greater good."[25] Greenberg and Weber ultimately take a hopeful tone and outline a political agenda for Generation We.

For Generation We advocates, then, Millennials might be engaged in institutional reform from the inside. With perhaps the exception of the

19. McGlone et. al, "Corporate Social Responsibility." McGlone et. al., 200, caution that their findings are not generalizable due to the sample size, however the fact that their study largely substantiated the Cone Study conclusions is instructive.
20. Ibid., 208.
21. Deloitte, "The Millennial Survey 2011," 5.
22. Strauss and Howe, *Millennials Rising*, 214.
23. Howe, *Millennials Go to College*, 16.
24. Ibid.
25. Greenberg and Weber, *Generation We*, 4.

institution of the Church and government, there is some evidence that bears out the supposition that generally Millennials are conducive to a vision of changing institutions from the inside and their participation in these institutions has led to an increase in positive views of them.

In contrast to the "Generation We" perspective is the "Generation Me" perspective advocated by Jean M. Twenge. In a series of academic articles and in her 2004 book *Generation Me: Why Today's Young Americans Are More Confident, Assertive, Entitled—And More Miserable Than Ever Before*, Twenge takes a distinctly more pessimistic perspectives on Millennials. Twenge (and her collaborators) argue that one can trace a significant increase in self-esteem and self-perception that equates to a significant increase in narcissism among Millennials as compared with Baby Boomers or Generation X. She argues that as a result Millennials are more individualistic and motivated by extrinsic rewards and materialistic culture.[26]

What Twenge concludes then is that Millennials value "money, image and fame over concern for others and intrinsic meaning."[27] This is particularly stark in a comparative generational framework. She notes "College students ranked the importance of being very well off financially No. 8 in 1971 but since 1989, have consistently ranked it No. 1."[28] Likewise, Millennials ultimately lack a civic concern for society or others. In a scathing summation she states Millennials are

> less likely to have donated to charities, less likely to want a job worthwhile to society or that would help others, and less likely to agree they would eat differently if it meant more food for the starving. They were less likely to want to work in a social service organization or become a social worker, and were less likely to express empathy for outgroups.[29]

The notion then that Millennials "will save us all" is not substantiated by Twenge and her collaborators' research.

In a more troubling work Twenge focuses on this question of millennial narcissism. In a 2008 article[30] followed by a 2010 book, *The Narcissism Epidemic*.[31] Twenge examines the claim that Millennials are a more narcissistic generation than either the two which preceded it. Her analysis, using multi-generational survey material, confirms this. She notes that narcissism

---

26. Twenge, *Generation Me*.
27. Twenge et al., "Generational Differences," 1050.
28. Ibid.
29. Ibid., 1054.
30. Twenge and Campbell, "Increases," 1082–86.
31. Twenge and Campbell, *Narcissism Epidemic*.

actually has some benefits for the individual, they tend to be more aggressive and goal-oriented. Yet she also notes that while "narcissism may be positive in the short term for individuals, [it is] negative for other people, for society and for the individual in the long term."[32]

Yet even more problematic is that in another study Twenge shows that among Millennials there has likewise been an uptick in mental disorders. On the MMPI Psychopathic Deviation scale (which measures psychopathic tendencies) 40% of college students in 2007 scored two standard deviations above normal. This is compared with college students 1938 where between 1% and 5% did.[33] She ultimately blames this rise on a cultural proclivity that has prioritized money and acquisition, concluding "As American culture shifted toward emphasizing individual achievement, money and status rather than social relationships and community, psychopathology increased among young people."[34]

The other drawback of the narcissism that Twenge highlights is a related sense of entitlement among Millennials. Millennial students expect grades for "trying" rather than performing. She notes generationally this is related to grade inflation, "they were given better grades for doing less work."[35] Additionally Millennials place a high value on leisure and "favor jobs that do not require overtime and allow for several weeks of vacation."[36]

The Generation Me view of Millennials seems to suggests that Millennials are more focused on making money and status but with an expectation that it will take less work than previous generations. Twenge suggests that given the level of narcissism and psychopathology, we might well have concern about what will happen to the Millennials when they confront the real world. Will employers likewise need to scale down expectations? Or will Millennials suddenly confront a cognitive dissonance between their expectations and reality? But in terms of institutions what we see is that this analysis corresponds to the data that indicates that Millennials are inclined to be supportive precisely of those institutions that seem to be supportive of success in the capitalist system and a social safety-net for when things do not work out.

Another proponent of the Generation Me perspective is Christian Smith. In their 2011 work Smith and Davidson likewise argue that

32. Twenge et al., "Egos Inflating Over Time," 892.
33. Twenge et al., "Birth Cohort Increases," 150.
34. Ibid., 152.
35. Twenge, "Generational Changes," 402.
36. Ibid.

Millennials are not the bright hope that Generation We observers expect.[37] They too argue that Millennials are highly materialistic and consumer-oriented. Additionally, in direct response to the Generation We perspective, they assert that Millennials are resolutely not civic minded. In fact, from the results of the National Youth Survey on Religion, Smith finds that 69% of Millennials categorically state that they are "not political." Drilling down further, Smith finds that even the minority who claim they are political overstate the facts, and ultimately concludes that in reality only 4% of Millennials are actually politically active, if the term is understood to include things like voting, calling one's congressperson, and regularly following political issues.

Smith however, goes one step farther to try to explain the reason for this civic incivility. He argues that there are several components to the Generation Me critique. First, there is a lack of moral reasoning among Millennials. By and large, Smith notes, Millennials are unable to formulate moral arguments for their positions. Many are flummoxed by the very notion. Instead Smith says that they are moral individualists[38]—they think that morality is an individual proposition and that it is ultimately relative. They are wary of imposing their moral position on anyone else and likewise are resistant to a moral position being imposed on them. Smith links this to an "educational agenda" that has postulated tolerance and pluralism.[39] While Smith sees advantages to this in Millennials' diminished racial and ethnic prejudice as compared to other generations, he sees this as also precipitating "sloppy and indefensible moral reasoning."[40] Smith doesn't blame Millennials per se, rather he sees moral reasoning as a skill to be taught and the public school system as intentionally shirking its responsibility therein.[41]

Additionally, the materialism that Twenge emphasizes is reiterated in Smith. Smith notes that in his survey "between one-half to two-thirds of emerging adults said that their well-being can be measured by what they own."[42] Further, emerging adults that Smith interviewed were unable to

---

37. Smith and Davidson, *Lost in Transition*.

38. Ibid., 71. This is a change from the language of moral intuitionists that Smith uses in *Souls in Transition*. However earlier in the book he talks about moral instinctiveness (52–56) which seems to more closely align with the notion of moral intuition that he discussed in Souls. The move to the language of "individualists" highlights a continuing theme that one sees in his work which is echoed in Twenge's work regarding the individualist perspective of Millennials.

39. Ibid., 34–35.
40. Ibid., 35.
41. Ibid., 62.
42. Ibid., 71.

lodge any sustained critique against run-away materialism. While they seemed uncomfortable with unrestrained acquisitiveness (shoes numbering in the hundreds or thousands seemed to be the example du jour) they often could not come up with a reason as to why such acquisitiveness might be a bad thing. Smith sees this as rooted in three foundational beliefs: First, money is the result of hard work. Second, society or other individuals do not have the right to limit the individual's spending. Third, and perhaps most importantly, "people are naturally driven by self-interested acquisitive motives, which ultimately cannot be denied or deterred."[43] The naturalizing of the capitalist notion of acquisition as ultimately instinctive highlights both the justification of consumerism and re-emphasizes the individualist perspective that conjoins moral disconnects, narcissism, and entitlement.

It is at this point that the Generation Me critique dovetails with the data we have seen regarding a distrust of governmental institutions. Smith argues that Millennials lack of civic responsibility is ultimately motivated by a "cynicism about the political leaders working the political system."[44] Millennials are both suspicious of the political system and despair of being able to change it. Additionally, their lack of moral reasoning ability makes it difficult to forward a critique of the political system. Smith notes, they also express a "dislike for the conflict and divisiveness that can result from politics."[45] This may, in fact, tie into the tolerance and plurality that was mentioned above. The diatribes that are often a part of the political shout fests so prevalent today often sound a lot like the very intolerance to which Millennials have an aversion. Smith summarizes,

> Politically distrustful emerging adults thus demonstrate suspicion and hostility with respect to politicians, the political system, and other people involved in politics—and say that this is the reason for their own lack of interest in being civically engaged. Though generally informed about political issues and even often passionate about the topic generally, these emerging adults seem alienated from greater political involvement by their pervasive distrust.[46]

The dreams of a politically active millennial generation postulated by the Generation We perspective seems problematic given the analyses of Smith and Twenge.

---

43. Ibid., 80.
44. Ibid., 202.
45. Ibid., 204.
46. Ibid.

DIFFERENCES IN INSTITUTIONS

What comes at the end of this analysis is that there are two categories of institutions that Millennials have very different feelings about. On the one hand, there is the capitalist marketplace. Millennials have fairly positive feelings about this. Their perspective on small business and labor unions appears to be generally positive and growing. While less than a majority have a positive view of the financial industry and large corporations even those institutions seem to be gaining ground.[47] On the other hand when it comes to governmental institutions and the church, these institutions move from negative to more negative. And while it is true that a positive view of the church as an institution still garners a majority, the downward trend is extreme.

How might we explain the different between these two categories of institutions? At a certain level we might suppose that participation makes the difference. As Millennials move into the workforce, we see the level of positive appreciation increase. Additionally, the value structure as argued above by Smith and Twenge conforms to this favorable view of business. If Millennials ultimately value acquisition as a signifier of self-worth, they are more likely to view institutions that contribute to their ability to do that in affirmative ways.

On the other hand, as Smith notes, there is a remarkable reticence to enter into the political arena among Millennials; the resistance to the kind of conflict that political difference entails, and a generally alienated perspective on politics in general spills into a very negative view of government. The millennial embrace of Bernie Sanders with his message that "the system is broken" indicates just that sort of alienation. At the same time "Bernie" supporters[48] at the Democratic National Convention weeping when at last it became clear to them that there was no magical way that Sanders would become the nominee indicates an additional level of simple ignorance of the modern political system. No convention in their lifetime has ever been more than an extended infomercial, that there was a faction of *convention delegates* that held out hope that this would be otherwise represents a painful millennial disconnect from political reality. All this may explain why

---

47. Fingerhut, "Millennials Views." Using Pew data, Fingerhut shows that the number of Millennials who think a given institution "has a positive effect on the way that things are going in the country" has increased 10 points for banks and financial institutions (35% to 45%) and 10 points for large corporations (28% to 38%). Labor unions and small business have increased by eight points each.

48. Bernie Sanders supporters often referred to Bernie Sanders (and were thus referred to themselves) by Sanders first name, "Bernie."

REED—*The Problem of Anti-Institutionalism in Millennials*

third party candidates in the fall of 2016 were running at 19% (Libertarian) and 9% (Green).[49] Almost a third of Millennials are opting out of the two party system. We have yet to see what effect this will have on Millennials' view of politics going forward, but it seems likely that this will not stem the trend seen heretofore.

Turning then to the institution of the church, the estrangement from the church may likewise be found in negative feelings towards the church as an institution. As noted above, Millennials have been significantly overrepresented among the religiously unaffiliated. Millennials are 10 points higher than Gen X and more than twice as likely as Baby Boomers to be unaffiliated.[50] Unsurprisingly then, Millennials likewise have the lowest percentage of weekly church attendance and the highest percentage of "seldom/never" attenders.[51] Thus it seems likely that the decrease in participation in religion in general and in church in particular should have the reverse effect of participation in the workforce, namely a decline in a view of its constructive effect in society.

Attendance at religious services by age group (2014)

Likewise, we might note that Millennials also lead in terms of those who say religion is "not at all important" or "not too important" and significantly lag behind the other generational cohorts who say religion is "very important." I also should note that the "somewhat important" category is marginally higher than in the other generational cohorts. Still the

---

49. Pew Research Center, "Voters' General Election Preferences." These numbers are significantly higher than other election cycles. In 2012 the Green and Libertarian parties won less than 2% between them. In the end however, while third parties did not get the double digit percentage the fall 2016 numbers predicted in the 2016 election, third parties did almost triple their millennial vote from 2012. Green, "How Millennials Voted."

50. Pew Research, "U.S. Public Becoming Less Religious."

51. Pew Research, "Millennials in Adulthood."

combination of "very" and "somewhat" make for a lower overall level than all other generational cohorts.

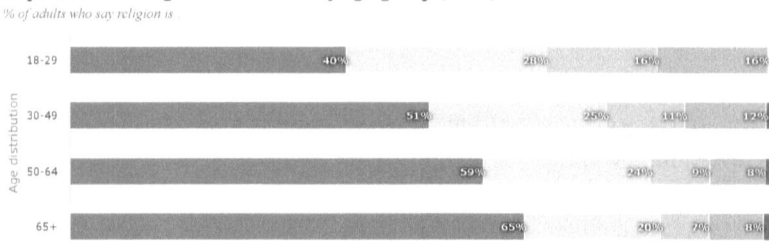

Importance of religion in one's life by age group (2014)

These factors together function as a basis of an explanation for why this second category of institutions, government and religion, have seen a much greater level of suspicion among Millennials. Millennial discouragement with and lack of participation in these institutions lead to cycle of greater and greater alienation from both institutions. However, this is by no means a complete explanation. To indicate a correlation between decreased church attendance, religious disaffiliation, and a diminished view of the importance of religion is perhaps to say the same thing thrice. The real question is why? Why have Millennials abandoned the church? It is here that we may profitably turn to qualitative work to look for answers.

MILLENNIALS AND INSTITUTIONS: QUALITATIVE ANALYSIS

I have been conducting interviews and focus groups with Millennials for the past two years. The subjects have all been Millennials with a mix of convenience sampled college students and millennial attendees at the Wild Goose festival which is held each summer in Hot Springs, NC. My work therefore centers on Southern Millennials for the most part, but I believe that this makes the work particularly relevant. The South remains the last stronghold of American Evangelicalism and there are a higher percentage of Millennial Evangelicals in the South than other regions.[52] The problems that Southern Millennials tell us they have with institutions and the church in particular are thus key pointers to where the church is failing to attract or keep Millennials.

---

52. Smith et al., "General Social Surveys, 1972–2014."

If we then begin to explore what these Millennials are criticizing about the church as an institution we must begin with the issue of sexuality. Southern Millennials are by and large affirmative of LGBT issues. While surveys indicate that those in the South lag behind their companions in the other regions, still a majority of southern Millennials agree with a right to marriage for homosexuals.[53]

Thus at some level when Millennials are asked about why the they are leaving the church, the issue of tolerance is on the forefront. One millennial put it fairly straightforwardly, "the recent gay marriage stuff has driven people out of the church." This sentiment was echoed by a large number of Millennials my research team talked to. The single biggest problem for the church as institution is without doubt the issue of the Church on homosexuality.

But interestingly this issue is not isolated. The respondent above who gave that direct answer did so as a way of clarifying the answer of another participant in the focus group who started with the more general complaint that the church was "judgmental." This category was often contrasted with a notion of "openness" that the church was seen to lack.

This notion of openness, sometimes discussed as tolerance, actually centers around a cluster of issues. It is not merely that the church is perceived as being backward on the issue of gay rights, it is also that the church is restrictive on doctrine, and uncompromising in its rejection of Millennials who express doubt. Millennials' experience of the church is that when they expressed issues of doubt about traditional doctrine they were often reprimanded and sometimes expelled. Other times if they revealed, or had friends who revealed, that they were homosexual or even struggling with their sexual identity they were likewise reprimanded or expelled (more often expelled for this).

Millennials perceive this issue of judgmentalism and intolerance operating in both the domain of theology and identity. One millennial put the connection clearly when they noted that their, "pastor preach[es] resurrection and all gay people are going to hell which is so ridiculous." Here we can see the intertwining of the categories of doctrine and identity both of which are ultimately dismissed as "ridiculous."

Of course at some level this does not come as a surprise. Certainly the position on homosexuality that many traditional churches hold is based on doctrine. It is not merely that they don't like gay people AND they hold problematic doctrines. The doctrines ultimately are determinative of the categorization and treatment of people. And yet Millennials do not seem

53. Ibid.

to recognize that this comes from a stance of doctrinal purity, rather they see this as a general attitude of judgmentalism that extends both to sexuality and doctrinal deviance. The problem is not that the church needs to change its doctrine, rather the problem is more affective—the church needs to change its attitude to one of openness in all areas and rid itself of the judgmentalism that is manifested in the different domains of theology, doctrine, and culture war sermons.

This then leads to another problem which is related to the first. When asked why they think Millennials stay in the church they point to the safety that tradition gives them. As one millennial suggested,

> I think it provides them with a set of, like, answers and security as to where we came from, and like what happens after we pass away, and it just, I don't know, it's very structured, and it just helps them get a sense of security and like an idea of what's going on. A lot of people don't like uncertainty.

The church provides structure and security. This is also coupled with familial pressure. Several Millennials we talked to mentioned they continued to attend because their family was part of the church, or that they had friends there.

What these Millennials are clearly pointing to is the comfort of community and the way that communities generally reproduce themselves through both familial and peer connections. Yet this wasn't seen by the Millennials as a positive thing. The language they use indicates that they do not see these communities as places to grow, but rather places to avoid growth. They see them more as enclaves that excuse judgment and intolerance rather the authentic places of connection.

Another particular kind of critique of the church came specifically from Millennials who had already left the church or were never part of one to begin with. These we might categorize as "nones" though they themselves would not always use that label (though several of them did). But beyond the problem of judgmentalism and intolerance, these Millennials expressed some apprehension about the institutional church particularly in relationship to its role in politics.

Kinnaman and Lyons early study *Unchristian* pointed the way to this problem.[54] Unchurched Millennials often expressed the opinion that the church was "too political." I wanted to explore this notion further with Millennials as to why this was a problem. Unchurched Millennials were

---

54. Kinnaman and Lyons, *Unchristian*, 153–80.

particularly worried about the church's participation in politics. As one participant commented,

> when you have a person [politician] who is voting and who's zealously religious and therefore opposed to letting the will of the people be heard, if a majority of the people are voting for an issue and the person disagrees on religious grounds, then you have a system of politics and religion that isn't working for anybody.

Here we note that the problem is that religious views are tainting both politicians and the electorate. There is an unspoken opposing term here as well. If religious views are not the foundation of good electoral politics then what is? And here the opposite terms appear to be reason and science.

What seems to be at bottom are a series of critiques raised by Millennials I interviewed such as:

> The church and the government are supposed to be separate entities and the questioning of rights of people to get married has nothing to do with religion. Marriage is not even constituted religiously it is a government action that allows to people to couple and share benefits it has nothing to do with religion

> I would have to say that I don't think a 3000-year-old document should be used in any current political whatever at all.

These two quotes point to a basic problem that these Millennials see with the church. The church is ultimately subject to an extra-rational force, be it understood as either God or God through the Bible. In both cases however, the position of the Church (and again gay marriage is the example that comes up most commonly) is not subject to rational discourse and debate. These Millennials perceive that institutional church is self-exempted from rationality and therefore unfit partners in the political process. Many of these Millennials straightforwardly held that the church should have no role in politics, while often despairing of the practicality of such a position.

When we look then at the problem of institutions vis-à-vis Millennials we see several factors. Millennials are not anti-institutional per se. They have, in fact, positive views of several institutions. But what seems to characterize the institutions which Millennials have a disregard for is located in the affective domain. Institutions, like government and church, that seem to ultimately be inspiring conflict, intolerance, and lack relevance to their lives have seen decreasing participation. The current struggle the democratic party is having getting the Millennials back on-board after the failed millennial embrace of Bernie Sanders highlights this in terms of politics (though clearly more work on this needs to be done). But likewise, we see particularly the more conservative church's perspective on homosexuality, its exclusion of those who are not like (or do not think) like its members, its political legacy that Millennials see as divisive and its rejection of science and reason in lieu of an extra-rational authority all function to move greater and greater numbers of Millennials out of the church. PRRI report released in late September 2016 put the number of millennial "nones" at 39% and showed them to be more than double the next largest religious affiliation among Millennials.[55] PRRI went even further and indicated that 74% of "nones" are what they term "rejectionists"—those who are intentionally not participating in the church.[56]

What I hope to have shown here, however, is that rejectionists have not rejected the church because of disagreements with doctrine, or because of specific congregational acts. Rather they have rejected the institution of church because they see at its core, in its DNA, a judgmentalism that is only manifested in acts and doctrines. The Millennial exodus from the church is focused on this broader affective perception. Thus a change in worship style or recasting doctrine ("love the sinner . . .") may have no effect on this generation. As long of the smell of judgement lingers in the air Millennials will see a problem and all evidence points to a continuation of a trend away from this institution.

ANTI-INSTITUTIONALISM AND THE EMERGING CHURCH

I would however end with a short discussion on the Emerging Church. In his early book *A New Kind of Christian*, Brian McLaren speaking through the character of Neo, talks about the particular problem of Hell. In so doing he advocates a new attitude for the church,

> It's none of your business who does and does not go to hell. It is your business to be warned by it and to run, not walk, in the opposite direction! It is your business to love God with all your heart, soul, mind, and strength, to love your neighbor as yourself, to have confidence in Jesus Christ and live as Jesus lived. Let the imagery of hell remind you that life is serious business, that there are real consequences to how we live and believe, that justice and injustice ultimately matter more than most of what

---

55. "Jones et al., "Exodus."
56. Ibid.

people worry about. Now stop speculating about hell and start living for heaven![57]

Here the issue is to whom the various prescriptions that the church offers are directed. For McLaren these have been too often directed outward at those outside the church. McLaren wants to take this mentality off the table, by saying "it's none of your business . . . it is your business to . . ." Judgment directed at outsiders is the replaced a mentality of introspection. This corresponds to a continuing theme throughout McLaren's book which indicates that modernist Christianity has become all-consumed with the micro-inspection of the individual acts and fates, and has therefore has failed to see the global responsibility that Christianity proposes.

This change in perspective might very well have the effect of reaching out to Millennials. In my research we have shown video and quotes of Emerging Church leaders to Millennials, and we have seen significantly more positive responses than negative.[58] To that end there is a general receptivity to many facets of the Emerging Church that appeal to Millennials. The combination of a rejection of judgmentalism and an embrace of issues like gay marriage and a highlighting of tolerance all connect with Millennials.

Other kinds of acts by the Emerging Church might also have implications. The move to non-traditional venues for services like Pub Churches, the abandonment of the agenda of the Christian Right and the embrace of social justice issues all might attract Millennials. But in terms of the work that has been reviewed in this paper and my research, it seems clear that the most important move the Emerging Church can make toward Millennials is the rejection of judgmentalism. If this move can be credibly conducted it would address a major complaint of Millennials and might function to change some millennial attitudes. However, heretofore, the rather limited number of Emerging Churches (which may be a structural feature, not a bug) may ultimately mean that while it may attract a millennial following, it will not actually move the needle on the broader millennial anti-institutionalism related to church.

BIBLIOGRAPHY

Cone Inc., and AMP Agency. "The 2006 Cone Millennial Cause Study, The Millennial Generation: Pro-Social and Empowered to Change the World."

---

57. McLaren, *A New Kind of Christian*, 180.
58. See chapter 2 in this volume.

Boston: Cone Communications, 2006. http://www.conecomm.com/2006-cone-communications-millennial-cause-study-pdf/.

Cooper, Betsy, Daniel Cox, Rachel Lienesch, and Robert P. Jones. "Exodus: Why Americans Are Leaving Religion—and Why They're Unlikely to Come Back." Public Religion Research Institute, September 22, 2016. http://www.prri.org/research/prri-rns-2016-religiously-unaffiliated-americans/.

Deloitte. "The Millennial Survey 2011 | Deloitte | Sustainable Brands." *Sustainablebrands.com*. http://www.sustainablebrands.com/digital_learning/research/millennial-survey-2011-deloitte.

Fingerhut, Hannah. "Millennials' Views of News Media, Religious Organizations Grow More Negative." *Pew Research Center*, January 4, 2016. http://www.pewresearch.org/fact-tank/2016/01/04/millennials-views-of-news-media-religious-organizations-grow-more-negative/.

Green, Matthew. "How Millennials Voted in the 2016 Presidential Election (with Lesson Plan)." *The Lowdown*, November 15, 2016. https://ww2.kqed.org/lowdown/2016/11/14/how-millennials-voted/.

Greenberg, Eric H., and Karl Weber. *Generation We: How Millennial Youth Are Taking over America and Changing Our World Forever*. Emeryville, CA: Pachatusan, 2008.

Harvard Institute of Politics. "Opinion among U.S. Millennials on How Often They Trust Major Institutions in 2016." 2016. https://www-statista-com.proxy006.nclive.org/statistics/540713/trust-among-us-millennials-of-major-institutions.

Howe, Neil. *Millennials Go to College*. 2nd ed. Great Falls, VA: Lifecourse Associates, 2007.

Howe, Neil, and Bill Strauss. *Millennials Rising: The Next Great Generation*. New York: Vintage, 2000.

Jones, Robert P. *The End of White Christian America*. New York: Simon & Schuster, 2016.

Jones, Robert P., Daniel Cox, Betsy Cooper, and Rachel Lienesch. "Exodus: Why Americans Are Leaving Religion—and Why They're Unlikely to Come Back." Public Religion Research Institute, September 22, 2016. http://www.prri.org/research/prri-rns-2016-religiously-unaffiliated-americans/.

Kinnaman, David, and Gabe Lyons. *Unchristian: What a New Generation Really Thinks about Christianity—and Why It Matters*. Grand Rapids: Baker, 2007.

McGlone, Teresa, Judith Winters Spain, and Vernon McGlone. "Corporate Social Responsibility and the Millennials." *Journal of Education for Business* 86.4 (2011) 195–200.

McLaren, Brian D. *A New Kind of Christian: A Tale of Two Friends on a Spiritual Journey*. San Francisco: Jossey-Bass, 2008.

Pearce, Lisa, and Melinda Lundquist Denton. *A Faith of Their Own: Stability and Change in the Religiosity of America's Adolescents*. First edition. New York: Oxford University Press, 2011.

Pew Research Center. "Millennials in Adulthood: Detached from Institutions, Networked with Friends." Pew Research Center, March 7, 2014. http://www.pewsocialtrends.org/files/2014/03/2014-03-07_generations-report-version-for-web.pdf.

———. "U.S. Public Becoming Less Religious," November 3, 2015. http://www.pewforum.org/2015/11/03/u-s-public-becoming-less-religious/.

———. "Voters' General Election Preferences." *Pew Research Center for the People and the Press*, August 18, 2016. http://www.people-press.org/2016/08/18/1-voters-general-election-preferences/.

Pew Research Center, 1615 L. "Religious Landscape Study." *Pew Research Center's Religion & Public Life Project: Religious Landscape Study*, May 11, 2015. http://www.pewforum.org/religious-landscape-study/.

Pew Research Center, Pew Forum On Religion and Public Life. "'None' on the Rise: One-in-Five Adults Have No Religious Affiliation." Pew Research Center, 2012. http://www.pewforum.org/files/2012/10/NonesOnTheRise-full.pdf.

Smith, Christian. "National Study of Youth and Religion, Wave 3 (2007–2008) | Data Archive | The Association of Religion Data Archives." The data were downloaded from the Association of Religion Data Archives, www.TheARDA.com. The National Study of Youth and Religion, http://youthandreligion.nd.edu/, whose data were used by permission here, was generously funded by Lilly Endowment Inc., under the direction of Christian Smith, of the Department of Sociology at the University of Notre Dame, 2008. http://thearda.com/Archive/Files/Descriptions/NSYRW3.asp.

Smith, Christian, and Hilary Davidson. *Lost in Transition: The Dark Side of Emerging Adulthood*. New York: Oxford University Press,, 2011.

Smith, Christian, and Patricia Snell. *Souls in Transition: The Religious and Spiritual Lives of Emerging Adults*. New York: Oxford University Press, 2009.

Smith, Tom W., Peter Marsden, Michael Hout, and Jibum Kim. "General Social Surveys, 1972–2014 [machine Readable Data File] /Principal Investigator, Tom W. Smith; Co-Principal Investigator, Peter V. Marsden; Co-Principal Investigator, Michael Hout; Sponsored by National Science Foundation. -NORC Ed.- Chicago: NORC at the University of Chicago [producer and Distributor]." NORC at University of Chicago, 2016. gssdataexplorer.norc.org.

Twenge, Jean. *Generation Me—Revised and Updated: Why Today's Young Americans Are More Confident, Assertive, Entitled—and More Miserable Than Ever Before*. Rev. ed. New York: Atria, 2004.

———. "Generational Changes and Their Impact in the Classroom: Teaching Generation Me." *Medical Education* 43.5 (2009) 398–405.

Twenge, Jean, and W. Keith Campbell. "Increases in Positive Self-Views Among High School Students: Birth-Cohort Changes in Anticipated Performance, Self-Satisfaction, Self-Liking, and Self-Competence." *Psychological Science (Wiley-Blackwell)* 19.11 (2008) 1082–86.

———. *The Narcissism Epidemic: Living in the Age of Entitlement*. New York: Atria, 2010.

Twenge, Jean, W. Keith Campbell, and Elise C. Freeman. "Generational Differences in Young Adults' Life Goals, Concern for Others, and Civic Orientation, 1966–2009." *Journal of Personality and Social Psychology* 102.5 (2012) 1045–62.

Twenge, Jean, Brittany Gentile, C. Nathan DeWall, Debbie Ma, Katharine Lacefield, and David R. Schurtz. "Birth Cohort Increases in Psychopathology among Young Americans, 1938–2007: A Cross-Temporal Meta-Analysis of the MMPI." *Clinical Psychology Review* 30.2 (2010) 145–54.

Twenge, Jean, Sara Konrath, Joshua D. Foster, W. Keith Campbell, and Brad J. Bushman. "Egos Inflating Over Time: A Cross-Temporal Meta-Analysis of the Narcissistic Personality Inventory." *Journal of Personality* 76 (2008) 875–902.

10

A Church for the De-Churched and Un-Churched

Sunday Assembly as a Response to and Space for the "Nones"

JOEL D. DANIELS

Abstract

Sunday Assembly (SA), a non-religious community established in 2013, was created to provide a "church" for the de-churched and un-churched, or the "nones." In a relatively short amount of time, SA has experienced significant growth by successfully appealing to people who have rejected traditional forms of religion. In order to better understand "nones" and organizational structures that foster community outside the Christian church, this essay examines SA's story, success, and professed goals. Therefore, I first explore SA's history, describing its genesis and its current structure and expression, and then I survey the sociological demographics of "nones," which explains where and why SA has grown. Next, I consider the larger theological claims present in SA's mission, such as an emphasis on feeling, freedom, and estrangement, through the theology of Friedrich Schleiermacher, Karl Rahner, and Paul Tillich. Indeed, there are notable similarities between SA and these theologians, likely helping "nones" naturally transition from traditional Christianity to SA's non-religious expression. I conclude by focusing on the sustainability of SA, acknowledging both the strengths and weaknesses of the community, and consider if the Emerging Church (EC) could adopt SA's model to better serve the "nones." Although many other religious communities could be included, I focus on the EC because of its congruence with SA's values, mission, and goals. SA is a vibrant multi-site "assembly" that creatively serves the "nones," making it a useful community to study by others who also want to better care for "nones."

Research has repeatedly confirmed that the "nones," those affirming no particular religious affiliation, are on the rise in English-speaking countries on both sides of the Atlantic.[1] The causes for this rise include issues like disillusionment, politics, and personal preference.[2] Sunday Assembly (SA),[3] a non-religious community established in London in 2013, was created to provide a "church" for the de-churched and un-churched, or the "nones."[4] Although SA is often referred to as an "atheist church," the founders, British comedians Sanderson Jones and Pippa Evans, rejected the title claiming that SA is a church for everyone[5]—including, but not limited to, atheists. By appealing to "nones'" desire for community without religion, SA has quickly grown into a community of thousands with over 70 assemblies or chapters around the world.[6]

This essay examines SA's history, success, and professed goals in order to examine how SA attempted to create a non-religious framework for "nones'" beliefs, desires, and actions. I first describe SA's history, beginning with SA's early history then transitioning to its more recent appearance. Second, I explore the sociological demographics of "nones," and using Friedrich Schleiermacher, Karl Rahner, and Paul Tillich, I consider the larger theological claims found in SA's mission—such as feeling, freedom, and estrangement. I conclude by focusing on the sustainability of SA, acknowledging both the strengths and weaknesses of the community, and

---

1. See Pew Research Center, "U.S. Public Becoming Less Religious," particularly chapters 1–2.

2. Ibid., particularly chapters 3–4; and Barna, "What Millennials Want When They Visit Church."

3. In the essay I use the following abbreviations: for Sunday Assembly, SA; for the Emerging/Emergent Church, EC; and for the Pew Research Center, PRC. I also indicate these abbreviations when I first introduce the terms.

4. Sunday Assembly, "Our Story."

5. Though, as I explain below, SA did start as an atheist church but quickly transitioned to a church for everyone.

6. Jones, "Changes to the Launch System."

consider if the Emerging Church (EC) could use SA's model to better serve the "nones." Though many other religious communities could be included, I focus on the EC because of its congruence with SA's values, mission, and overall model. SA is a vibrant multi-site "assembly" that creatively serves the "nones," making it a useful community to study by others who hope to better care for "nones" as well.

WHAT IS SUNDAY ASSEMBLY?

SA began as an organic community that embraced ideals such as subjectivity and deconstructionism.[7] The founders, Jones and Evans, expressed SA's vision in three parts: Live Better, Help Often, and Wonder More. With that ethos, SA quickly grew and began to organize; however, as the recent history shows, the growth has slowed, particularly in relation to SA's stated expectation. Nevertheless, SA is an important and vibrant non-religious community that is affecting people throughout the world.

SA was initially known as an "atheist church," but that moniker was mainly used for marketing. Atheist activist Hemant Mehta explains, "There's a simple reason [SA's] getting that label: It's sexy. No one's Googling the 'Sunday Assembly,' which is the official name for these events. But 'atheist church,' which I've used . . . is just more clickable. People *want* to read articles about 'atheist churches,' not 'Sunday assemblies.'"[8] Mehta is correct—when it began on January 6, 2013 in London, SA was an instant success. Just nine months after their launch, SA boasted about its growth saying, "The 3,000 percent growth rate might make this non-religious Assembly the fastest growing church in the world."[9] Due to the rapid growth, SA recognized that it needed to transition away from its organic model to ensure continued success.

---

7. These ideals—subjectivity and deconstructionism—tend to be associated with postmodernity. For a more in-depth look at postmodernity, see Ciochina, "Communicating Postmodernity," 932–40. Nevertheless, subjectivity and deconstructionism span eras and there are not strict lines that divide postmodernity from modernity. See Swidler, "Postmodernity—or Expanding Modernity," 1–4. Additionally, Sanja Ivic and Dragan D. Lakicevic argue that Europeans, SA's original context, cannot identify with either modernity or postmodernity but should be viewed as existing in a "dynamic and shifting concept of identity." See Ivic and Lakicevic, "European Identity: Between Modernity and Postmodernity," 395–407.

8. Mehta, "The Sunday Assembly Isn't an Atheist Megachurch, No Matter What the Media Says."

9. Engelhart, "Atheism Starts Its Megachurch."

One of the first changes for SA was its connection to atheism. Explaining the change, Pippa Evans said, "'Atheist Church' as a phrase has been good to us. It has got us publicity. But the term 'atheist' does hold negative connotations...We hope that eventually we will be able to drop it all together and simply be known as the 100%-celebration-of-life-party-fun-times-place-of-friendship-and-love-community-support-awesome Church."[10] SA was not restricted to the atheist community; rather, SA had a vision for including everyone, regardless of beliefs: "The Sunday Assembly denies any backsliding or apostasy, and argues that, by not focusing on 'the atheist community', it is merely trying to be as inclusive as possible."[11] SA's inclusivity, however, was not without critics.

After expanding into the U.S., SA experienced its first significant conflict: "Three former members of the New York franchise broke away and formed a group called 'Godless Revival,' complaining about the institutionalization of what they had assumed would be nothing more than a parody church."[12] Lee Moore, one of the original board members for the New York community, led the split. Moore believed that Jones and Evans improperly superseded the board's majority decision concerning the direction of the community.[13] Moore furthered his complaint by suggesting that Jones and Evans were only expanding SA in order to "get rich." As a result, Moore, and others, started 'The Godless Revival,' explaining, "We have no centralized leadership or rules to follow, we are not trying to get a paycheck out of it. The sole goal is to promote a godless celebration of life."[14] At the time of the schism, many popular news outlets like CNN, Huffington Post, and NPR reported on the story; hoping to remove the negativity from the split, Mehta said, "You rarely see headlines saying there's a 'schism' in the Christian community just because a university has both a Campus Crusade for Christ and InterVarsity Christian Fellowship group...I don't see the difference here—if anything, it's at a massively smaller scale."[15] In other words, SA, while try-

---

10. Evans, "How to Build an Atheist Church: Day 4, Atheist Church."

11. Watts, "The Church of Self-Worship." Engelhart explained SA as "a kind of atheist version of Unitarian Universalism: irreligious, but still eager to include everyone." Engelhart, "After a Schism."

12. Ibid.

13. Moore said, "A minority of organizers wished to make the event not a show but an actual church service and agreed with Jones about cutting out the word Atheist, not having speakers from the Atheist community, avoiding having an Atheist audience, and moving the show out of a bar setting to a more formal church-like setting." Moore, "Sunday Assembly Has a Problem with Atheism."

14. Ibid.

15. Clark, "Atheist Sunday Assembly Sees 'Church' Split Due to Ideological Differences."

ing to correct organized religions' failures, remained susceptible to internal division and conflict.

Due to both the schism and rapid growth, SA established concrete parameters for the organization—the organic, loosely controlled community needed to adjust to avoid additional threats. Thus, SA established a "Sunday Assembly Everywhere" accreditation process for new SA chapter leaders, which includes a three to six month peer review process before a group or leader can be eligible for "Sunday Assembly" status. This training also provides the new chapter leaders "the right to use all the Sunday Assembly materials, logos, positive vibes and good will."[16] Additionally, on April 28, 2014, SA held its first "General Assembly" in order to "set up a system of church-like management, an event that the group's organizers acknowledge will be compared to the Church of England's General Synod."[17] At the time, SA predicted that it would have 100 communities on five continents by the end of the year.[18]

After its launch and initial growth, SA has restructured and transitioned into a more traditional church/business model. One significant change for SA is that co-founder Pippa Evans is no longer with SA; at the same time, Sanderson Jones's role has expanded to "Co-founder and CEO." Additionally, SA added three other full-time staff.[19] Since SA has multiple communities around the world, it is possible that there are many others who are paid staff in local expressions. Hence, SA's structure is hierarchical and traditional. That is noteworthy because when SA began, SA touted itself as more authentic than religious communities because it was "volunteer led."[20]

Another way SA originally differentiated itself from religious communities concerned money. Unlike traditional churches, SA would not insist on financial support. Yet, in his blog post communicating SA's vision, Jones made a different plea. Softening the blow with humor, Jones began his conversation on money by saying, "We didn't want people to think we were like those televangelists with big hair and bigger grins."[21] He goes on, however, to ask for those in the community to give something like a tithe, even

---

16. Engelhart, "After a Schism." SA's "Launch System" has since changed; see Sanderson Jones, "Changes to the Launch System: Learning, Changing, Growing."

17. Addley, "Atheist Sunday Assembly."

18. Ibid.

19. Liz Slade (COO), Jacqueline Gunn (Chief Community Creator), and Ruth Moir (Community Creator-London).

20. Sunday Assembly, "About." It is also worth noting that SA's leadership fits the "nones" demographic.

21. Jones, "Our Vision."

referencing "tithing" specifically.[22] Jones concludes saying one's checkbook should reflect what one values.

From the beginning, this tension between rejecting traditional religion while simultaneously needing the model for funding has existed. Reporter Katie Engelhart described her experience attending one Sunday Assembly in 2014 saying, "Instead of receiving self-improvement nudges or engaging in conversation with strangers, I watched the founders fret (a lot) over technical glitches with the web streaming, talk about how hard they had worked to pull the service off, and try to sell me on Sunday Assembly swag."[23] Money, regardless of how badly one wants to ignore it, is important for any organization—particularly a non-profit.[24]

Nevertheless, SA has continued to flourish, although not to the degree its founders believed it would. SA's leadership predicted that it would have over 100 "assemblies" by the end of 2014.[25] By 2016, they had not reached that number, though SA's success is impressive: approximately 90 communities in 70 cities in 11 countries. Nonetheless, Hemant Mehta, arguing that SA is not a mega-church, says that the vast majority of SA communities have twenty or fewer people.[26] And while SA received extensive media coverage initially, there have been no popular articles written about SA since 2014. As all organizations must do, SA is transitioning from startup to established entity.

WHAT CONTRIBUTES TO SA'S SUCCESS?

Though it started as an atheist community, SA exists to provide space and relationships for people of all backgrounds. Indeed, SA openly rejected the title of "Atheist Church." For this essay's purposes, investigating who

---

22. Jones says, "This is partly because I had never really gone to a fun congregation and understood that they rely 100% on donations from attendees." Ibid.

23. Engelhart, "After a Schism."

24. Engelhart writes, "There's more to come: In October, the Sunday Assembly (SA) will launch a crowd funded indiegogo campaign, with the ambitious goal of raising $793,000. This will be followed by a second wave of [Sunday Assembly] openings. The effort reads as part quixotic hipster start-up, part Southern megachurch." Engelhart, "Atheism Starts Its Megachurch." She goes on, "Eventually, Jones and Evans hope their Assemblies will offer more church-like services: Sunday school, weddings, funerals." Interestingly, the indiegogo page closed after raising 33,668 pounds—the goal was 500,000 pounds (7%). For the Indiegogo page, see Jones, "Godless Congregations for All."

25. Addley, "Atheist Sunday Assembly."

26. Mehta, "Atheist Megachurch?"

comprises SA is beneficial and necessary: to whom does SA appeal? SA's model, while desiring to include people from any and all demographics, has primarily attracted "nones." Though that is perhaps an obvious discovery, it is valuable to specifically identify it so that additional investigations into the "nones'" desires and motivations can be conducted.

SA'S HISTORY AND "NONES"

The decline of Christianity in Europe, and particularly England, has created space for a community like SA to exist. According to the Pew Research Center (PRC), the Christian population in Europe will diminish by close to 100 million people by 2050[27]; however, during that same period the religiously "unaffiliated"—or "nones"—will grow by over 22 million people, meaning nearly a quarter of the population will identify as "nones."[28] Alain De Botton, author of *Religion for Atheists*,[29] discussed this religious transition saying, "A survey published in the U.K. in January (2012) predicted that within 20 years, the majority of the British population will define themselves as having no religion. In the British isles, religion has become something of a sideshow, even a joke."[30] As noted earlier, the following year, on January 6, 2013, English comedians Sanderson Jones and Pippa Evans started SA, a church for the non-religious. It seems appropriate that comedians would make use of the "joke" of religion in England!

Since the 1960s, scholars have referred to the segment of the population that does not affirm any particular religious tradition as "nones."[31] Kimberly Winston said in 2012 that "nones" then totaled 46 million people.[32] In 2014, PRC found that 22.8% of the population of the USA was religiously unaffiliated,[33] meaning roughly 56 million Americans were considered "nones" then. If those numbers are an accurate representation of growth, "nones", in 2016, approached 70 million.

While they are religiously unaffiliated, "nones" are not opposed to God or other traditional religious ideas; as Chaeyoon Lim et al. explain, "Using

---

27. Pew Research Center, "Europe Projected to Retain its Christian Majority."

28. The only other group that is projected to grow more than the "nones" in Europe is Islam; however, Muslims are only projected to make up slightly over 10% of the population.

29. Botton, *Religion for Atheists*.

30. Botton, "The Wisdom of Faith."

31. Lugo, director, "'Nones' on the Rise," 7.

32. Winston, "The Rise of the 'nones,'" 14.

33. This was up from 16.1% in 2007.

data from three separate panel data sets, we found that religious 'nones' comprise two distinct groups: one whose members consistently claim no religious preference and the other whose members do so in one wave but choose something else at another time, despite that they did not appear to have experienced significant religious changes between the waves."[34] Nancy Ammerman offers an explanation for why this is happening, stating, "In Europe and in the United States, both scholarly and popular perceptions seem to tell a story of declining 'religion' and growing 'spirituality'—a zero-sum movement from one to the other. What is declining in this picture is 'religion,' usually assumed to be organized, traditional, and communal, while 'spirituality' is often described as improvised and individual."[35] Thus, while "religion" might be declining, "spirituality," which often includes God, appears to be increasing.

According to PRC, over 60% of "nones" claim belief in God.[36] It is worth noting that this percentage is down from 70% in 2007. Although this clearly suggests diminishing belief as PRC acknowledges, some of the difference *could* be etymological.[37] The question PRC posed appears to ask about the "certainty" of God. The concept of "certainty" has likely changed or at least been challenged in recent years causing people to be less willing to use it in any context. While that theory would need further investigation to substantiate, PRC's research at the very least *suggests* its validity by stating that belief in God has dropped at a similar rate for mainline Protestants, Catholics, and Orthodox Christians as well.[38] Nevertheless, according to Michael Hout and Claude S. Fischer's research, the "beliefs, practices, attitudes, and origins of persons who have no religious preferences have shown the majority to be 'unchurched believers'—only a minority appear to be 'atheist,' 'agnostic,' or 'skeptical.'"[39] They add that many "nones" are frustrated with church leadership and not with God. They conclude by averring, "The most distinct fact about people with no religious preference is their lack of participation in

---

34. Lim et al., "Secular and Liminal," 613.

35. Ammerman, "Spiritual but not Religious?," 259.

36. Pew Research, "U.S. Public Becoming Less Religious," 47.

37. Pew noted that some argue that changes are the result of terminological changes and not actual belief. In other words, U.S. religion could be identical to 2007 except cultural understanding of words has changed. Ibid., 25.

38. Mainline Protestants (down from 73% in 2007 to 66%); Catholics (from 72% to 64%); and Orthodox Christians (from 71% to 61%). Ibid., 47.

39. Hout and Fischer, "Why More Americans Have no Religious Preferences," 178.

organized religion."[40] In other words, "nones" and disbelief are not necessarily synonymous.[41]

Other demographics like age, socioeconomics, marital status, politics, and race are also important for identifying "nones." According to PRC, the majority (72%) of "nones" are under the age of 50, with 35% coming from the 18 to 29 demographic.[42] Socioeconomically, "nones" earn similar salaries and are slightly more educated than the general population (31% to 28%).[43] Concerning marriage, "nones" are less likely to marry than their religious counterpart (39% to 51%),[44] though PRC admits that this statistic is potentially misleading since "nones" come from a younger demographic. It is possible that the long-term data will show that "nones" are as likely to marry as religious Americans. Likely also due to age, "nones" tend to be slightly more liberal than the general population (54%).[45] A statistic that is less equivocal, though, is race. The majority of "nones" in the U.S. are non-Hispanic whites (71%).[46] One additional factor appears to be location—"nones" are more prevalent in urban areas,[47] particularly in Seattle, San Francisco, and Boston.[48] Thus, "nones" tend to be young, middle-class, single, liberal, urban, and white.

During SA's enormous growth in its first several months of existence, SA co-founder Jones declared that SA was preparing to launch new SA

40. Ibid., 174.

41. Baker and Smith suggest that atheists are different in that they typically are oppositional toward religion, "Atheists are the most vehemently nonreligious . . . atheists are sharply opposed to religion in the public sphere." See Baker and Smith, "None Too Simple: Examining Issues of Religious Nonbelief and Nonbelonging in the United States," 731.

42. Pew Research Center, "'Nones' on the Rise," 33.

43. Ibid., 35. Also see Fry and Kochhar, "America's Wealth Gap."

44. Pew Research Center, "'Nones' on the Rise," 39.

45. Pew Research Center, "U.S. Public Becoming Less Religious," 99.

46. Pew Research Center, "'Nones' on the Rise," 36.

47. Southern cities are less likely to fit into this claim—particularly Dallas, Houston, Atlanta, and Nashville.

48. Lipka, "Major U.S. Metropolitan Areas Differ in their Religious Profiles"; and Piacenza and Jones, "The Top Two Religious Groups that Dominate American Cities." Additionally, there are many factors that have caused this particular population to become "nones." Providing one theory, Neil Pembroke suggests technology has led to a larger displacement that encompasses religion: "Here we have been given a rather difficult task, as the technology revolution has resulted in general sense of uprootedness." Pembroke, "John Stott and Erik Erikson on the Problem of Modernity," 239. Furthermore, according to Allen B. Downey's research, Internet usage is linked to religious affiliation—the more time one spends on the Internet, the less likely one is to affiliate religiously. Downey, "Religious Affiliation, Education and Internet Use," 1–12.

expressions in "non-Western" countries—meaning countries that do not fit into the "nones" demographic—like Kenya, Malaysia, and Brazil.[49] Up to this point, however, SA has only experienced success in more "Western" contexts: North America, Western Europe, South Africa, Australia, and New Zealand.[50] The two most receptive areas of the world, at least numerically, are the U.S. and the UK. Of the roughly 90 SA communities, twenty-five are in the UK and forty-four in the United States.[51] Furthermore, in these "Western" contexts, SA is found in urban centers—SA even describes itself as "a secular urban oasis."[52]

Sanderson Jones explained SA's appeal, saying, "I don't expect much objection from religious communities. They are happy for us to use their church model. I think it's more aggressive atheists who will have an issue with it."[53] In other words, SA's congregation is not filled with atheists—which accords with the "nones" demographics. SA's organizational split in New York City also expresses SA's desire to extend beyond the atheist community.

Based on media reports and posted photos on SA's website, it appears that SA's community is comprised primarily of "nones." Adam Watts, a reporter observing one of SA's gatherings, described the participants as "mostly young, white and hip—there is a lot of facial hair among the men, and everyone seems to be wearing quirky spectacles and vintage [clothing]."[54] The photos on SA's website affirm Watts report: the majority of the people are young, white, and trendy.

SA appears to be a community comprised of "nones" or the un-churched and de-churched. It is primarily white, young, and urban. Additionally, with SA's stated commitment of social justice, SA appears to also attract a more liberal crowd.

---

49. Addley, "Atheist Sunday Assembly," 7.

50. As of this essay, SA has only produced assemblies in the "West": Europe, North America, Australia, New Zealand, and South Africa. The numbers breakdown: 36 in Europe (25 in UK and all in western Europe), 3 in Canada and 44 in USA, 6 in Australia, 1 in New Zealand, and 1 in South Africa (Cape Town).

51. Sunday Assembly, "Global Assembly List."

52. Engelhart, "After a Schism."

53. Engelhart, "Atheism Starts Its Megachurch."

54. Watts. Furthermore, the community composition is not surprising: "[According to recent surveys], younger people, men, whites, political liberals, biblical skeptics, the highly educated, and those raised in nonreligious homes are more likely to identify as nonreligious in adulthood." Vargas, "Retrospective Accounts of Religious Disaffiliation in the United States: Stressors, Skepticism, and Political Factor," 201.

Part 3: The Emerging Church and Millennials

THEOLOGICAL INVESTIGATION

Since "nones" oppose traditional religion and not necessarily God or spirituality, investigating SA's theological position is relevant. SA clearly rejects theological language and restrictive categories; nonetheless, SA's values and ideals align well with versions of Christian theology—particularly through theologians like Friedrich Schleiermacher (feeling), Karl Rahner (freedom), and Paul Tillich (estrangement). While these theologians represent a more "liberal" expression of Christianity, they remain important voices in the tradition. Moreover, their interpretation of Christianity provides a rich corollary between Christianity and SA. Lastly, since SA has been successful in Western contexts, primarily those that have historically been Christian, it is unsurprising that SA's theological connection has attracted "nones" that still believe in God but no longer in the church.

Feeling and Schleiermacher

SA's organizational model—radical inclusion of the whole person[55]—is not a contemporary phenomenon. Though one could find other similar movements in history, Romanticism, which took place in the late eighteenth and early nineteenth centuries, is one of the clearest examples.[56] Romanticism valued "the individual as a whole—not merely the mind, but also the body; not only the reason, but also the emotions, the passions and, crucially, the imagination."[57] Friedrich Schleiermacher, writing and ministering in this era, hoped to provide the Romantic community with meaning through his work, *On Religion*. In response to Kantian philosophy, Schleiermacher emphasized the role of feeling—as opposed to knowing or doing—in his theology. Unfortunately, many have misunderstood Schleiermacher's "feeling" as subjective, interior emotion, which not only misrepresents Schleiermacher but also his audience. Schleiermacher's statement that religion is "neither thinking nor action, but intuition and feeling" is associated with the "intuition of the universe" that each person "must be conscious of," although each person's feeling is "only a part of the whole."[58] By refusing to constrain

---

55. See Jones, "How to Sum Up a Conference Called Wonder?"

56. Muers and Higton, *Modern Theology*, 62.

57. Ibid., 62. Julia A. Lamm adds, "While emotions and sentiments were important to the Romantics, the Romantics genius was the one who would draw back from the immediacy of emotion and experience into a contemplative moment, reflect on those emotions and sentiments, and then give thoughtful expression to them, shaping them into a new work of art." Lamm, *Schleiermacher*, 13.

58. Schleiermacher, *On Religion*, 22–27.

religion to what one does or intellectualizes, Schleiermacher argues for a different understanding of religion: feeling.

Similarly, SA wants to remove the requirements found in many religions, such as doctrines and divinity; nevertheless, SA values the religious form and model. As Ian Dodd, founder of a SA chapter, said, "The church model has worked really well for a couple of thousand years. What we're trying to do is hold on to the bath water while throwing out the baby Jesus."[59] In other words, SA believes there is something about gathering together, singing, listening to a speaker, and communing with others that has a deeper value, which transcends Christianity and religion as a whole.

Schleiermacher's "feeling/intuition" includes that same notion. Discussing the universality of intuition, Schleiermacher says, "The basic intuition of every positive religion is eternal in itself because it is a supplementary part of the infinite reality...[thus] innumerable forms of religion are possible."[60] This deeper-than-Christianity feeling/intuition is what SA affirms and pursues. As Jones proclaimed at one of their inaugural gatherings, "If you leave here feeling a little more whizzy about life . . . then that would be great."[61] SA believes that by "living better, helping often, and wondering more," people can discover the universal feeling of goodness and life. And while it claims to be "non-religious," Schleiermacher would say SA evokes the very essence of religion.

Freedom and Rahner

One of SA's foundational commitments is freedom: "We won't tell you how to live, but we will try to help you do it as well as you can."[62] Rahner appears to affirm that notion when saying, "In real freedom the subject always intends himself, understands and posits himself. Ultimately he does not do *something*, but does *himself* . . . Freedom is the capacity of the one subject to decide about himself in his single totality."[63] On the surface, both SA and Rahner seem to argue for individual freedom that expresses itself through independence. For SA, no one should be able to tell another how she or he should live. As a community, SA promotes individual beliefs and lives, and, according to this value, exists to support people in their quest for individual meaning.

59. Engelhart, "Atheism Starts a Megachurch."
60. Schleiermacher, *On Religion*, 122–23.
61. Kamer, "Atheist Church First Sunday Assembly."
62. Sunday Assembly, "About."
63. Rahner, *Foundations of Christian Faith*, 95.

Rahner, however, did not reduce freedom to individuality; instead, he located it within community: "For whenever I act freely as a subject, I always act into an objective world, I always, as it were, leave my freedom and enter into the necessities of this world."[64] For Rahner, the self is not independent because it interacts with the world—the self necessarily concedes freedom, in an individualist sense, in order to exist within a diverse world. Moreover, Rahner values the "other" because it is through the other that one encounters God.[65] Therefore, God and freedom are not competing but instead intertwined—to be free is to encounter God in all things.[66]

Though refusing to acknowledge any idea of encountering God, SA believes, like Rahner, in community. On March 10, 2016, Jones wrote a blog post entitled "Our Vision," which outlined SA's purpose and goals. Jones says the "first principle" for SA is to help everyone, not just those in the SA community, live as fully as possible.[67] Jones adds that his SA community in England has grown and they expect to move to two Sunday morning services saying, "Bring your hangovers to Sunday Assembly!" Jones also spends significant time in his blog post promoting SA's small groups. SA did a social impact study and determined that interacting with a community improves life satisfaction and happiness. In fact, the study stated that the most important factors to "reduce your chances of dying" are social integration, strong relationships, and social support. As a result, SA launched an 8-week "Life Course" based on Martin Seligman's P.E.R.M.A. psychological model along with the meeting structure of the Alpha Course.[68] On a very basic level, SA and Rahner both support freedom through community.[69]

---

64. Ibid., 97.

65. For Rahner, through the "other" is how we all encounter God: "In this sense we encounter God in a radical way everywhere as a question to our freedom, we encounter him unexpressed, unthematic, unobjectified and unspoken in all of the things of the world, and therefore and especially in our neighbor." Ibid., 98–99.

66. Ibid., 105.

67. Jones, "Sunday Assembly London: Our Vision."

68. For more on P.E.R.M.A., see Seligman, *Flourish*; for Alpha, see Alpha, "About."

69. Another important aspect of freedom for both Rahner and SA, although not as relevant for the current discussion, is love. For Rahner, confessional salvation comes through freely expressing love: "But wherever a free and lonely act of decision has taken place in absolute obedience to a higher law, or in a radical affirmation of love for another person, something eternal has taken place." Rahner, 439. SA takes a similar stance: "[Sunday Assembly] has a mission. . .with your involvement. The Sunday Assembly will make the world a better place." Sunday Assembly, "About," Jones adds, "We are a movement that is set to unleash the pent up capacity for love and wonder and community that lies latent in towns, cities and countries across the world. Jones, "How to Sum Up a Conference Called Wonder?" While it does not believe in a "higher law," at least not in a religious sense, SA definitely believes love has power to bring about

Estrangement and Tillich

The concept of community suggests that SA, like Paul Tillich, believes estrangement is a significant problem in the world. SA argues that people feel estranged because they do not have a community of support. Moreover, SA states that people should invest in "the one life we know we have."[70] In other words, one can become estranged from oneself by focusing on an "afterlife" that is not guaranteed. Though not identical, both SA and Tillich want to alleviate estrangement.

With its statement about fully living "the one life we know we have," SA is acknowledging the reality of finitude. Regardless of what any other individual or religious community might say, every person is limited to a relatively short amount of time on earth.[71] For Tillich, estrangement is connected with finitude: "Man knows that he is finite, that he is excluded from an infinity which nevertheless belongs to him. He is aware of his potential infinity while being aware of his actual finitude."[72] SA, in many ways, is attempting to offer an alternative narrative to Tillich's—rather than being concerned with infinite existence, one should fully invest in the present.[73]

While this initial reflection appears to put SA and Tillich at odds, further investigation reveals philosophical concord—both SA and Tillich believe in a kind of healing and "salvation." Tillich says, "With respect to both the original meaning of salvation and our present situation, it may be adequate to interpret salvation as 'healing.'"[74] Salvation, for Tillich, is a kind of confession of being. According to Tillich, "God does not exist. [God] is being-itself beyond essence and existence."[75] If one accepts Tillich's project, the idea of "a" God that exists somewhere can be abandoned and replaced by "being-itself." SA's ideology, which affirms connecting with the depths of full living, fits within Tillich's system. Like Tillich, SA exists to provide the world with healing: "Since our launch in 2013 we have launched 70 communities worldwide and now Sunday Assembly is being commissioned as

positive change in the world.

70. Sunday Assembly, "About."

71. Certainly there are other philosophies, particularly East Asian, which would challenge that statement; nevertheless, for this paper's sake, I will not challenge the notion of finitude in the way SA and Tillich define it.

72. Tillich, *Systematic Theology*, vol. 1, 206.

73. SA connects being present with Buddhist meditation, which they apparently do not view as a problematic religion.

74. Tillich, *Systematic Theology*, vol. 2, 166.

75. Tillich, *Systematic Theology*, vol. 1, 205.

a community-building, health-promoting tool."[76] Although it might refute the terminology, SA believes in salvation and healing through its community and ideology.

Additionally, like Tillich, SA also rejects the notion that full living exists in a God that exists somewhere; instead, SA calls people toward the deeper life found in community. In this way, individuals can access true being-itself. Tillich agrees saying, "This possibility is excluded from the Spiritual Community because religion in the narrower sense is excluded from it. On the other hand, the unity of religion and morals expresses itself in the character of morals in the Spiritual Community."[77] Tillich's utilization of the word "Spiritual" fits well considering "nones," which make-up the vast majority of SA's community, often identify as spiritual but not religious. There appears to be a clear connection between SA's ideology and Tillich's theology.

WHAT CAN BE LEARNED?

SA's ideology shares aspects of Schleiermacher, Rahner, and Tillich's theologies. All three desire, like SA, to move people from estrangement to meaning and life. Likewise, they all identify healing and salvation through, on some level, community. Nevertheless, there is a major divide between SA's ideology and Schleiermacher, Rahner, and Tillich's theology: motivation. I begin this section, therefore, by exploring potential problems with SA's philosophy based on Schleiermacher, Rahner, and Tillich's thought. Second, while it has problems, mostly because there is no perfect structure, SA's model can be integrated into the Emerging Church (EC), perhaps more easily than other religious communities, in order to better communicate to "nones." Lastly, I propose three areas for the EC to consider moving forward based on SA's success: (1) recognition that tradition, organization, and format are not the church's problem, (2) that there is important concord between SA and EC, and (3) that the EC, as well as other communities, can better communicate to the "nones" by implementing two SA values—constant wonder and humor.

---

76. Jones, "Hiring: Business Development Manager."
77. Tillich, *Systematic Theology*, vol. 3, 159.

Problems?

Motivation, particularly as it related to community involvement, is convoluted and intricate; however, SA has a vastly different approach than Schleiermacher, Rahner, and Tillich concerning motivation. For SA, one's desire for a full life is the end in itself. SA emphasizes this point saying, "*We are obsessed with trying to help you—yes, YOU!—to live your life as fully as possible.*"[78] This vision has been responsible for substantial growth; yet, as I discuss below, that same vision does not support long-term growth or possibly even sustainability.

Rahner, like SA, says estrangement is a "journey into the future [with] the constant effort to lessen the distance between what he is and what he should be and wants to be."[79] SA wants to help each person be whatever she or he desires. That focus, however, inevitably reduces the world to the self, disallowing personal desire to transition into purpose and meaning. While it promotes a vision of community, in actuality SA appears to exist as a collection of individuals. Consequently, each individual participates in the community for the way it benefits the self. The difficult hurdle, then, is getting people to commit to serving, financially supporting, and ultimately sacrificing the self for the community.

Rahner, alternatively, did not end by promoting a better self at all cost; instead, he says, "Love for everything must always become concrete in the love of a concrete individual. Consequently, in the single human race the God-Man made possible the absoluteness of the love for a concrete individual."[80] For Rahner, Jesus is the model of how love truly works: one moves from love of self to love of a "concrete" other. Tillich explains what occurs when this does not happen:

> The destructive character of existential insecurity and doubt is manifest in the way man tries to escape despair. He tries to make absolute a finite security or a finite certainty. The threat of a breakdown leads to the establishment of defenses, some of which are brutal, some fanatical, some dishonest, and all insufficient and destructive; for there is no security and certainty within finitude.[81]

Like Rahner, Tillich argues that one must move past love for self and the world, ultimately accepting Jesus' mission of loving others or the

---

78. Emphasis original; see Jones, "Sunday Assembly London: Our Vision."
79. Rahner, *Foundations of Christian Faith*, 297.
80. Ibid., 296.
81. Tillich, *Systematic Theology Vol 2*, 73.

"blessedness of the divine life."[82] Schleiermacher suggests something similar saying that ultimately everyone hungers for something greater than the self.[83]

The challenge for SA is moving people from self-focus to self-sacrifice for the sake of the community and world. However, with SA's basic premise—helping each individual have the best life possible—it is difficult to explain why participants should give up their individual benefits for the sake of helping *someone else* find her or his individual benefits. According to Tillich, true peace and life only comes in the collective: "But in this surrender the individual is accepted not by any other individual but only by that to which they have all surrendered their potential solitude, that is, the spirit of the collective."[84] Can SA create a community where *all* participants recognize the need and value of surrender when the reason they initially joined was for their individual lives to be full? Though challenging, I think, with the right commitment from the leaders, it is possible; however, it would take significant time and effort to communicate how self-surrender for others *is how one fully lives*—especially when the only guaranteed life a person has is short and is already influenced by similar messages in religion, the very thing SA is supposedly not.[85]

What's not the Problem?

SA suggests that "nones" are not leaving the church because the church is outdated in its expression. Indeed, according to Barna, only 8% of millennials who claim to "not value participating in a church community" cite feeling like the church is out of date.[86] The church expression is not the problem; rather, millennials claim that the main reason they do not attend church is because they find God in other places (39%).

82. Ibid., 48.
83. Schleiermacher, *On Religion*, 23.
84. Tillich, *Systematic Theology*, vol. 2, 72.
85. Thomas Hobbes suggests similar things as Tillich and Rahner: "From this equality of ability, ariseth equality of hope in the attaining of our ends. And therefore if any two men desire the same thing, which nevertheless they cannot both enjoy, they become enemies; and in the way to their end, which is principally their own conservation, and sometimes their delectation only, endeavor to destroy, or subdue one another. . .Again, men have no pleasure, but on the contrary a great deal of grief, in keeping company, where there is no power able to over-awe them all." In other words, what is the "great" good worth joining? Hobbes, *Leviathan: Or the Matter, Forme and Power of a Commonwealth, Ecclasitcall and Civil*, 81.
86. Barna, "What Millennials Want When They Visit Church."

The church expression appears quite attractive to "nones." As SA has shown, people desire to come together (on a Sunday morning no less) to sing, give of their time and resources, and listen to someone share about how to live fully. Whether it is cultural or psychological, humans often gravitate toward communities that are committed to bringing about positive change in the world. Thus, the notion that a church must reformat, rebrand, or become a more relevant Sunday experience—filled with lighting, set designs, and free coffee—is not necessarily true or even helpful. In other words, a church can include these things and many others, but they should do so as values in themselves and not a means to reach "nones." SA has demonstrated that the church's expression is not the problem.

Concord and Response

The Emerging Church (EC) has been an identifiable community for nearly twenty years. Led by Brian McLaren, among others, the EC has experienced significant growth as well as controversy. The reasons for both appear to be found in the EC's core values: relativism, inclusivism, mission, and discussion.[87] Relativism often has a negative connotation within Christianity because it appears to reduce God's truth; however, similar to what SA has done with the "unknowability" of what happens after death,[88] the EC acknowledges human limitation. For the EC, relativism does not necessarily connote the absence of truth. Rather,, relativism embraces uncertainty while refusing to assume that finite humans can do more than simply pursue knowing God. Similarly, inclusivism attempts to reconcile Jesus' death and resurrection, which is believed to bring life and freedom from sin and death, with the many world religions.[89] Schleiermacher offers important insight to this point saying, "The religion of religions cannot gather enough material for the truest aspect of its innermost intuition, and just as nothing is more irreligious than to demand uniformity in humanity generally, so nothing is

---

87. See Burge and Djupe, "Emergent Church Practices in America"; for similar evaluations, see Keuss, "The Emergent Church and Neo-correlational Theology"; Hawtrey and Lunn, "The Emergent Church, Socio-Economics and Christian Mission"; and Burge and Djupe, "Truly Inclusive or Uniformly Liberal?"

88. SA emphatically states that their community "is 100% celebration of [this] life" because "we are born from nothing and go to nothing. Let's enjoy it together. Sunday Assembly, "About."

89. I recognize that terms like "religion" and even "world religion" are problematic. See Masuzawa, *The Invention of World Religions*.

more unchristian than to seek uniformity in religion."[90] Jesus opened grace to all, meaning a single expression is necessarily insufficient.

With this immense grace comes a new form of mission and discussion. For the EC and SA, mission and discussion are social in nature. Instead of mission being about presenting a monologue to an "unbeliever" about her or his destiny without Jesus, mission is about ecological and social justice, which means having honest dialogues with others—allowing the other to change the self. It is through mutually beneficial dialogue , the EC and SA maintain, that true change can occur.

While there are important areas of concord, the EC can also learn from how SA has used both wonder and humor. It is important, however, to state that these are not strategies for numeric growth. As SA has shown, while it has expanded, SA is not a mega-church. Including wonder and humor to the other EC values is still less effective at drawing large crowds than messages of prosperity and the threat of hell—though drawing large crowds is not necessarily a EC value anyway. Nevertheless, SA's success, particularly with "nones," indicates that wonder and humor are vital to a community hoping to effectively communicate to that population.

One of SA's taglines is, "A global community for wonder and good." Wonder is not simply an attractive word that is used to convince onlookers that SA is creative and artistic. SA is so committed to wonder that they host an annual conference titled, "Wonder." The conference is SA's General Assembly meaning, while there are likely conversations on business matters and other necessary organizational discussions, the goal, as they state, is "to unleash the pent up capacity for love and wonder and community that lies latent in towns, cities and countries across the world."[91] The conference is dedicated to sharing stories of life change, singing together, and listening to speakers talk about neurological and philosophical marvels. Wonder for SA is an end—it does not point to something else. In this way, wonder serves a similar function as God in the EC; hence, wonder does not relativize the world, in a negative sense, but unites it and gives it meaning.

The EC has been an important part of the Church because it has challenged potentially problematic epistemologies and doctrines. The result, however, tends to be a deconstructed gospel. Though certainty can be problematic, people still need something to adhere to. In the EC, wonder can function as that "thing." According to PRC, the percentage of people saying they feel a sense of wonder has grown in every major Christian

---

90. Schleiermacher, *On Religion*, 123.
91. Jones, "How to Sum Up a Conference Called Wonder?"

denomination over the past seven years.[92] Perhaps more importantly, however, is that this statistic is true for "nones" as well. Furthermore, PRC says "self-described atheists and agnostics are somewhat more likely than members of most religious groups to say they often experience such a sense of wonder."[93] The EC can allow wonder to undergird its deconstruction so its participants can still find support in its questioning.

One of the wonder-full things in life is humor, and SA has utilized it brilliantly. Granted, two comedians founded SA; nevertheless, humor is valuable within any community. Laughter transcends difference and removes barriers. According to PRC, "nones" are most frustrated by the church because they view the church as "focused too much on rules."[94] In other words, "nones" perceive the church to be rigid and stuck. The second leading reason millennials are leaving the church, according to Barna, is boredom.[95] Humor acknowledges the nuances of actual living. Life is not rigid and static—it is filled with mistakes, failure, and self-consciousness. Humor is filled with wonder: it soothes pain, reconstructs situations, invites, includes, and reinforces the hope that there is something good here.

CONCLUSION

SA presents the EC with an important model for communicating with and, more importantly, caring for the un-churched and de-churched. By including wonder and humor, the EC can provide support to its deconstruction while also laughing when things do not come together perfectly. People want to be invited into wonder and meaning without pandering. The EC is uniquely positioned to successfully include "nones" through its philosophy of relativism, inclusion, mission, and discussion. Furthermore, by allowing people to find a deeper meaning of wonder—connected to grace, forgiveness, and love—the EC can provide hope to the many who are searching.

---

92. Pew Research Center, "U.S. Public Becoming Less Religious," 168–69. The only community that did not experience growth was a subgroup within Restorationist, which was up overall, called "Restorationist in the mainline tradition."

93. Ibid., 89–90.

94. Ibid., 95.

95. Barna, "What Millennials Want When They Visit Church."

BIBLIOGRAPHY

Addley, Esther. "Atheist Sunday Assembly Prepares for First 'Synod' as Expansion Continues." *The Guardian*. Last modified April 28, 2014. http://www.theguardian.com/world/2014/apr/29/atheist-sunday-assembly-first-synod.

Alpha. "About." http://alpha.org/about/.

Ammerman, Nancy. "Spiritual but Not Religious? Beyond Binary Choices in the Study of Religion." *Journal for the Scientific Study of Religion* 52.2 (2013) 258–87.

Baker, Joseph O. and Buster G. Smith. "None Too Simple: Examining Issues of Religious Nonbelief and Nonbelonging in the United States." *Journal for the Scientific Study of Religion* 48.4 (2009) 719–33.

Barco, Mandalit Del. "Sunday Assembly: A Church for the Godless Picks Up Steam." *National Public Radio*. Last modified January 7, 2014. http://www.youtube.com/watch?v=7eF8x2wwLkM.

Barna. "What Millennials Want When They Visit Church." *Millennials & Generations*. Last modified March 4, 2015. https://www.barna.org/barna-update/millennials/711-what-millennials-want-when-they-visit-church#.V5NusleeOf5.

Botton, Alain De. *Religion for Atheists: A Non-believers Guide to the Uses of Religion*. New York: Pantheon, 2012.

———. "The Wisdom of Faith: What Religion Can Teach Us." *National Public Radio*. Last Modified March 16, 2012. http://www.npr.org/2012/03/16/148599023/the-wisdom-of-faith-what-religion-can-teach-us.

Burge, Ryan P., and Paul A. Djupe. "Emergent Church Practices in America: Inclusion and Deliberation in American Congregations." *Religious Research Association* 57 (2014) 1–23.

———. "Truly Inclusive or Uniformly Liberal? An Analysis of the Politics of the Emerging Church." *Journal for the Scientific Study of Religion* 53.3 (2014) 636–51.

Ciochina, Raluca. "Communicating Postmodernity." *Contemporary Readings in Law and Social Justice* 5.2 (2013) 932–40.

Clark, Heather. "Atheist Sunday Assembly Sees 'Church' Split Due to Ideological Differences." *Christian News Network*. Last modified January 12, 2014. http://christiannews.net/2014/01/12/atheist-sunday-assembly-sees-church-split-due-to-ideological-differences/.

Downey, Allen B. "Religious Affiliation, Education and Internet Use." *Cornell University* (March 21, 2014) 1–12. http://arxiv.org/pdf/1403.5534v1.pdf.

Engelhart, Katie. "After a Schism, a Question: Can Atheist Churches Last?" *CNN*. Last modified January 4, 2014. http://religion.blogs.cnn.com/2014/01/04/after-a-schism-a-question-can-atheist-churches-last/.

———. "Atheism Starts Its Megachurch: Is It a Religion Now?" *Salon*. Last modified September 22, 2013. http://www.salon.com/2013/09/22/atheism_starts_its_megachurch_is_it_a_religion_now.

Evans, Pippa. "How to Build an Atheist Church: Day 4, Atheist Church—the Double Edged Sword." *New Humanist*. Last modified August 5, 2013. Accessed July 23, 2016. https://newhumanist.org.uk/articles/4256/day-4-atheist-church-the-double-edged-sword.

Fry, Richard, and Rakesh Kochhar. "America's Wealth Gap Between Middle-Income and Upper-Income Families is the Widest on Record." Pew Research Center:

Fact Tank. Last modified December 17, 2014. http://www.pewresearch.org/fact-tank/2014/12/17/wealth-gap-upper-middle-income/.

Hawtrey Kim, and John Lunn. "The Emergent Church, Socio-Economics and Christian Mission." *Transformation* 27.2 (2010) 65–74.

Hobbes, Thomas. *Leviathan: Or the Matter, Forme and Power of a Commonwealth, Ecclasitcalland Civil*, edited by Mil Oakeshott. Oxford: Blackwell, 1946.

Hout, Michael, and Claude S. Fischer. "Why More Americans Have No Religious Preferences: Politics and Generations." *American Sociological Review* 67 (2002) 165–90.

Ivic, Sanja, and Dragan D. Lakicevic. "European Identity: Between Modernity and Postmodernity." *The European Journal of Social Science Research* 24.4 (2011) 395–407.

Jones, Sanderson. "Changes to the Launch System: Learning, Changing, Growing." *Sunday Assembly Blog*. Last modified January 21, 2016. https://www.sundayassembly.com/blog/author/sanderson.

———. "Godless Congregations for All: The Sunday Assembly Global Platform." *Indiegogo*. Accessed August 12, 2016. https://www.indiegogo.com/projects/godless-congregations-for-all-the-sunday-assembly-global-platform#/.

———. "Hiring: Business Development Manager." *Sunday Assembly Blog*. Last modified January 21, 2016. https://www.sundayassembly.com/blog/author/sanderson.

———. "How to Sum Up a Conference Called Wonder?" *Sunday Assembly Blog*. Last modified June 4, 2015. https://www.sundayassembly.com/blog/author/sanderson.

———. "Sunday Assembly London: Our Vision." *Sunday Assembly Blog*. Last modified March 10, 2016. https://www.sundayassembly.com/blog/author/sanderson.

Kamer, Nimrod. "Atheist Church First Sunday Assembly: Don't Panic." YouTube video, 5:00, posted by Nimrod Kamer, January 16, 2013. http://www.youtube.com/watch?v=7eF8x2wwLkM.

Keuss, Jeff. "The Emergent Church and Neo-correlational Theology after Tillich, Schleiermacher and Browning." *Scottish Journal of Theology* 61 (2008) 450–61.

Lamm, Julia A. *Schleiermacher: Christmas Dialogue, The Second Speech, and Other Selections*. New York: Paulist, 2014.

Lim, Chaeyoon, Carol Ann MacGregor, and Robert D. Putnam. "Secular and Liminal: Discovering Heterogeneity Among Religious 'nones.'" *Journal for the Scientific Study of Religion* 49 (2010) 596–618.

Lipka, Michael. "Major U.S. Metropolitan Areas Differ in their Religious Profiles." Pew Research Center: Fact Tank. Last modified July 29, 2015. http://www.pewresearch.org/fact-tank/2015/07/29/major-u-s-metropolitan-areas-differ-in-their-religious-profiles/.

Lugo, Luis, director. "'nones' on the Rise: One-in-Five Adults Have No Religious Affiliation." *Pew Research Center* (October 9, 2012) 1–80.

Masuzawa, Tomoko. *The Invention of World Religions: Or, How European Universalism Was Preserved in the Language of Pluralism*. Chicago: University of Chicago Press, 2005.

Mehta, Hemant. "Atheist Megachurch? 9 Reasons Why the Sunday Assembly is NOT a Mega-Church." YouTube video, 9:39. November 19, 2013. https://www.youtube.com/watch?v=Zy-l14kCnX4.

———. "The Sunday Assembly Isn't an Atheist Megachurch, No Matter What the Media Says." *Patheos*. http://www.patheos.com/blogs/friendlyatheist/2013/11/11/

the-sunday-assembly-isnt-an-atheist-megachurch-no-matter-what-the-media-says/.

Moore, Lee. "Sunday Assembly Has a Problem with Atheism." *A News Reports.* October 23, 2013. http://anewsreports.com/?p=2810.

Muers, Rachel, and Mike Higton. *Modern Theology: A Critical Introduction.* New York: Routledge, 2012.

Neuman, Scott. "Millennials 'Talk to God,' but Fewer Rely on Religion, Survey Finds." *NPR.* April 11, 2014. http://www.npr.org/blogs/the-two-way/2014/04/11/301969264/millennials-talk-to-god-but-fewer-rely-on-religion-surveyfinds?sc=17&f=1001&utm_source=iosnewsapp&utm_medium=Email&utm_campaign=app.

———. "Young 'nones' Set to Transform the Political Landscape." *NPR.* Last modified October 12, 2012. http://www.npr.org/blogs/itsallpolitics/2012/10/09/162582670/young-"nones"-set-to-transform-the-political-landscape.

Pembroke, Neil. "John Stott and Erik Erikson on the Problem of Modernity: Applications for the Ministry of the Church." *Journal of Psychology & Theology* 18 (1990) 237–43.

Pew Research Center. "Europe Projected to Retain its Christian Majority, but Religious Minority will Grow." *Fact Tank.* Last modified April, 15, 2015. http://www.pewresearch.org/fact-tank/2015/04/15/europe-projected-to-retain-its-christian-majority-but-religious-minorities-will-grow/.

———. "U.S. Public Becoming Less Religious." *The Pew Forum on Religion and Public Life* (2015) 1–265.

Piacenza, Joanna, and Robert P. Jones. "The Top Two Religious Groups that Dominate American Cities." Public Religious Research Institute. Last modified August 3, 2015. http://www.prri.org/spotlight/the-top-two-religious-traditions-that-dominate-american-cities/#.VcTv9xNVhBc.

Rahner, Karl. *Foundations of Christian Faith: An Introduction to the Idea of Christianity.* New York: Seabury, 1978.

Rose, Matthew F. "Hobbes as Political Theologian." *Political Theology* 14 (2013) 5–31.

Schleiermacher, Friedrich. *On Religion: Speeches to Its Cultured Despisers.* Translated and edited by Richard Crouter. Cambridge Texts in the History of Philosophy. Cambridge: Cambridge University Press, 1996.

Seligman, Martin E. P. *Flourish: A Visionary New Understanding of Happiness and Well-being.* New York: Free Press, 2011.

Sunday Assembly. "About." http://sundayassembly.com/about/.

———. "Find Your Nearest Assembly." Community. http://sundayassembly.com/assemblies/.

———. "Global Assembly List." Community. http://www.sundayassembly.com/assemblies.

———. "Our Story." About. http://sundayassembly.com/story/.

Swidler, Leonard. "Postmodernity—or Expanding Modernity." *Journal of Ecumenical Studies* 46 (2011) 1–4.

Tillich, Paul. *Systematic Theology.* Vol. 1. Chicago: Chicago University Press, 1951.

———. *Systematic Theology.* Vol. 2. Chicago: Chicago University Press, 1957.

———. *Systematic Theology.* Vol. 3. Chicago: Chicago University Press, 1963.

Vargas, Nicolas. "Retrospective Accounts of Religious Disaffiliation in the United States: Stressors, Skepticism, and Political Factor." *Sociology of Religion* 73 (2012) 200–223.

Watts, Adam. "The Church of Self-Worship: Sunday Morning with the Atheists." *Spectators*. Last modified February 21, 2014. http://www.spectator.co.uk/features/9141372/so-tell-me-about-your-faith-journey-sunday-morning-at-the-atheist-church/.

Winston, Kimberly. "The Rise of the 'Nones.'" *Christian Century* 129.22 (2012) 14.

11

Race and the Emerging Church
A View from South Africa

RACHEL C. SCHNEIDER

Abstract

This chapter discusses the role of race in the Emerging Church Movement (ECM) in South Africa. Over the last decade, the ECM has sparked numerous religious and theological experiments intended to rethink the meaning of "church." Initially a response to conservative evangelicalism in the United States and stagnant Protestant mainline denominations in the United Kingdom, ECM leaders view social changes associated with late modernity, such as fluidity and pluralism, as having the potential to give birth to religious renewal in the West. In 2013–2014, I conducted ten months of fieldwork in Johannesburg, interviewing and observing progressive white South Africans involved in social justice and development work. I soon discovered that many of my interlocutors were part of networks with ties to the ECM. Moreover, they exhibited characteristics of Emerging Christianity, such as a yearning to embody an alternate religious subjectivity that could serve as a form of cultural critique of white, middle-class, suburban life. Drawing on archival data from digital media sources as well as my own data, this chapter first maps the rise of South Africa's "emerging conversation" (2003–2011). I then discuss how issues of race, colonialism, and white supremacy were addressed by those involved in the conversation. While scholars often note the predominantly white, Western character of the ECM, attention to how race (particularly whiteness) shapes Emerging Church practices and culture has not been addressed in any sustained way. The South African case raises a number of issues regarding race and power in the ECM, which I address in my final section. Ultimately, I argue that though the ECM appeals primarily to middle-class whites, this need not disqualify the ECM as a significant movement provided that it retains a critical orientation toward power. Participants must commit themselves to interrogating how white normativity influences ECM culture and practices.

INTRODUCTION

This chapter discusses the role of race in the Emerging Church Movement (ECM) in South Africa. As a scholar who works at the juncture of critical race studies and the anthropology of religion, I am interested in how white, Western subjectivity has influenced the spiritual and social ideals of the ECM and what happens when the ECM intersects with contexts that are not predominantly white. The Emerging Church Movement is a "discernable, transnational network" of Christians who, despite holding diverse beliefs and practices, share a desire to resist dominant religious, theological, and social narratives.[1] Over the last decade, the ECM has sparked a number of religious and theological experiments intended to rethink the meaning of "church" in response to late modern (or post-modern) conditions. Initially growing out of reactions to conservative evangelicalism in the United States and stagnant Protestant mainline denominations in the United Kingdom, ECM leaders view social changes associated with late modernity, such as fluidity and pluralism, as having the potential to give birth to religious renewal in the West.[2]

In 2013–2014, I conducted ten months of fieldwork in Johannesburg, interviewing and observing progressive white South Africans involved in social justice and community development work. My goal was to explore how religion and spirituality informed their ethics and visions of social change. I did not set out to study the ECM, but I soon discovered that many of my interlocutors were part of networks and organizations with ties to the ECM. They also exhibited characteristics of Emerging Christianity, such as a yearning to embody an alternate religious subjectivity that could serve as a form of religious and cultural critique of white, middle-class, suburban life.[3]

---

1. Martí and Ganiel, *The Deconstructed Church*, 8, 26.

2. Usually understood by commentators as Europe, North America, Australia, and New Zealand.

3. Bielo, *Emerging Evangelicals*, 2011, 5.

Drawing on archival data from digital media sources as well my own data, this paper begins by mapping the rise of South Africa's "emerging conversation" (2003–2011).[4] I then discuss how issues of race, colonialism, and white supremacy were addressed by those involved in the conversation. While scholars often note the predominantly white and Western character of the ECM,[5] attention to how race (particularly whiteness) shapes Emerging Church practice and culture has not been addressed in any sustained way. The South African case raises a number of issues regarding race and power in the ECM, which I discuss in my final section.

Though the ECM aspires to be diverse and transnational, its appeal has been predominately among white, middle-class, well-educated, North American, and Western populations. At the same time, the ECM's interest in social justice, pluralism, and the reconfiguring of personal and social relationships, both within and beyond Christian ecclesial spaces, would seem to provide resources for critiquing the relationship between conservative religion, neoliberalism, and white supremacy. Certainly, my South African interlocutors stood out from their white suburban peers in their willingness to question white superiority, privilege, and normativity; their desire to engage with and learn from black South Africans; and their rejection of racial fear and paranoia. However, certain attributes of the ECM, such as a high emphasis on experimentation and reflexivity, rendered their efforts unstable.[6] To the extent that my interlocutors pursued concrete actions aimed

---

4. I surveyed over 200 online posts and documents related to the ECM in South Africa published from 2004–2014. Due to my desire to maintain the anonymity of my fieldwork interlocutors—and given that many either participated in the emerging conversation in South Africa or were related to key players in the conversation—I have chosen to keep my digital sources anonymous unless directly quoting from these sources. That being said, South African bloggers very much relied on the public nature of their reflections to forge connections with like-minded individuals in South Africa and abroad.

5. See for example, Gibbs and Bolger, *Emerging Churches*, 11. Gibbs and Bolger note, "Our research identified that many emerging churches are led by white, anglo, middle-class males. Consequently, some may judge the movement to be deficient multiculturally. At this point in time, the detractors may be right. Part of the reason this particular culture predominates is that many of the pioneering emerging churches arose out of the evangelical charismatic subculture, which has these same characteristics." Bielo, *Emerging Evangelicals*, 2011; Martí and Ganiel, *The Deconstructed Church*; Packard, *The Emerging Church*. Packard has a very thoughtful discussion of diversity on 11–12.

6. Martí and Ganiel draw on sociologists Stephan Fuchs and Steen Ward to define "deconstruction" as a form of micropolitics that responds to pressures to conform through the creation of alternate frameworks and spaces. They consider practices of deconstruction to be fundamental to the ECM. Martí and Ganiel, *The Deconstructed Church*, 26.

at challenging the boundaries and norms of middle-class whiteness, such actions produced significant personal costs and social consequences that could serve to unwittingly reinforce, rather than deconstruct, racial divides.

THE RISE OF THE EMERGING CONVERSATION IN SOUTH AFRICA

The immediate backstory of South Africa's emerging conversation begins in the 1990s. Like most South African stories, it is thoroughly entangled with the country's racial history. In 1994, South Africa emerged from decades of apartheid: a brutal system of racial segregation designed to maintain the dominance of the minority white population vis-à-vis the black majority and other racial groups. While most South Africans welcomed the arrival of a "new" South Africa, a mood of anxiety, and even pessimism, percolated among the privileged white populace. No longer could the advantages attached to white skin—advantages forged through Dutch and British colonialism and legislated under apartheid—be taken for granted, leaving many white South Africans to perceive their future as precarious and unstable. In response, many whites chose to leave South Africa, emigrating to the United Kingdom, North America, New Zealand or Australia, or they actively withdrew to spaces of racial and cultural familiarity, including wealthy suburbs and churches.[7]

As white theologians and church leaders from historic mainline denominations (Anglican, Methodist, Reformed, Baptist, Lutheran, Congregationalist etc.) took stock of the current moment, the situation seemed dire. Much like the nation itself, and the fate of whites in it, the long-term choice facing mainline denominations seemed stark: "adapt or die."[8] On a

---

7. Statistics on white emigration are very difficult to find, but there is a difference of 600,288 whites between the 1991 and 1996 censuses. Some of this difference may be due to respondents choosing to not identify their race in the census. Hendriks and Erasmus, "Interpreting the New Religious Landscape in Post-Apartheid South Africa," 42.

8. Ibid., 61; Tutu, *Bishop Desmond Tutu*. The "adapt or die" discourse goes back to the anti-apartheid struggle of the 1980s where activists warned the white public that if power relations were not shifted voluntarily a bloodbath was sure to follow. For example, Anglican Archbishop Desmond Tutu continually reminded the white public (and the world) that South Africa was dangerously poised between two alternatives. Tutu told whites: "You have to decide which way you want to go. It is possible in our country to choose the path that leads to a new and more open society—a society that is more just, where people matter because they are created in the image of God. Equally, it is possible to choose the road that leads to our destruction, because it is the road of injustice and oppression." The only option for avoiding a "bloodbath" was "real change"

political level, leaders were acutely aware of needing to come to terms with the apartheid past and engage with (or at least not appear to be obstructing) the national social-political transformation project. Many also realized that the path to denominational growth and survival necessarily involved the inclusion of black South Africans at every level. However, strong counter-pressures came from traditional white and middle class constituencies who sought comfort and stability in the midst of rapid social change.[9] Simultaneously, the white religious "market share" was also being impacted by global trends such as the rise of megachurches, the spread of charismatic forms of Christianity, and an increase in those who claimed no religious identification.[10]

The perceived crisis in mainline denominations was intensified due to varying levels of guilt and denial about the role of churches in supporting systems of white supremacy. Prior to the arrival of democracy in 1994, "English" mainline traditions—such as Anglican and Methodist—had occupied powerful social positions. Under colonialism and apartheid, they were key missionizing agents: often partners with the state or alternatives to the state in overseeing projects of education and health care. Though these denominations were critical of racial discrimination, officially anti-apartheid, and counted many black members, leadership remained firmly in the hands of white elites. As a result, they tended to reinforce, rather than subvert, the dominant racial hierarchy. More notoriously, the Dutch Reformed Church, the historic denomination of white Afrikaners, had the unenviable reputation of providing theological justifications for apartheid and served as the

---

(39). For Tutu, the national crisis provoked by apartheid repression provided an "opportunity" for whites to take the side of justice, peace, and security for all (34).

9. For how this dynamic played out in the Dutch Reformed Church in the late 1990s and early 2000s, see De Wet, "Dealing with Corruption in South African Civil Society," 5–7; Kuperus, "The Political Role and Democratic Contribution of Churches in Post-Apartheid South Africa," 285–89. An entire journal issue of *Scriptura* was devoted to exploring the fate of the DRC church. It addressed issues such as shifting spirituality and dissatisfaction among DRC youth populations; the need to deal with the DRC history of racial segregation and the apartheid past; and the need to "reclaim" the Reformed Tradition and adapt it in ways that would allow it to be relevant, credible, and applicable to the new social and political context, which would involve participating in ecumenical, African, and public discourses. See Wolfram Weisse, "Introduction," *Scriptura* 83 (2003): 189–91.

10. Hendriks and Erasmus, "Interpreting the New Religious Landscape in Post-Apartheid South Africa," 55–56.

de facto state church during apartheid.[11] Now, both English and Afrikaner churches had to come to terms with their place in a changing South Africa.[12]

But all was not doom and gloom. In the early 2000s, a small network of young white pastors, theology students, and lay people began their own conversation: one much more optimistic about the future of "the church" in South Africa. This network was convinced that death or growing irrelevance need not be the fate of the church in South Africa. A new church was being born, or needed to emerge, out of the ashes of apartheid. Influenced by the ECM in the United States and Europe, those attracted to this conversation were predominantly white, male, and educated. While hailing from a variety of traditions—Reformed, Orthodox, Anglican, Baptist, Methodist, Pentecostal, and evangelical—they were united by a sense that the church in South Africa needed to change in order to remain spiritually fulfilling and socially relevant. Though wrestling with many of the same questions as mainline leaders, this group interpreted South Africa's changing social and political environment as providing opportunities to develop more authentic expressions of Christian faith.

Interest in the ECM among South Africans began as early as 2003. By the mid-2000s, a virtual network of blogs and websites devoted to the emerging conversation in South Africa existed. Here, participants reflected on and transmitted the thought of key ECM leaders such as Brian McLaren, Tony Jones, Scot McKnight, and Dan Kimball and discussed application in the South African context. Similar to what McLaren narrates in *The Justice Project*, initially the emerging conversation in South Africa was focused primarily on doing "church" differently and creating "safe space" for critical questions not allowed in traditional religious spaces.[13] Participants expressed frustration with the commodified culture of evangelical and charismatic megachurches, the homogeneity of suburban life, and the conservative dogmatism found in both. Together, they dreamed of an alternate "church" in South Africa, understood more as a web of individuals and communities than a set of institutions, which would be more receptive to

---

11 For further discussions on the relationship between Christianity, colonialism and apartheid, see Elphick, *The Equality of Believers*; Elphick and Davenport, *Christianity in South Africa*; Prozesky, *Christianity amidst Apartheid*. For discussion of "English" mainline traditions specifically, see Cochrane, *Servants of Power*; Comaroff and Comaroff, *Of Revelation and Revolution*, vols. 1 and 2.

12. In contrast to previous understandings of South Africa as a white "Christian" nation, democratic South Africa is officially a secular state that celebrates religious pluralism, leading some to worry that a post-apartheid South Africa would mean a post-Christian South Africa.

13. McLaren, "Introduction," 15.

questioning, more responsive to the youth, and take seriously the life and teachings of Jesus.

By 2006, several ecclesial experiments influenced by the ECM were active in the Johannesburg/Pretoria area where I conducted my research. Following church plant, house church, and neo-monastic models, the focus of these experiments was to intentionally bring together people who were committed to exploring what it meant to be a "missional" in their local context. Being missional meant, in part, committing oneself to critical engagement with one's culture and society, rather than withdrawing.[14] These groups were especially interested in developing practices and forms of community that could address the impact of consumer capitalism on Western Christianity, which they saw as corrosive to their spiritual health and South African society at large. In their view, Christianity was not a religious product to be consumed or a quick emotional release, but rather an invitation to a life of adventure, service, and personal growth with high demands. Following Jesus meant active commitment to a specific locale as well as deep commitment to a specific *community* of people (rather than to an institution).

RACE AND THE EMERGING CONVERSATION IN SOUTH AFRICA

Interest in the emerging conversation grew from 2003–2010, though core participants remained an extremely small segment of the white Christian population.[15] As participants explored what it meant to be "missional" in their local context, they increasingly began to engage with 1) apartheid, colonial, and Christian mission histories; 2) their relatively wealthy class positions; and 3) their racial and ethnic identities as white South Africans. The increased attention to race and class can be linked to several factors. First, broader ECM critiques of consumerism and commodification as well as ECM values of inclusion and diversity implicitly opened the door for participants to wrestle more actively with issues of race and class. In South Africa, like the United States, class remains indexed by race, but unlike the

14. Packard, *The Emerging Church*, 43. For a longer discussion of how being "missional" manifests in Emerging Christian thought and practice, see Bielo, *Emerging Evangelicals*, 2011, chaps. 5–6.

15 Martí and Ganiel underscore how conferences/gatherings and virtual networks were key ways of spreading ECM influence in the US and UK. The same appears to be true in South Africa: both at a local level through the establishment of experimental communities but also at a national and transnational level through conferences, gatherings, and the blogosphere. See Martí and Ganiel, *The Deconstructed Church*, 10

US, embodied confrontation with extreme racialized poverty and wealth (regardless of how these facts are interpreted) is a constant part of white middle-class life. The more participants sought to be socially engaged, the more issues tied to colonialism and apartheid, such as poverty and HIV/AIDS, could not be ignored. Second, ECM desires to develop a more tolerant and inclusive Christian identity dovetailed with a national emphasis on tolerance and inclusion following apartheid. Finally, as participants began to note the uniqueness of their South African (and African) context relative to North America and Europe, they could not help but reflect on the white and Western makeup of the ECM.

Perhaps the most reflexive engagements regarding the ECM and race came from young Afrikaners during the years of 2006–2010. While both English and Afrikaner white South Africans experienced "an acute sense of loss of the familiar, loss of certainty, loss of comfort, loss of privilege, [and] loss of well-known roles," young Afrikaners found themselves facing a future where they could no longer rely on the sacred canopy of apartheid that provided their parents and grandparents with a sense of order and ethnic pride.[16] For example, Cobus van Wyngaard, a theology student at the University of Pretoria was quite explicit about where he hoped the emerging conversation in South Africa would go and his desires to wrestle with his white, Dutch Reformed, and Afrikaner background.[17] Asking what it would mean to be church and live faithfully as a Christian in a "changing" environment and a "new" world, it was clear that the answers he had in mind did not simply involve engaging with postmodern epistemologies or aesthetics, but rather a shift away from the modernist legacy of colonialism and racism that had deeply compromised white Christian credibility in South Africa. Cobus worried that without intentional efforts to engage histories of racial oppression, the ECM in South Africa would retain and incorporate this modernist legacy. Describing a conversation with a religiously disillusioned black peer, Cobus writes, "Sadly, I had to admit that the emerging church conversation is a primarily white, western conversation. Not that we don't want people from other cultures, but simply that we don't seem able to make them part of the conversation on a really significant level. *But in South Africa we cannot afford to have just another white conversation.*" Leaving aside the question of

---

16. Steyn, *Whiteness Just Isn't What It Used to Be*, 156.

17. Cobus one of the most prolific bloggers on race and the emerging conversation in South Africa and became one of my most valued interlocutors during my field research. While Cobus has gone on to become an academic theologian, when he started his blog in 2006 he was primarily focused on exploring the personal and practical implications of the emerging conversation for South Africa, especially in relation to the struggling Dutch Reformed Church (DRC).

whether those in the Global North could afford to have just another white conversation, Cobus goes on: "I believe that an emerging church in South Africa needs to be inter-cultural. In a society still plagued by racism, people following Christ need to open new doors of genuine community across cultural barriers. Now, I've lived here long enough to know how easy it is to get people from different racial backgrounds to belong to a single institution, even recite creeds together, but still keep their lives completely apart." He hoped that the emerging conversation in South Africa would push the ECM more broadly to have "real multi-racial and multi-cultural conversation," which, in his view, will takes deep commitment from people on all sides.[18]

Cobus' reflections are noteworthy because they articulated an implicit critique of the ECM and a suspicion about the impact of uncritically importing ECM frameworks and terminology from the Global North into South Africa. Further, his concerns overlapped with concerns emerging in the North American ECM. In the US, there was growing recognition that the ECM had a race problem.[19] Because it started as a reaction to conservative evangelicalism, the ECM in the US tended to be majority white, and critics of color started to raise questions about whether the ECM had failed, despite their interest in deconstruction, to come to terms with how white, middle-class norms and values shaped emerging theology and practice. In response, North American leaders like Brian McLaren increasingly sought to connect the ECM with global conversations regarding social justice and neo-imperialism.[20]

One way this happened was through the creation of Amahoro Africa. Started by Burundian Claude Nikondeha, Amahoro sought to bring the ECM into dialogue with the African context and explicitly link deconstructionism with postcolonial concerns. Beginning in 2006 and active until 2013, the Amahoro network organized virtual dialogues and concrete gatherings in places such as Uganda, Rwanda, and Kenya. These gatherings became important spaces for white South Africans (and white North Americans

---

18. Van Wyngaard, "Conversations with Some Black People."

19. Soong-Chan et al., "Is the Emerging Church for Whites Only?" The May 2010 article sparked a number of blog posts in response, both on Sojourners website and in the larger ECM blogosphere.

20. McLaren narrates some of this journey and the reasons for his shift in focus in his introduction to *The Justice Project*. The influence of Brian McLaren personally on the South African and African emerging conversation is significant. McLaren visited South Africa in 2007 to host a gathering of about 100 South Africans (all white, only a few women) to discuss the ECM. For many who attended, this was the first time they translated their online relationships to in-person relationships. Brian McLaren also actively supported the creation of Amahoro Africa and helped connect South Africans to the Amahoro network.

and Europeans) to wrestle with how an ideology of white supremacy had shaped Western Christianity and the negative social impact of this ideology on the rest of the world. Andrew Jones remarked after the 2007 Amahoro gathering that what was being asked of the ECM was to "shift from the issue of knowledge to the issue of power" because "the Western church has gotten stuck on the epistemological questions of knowledge to the neglect of justice and power." He hoped that "maybe the African church will show the Western church how to navigate these waters."[21] Amahoro's explicit focus on power divides between the Global North and South, attention to poverty and violence, and exploration of Africa through the eyes of those on the undersides of colonialism and apartheid left a powerful impression on white and Western participants.

Amahoro's third major gathering took place in South Africa in 2009. A focus on learning about postcolonial reconstruction and racial reconciliation was perceived as a turning point for many white South African attendees. Cobus called the event a "conversion" in that he realized that being missional meant both claiming his white identity and re-orienting himself to the African continent.[22] He reflected:

> While it is popular for young Afrikaners to reject the past by saying that they had nothing to do with Apartheid, if I want to be in Africa I cannot say this. In Africa I cannot reject my past, I cannot be totally individualistic, what my people did is part of me. This said before I even start looking at all the practical ways in which Apartheid is still part of my daily life, in where I live, how I live etc. [. . .] Suddenly our place in this conversation seemed so clear. We do not take part in this African conversation by forgetting Apartheid, by forgetting our past. We take part in this conversation by *remembering* our past. By telling our story, so that this may never happen again.

Cobus concluded that the only way to "take the side" of the have-nots and the oppressed was as a "child of the iconic oppressor of the past."[23]

LESSONS FROM SOUTH AFRICA

Cobus was not alone in his desire to become a different kind of white South African: one open and committed to a racially inclusive and pluralistic

---

21. Jones, "Amahoro Africa and Postcolonialism."
22. Van Wyngaard, "Afrikaners."
23. Van Wyngaard, "How One Afrikaner Became an African Theologian."

South Africa and responsive to the wounds of history. Though a self-identified emerging conversation in South Africa had largely evaporated by 2011, the influence of the ECM remains visible in the experimental communities and faith-based development organizations (FBOs) I studied in 2013–2014. Though space does not permit me to go into the details of my research, in what follows I explore three questions regarding race, power, and the ECM prompted by my analysis of the South African emerging conversation and observations made during my fieldwork. I have already noted that at the end of the twentieth century, South Africa experienced dramatic social change. South Africans of all races went from living in a society dominated by whiteness and Christian nationalism to living in a multicultural and religiously plural society aspiring to be "non-racial" through a politics of redress. This process was and continues to be tumultuous. For some, social change is experienced as holding forth new subjective possibilities and freedoms; for others, it comes with a sense of humiliation and defeat.

On the one hand, white people struggle to hold onto a sense of identity and social/national belonging in light of public challenges to white supremacy. On the other hand, South Africa remains marked by extreme racialized inequality, fueled by neoliberal economic policies and global capitalism. Whites, for all their social insecurity, have continued to dominate in educational, cultural, and economic spheres. This fact has produced new forms of political activism led by black South Africans demanding "decolonization" of historically white institutions and increased redistribution of wealth. This charged environment has a lot of similarities to both the US and UK where in the past several years white power has been actively debated and contested through activism by people of color in the public sphere. Thus, I believe South Africa offers important lessons for how white interrogations of race and power might impact the ECM more broadly.

Can the ECM Contribute to Postcolonial Forms of Christianity?

By postcolonial, I mean the creation of forms of Christianity that 1) recognize and wrestle with the relationship between Christianity, modernity, and colonialism, both at home and around the world, and 2) seek to interrogate and disrupt colonial logics as expressed in and reinforced by Christian theology and ecclesial spaces. In South Africa, as in the US, colonial logics manifest in inherited notions of white racial and cultural superiority, as well as a persisting sense of white entitlement to property ownership, job opportunities, social capital, economic resources, and religious authority. Such entitlement is often expressed negatively through pessimism about the rising status of racial others, suspicion and derision of racial others, and resistance to redressive policies. One additional colonial legacy with pertinence to the ECM is what anthropologist Webb Kean calls the "moral narrative of modernity:" the idea that Western subjects, by virtue of their access to material and immaterial goods, can lead the world in a quest for "human liberation from a host of false beliefs and fetishisms."[24] Such views can find their way into the most liberal, progressive, post-modern, or deconstructionist of movements and often work to keep white people, however unintentionally, at the center of knowledge production.

From 2006–2010, the emerging conversation in South Africa increasingly adopted a self-reflexive tone with a postcolonial edge. White participants began to increasingly think of themselves more as "South African" and even "African" rather than "Western" and sought to shift their frame of reference from the Global North to the Global South. They asked what it might mean to develop a distinctly South African contribution to the ECM, given their placement on the African continent and immersion in a diverse national context. They also wondered what it would mean to be engaged with both environments, given the deep and problematic history of colonization and Christian hegemony to which they as white subjects were inextricably tied.

The desire to engage with the "real" South Africa and to ensure that the ECM was not simply a white, Western movement prompted concrete efforts to face past and present racial injustice as well as confront white fear and denial. In efforts to break from the "ignorance contract"—collective denial about the horrific impact of colonialism and apartheid on nonwhite populations—some began to seek out alternate forms of knowledge through practices such as "pilgrimages" to the Apartheid museum in Johannesburg or talking directly with black South Africans about their memories and experiences of apartheid.[25] Though this process involved many short-term experiments, such as visits to black urban centers, visits to "squatter camps" (informal black communities), or participating in interracial "reconciliation" dialogues and charity work—which yielded the surprising insight that black spaces were indeed "safe" and black people friendly!—they remain significant. Even symbolic acts of crossing white borders exposed deep seated racial fears and misperceptions and challenged white participants to reflect on dynamics of privilege and oppression.[26]

---

24. Keane, *Christian Moderns*, 5.

25. Steyn, "The Ignorance Contract."

26. For a longer discussion of this, see Van Wyngaard, "White Christians Crossing Borders," 2014.

At the same time, not all those involved in the emerging conversation allowed their initial interest in postmodernity to lead to long-term interrogation of race, whiteness, apartheid, and colonialism. In fact, the emerging conversation in South Africa could just as easily work to maintain and reinforce cultural, philosophical, theological, and aesthetic links between white South Africans and North America, Europe, and other settler colonies and easily shift attention away from race by providing a sense of diversity through transnational flows. Further, as Reggie Nel, a Black South African theologian, points out, the missional/emerging conversation in South Africa actually worked to reproduce apartheid and colonial era power dynamics in South Africa because initially contact between North American ECM leaders and South Africa came through white churches who took the "lead" in trying to promote the ECM and its vision to Black networks.[27] Nel critiques the way that the emerging-missional conversation in its early incarnations in South Africa was plagued with the assumption that Black and African churches needed to "catch up" to what was happening in white, Western, and Euro-American circles or risk missing the "Great Emergence."[28]

Given the origins of the emerging conversation in South Africa, and the fact that it relied on forms of knowledge production and circulation readily available to white elites, such as blogs and books, it makes sense that movement had difficulty recruiting and integrating a racially diverse set of participants. Nevertheless, the fact that some white participants were asking what a post-colonial and post-apartheid emerging church might look like and naming white supremacy as being *their* responsibility to address, not only in South African society but within white religious communities, remains noteworthy and not without costs.

In the case of one emerging congregation in Johannesburg, which lasted from 2003–2011, a desire by white Afrikaner leaders to become more culturally and racially inclusive eventually led to its formal disintegration. As the congregation sought to embody a value of inclusion, first through changing their primary language from Afrikaans to English, then through building friendships with black congregations in poor areas, and finally through explicit dialogues focusing on interrogating the apartheid past alongside black peers, each stage was met with resistance. Congregants were all for experimenting with ecclesial forms and seeking a more authentic spirituality as long as it stayed within familiar Afrikaner, white, and

27. Nel, "A Piece of My Mind . . ." Inspired by the Black Consciousness movement, Black is a broader political identity category in South Africa that those who were oppressed during apartheid, even if from a variety of racial, cultural, and ethnic backgrounds, adopt.

28. Tickle, *The Great Emergence*.

Western frameworks, but they resisted more sustained efforts to promote cultural and racial inclusion through acts that de-centered white identity and authority. As race and apartheid became explicit objects of reflection and intervention, and more radical practices like residential relocation were discussed, resistance among white members increased and numbers dwindled. This example offers a cautionary tale regarding how far subjects are willing to go when it comes to interrogating and actively disrupting/deconstructing their own racial identities. Even the most dedicated white participants struggled with how to move beyond symbolic gestures of rebellion towards embodiment of new (and sustainable) ways of being.[29]

Can the ECM Build and Sustain Spiritual Communities across Race and Class Divides?

The two primary groups I studied in the Johannesburg area composed a network of about fifteen to twenty people actively engaged in community development work in black majority contexts.[30] Leadership in these groups skewed white, but given the highly segregated nature of South African society, the fact that these groups had managed to recruit and integrate black members from a variety of social classes was striking.[31] Though small, the influence of this network was felt more widely through connections to other churches, FBOs, and activist circles. Started by white South Africans disillusioned with the narrow confines of white suburban life and conservative Christianity, these groups were heavily influenced by the neo-monastic and missional streams found in the ECM. Though focused on the day-to-day work of supporting development projects, core members understood themselves to be part of, and contributing to the building of, a diverse spiritual "community" composed of individuals who were committed to a "shared way of life."

Those I engaged with did not necessarily seek to sever all ties with suburbia or reject all middle class comforts. Rather, they were seeking a new orientation that could ground them amidst the complexities of South African life. Similar to the urban missional communities that anthropologist

---

29. Steyn, *Whiteness Just Isn't What It Used to Be*, xv.

30. Initially, the groups I studied were not well acquainted, but by the time I left, they were increasingly linked with one another. Due to the intensive, unique, and relatively radical nature of their ethical orientations vis-à-vis dominant norms in white society, most sought like-minded collaborators and conversation partners wherever they could find them.

31. The network was roughly 60% white and 40% black.

James Bielo describes, many had chosen to intentionally live near one another and/or commit to working in a specific locale or neighborhood. This often involved relocating from white and wealthy suburbs to majority black, mixed-income and poor areas. Members also encouraged one another to free up as much time and as many resources as possible in order to invest in community development and the development of alternate (non-mainstream) expressions of Christian faith.

The daily work of creating a "shared way of life" across race and class lines—one grounded in a holistic sense of Christian spirituality that drew freely from Protestant, Catholic, and pre-Reformation traditions—was experienced by white members as difficult but enriching. Individual and collective practices, such as intentional reflection, communal meals, informal gatherings, hospitality to visitors, the sharing of resources, and seeking to be as self-sustainable as possible (sometimes through social entrepreneurship) so as not to detract money and resources from community development projects, sustained their visions of spiritual and social transformation. Members dreamed of becoming the kinds of subjects whose conduct could help practically bridge the gaps between white and black, wealthy and impoverished, that constantly threaten to tear South Africa apart. They also dreamed about being the kinds of subjects whose commitment to following Jesus and modeling his concern for the poor, excluded, and marginalized might contribute to national healing and social integration.

By seeking to understand the lived realities of those who "had more" and those who "had less," the groups I studied aspired to live lives that transcended racial, ethnic, national, economic and religious lines and to be active citizens who advocated for the realization of social justice. No doubt my interlocutors would emphatically agree with critical race scholar Melissa Steyn's reflections on her anti-apartheid activism: "working along with South Africans of all cultural groups towards a common cause, greatly deepened my insight into what my whiteness had cost me: the sense of community I had been deprived of; the friends I could have had; the freedom I have never known to inhabit my land other than as some sort of psychological squatter."[32] Steyn goes on to describe the benefits of coming to know "in a new way through personal relationships, the deep humanity of the African people I had been raised to fear," of breaking with social taboos to see the "normalcy and complexity" of black lives.[33]

---

32. Steyn, *Whiteness Just Isn't What It Used to Be*, xvi.

33. Ibid.

In our conversations, my interlocutors described to me the painful joy of learning about and from the "other."[34] Exposure to new foods, new cultural practices, new spaces, and new communities was experienced as liberating. For example, one person understood themselves as finally being able to "dream" again. Another reported a sense of becoming more authentically "human" as a result of their engagement with black South Africans. I was particularly struck by how my interlocutors described their journeys in conversion terms. Those familiar with the ECM know that deconversion narratives feature prominently,[35] but perhaps more important for my interlocutors was the sense that, to use McLaren's terms, "margins" could indeed become "horizons," if they had eyes to see.[36] Almost all my interlocutors reported a series of "waking up" experiences. The more they asked what it meant to "follow Jesus in South Africa," the more they sought to come to terms with the evils of apartheid, the pain and suffering endemic to black life, and the ignorance and apathy of white family, friends, and churches.

While a collective process of waking up among white populations might greatly increase the chances of building and sustaining racially diverse communities in the long-term, at an individual level it brought many challenges. As Steyn notes: "A white skin is not skin that can be shed without losing some blood."[37] Waking up to the "real South Africa" meant constantly facing the harsh reality that the "past" (a code word for apartheid) continued to reassert itself. Living and working in majority black areas daily showcased the ways apartheid-era divides and power structures were still in place. Added to this was the cognitive dissonance produced by having access to and moving between different worlds: white and black, urban and suburban, rich and poor.

Though many black South Africans are forced to regularly navigate and adapt to white cultural environments and suburban worlds—necessitating collective strategies for survival—the choices made by my interlocutors were voluntary and, as such, much more solitary and fragmented. I do not seek to downplay the privilege and asymmetrical power they exercised in adopting the value of "downward mobility," but I do want to highlight the challenges it produced. The most radical of my interlocutors often expressed an acute sense of "misplacement" and exhibited visible physical and mental exhaustion that was very similar to the "tenuousness, unpredictability, and

34. Ibid.

35. See for example, Bielo, *Emerging Evangelicals*, 2011; Bielo, "Belief, Deconversion, and Authenticity among U.S. Emerging Evangelicals"; Harrold, "Deconversion in the Emerging Church."

36. McLaren, "Turning the Tables of White-European-Male-Privilege."

37. Steyn, *Whiteness Just Isn't What It Used to Be*, xvii.

exhaustion" Bielo discusses in his study of US emerging evangelicals trying to be missional in racially diverse and economically depressed areas.[38] The further my interlocutors moved towards racial and cultural others, and the further away they moved from white centers of power, through actions such as buying homes and living in majority black communities and engaging in political activism aligned with "radical" black politics, the more they were forced to confront myths of white innocence and the reality of white complicity. And the more they identified themselves with the experience of poor and black communities, the more they found themselves alienated from mainstream white communities, facing hostility, resistance, and fear from friends and family. At the same time, power differentials, cultural differences, and histories of oppression created significant challenges to building long-term trust and rapport with black South Africans. These dynamics meant that the work of racial self-excavation required a high degree of willingness by white subjects to face discomforting truths, regardless of recognition or embrace by others.

I often wondered whether the high degree of religious experimentation, social transgression, and political engagement I observed among my interlocutors would lead to eventual disenchantment, withdrawal, and even backlash that could ultimately undermine ideals of diversity, inclusion, and justice. As Packard notes, ECM preference for the organic over the institutional means activities are often determined by the energy/capacity/interest of participants, and when these shift, so do activities.[39] These dynamics certainly influenced the groups I studied. The kinds of activities and organizations my interlocutors were involved in necessitated living "unsettled lives" with high energy and time investments.[40] Small numbers and reliance on the "labor of the willing" (often aged twenty-five to thirty-five) made things unpredictable, especially when decisions about family, education, and finances came into the mix.[41] Further, white members in particular were often caught between their desire to live in solidarity with the poor and marginalized and the centripetal force of middle-class norms and expectations. A sense of being stretched thin due to competing aspirations

---

38. Bielo, *Emerging Evangelicals*, 2011, 126.

39. Packard, *The Emerging Church*, 111–16.

40. Ibid., 62–84.

41. Ibid., 83–84. As Packard concludes that ECM functionally precludes many from participating in the time-intensive activities necessary to sustain an unsettled life. "To the extent that this life station matches up with class, racial and ethnic divides, the Emerging Church will never be able to successfully court the kind of diversity it professes to desire, at least here in the United States." (84)

and demands became even more intensified when combined with the sense of displacement produced by living and working in majority black contexts.

For some, the strain proved too much. One black development worker expressed his frustration to me that white leaders often found it difficult to be present in day to day community development operations due to their entanglement with outside commitments, networks, and projects. This left him with a heavy load and increased frustration over constantly shifting organizational priorities. When white leaders had to step down due to personal circumstances and capacity issues, this left development projects in a bind and paid black staff stood to lose their employment. Thus, the combined impact of misplacement, exhaustion, and class-based entanglements among white members could work to reinforce, rather than mitigate, racial tensions and, in so doing, jeopardize long-term development goals. Perhaps unfairly, black perceptions of white liberals as constantly vacillating between two worlds while "skillfully extracting whatever suits them from the exclusive pool of white privilege" could all too easily be reinforced.[42]

Can the ECM Support White Transformation?

Philosopher Shannon Sullivan has argued that shifting motivation for engaging with racial justice from shame or guilt to "bestowing" self-love is an important component of sustaining commitment to antiracism among white subjects.[43] The emerging conversation in South Africa provided white subjects not only with the initial means through which to push against/move away from the political, social, and theological conservatism that undergirded apartheid and colonial mindsets but also with an idealistic vision that could frame shifting power relations as part of a transcendent process. White members were able to positively respond to wider social and political processes of white relativization, in part, because these changes were seen as having the potential to move them closer to experiencing God's "Kingdom" in the here and now rather than as "reverse-racism."

While exhibiting a familiar ECM deconstructionist impulse, participants also exhibited a deep commitment to the work of reconstruction through community development projects and their ethics.[44] I was profoundly struck by the sense among those I worked with that they were "in it for the long haul," which in light of pressures to withdraw to white-dominated contexts was a powerful political statement. My interlocutors did not

42. Biko, *I Write What I Like*, 23.
43. Sullivan, "On the Need for a New Ethos of White Antiracism," 22.
44. Labanow, *Evangelicalism and the Emerging Church*, 98–124.

view what they were doing as charity work; rather, they saw the sharing of their skills and resources with marginalized communities as a form of redress that was about securing their own future flourishing through signaling their commitment to living in a "transformed" South Africa. This meant weighing opportunities for their own economic advancement alongside the need to advance those who had been oppressed by their parents and grandparents and staying present with the messy, painful, and complex subjective realities that define South Africa.

Without a doubt, the quest to move beyond a whites-only and Western form of life created many unanticipated challenges and contradictions for my interlocutors.[45] In my previous section, I discussed how creating spiritual community across racial and economic borders and problematizing whiteness in South Africa remains immensely difficult. I saw my interlocutors responding to the challenges created by their contradictory social locations in several ways: 1) They primarily interpreted resistance from black and white communities as confirmation of urgent work needed to build partnerships across racial lines. 2) Experiences of alienation, in both white and black contexts, served only increase their motivation to develop shared practices and meaningful forms of community alongside black peers that could reinforce alternate ideals and values. 3) Participants who once felt very critical, and even sought to distance themselves from the white suburbs, begin to reframe the work of being missional as oriented *towards* the white suburbs. The latter strategy intrigued me because it involved a renewed emphasis on engagement with white communities in order to spread the message that transformation was necessary. Being committed for the long haul increasingly meant fostering connections to white institutions, including suburban churches, in order to be voices for change.

I interpret a renewed focus on white networks and communities several ways. First, there was a growing awareness in the groups I studied of the need to promote black leadership. Thus, many white members were moving into support and fundraising roles within their organizations and focusing on using their access to resources and opportunities strategically to support black empowerment (one informant called this being "Robin Hood"). Second, living and working in majority black spaces gave my informants a great sense of responsibility because they often knew in an intimate way the kinds of precarities that were foreign to most in the suburbs. Increased efforts to engage with white communities, especially white church communities, certainly exacerbating the ever-present temptation to return to spaces of white comfort and safety and offered a pious rationalization for doing so.

45. Krog, *Begging to Be Black*, 92.

Yet, it also provided white members a way of using the awareness they had gained through their work and relationships in the service of white transformation in spaces where were likely to be highly effective given their cultural familiarity and the authority attached to white skin. In a way, I believe my interlocutors had internalized some of Black Consciousness activist Steve Biko's 1970 admonition to white liberals:[46]

> No true liberal should feel any resentment at the growth of black consciousness. Rather, all true liberals should realize that the place for their fight for justice is within white society . . . The liberal must apply himself with absolute dedication to the idea of educating his white brothers that the history of the country may have to be rewritten at some stage . . . the liberal must serve as a lubricating material so that we can change the gears in trying to find a better direction for South Africa.

Renewed connection to white networks in hopes of playing a long-term bridging and reconciling role allows for targeted critiques of dominant white norms, values and habits. It also mitigated some of the loss, alienation, and displacement that I saw lead to burn-out and withdrawal, because, just as Cobus described after attending the 2009 Amahoro Gathering, it gave them a meaningful and more sustainable "place" in wider processes of transformation without denying their identities, histories, and networks.

CONCLUSION

Steyn observed in 2001 that "South Africans, willingly or unwillingly, successfully or unsuccessfully, are engaged with one of the most profound collective psychological adjustments happening in the contemporary world." In response to the social changes brought about by political realignment, South Africans of all races are engaged in a process of "selecting, editing, and borrowing from cultural resources available to them in light of new knowledge and possibilities, while yet retaining a sense of personal coherence."[47] For white South Africans, this process involves coming to terms with a country redefining itself as African, rather than Western, and acknowledging their interdependence with other racial groups. It also involves acknowledging entanglement with histories of racism and colonialism. One resource available to young white South Africans trying to redefine themselves within the "emerging" South African society was the ECM, and this helps explain its

---

46. Biko, *I Write What I Like*, 27–28.
47. Steyn, *Whiteness Just Isn't What It Used to Be*, xxi–xxii.

particular appeal from 2003–2010 and its ongoing influence in the groups I studied.

The emerging conversation created space for young progressive-minded white Christians to challenge the master narratives they had inherited, which connected Christianity and white supremacy together in a political theology of racial and cultural separatism. To greater and lesser degrees, white South African Emerging Christians began the difficult and painful work of confronting "the extent to which their identities and personal expectations had been shaped through asymmetrical power relations."[48] Notably, the desire expressed by Emerging Christians to engage with social change differed from their white peers who tended to fear the future, anticipate increased racial tension, and worry over the threat of 'reverse racism,' while defending their English and Afrikaans identities.[49] Reflections on apartheid and the church, as well as discussions with black friends and neighbors about their memories of apartheid, brought soberness, humility, and hope to white South Africans involved in the emerging conversation, which differed from white discourses of colorblindness, denial, and victimization heard more widely.

Steyn notes that one of the most difficult aspects of her journey to divest from white supremacy was learning to break "the law of the father": learning to challenge the men who, in her cultural background, were given so much authority.[50] Similarly, the emerging conversation in South Africa allowed younger white South Africans to question centers of power that reinforced apartheid theology and post-apartheid withdrawal. Part of what motivated them to wrestle with questions of white complicity was a desire to be authentic followers of Jesus in South Africa and the belief that this meant orienting oneself towards the poor, excluded, and marginalized. Within communities influenced by ECM, participants sought to challenge not only secular-profane divides but also white-nonwhite divides through emphasis on holistic spirituality. They pushed themselves to think not only about "church" but also about "community" in new ways that challenged historic divides founded on ideas of absolute racial and cultural difference.

The groups I studied, inspired by the ECM and its growing emphasis on social justice, sought to help create a more just and equitable South Africa. Involvement in local community development work allowed for a renewed sense of agency and relevance at a time where white dominance and superiority were being challenged in many other spheres. While participation

---

48 Steyn, *Whiteness Just Isn't What It Used to Be*, xxii.

49. Van Wyngaard, "Youth in South Africa."

50. Steyn, *Whiteness Just Isn't What It Used to Be*, xiv.

in these groups allowed white subjects to exercise more control over the process of inclusion and integration, those who allowed the memories and experiences of racial others to alter their way of life often set out to practice deconstruction in their most intimate spheres. Through intentional practices of emplacement in black majority contexts, white Emerging Christians were learning to embrace the rise of black consciousness and simultaneously recognizing the role they had to play in preparing their white friends, families, and churches for the ongoing process of shifting power relations.

Yet the daily work of balancing competing obligations and maintaining awareness how one's values/preferences were shaped by race required exhausting levels of reflexivity and an extremely high tolerance for ambiguity. Already, emerging communities by virtue of their high level of commitment, high levels of self-reflexivity, and reliance on young labor tend to be fluid and unstable. What this means in the long term—for my interlocutors and those they interact with—remains to be seen. Interestingly, the option that does not seem to be on the table is the creation of alternate communities where whites are fully subordinate to the leadership and direction of black subjects. Arguably, this may not be the most effective in terms of wider impact on white society, though certainly this would be a radical way to embody a personal rejection of white supremacy. The choice to re-engage with white churches and white suburban culture provided one way of coping with the strains and tensions produced by a sense of being "unsettled." However, my observations lead me to believe that unless long-term emplacement in non-white and/or non-suburban spaces occurs alongside efforts to engage broader white communities, it will be difficult to sustain a commitment to racial justice that extends beyond the short-term and symbolic. Continued investment in black majority contexts and conversations provide crucial opportunities to critically reflect on white norms and assumptions and learn from the experiences of others.

Whatever religious/ethical communities are still "emerging" in South Africa and elsewhere, while certainly more multicultural and multiracial than the institutions they grew out of, they remain in a white key. In my view, the assertion that the ECM appeals primarily to white people need not disqualify the ECM as a significant social and spiritual movement provided that participants and observers understand the ECM as primarily a movement in response to white, Western Christianity, and they commit to interrogating how notions of white normativity and superiority might consciously and unconsciously influence ECM norms and practices. I have argued that the dispositions, habits, and practices that the ECM encourages may help to promote white antiracism and postcolonial forms of Christianity among white populations, but only if the tensions produced by living unsettled lives encourages renewed commitment rather than withdrawal. It is here that the ECM might play an important role in equipping white individuals with the theological resources and sense of community needed to develop sustainable and embodied critiques of white supremacy within an unequal world.

BIBLIOGRAPHY

Bielo, James S. "Belief, Deconversion, and Authenticity among U.S. Emerging Evangelicals." *Ethos* 40 (2012) 258–76.

———. *Emerging Evangelicals: Faith, Modernity, and the Desire for Authenticity*. New York: New York University Press, 2011.

Biko, Steve. *I Write What I Like*. Edited by Aelred Stubbs. Johannesburg: Picador Africa, 2006.

Cochrane, James R. *Servants of Power: The Role of English-Speaking Churches in South Africa, 1903–1930*. Johannesburg: Ravan, 1987.

Comaroff, Jean, and John Comaroff. *Of Revelation and Revolution*. Vol. 1, *Christianity, Colonialism, and Consciousness in South Africa*. Chicago: University of Chicago Press, 1991.

———. *Of Revelation and Revolution*. Vol. 2, *The Dialectics of Modernity on a South African Frontier*. Chicago: University of Chicago Press, 1997.

De Wet, Friedrich W. "Dealing with Corruption in South African Civil Society: Orientating Christian Communities for Their Role in a Post-Apartheid Context." *Verbum et Ecclesia* 36.1 (2015) 1–11.

Elphick, Richard. *The Equality of Believers: Protestant Missionaries and the Racial Politics of South Africa*. Charlottesville: University of Virginia Press, 2012.

Elphick, Richard, and T. R. H Davenport. *Christianity in South Africa: A Political, Social, and Cultural History*. Berkeley: University of California Press, 1997.

Gibbs, Eddie, and Ryan K. Bolger. *Emerging Churches: Creating Christian Community in Postmodern Cultures*. Grand Rapids: Baker Academic, 2005.

Harrold, Philip. "Deconversion in the Emerging Church." *International Journal for the Study of the Christian Church* 6 (2006) 79–90.

Hendriks, Jurgens, and Johannes Erasmus. "Interpreting the New Religious Landscape in Post–Apartheid South Africa." *Journal of Theology for Southern Africa* 109 (2001) 41–65.

Jones, Andrew. "Amahoro Africa and Postcolonialism." *TallSkinnyKiwi*. http://tallskinnykiwi.typepad.com/tallskinnykiwi/2007/05/amahoro_ africa_.html.

Keane, Webb. *Christian Moderns: Freedom and Fetish in the Mission Encounter*. Berkeley: University of California Press, 2007.

Krog, Antjie. *Begging to Be Black*. Cape Town: Random House Struik, 2012.

Kuperus, T. "The Political Role and Democratic Contribution of Churches in Post-Apartheid South Africa." *Journal of Church and State* 53 (2011) 278–306.

Labanow, Cory E. *Evangelicalism and the Emerging Church: A Congregational Study of a Vineyard Church*. New York: Routledge, 2016.

Martí, Gerardo, and Gladys Ganiel. *The Deconstructed Church: Understanding Emerging Christianity*. Oxford: Oxford University Press, 2014.

McLaren, Brian D. "Introduction: A Conversation about Justice." In *The Justice Project*, edited by Elisa Padilla, Ashley Bunting Seeber, and Brian McLaren, 13–20. Grand Rapids: Baker, 2009.

———"Turning the Tables of White-European-Male-Privilege: 'Our' Tables, 'Their' Tables, and New Tables." *Sojourners*, April 22, 2010. https://sojo.net/articles/turning-tables-white-european-male-privilege-our-tables-their-tables-and-new-tables.

Nel, Reggie. "A Piece of My Mind . . . : Missional Is Still in White Hands, Purposefully." *A Piece of My Mind . . .* , February 6, 2009. http://rwnel.blogspot.com/2009/02/missional-is-still-in-white-hands.html.

Packard, Josh. *The Emerging Church: Religion at the Margins*. Boulder, CO: First Forum, 2012.

Prozesky, Martin. *Christianity Amidst Apartheid: Selected Perspectives on the Church in South Africa*. New York: St. Martin's, 1990.

Soong-Chan, Rah, Jason Mach, Brian McLaren, Debbie Blue, and Julie Clawson. "Is the Emerging Church for Whites Only?" *Sojourners*, May 2010. https://sojo.net/magazine/may-2010/emerging-church-whites-only.

Steyn, Melissa. "The Ignorance Contract: Recollections of Apartheid Childhoods and the Construction of Epistemologies of Ignorance." *Identities* 19.1 (2012) 8–25.

———. *"Whiteness Just Isn't What It Used to Be:" White Identity in a Changing South Africa*. Interruptions—Border Testimony(ies) and Critical Discourse/s. Albany: SUNY Press, 2001.

Sullivan, Shannon. "On the Need for a New Ethos of White Antiracism." *philoSOPHIA* 2.1 (2012) 21–38.

Tickle, Phyllis. *The Great Emergence: How Christianity Is Changing and Why*. Grand Rapids: Baker, 2012.

Tutu, Desmond. *Bishop Desmond Tutu, the Voice of One Crying in the Wilderness: A Collection of His Recent Statements in the Struggle for Justice in South Africa*. Edited by John Webster. London: Mowbray, 1982.

Van Wyngaard, George Jacobus (Cobus). "Afrikaners: Remember the Story of Your Tribe." *My Contemplations*, October 30, 2009. https://mycontemplations.wordpress.com/2009/10/30/afrikaners-remember-the-story-of-your-tribe/.

———. "Conversations with Some Black People." *Emerging South Africa*, November 30, 2006. https://emergingsa.wordpress.com/2006/11/30/conversations-with-some-black-people/.

———. "How One Afrikaner Became an African Theologian." *My Contemplations*, June 17, 2009. https://mycontemplations.wordpress.com/2009/06/17/how-one-afrikaner-became-an-african-theologian/.

———. "White Christians Crossing Borders: Between Perpetuation and Transformation." In *Unsettling Whiteness*, edited by Samantha Schulz and Lucy Michael, 191–202. Oxford: Inter-Disciplinary, 2014. http://www.inter-disciplinary.net/critical-issues/wp-content/uploads/2013/05/Van-Wyngaard-white3-wpaper.pdf.

———. "Youth in South Africa." *My Contemplations*. August 10, 2007. https://mycontemplations.wordpress.com/2007/08/10/youth-in-south-africa/.

Weisse, Wolfram. "Introduction." *Scriptura* 83 (2003) 189–91.

12

Emerging Out of Patriarchy?
The Emerging Church Movement from a Feminist Practical Theological Perspective

Xochitl Alvizo and Gerardo Martí

Abstract

The Emerging Church Movement (ECM) is a loosely formed network of relationally connected congregations seeking to rethink and reform church in light of a changing culture. The popular literature on the ECM—often written by white male leaders in the movement—touts its commitment to radical inclusivity, egalitarian structures, and participatory forms. But does the ECM interrogate its own gender norms? In this chapter, we ask: To what extent does Emerging Christianity include the overcoming of deeply ingrained and highly institutionalized gendered oppressions? Is the ECM a new form of Christianity "emerging" out of patriarchy? Drawing from feminist theology developed post-Women's Liberation, Alvizo and Martí find that the Emerging Church Movement represents a unique opportunity to apply a feminist perspective of church, one that envisions new imperatives that can help it fulfill its desire for a radically inclusive, egalitarian church.

Broadly speaking, the Emerging Church is a loosely formed network of relationally connected congregations that seeks to rethink and reform within Western Christianity in light of what it understands to be important elements of a changing culture and in response to experiences of Christianity and church it deems to be unchristian.[1] Just mention the "Emerging Church" among leaders and observers of contemporary Christianity, and a stereotypical image of who belongs to the Emerging Church Movement (EMC) comes to mind. That image invariably consists of a white, middle-class, and college-educated hipster. While a closer observation of those who participate in the ECM shows significantly more diversity than mainline Christianity,[2] the most visible leaders of the ECM featured in events, conferences, and published books are white men—perhaps with the exception of one high-profile white woman (more on this below). Ironically, the popular literature on the Emerging Church, often written by white male leaders in the movement, touts commitment to radical inclusivity, egalitarian structures, and participatory forms. In this chapter, we ask: To what extent does Emerging Christianity include the overcoming of deeply ingrained and highly institutionalized gendered oppressions? Is the ECM a new form of Christianity "emerging" out of patriarchy?

INTRODUCING A FEMINIST PRACTICAL THEOLOGICAL PERSPECTIVE

To answer the question we posed above, we employ a feminist practical theological perspective to analyze the ECM. Not only does the recent phenomenon of the ECM provide a strategic opportunity to further apply a feminist lens to a contemporary embodiment of the Christian church, we also believe it offers an especially insightful and productive way for understanding the movement itself. Using a feminist practical theological perspective does not necessarily result in a full comprehension of all aspects of the ECM but rather draws attention to particular aspects of theological and theoretical concern (i.e. gender and patriarchy) in order to pursue new insights of profound salience to Christian life today. Therefore, the task we adopt in this chapter is to focus on observations of the ECM and enact a

---

1. For more on the Emerging Church Movement, see Alvizo, "A Feminist Theological Analysis of the Leadership Structures of the Emerging Church." Also, Martí and Ganiel, *The Deconstructed Church*; Martí, "New Concepts for New Dynamics: Generating Theory for the Study of Religious Innovation and Social Change"; Clawson and Stace, *Crossing Boundaries, Redefining Faith*; and Jones, *The Church Is Flat*.

2. See Martí and Ganiel, *The Deconstructed Church*, 23, 42, 111, 205.

feminist practical theological vision of church—a project that is never complete but ongoing and always open to further construction.

What makes a feminist practical theological perspective significant is the value of its critique of contemporary systems. More specifically, it critiques much of what passes as standard and generally unquestioned theological work for its failure to address systemic sexism. Scholars who adopt a feminist practical theological perspective have as their project to move the church away from the patriarchy historically embedded within it and instead move the church toward becoming a liberative institution. It seeks to create conditions such that all persons experience a full life. At its root, a feminist practical theological lens provides a framework and language for analyzing structures and patterns of patriarchy.

The ECM has been motivated to avoid replicating the rigid theologies and practices of "conservative/evangelical/fundamentalist Protestantism . . . [and] other forms of traditional Christianity that they have experienced as stifling or inauthentic."[3] Emerging Church congregations have therefore sought to form church in ways that are more *organic* (responsive to its context, fluid in form and expression), *relational* (participatory in structure, leadership, and decision-making), and *inclusive* (of diversity, questioning, and change as a result of new encounters) as a way to counter the damaging habits and patterns its participants have experienced in previous churches. Consistent with the expressed values of ECM leaders, a feminist lens expresses commitment to an egalitarian leadership structure, to a fluid form of church, and to a radical inclusivity, particularly for those typically marginalized in society.

A feminist practical theological perspective applied to the ECM leads to questions about how its public presentation and leadership relates to its expressed commitments and in turn its structures. Its seeming domination by male leaders invites a feminist analysis of the nature of its self-understanding and potentially problematic patriarchal habits and patterns it has inherited and perpetuated. Feminist practical theology becomes a tool for the continuation of the ECM's project as an inclusive, egalitarian, transforming church. A feminist theological engagement to the ECM draws out the subtleties of patriarchy deeply embedded in the church and the history that has created and perpetuated this environment, which many, including those within the EMC, have not yet fully taken into account. By analyzing the ECM from a feminist practical theological lens, we draw attention to particular aspects of the movement to resource and strengthen its desired goals. Ultimately, by bringing two projects together, that of eliminating patriarchy

---

3. Martí and Ganiel, *The Deconstructed Church*, 26.

through a feminist practical theology and that of radical inclusivity through ECM structures, we hope to move both forward in mutually beneficial ways.

UNCOVERING PATRIARCHY IN THE CHURCH

Like the rise of the Emerging Church Movement, the feminist practical theological lens is fairly recent. Early feminist theologians, ignited by the Women's Liberation Movement of the time, began the work of exposing the largely overlooked sexism and misogyny embedded within church teachings and doctrines, calling the church to repent of these sins. These theologians gave voice and visibility to the patriarchal patterns and habits embedded within the church's language and symbol systems, its leadership structure, and its rigid institutionalization, which, in step with the larger society within which it exists, relegated women to a status inferior to that of men. These early feminist theologians expected that such uncovering and calling out would result in theological renewal and reform of the church. Now, the ECM, a group committed to a flat organizational structure, has actively tried to be sensitive to patriarchal relationships. Yet such patterns continue, and the ECM's attempts to respond to criticisms regarding women's experience has been insufficient.

The most important contributor to the formation of a feminist practical theological perspective is Mary Daly. As a feminist catholic theologian in the late 1960s, she brought sharp attention to the largely normalized patriarchal habits embedded within the Catholic Church's structure, theology, and practice. In 1968, Daly published her first book, *The Church and the Second Sex*,[4] which represented the most robust challenge raised against the church's patriarchal practices to date. The book was as controversial as it was powerful. She challenged the church on its systematic valuing of men over women, its hierarchical structures of power in which men hold highest place, and its restrictive gender roles and relations. Extending her charge to all the religions of "God the Father," she called on the church to exorcise "the 'demon' of sexual prejudice" from itself.[5] In this first, and her only decidedly Christian, book, Daly effectively set the theological and practical groundwork for a feminist reformation of the church. The diagnosis and agenda for change embedded in this work provided a platform for the continual development of feminist practical and ecclesiological work to come.[6] Though she spent

---

4. Daly, *The Church and the Second Sex*.
5. Daly, *The Church and the Second Sex*, 193.
6. Daly would soon supersede this theological work with her post-Christian philosophy, introduced in *Beyond God the Father*, as she concludes that Christianity,

much of her narrative making her case against the Church, her ultimate objective was reforming the Church, which, amidst the Women's Liberation Movement and the upcoming Second Vatican Council, she believed to be imminent.[7]

Mary Daly described the antagonism evident in the relationship of the Catholic Church with women by saying that the Church's teachings perpetuated a "traditional view of woman" that both "pretends to put woman on a pedestal but which in reality prevents her from genuine self-fulfillment and from active, adult-size participation in society."[8] Building on her contemporary Simone de Beauvoir's work, *The Second Sex*,[9] Daly pointed out ways in which Christianity served as an instrument of women's oppression. While she drew on insights from de Beauvoir to make her case against the Church and writes her book with the conviction that there have been "harmful distortions of doctrine and practice" within the Church, Daly did not see the Church as static and believed it possible to purify and reform its teachings so that the promising elements of Christian thought could still be restored as sources for a "genuinely life-fostering evolution" in the situation of women and of the Church.[10]

Among the charges made against the Church by Daly, the following three are most relevant for our task in this chapter. First, Christianity in general and the Catholic Church in particular implicitly convey that women are naturally inferior to men. Christianity does this by identifying women with the image of Mary the Mother of God who has the lesser role of "merely supplying the matter" in procreation and in God's incarnation in Jesus. As such, "For the first time in human history the mother kneels before her son," effectively only glorifying Mary—and by extension women—inasmuch as she accepts "the subordinate role assigned to her" in relation to her son.[11]

Second, Christianity perpetuates women's oppression through the psychological impact of an exclusively male divinity that is reinforced in

---

along with the other religions of "God the Father," is ultimately irredeemable. Feminist theologians who likewise judge Christianity to be patriarchal but nonetheless continue to work for change within their religious tradition, while they do not follow in Daly's direction, recognize the value of Daly's work for laying the foundations on which they will build their own work toward a renewed church.

7. By the publication of her second book, just a few years following the Second Vatican Council—which offered no new position in respect to women's ordination or leadership roles within the church, Daly judged the church to be irredeemably patriarchal and effectively left Christianity.

8. Daly, *The Church and the Second Sex*, 53.

9. De Beauvoir, *The Second Sex*.

10. Daly, *Church and the Second Sex*, 73.

11. Daly, quoting de Beauvoir, *Church and the Second Sex*, 61.

women's exclusion from that hierarchy as well as "the fact that God is called Father, that Christ is male, and that the angels, though they are pure spirit, have masculine names," creating an "inextricable confusion between man and God."[12] And third, the exclusion of women from the hierarchy creates a physical, material, and visual manifestation of male superiority that places men in roles not permitted (or practically available) to women. Further, Daly (along with de Beauvoir) asserts that this gender exclusion has specific psychological effects on women that are qualitatively different from other instances they may experience because "it is linked with an idea of divinity as male."[13] The ever-present male-dominated language and symbolism for the divine continually exacerbates the effects of exclusion. In addition, the Church asserts that feminine inferiority is inherent to the structure of their metaphysical reality. Daly shows how both the Hebrew tradition and Greek philosophy lay foundations for the view of human's fixed natures according to sex and the idea of women as the weaker or lesser sex.[14] Daly (and de Beauvoir) see philosophy and theology as key in laying "the misogynistic caste" of the Christian tradition. In the cases of both Eve and Pandora, women are the ones through whom sin or evil find its way into the world. Put simply, women are divinely established as being unequal to men due to their corruptibility and their subordination is thought to be "inscribed in the heavens."[15] The idea of women's inherent inferiority is built upon and continued by highly esteemed church fathers such as Ambrose, Clement of Alexandria, Jerome, and Augustine.[16]

Essentially, Daly's book powerfully explicated a single, significant, and core concern: Christianity's collusion with broader society in perpetuating women's second-class citizenship status, a firm conclusion she exposed in a systematic and damning way. The same patterns of prejudice, chauvinism, and hierarchical power structures based on notions of sexual difference that plagued society generally—beliefs that are materially detrimental to women and other marginalized persons—were revealed to be embedded in the church, and, worse, shown to be theologically justified and perpetuated. To overcome the Church's oppression of women, Daly proposed that "exorcising the evil of sexual prejudice" should begin with women themselves and their own consciousness-raising. She called for women already aware of the

---

12. Daly, *Church and the Second Sex*, 65–66.
13. Daly, *Church and the Second Sex*, 66.
14. Daly, *Church and the Second Sex*, 62–63.
15. In reference to the work of Plato, Aristotle, and Thomas Aquinas, see Daly, *Church and the Second Sex*, 62–63.
16. Daly, *Church and the Second Sex*, 63–64, 85–90.

prevailing sexual prejudice to be creatively vigorous and take on "the responsibility of changing the image of woman by raising up their own image, giving an example to others, and especially to the young."[17]

Such a comprehensive project—creating an atmosphere to foster the full evolution and human potential of women—required both theoretical and practical change.[18] Regarding theory, Daly saw a need to combat the idea of God as immutable, an image that results in a static view of the world, one where divine revelation was given in the past once and for all. Also, a "regressive, sin-obsessed view of human life" needed to shift decisively toward a view of the Incarnation, which allows for continued betterment of the human condition and the moral evolution of all people.[19] On a practical level, Daly argues for eradicating role-specific discrimination of women at various levels of service, from that which is assigned to her in the family structure to that from which she is excluded in church offices and functions.[20]

Despite her emphasis on the sins of church, her practical emphasis on change demonstrates how Daly remained optimistic for the future.[21] Daly's objective in *The Church and the Second Sex* is to convince readers that the seeds of the "democratized Church of the future" were present, though not yet made manifest, in "the living faith, hope and courage of the Christian community."[22] She reflected a positive, not sin-obsessed, understanding of the "nature" of humanity that affirmed the image of the divine in all persons. The divine is both accessible and actively present, and the power of divinity offers us the possibility that this should (and ultimately would) lead to transformation. Hers is an eschatological vision of a people of the democratized church that was indeed available; nevertheless, it is the responsibility of the church to embody and reflect this possibility of transcending sexual prejudice by reforming its doctrine and practice.

---

17. Daly, *Church and the Second Sex*, 177.
18. Daly, *Church and the Second Sex*, 177–78.
19. Daly, *Church and the Second Sex*, 182–85.
20. Daly, *Church and the Second Sex*, 195.
21. Again, Daly remained optimistic at the moment of writing this first book, though not at the time of writing her second book.
22. Daly, *Church and the Second Sex*, 213.

UNCOVERING PATRIARCHY IN THE EMERGING CHURCH MOVEMENT

Using the sensitizing work of Mary Daly as a foundation, how does the Emerging Church Movement understand itself in relation to the patriarchal hierarchy of contemporary society? First, the ECM can be difficult to define. In *The Deconstructed Church: Understanding Emerging Christianity*, Gerardo Martí and Gladys Ganiel refer to the ECM as "deconstructed" in order to describe its most fundamental characteristic—the willingness to raise questions, critiques, and doubts within the church. The "deconstructed" church refers to the phenomenon among Emerging Christians who read their tradition and the theologies that undergird their church structures and practices "meticulously, feeling about for its tensions, releasing what it itself may not want to disclose, remembering something it may not want to recall."[23] This default posture among ECM participants is what makes the ECM stand out as a "movement" in the first place; the Emerging Church Movement is made up of communities of people, congregations, among whom deconstruction is happening—not necessarily as an intentional act, but as something that cannot be helped. Deconstruction is core to their religious identity. The ubiquitous practice of deconstruction makes it possible to raise questions and critiques not only at the congregational level but at the theological and normative level of "Church" as well. ECM participants raise questions about the forms and structures of church, about theological issues like the nature of God, of faith, and of many other taken-for-granted doctrines within various strands of Christianity. ECM communities include many who are disaffected and disaffiliated from other forms of Christianity: *disaffected* because of the negative experiences they experienced in church structures (including abusive and traumatic experiences) and because of the incongruity between their understanding of what it means to be a church and concrete experiences of church; *disaffiliated* because of their decision to exit from other churches, sometimes from a series of churches and denominational orientations. Among ECM congregations, participants accept that their new ECM religious community represents a disruption of what they have previously known as normal and unquestioned faith. Their new ECM communities enact an active re-imagining of the Christian tradition.

---

23. Here I (Alvizo) draw from John D. Caputo's description of deconstruction during an interview with Gary Gutting for *The New Times*. While Caputo's work with Jacques Derrida and deconstruction is not necessarily widely read by those within the Emerging Church Movement, he is an explicit resource to some of its more philosophically inclined leaders. Gutting, "Deconstructing God," para. 24.

There are several dominant themes that recur in ECM publications and the qualitative research conducted on ECM congregations regarding their self-description and self-claimed commitments. For our understanding of the ECM, we draw from exhaustive reviews of the writings from ECM-affiliated leaders, and we also engage in systematic observation using the social scientific tools of ethnography (to avoid confusing the values promoted among the ECM and the actual behaviors of ECM participants).[24] The ECM is not a monolithic entity; rather, it represents a loose affiliation of different gatherings of people from various backgrounds and denominations, often younger but also older men and women whose children have grown and left the house. Together, they question their inherited tradition, raise concerns of their inherited theologies, and interrogate the incongruities experienced between their tradition's theological claims and the ways in which their churches are (or are not) embodying those claims. The reflexivity evident in their gatherings is continuous and palpable.

For our purposes, three recurring ECM themes stand out: 1) claims that the Emerging Church is more localized and fluid in form and expression, 2) attempts to put into practice more relational and participatory structures of participation and leadership, and 3) desire for greater inclusion of diversity, welcoming the questioning and change that is brought about by encounters with difference within the church as well as engaging with diversity outside of it. These three overarching characteristics, which we label here as *organic, relational,* and *inclusive,* reflect ECM's inclination for deconstruction and echoes commitments found in the ecclesiological work of feminist theologians.[25] Despite the ECM's self-claimed commitments of being more organic, relational, and inclusive, ECM leaders struggle to overcome the public perception that it is a movement dominated and led by a handful of white men. For example, in the United States, several of the most prominent figures recognized as representing the ECM are the oft cited Brian McLaren, Tony Jones, Doug Pagitt, Jay Bakker, Rob Bell, and Peter Rollins. Its public presentation on platforms at events, conferences,

---

24. For methodological guidance on the role of ethnography in practical theological scholarship, see Martí. "Found Theologies versus Imposed Theologies: Remarks on Theology and Ethnography from a Sociological Perspective," 157–172. Examples of ethnographic research that pays close attention to theological orientations, see Martí, *A Mosaic of Believers*; Martí, *Hollywood Faith*; Martí, *Worship Across the Racial Divide*; Jenkins and Martí, 'Warrior Chicks: Youthful Aging in a Postfeminist Prosperity Discourse'; Martí and Ganiel, *The Deconstructed Church*; Martí, "'I Was a Muslim, but Now I Am a Christian'"; Martí, "*Maranatha* (O Lord, Come)" .

25. For more on the Emerging Church's characteristics of being "organic," "relational," and "inclusive," see Alvizo, "A Feminist Theological Analysis of the Leadership Structures of the Emerging Church."

and congregational meetings, as well as the authorship of an extensive literature by leaders, often follows the pattern of a few high-profile white men standing in for the many—effectively erasing women. (Recently coming into more prominence after publication of new books and wider media coverage, Nadia Bolz-Weber and Rachel Held Evans are women now more visible in the ECM—see below.) Many others, who are recognized leaders in the movement and make up a great part of the emerging church, are also often missing.

The prominence of white male leadership in the ECM—something which these leaders have made efforts to overcome and who therefore resist such characterization—can be partly explained by recalling a popular telling of the history of the Emerging Church.[26] The ECM is most often traced back to events initiated by the Leadership Network, "a private parachurch evangelical organization that stimulates innovation and dialogue among church leaders."[27] The Leadership Network called together persons such as Brian McLaren, Tony Jones, Doug Pagitt, and Dan Kimball to form the Young Leaders Network, characterized as "advance scouts for the emerging church."[28] A project geared toward generational succession (and fear of losing the youth of America), this new alliance sought to empower emerging leaders to help them innovate evangelical Christianity in an increasingly "postmodern" culture. From this effort, the Leadership Network hired Doug Pagitt in 1997 to "scout" emerging church leaders—mostly youth pastors from moderately conservative churches who focused their ministry on the "baby busters and Generation X."[29] This first iteration of emerging leaders, comprised of young white men, played a formative role in the ECM. However, this oft-cited history is only a partial representation of the roots of the ECM.

In actuality, the origins, motivations, and participants of the ECM are more diverse and expansive than this anecdote reflects; thus, the legacy and impact of the usual origin story has been in some ways damaging. The pattern of male public representation, and the resulting popular perception of

---

26. One specific to the Emerging Church and not simply the default historical reality of white male dominance in the United States.

27. Martí and Ganiel, *The Deconstructed Church,* 22.

28. This was the tagline used on their website, which they have since changed, but which is documented by Dan Kimball in *Listening to the Beliefs of the Emerging Church* (83) and in his blogpost "Origin of the Terms "Emerging" and "Emergent" Church—Part I."

29. Dan Kimball, "Origin of the Terms "Emerging" and "Emergent" Church—Part I."

the ECM as orienting itself around those who are white and male, has been a point of discussion for a long time.

In the activities of the ECM, women overwhelmingly have reported positive and at times healing and transformative experiences with their individual congregations. However, within the movement, there are persistent reports of exclusion and marginalization of women. More specifically, recurring charges are made that the panels at Emerging Church conferences are largely made up of men, that Emergent events resemble "frat parties," and that when women do speak at events, men do not take them seriously. Julie Clawson, an early and active participant and once an avid blogger and founder of "Emerging Women" (an informal gathering of women who maintained a blog by the same name) was among the most outspoken about the embedded sexism evident at Emerging events.[30] Comments on her blog posts from other Emergent women confirm exclusionary experiences as being more than a few isolated incidents; women often expressed frustration about the experiences in regional and national gatherings where panels and plenary sessions predominantly feature male speakers. The prevalence of males on the stages of EMC-related gatherings created a public witness that the Emerging Church at large devalued women's contributions.

For example, in 2012, at an Emergent Village event at the Claremont School of Theology, women's frustration regarding the gendered dynamics of the ECM was an open point of discussion.[31] Roughly 40 percent of both the attendees *and* the presenters were women. Throughout the three days of the conference, the proportion of women represented a significant difference from what had been the case in earlier years; previous conferences were much less balanced, and women were vastly underrepresented. During one panel at a previous conference, a handful of outspoken women interrupted an all-male panel to raise the concern that the conference speakers were, yet again, all men. Conference organizers called for a short break, using the time to diversify the panel on the spot, with some men stepping down from the stage and some women stepping in to take their place. As a result, at the 2012 event, explicit efforts were made by the conference organizers to include women intentionally on the panels from the start.

Women's ECM conference experiences illustrate frustrations stemming from the tensions between commitment to the values of inclusivity

---

30. Julie Clawson, "Onehandclapping" website, http://julieclawson.com/, accessed March 1, 2015. Clawson is also author of the following books: *Everyday Justice* and *The Hunger Games and the Gospel*.

31. Xochitl Alvizo spoke with both women and men there expressing their frustrations, some of whom are referenced in this piece.

and egalitarianism alongside the systematic marginalization and exclusion of women. In one of her blog posts, Clawson puts it this way:

> So why isn't the message of welcome and inclusion being heard (if it does exist)? The most common answer still is because most of the authors and speakers are male—they are the voice that gets heard no matter who else is out there. Even at the recent Midwest Emergent Gathering where we attempted to be very deliberate about giving women a voice, the upfront presence was still predominantly male . . . It's not that there is anything wrong with the male leaders, they are great guys . . . I personally greatly appreciate the work they have done and the contributions they have made. But as popular as they [are] . . . we women don't have a place. We don't fit in with the boys' clubs and the male bonding experiences (which is what even many public events seem to be).[32]

Clawson is not alone in her frustrations. Stephanie Spellers, an ordained priest in the Episcopal Church and (former) lead organizer of The Crossing (an emergent community in Boston, Massachusetts) expresses a similar sentiment, this time emphasizing race. Expressing her concern that people disregard the reality that not all "Emergent Christians" are white, she asks:

> Is the emerging church a whites-only movement? Some savvy observers say so.1 Perhaps because I'm a black woman serving as priest and lead organizer with an Anglimergent community in Boston, I get peppered with questions like "Aren't they racists? What are you doing with them?" My more skeptical Episcopal colleagues are almost giddy with the news, as if they're grateful to see cracks in the revolutionaries' ranks.[33]

For Spellers, the general perception of the ECM as "white-only" is problematic in that it effectively erases all other participants who are not white and male. And because the ECM generally has limited public exposure, and because the popular few tend to be white and male, Spellers' own participation is looked upon with curious skepticism.

---

32. Clawson, "Women in the Emerging Church."

33. Spellers, "Monocultural Church in a Hybrid World," 12. Quote includes footnote 1: Rah, *The Next Evangelicalism*. See also, Rah and Mach, with responses by Debbie Blue, Julie Clawson, and Brian D. McLaren, "Is the Emerging Church for Whites Only?" 16–21. This article created a stir among Emerging Church leaders and participants, responses to which exploded on the blogosphere for months to follow.

From outside the movement, sociologist Gladys Ganiel also affirms the lack of priority given to women's visibility in the Emerging Church. Referencing a discussion with Peter Rollins, Ganiel notes that, "the group with which Rollins is associated in Belfast, Ikon,[34] seems to me quite gender-balanced. A number of women are involved in planning and organizing its events." She continues, saying, "But as Rollins wryly acknowledged, the Insurrection Tour—a sort of portable Ikon featuring Rollins, Pádraig Ó Tuama, and Jonny McEwen—was fronted by three white guys."[35]

What little attention is given to women in the movement can leave people scratching their heads. For example, at the 2014 annual meeting of the American Academy of Religion, the Critical Research in Religion group held a session titled, "Is the Emergent/ing Church Important?" where an early version of this chapter was presented. Titled "Is the Emerging Church Important from a Feminist Practical Theological Perspective," with its explicitly feminist analysis, the presentation was received with awkward commentary. Homebrewed Christianity, a community of podcasts, bloggers, and regular listeners "invested in expanding and deepening the conversation around faith and theology," recorded a podcast following the session that included brief comments about the panel's content.[36] Hosted by Tripp Fuller, the podcast consisted of a conversation between him and Tony Jones offering their reaction to the panel's topic. Both are active ECM participants, and their exchange regarding the paper on feminism and the Emerging Church offers a glimpse into the disregard of hetero/sexism and misogyny. Jones briefly introduced the topic of each of the papers, and as he introduced the paper written from a feminist perspective, this was the exchange:

> Jones: There was another one about, a paper on—is the Emerging Church a place where feminism can thrive, that's actually open to overthrowing patriarchal systems and patterns in the conventional church.
>
> Fuller: Was the subtitle, 'Tony Jones saves women'?
>
> Jones: It wasn't.
>
> Fuller: Oh my bad—
>
> Jones:—Actually, it wasn't.

---

34. According to its "About Ikon" page of its website, Ikon is a "Belfast-based collective who offer anarchic experiments in transformance art," accessed December 31, 2014, http://ikonbelfast.wordpress.com/about/.

35. Ganiel, "Emerging Women?," para. 4.

36. Homebrewed Christianity, Homebrewed Christianity website, http://homebrewedchristianity.com/.

Fuller:—I was too busy reading the internet.[37]

This moment, while brief and seemingly lighthearted, is an apt illustration of the "boys club" environment contributing to the negative public image of the ECM. It is the type of masculine play that supports the perception of the ECM as "just more patriarchy."[38]

What about some of the prominent women associated with the movement? Nadia Bolz-Weber is a high-profile writer and speaker and one of the very few women leaders viewed as core to the ECM. Bolz-Weber, a Lutheran minister, is the founding pastor of an emerging congregation named House for All Sinners and Saints, who seemingly disproves the gendered characterization made throughout this paper. She has an active public ministry, often featured in such mediums as "BBC World Service, The Washington Post, Bitch Magazine, NPR's Morning Edition, Fresh Air, More Magazine, The Daily Beast, and CNN."[39] She is easily recognizable because of her eye-catching style in fashion, strong physique, and extensive tattoos, which are made all the more striking by her regular use of a clerical collar (even when wearing cutoff sleeve shirts revealing the ink on her arms). Known for her sarcasm[40] and "foul mouth," she maintains a busy public speaking schedule touring the United States and other parts of the world to speak about her books, her spiritual memoir *Pastrix: The Cranky, Beautiful Faith of a Sinner & Saint* and *Accidental Saints: Finding God in All the Wrong People*—all while unabashedly upholding her Lutheran tradition.[41]

Unlike others in the ECM who have outspokenly troubled the theological waters they swim, Nadia Bolz-Weber does not raise questions of her denomination's theology, making her someone who gets disproportionate attention but is also theologically safe to the institution—emerging or mainline. House for all Sinners and Saints was founded as a mission and financially supported by the Evangelical Lutheran Church of America. While her presentation is progressive, so much so that "Nobody really believes she is an ordained pastor in the ELCA,"[42] she holds firmly to her Lutheran theology

37. See Homebrewed Christianity website, "Theology for the People: Publishing, Emergent and God," minute: 44:15–44:25.

38. "Just more patriarchy" is a quote from a woman minister of an ECM congregation whom I (Alvizo) interviewed during my research study with Emerging Church congregations. She made this statement in regard to her impression of the ECM at large and why she was reluctant to overtly affiliate and participate in ECM events.

39. Nadia Bolz-Weber website, http://www.nadiabolzweber.com/.

40. She is known on social media as the "sarcastic Lutheran"—a name she uses for herself.

41. Bolz-Weber, *Pastrix*; and Bolz-Weber, *Accidental Saints*.

42. Nadia Bolz-Weber, personal website, http://www.nadiabolzweber.com/.

and understands herself to be the "theological center" of her congregation. Thus, even while Nadia Bolz-Weber is a high profile woman counted in the fold of the ECM—a conspicuous contrast to the general public perception—she is strongly institutionally affiliated.

Rachel Held Evans is another high profile woman connected to the ECM.[43] She and Bolz-Weber partnered to organize a 2015 conference featuring only women speakers. This conference, titled "Why Christian," now an annual event,[44] was the second conference featuring all women speakers. In 2009, the JoPa Group (co-founded by Tony Jones and Doug Pagitt), organized the first such event, Christianity 21, with all women presenting in an effort to actively bring Emerging Church women to the forefront, "to imagine a 21st century Christianity with 21 speakers who deliver 21 big ideas in 21 minutes each."[45] Julie Clawson recalls Christianity 21, saying,

> In the lead-up to the conference I was part of numerous discussions regarding the need to give the stage so deliberately to a group of women. I get the desire to be at a point in the conversation where women's voices don't have to be highlighted but are just a normal part of things. Or to be at a place of if there is a Christian conference where the main speakers are women people don't assume that it's a women's conference. I'd love that, but we aren't there yet. I think C21 moved us forward in that direction, but women's voices had to be highlighted this time in order for that to happen. And I love that men who typically speak at these sorts of conferences came instead to serve at this one—doing all the behind the scenes stuff that we women often end up doing.[46]

This desire that Julie Clawson expressed in 2009—that people not assume that a conference in which the main speakers are women is a "women's conference"—continues to be unfulfilled. When the all-women speaker Why Christian conference was publicized in 2015, Rachel Held Evans noted precisely this assumption, raising the point that the same thing is not assumed for conferences with an all-men line up. Evans writes, "Observation: An all-woman speaker lineup at a conference generates the question "Is this

---

43. Rachel Held Evans (blog), "What Is Changing in the Church, April 19, 2010."

44. Why Christian, conference webpage, https://whychristian.net/, accessed June 6, 2017.

45. JoPa Group, "C21—2009," http://c21.thejopagroup.com/c21-2009/, accessed June 6, 2017.

46. Clawson (blog), "Thoughts on Christianity 21," October 14, 2009, http://julieclawson.com/2009/10/14/thoughts-on-christianity-21/.

a women's conference?" Would an all-male lineup?"[47] Women continue to be considered a class apart in a way men are simply not.

So, while the answer to the question "Is the Emerging Church for white men only?" can be said to be "No," that answer is not unequivocal. The integration of women to the public face and leadership of the movement has been difficult and contested. And recognition of prominent women has been slow to come. While emerging women's frustrations are not as dominant (or as public) as they once were, we find that their occasional inclusion is not a sufficient indication that those who have long represented the ECM in the *public's* perception have actively worked to address the concerns and experiences of women regarding sexism, heterosexism, and misogyny within the movement.[48] To accomplish this will likely require the ECM to take on an even deeper layer of theological deconstruction.

SENSITIVITIES FOR THE EMERGING CHURCH MOVEMENT FROM A FEMINIST PRACTICAL THEOLOGICAL PERSPECTIVE

Early feminist practical theologians oriented their work to intentionally address the context and the material effects of patriarchy. They focused their work and critiques on the *underlying structures* that created the conditions that distorted the church's constitution, and intentionally re-imagined and set forth the reforms needed at a practical level to contra-indicate the distortions. These efforts are echoed in certain imperatives of the ECM—commitments to such things as a flat leadership structure, participatory decision-making, and radical inclusivity (although the catalyst among ECM participants differs). While the ECM has successfully provided many positive and healing experiences, providing new avenues for participating in a church community, and while it has sought to be relational and egalitarian in leadership and structure, its efforts are nonetheless deficient. Knowing the frustrations women within the ECM have expressed, the lack of significant

---

47. Rachel Held Evans (Twitter), @rachelheldevans, January 12, 2015, https://twitter.com/rachelheldevans/status/554711049942106112?ref_src=twsrc%5Etfw&ref_url=https%3A%2F%2Fwww.christiantoday.com%2Farticle%2Fwhy.christian.nadia.bolz.weber.and.rachel.held.evans.launch.new.conference%2F45930.htm

48. See: Holly Roach, "Journeying Through the Dark Side of Emergent Christianity (Toward the Light!)," Emerging Voices: Riding a New Wave of Emergence website, http://www.patheos.com/blogs/emergentvillage/2014/10/the-dark-side-of-emergent-christianity/, October 1, 2013; Kim Roth, "I Am Emergent Village," Emerging Voices: Riding a New Wave of Emergence website, June 3, 2013, http://www.patheos.com/blogs/emergentvillage/2013/06/i-am-emergent-village/.

change on the part of its male leadership, and the insufficiency of all-women events, the need for a deeper level of deconstruction persists.

We propose three sensitivities drawn from early feminist practical theological work. These sensitivities effectively generate analytical questions and more properly motivate the development of the ECM:

- *We are embodied persons*: First, the primacy of embodied experience; this includes both concern for concrete reality, especially of the lives of those who have been systemically neglected, i.e. women, children, people of color, etc., and concern for physical human bodies—what they experience and what is done to them.
- *We are enmeshed in systems of power*: Second, the continual need for a systemic analysis of power dynamics; this includes both the role of institutional power differentials and the power differentials embedded in the social construction and employment of gender.[49]
- *We must prioritize the practice of reflexivity:* Third, the insistence that self-reflexivity, engaged in community, pertaining to one's theologizing and praxis, is imperative; including the recognition that one's inherited religious practices and theologies are born of and formed by particular socio-political contexts, interests, and locations and require critical reflection and interrogation.

These three sensitivities capture how feminists see and continually critique the deeply embedded historical pattern of structuring society—political and social units such as family, household, monarchy, nation—in such a way that some persons are more highly valued than others based on notions of sexual difference and are by default attributed more power and privilege. Entrenched patriarchalism exists both *interpersonally* in our attitudes and actions and *institutionally* in our macro-social and political structures, organizing power from the top-down. The system, therefore, is not only in reference to male-female social dynamics but also to all structures that set up a dynamic in which some effectively "lord" over others, whether based on sex differentiation, race, or socio-economic status.

Acknowledging the complexity of our bodies and their enmeshment with societal systems of power, Elisabeth Schüssler Fiorenza passes over the term "patriarchy" to use "*kyriarchy*." *Kyriarchy* is defined as "the structures of domination working together as a network—its branches include but are not limited to racism, sexism, classism, heterosexism, ageism, and

---

49. Ackermann and Bons-Strom, *Liberating Faith Practices*, 5.

ableism."⁵⁰ The term accentuates that patriarchy is a *system*. Kyriarchy is not simply about one group dominating another; it represents an interlocking web of oppressive social systems working together to preserve a perpetual condition of inequity. She names the entrenched patriarchal sexism of the church as a "structural sin" and an ultimately "life-destroying power."⁵¹ As structural sin, patriarchalism is inherited in "the dehumanizing trends, injustices and discriminations of institutions" and in "the theology and symbol system that legitimates these institutions."⁵² It also results in "false consciousness"—both collective and personal—that permits the acceptance and internalization of oppressive values.⁵³

The challenge for the ECM (and the whole of progressive efforts bringing attention to gender issues evident among many strands of contemporary Christianity) is to accept that our societal patriarchal inheritance requires more than just intentional effort. It requires active counter-practices of thoughtful resistance at the *structural* level. Even the early feminist theologians recognized the obduracy of this structural environment, one within which the church takes form and by which it continues to be shaped. The force of these gendered structures cannot be overstated or taken for granted.

Therefore, even among the most enlightened leaders of the ECM, it must be recognized that patriarchal patterns have so successfully structured the entirety of the Christian church that associated dynamics continually reemerge—even when they are understood to be theologically contrary to a particular church's desire. So, as a means of encouraging reflexivity, we encourage Emerging Christians to interrogate themselves and ask: Is the ECM taking seriously the concrete reality of women's embodied experience regarding their role and participation? Is it willing to look at its overarching patterns, systemically/collectively speaking, and not rest on its few notable exceptions? In the larger historical context of the prevailing sexual prejudice, what concrete action will it take to, as Mary Daly charges, take responsibility to raise the image of women, "giving an example to others, and especially to the young"?⁵⁴ Is it willing to do this at both structural and theological levels? For example, what are the underlying theologies regarding the nature of God and humanity implicitly and explicitly at work in the church's rhetoric, metaphors, song lyrics, liturgies, symbols? How may these reinforce or challenge patterns of oppression impacting embodied experience?

50. Schüssler Fiorenza, *Discipleship of Equals*, 131.
51. Ibid., 140
52. Ibid.
53. Ibid.
54. Daly, *Church and the Second Sex*, 177.

Even further, does the ECM, as a continually deconstructing church, deconstruct their decision-making and leadership structures from the lens of gender, sexuality, and race? What do their visible structures reveal about its connection between its theory and its practice? As the ECM interrogates its power dynamics, is it willing to make changes in order to better reflect its diverse community? And regarding its inclusivity—to what extent is the ECM as a collective willing to listen deeply to the voices, experiences, and contributions of all its participants? Are the voices of its broad range of participants having a shaping effect in the incarnation it takes as a religious body? Does the ECM's commitment to inclusion, particularly of those typically marginalized in society actually impact the way leadership looks and works? Who gets to see themselves reflected at the decision-making level and in the language and symbols of the church? What patterns of visibility are embodied in its public face to the world and how are these connected to its everyday reality? Whose work and contributions are celebrated and highlighted? Who is being overlooked and underappreciated? What are the images of power and relationality embedded in the language, symbols, and metaphors within its rhetoric, liturgies, and songs? Who is represented and actively involved in its day-to-day planning and whose labor is monetarily compensated?

The self-reflexivity that feminist practical theology insists upon invites questions like those posed above in order to generate heuristic connection between the stated ideals of the ECM and the reality of its concrete embodiment. Emerging Christians are encouraged to confront the depth of the problem before it is able to successfully address it. Moreover, in accomplishing the work of reflexivity, it is not sufficient to pose large, abstract questions. It is imperative to bring the focus down the ladder of abstraction to become even more perceptive of small, everyday nuances where social hierarchies are manifest, noticing and then challenging the conditions that facilitate the valuing of some people over others and perpetuating their second-class citizenship.

In short, a deconstructing church has a duty to take these realities into account and bring them to bear on its analysis of church and recommendations made for re/forming church theory and practice at the congregational level. A feminist practical theological perspective, then, reveals that on the whole, the leadership of the ECM has not adequately taken into account the insidious nature of patriarchy and its self-perpetuating character—patriarchy as structural sin—and has therefore not adequately responded to it. This deeper level of analysis from a feminist practical theological perspective invites the ECM to raises questions about the disconnection between its theory and its practice regarding its organic, relational, and inclusive character. The ECM must take seriously that church and Christianity are and always have been historically situated. In a context of patriarchal kyriarchy, the ECM must seek to transform the church in ways that address the particular distortions of said environment.

CONFRONTING PATRIARCHY AND CREATING OUR FUTURE TOGETHER

One of the primary tasks feminist theologians take on is to re-discover the past and face the unseen history of the church's complicity with sexism, marginalization, and domination. Mary Daly rightly noted that it takes courage to see—it is not easy to dis-cover and come face to face with one's own nonbeing in one's own religious tradition, with the many ways one has not been considered to be fully human.[55] It is the case that Christianity and the church contain the roots of patriarchy within its history and foundational texts and has in concrete ways explicitly and implicitly dehumanized women.[56] However, the church's willingness to discover and reveal what has been covered over is necessary for the discovery of an alternative future.[57] Transformation requires discovering the "previously unknown into that which we explicitly know, and therefore can reflect upon, criticize," to then "spark new visions . . . creative crystallizing."[58] Our deep understanding precedes our creative reimaging and transformation. The ECM can actively discover and explicitly critique the patriarchal patterns and structures embedded in Christianity to reach forward.

Feminist theologians have long noted the difficulty of facing and rejecting the deeply ingrained patterns of hierarchical structuring and sex-based valuing that have historically governed church leadership, decision-making, and theological interpretation—and the ECM is not immune to such deeply historic patterns. Indeed, entrenched habits are often thought to be intrinsic to the Christian tradition and challenging these patterns disrupts familiar habits of the church that are largely upheld even among Emerging Christians. Mary Daly notes: "[s]eeing means that everything changes: the old identifications and the old securities are gone."[59] In the case of the ECM, which strives to be a different kind of church—relational, organic, and inclusive—*seeing* and bringing an explicit critique of patriarchy is precisely

---

55. Daly, "The Women's Movement," 331.
56. See Schüssler Fiorenza, *The Power of the Word*.
57. Daly, *Gyn/Ecology*, in *The Mary Daly Reader*, 152.
58. Daly, *The Mary Daly Reader*, 152.
59. Daly, "The Women's Movement," 331.

the deeper layer of theological deconstruction it needs in order to shape new imperatives that can lead it to displace the habits and patterns that perpetuate implicit gender and race prejudices. A feminist practical theological lens proves fruitful to help see patriarchy, providing a conceptual language and framework of analysis for discerning the nature of these patterns and the depth of their entrenchment in the church.

The ECM represents a unique opportunity to apply and test a feminist perspective of church, analyze its structures and patterns of patriarchy, and interrogate how these continue to exist within it so it may envision new imperatives to help it move into its vision of a radically inclusive, egalitarian church. Despite the aggressive critique reported above, we believe that Emerging Christians can build on their commitment to inclusion of diversity, egalitarian leadership, and participatory structures. Clearly, more must be done than to simply acknowledge that a problem exists. Women within ECM congregations do report positive experiences and deep appreciation of the creative forms their churches take in comparison to others they have previously experienced or thought possible. And observation readily reveals male leaders attempting to address charges raised against them and to forge new paths that break away from inherited patterns of patriarchalism and structural sexism.

Change for such deeply entrenched structures is not accomplished by good will alone. Practices are laden with theory, reflect positionality and bias, and must therefore be made explicit and/or interrogated for the sake of addressing situations of inequality, oppression, and alleviating suffering.[60] The ECM, which has proved to be amenable to deconstruction and change, represents, from a feminist practical theological point of view, communities of faith with the potential to actively dismantle the patriarchal inheritance of their forms and structures. As the ECM names and employs an explicit critique of patriarchy to its own forms and structures, it not only resists kyriarchal ways of being and relating, it builds the potential for uprooting them so as to form a political body disentangled of patriarchal distortions that more faithfully represents the creative alternative church is designed to embody. As with feminist theologians and the critiques they raised of church decades before its formation, the ECM needs to now focus on the underlying structures creating the conditions that distort its constitution and the re-imagining and reforms needed at a practical level to contraindicate those patriarchal distortions.

---

60. See Ackermann and Bons-Strom, *Liberating Faith Practices*; Miller-McLemore and Gill-Austern, *Feminist and Womanist Pastoral Theology*; and Mercer, *Welcoming Children*.

A feminist practical theological perspective contributes to decentering the patriarchalism of the church and opening up more progressive Christian orientations like that of the ECM to exercise a timely and historically relevant theological imagination, so that the church may be the living, changing organism it is intended to be, one that values and is radically liberating to all its participants. Facilitated by the framework of analysis and conceptual vocabulary of a feminist practical theological perspective, the church of the near future will deepen its understanding of the subtleties of patriarchy embedded in the forms, structures, language and symbol systems and be inspired to dismantle environments where only male persons (as our primary example) are consistently privileged and valued over others.

In the end, bringing a feminist practical theological perspective to the Emerging Church Movement allows us to glimpse the subject matter from a different point of view, one that contributes both to advancing the ECM's self-proclaimed imperatives and feminist theologians' vision of a repentant and transformed church. If the Emerging Church is to be important from a feminist practical theological perspective, it must be able to constantly build a vision of itself beyond patriarchal kyriarchy—reject this inheritance of the historical Christian tradition—and actively engage in efforts to dismantle those systems in order to collectively create new ones. Feminist theologian Rosemary Radford Reuther points out that "patriarchy is too old and too deeply rooted both in our psyches and in our culture and collective life to be quickly analyzed, rejected, and then overcome."[61] If the emerging church is to emerge out of the patriarchal inheritance embedded in Christianity, to more faithfully embody its own vision, it must engage in some of the same deconstruction feminists been conducting since the Women's Liberation Movement of the late 1960s and early 1970s and move into an equally exciting future.

BIBLIOGRAPHY

Ackermann, Denise M., and Riet Bons-Strom, eds. *Liberating Faith Practices: Feminist Practical Theologies in Context.* Leuven: Peeters, 1998.

Alvizo, Xochitl. "A Feminist Theological Analysis of the Leadership Structures of the Emerging Church." In *Crossing Boundaries, Redefining Faith: Interdisciplinary Perspectives on the Emerging Church Movement,* edited by Michael Clawson and April Stace, 92–119. Eugene, OR: Pickwick, 2016.

Bolz-Weber, Nadia. *Pastrix: The Cranky, Beautiful Faith of a Sinner & Saint.* New York: Jericho, 2013.

---

61. Reuther, *Women–Church*, 62.

———. *Accidental Saints: Finding God in All the Wrong People*. New York: Convergent, 2015.

Clawson, Julie. *Everyday Justice: The Global Impact of Our Daily Choices*. Downers Grove, IL: Intervarsity, 2009.

———. *The Hunger Games and the Gospel*. Englewood, CO: Patheos, 2013.

Daly, Mary. *Beyond God the Father: Toward a Philosophy of Women's Liberation. With an Original Reintroduction by the Author*. Boston: Beacon, 1985 (original 1973).

———. *The Church and the Second Sex; with a Feminist Postchristian Introduction and New Archaic Afterwords by the Author*. Boston: Beacon, 1985.

———. *Gyn/Ecology: The Metaethics of Radical Feminism, With a New Intergalactic Introduction by the Author*, in *The Mary Daly Reader*, eds. Jennifer Rycenga and Linda Barufaldi, 152. New York: New York University Press, 2017.

———. "The Women's Movement: An Exodus Community." In *Religious Education* 47 (1972) 327–33.

De Beauvoir, Simone. *The Second Sex*. Translated by Constance Borde and Shiela Malovany-Chevallier. New York: Vintage, 2011.

Ganiel, Gladys. "Emerging Women? Is the Emerging Church Dominated by White Men?" Website, *Gladys Ganiel: Building a Church Without Walls*. http://www.gladysganiel.com/churches-reconciliation/emerging-women-is-the-emerging-church-dominated-by-white-men/.

Gutting, Gary. "Deconstructing God." In *The Stone* (blog), *The New York Times,* March 9, 2014. https://opinionator.blogs.nytimes.com/2014/03/09/deconstructing-god/?mcubz=0.

Jenkins, K. E., and Gerardo Martí. "Warrior Chicks: Youthful Aging in a Postfeminist Prosperity Discourse." *Journal for the Scientific Study of Religion* 51 (2012) 241–56.

Martí, Gerardo, and Gladys Ganiel. *The Deconstructed Church: Understanding Emerging Christianity*. New York: Oxford University Press, 2014.

Martí, Gerardo. "Found Theologies versus Imposed Theologies: Remarks on Theology and Ethnography from a Sociological Perspective." In *Ecclesial Practices* 3 (2016) 157–72.

———. *Hollywood Faith: Holiness, Prosperity, and Ambition in a Los Angeles Church*. New Brunswick, NJ: Rutgers University Press, 2008.

———. "'I Was a Muslim, but Now I Am a Christian': Preaching, Legitimation, and Identity Management in a Southern Evangelical Church." *Journal for the Scientific Study of Religion* 55 (2016) 250–70.

———. "*Maranatha* (O Lord, Come): The Power/Surrender Dynamic of Pentecostal Worship." *Liturgy* 33:3 (2018) 20–28.

———. *A Mosaic of Believers: Diversity and Innovation in a Multiethnic Church*. Bloomington: Indiana University Press, 2005.

———. "New Concepts for New Dynamics: Generating Theory for the Study of Religious Innovation and Social Change." In *Journal for the Scientific Study of Religion* 56:1 (2017) 6–18.

———. *Worship across the Racial Divide: Religious Music and the Multiracial Congregation*. New York: Oxford University Press, 2012.

Mercer, Bonnie J. *Welcoming Children: A Practical Theology of Childhood*. St. Louis: Chalice, 2005.

Miller-McLemore, Bonnie J., and Brita L. Gill-Austern. *Feminist and Womanist Pastoral Theology*. Nashville: Abingdon, 1999.

Rah, Soong-Chan. *The Next Evangelicalism: Freeing the Church from Western Cultural Captivity*. Downers Grove, IL: InterVarsity, 2009.

Rah, Soong-Chan and Jason Mach, with responses by Debbie Blue, Julie Clawson, and Brian D. McLaren. "Is the Emerging Church for Whites Only?" *Sojourners* (May 2010) 16–21.

Schüssler Fiorenza, Elisabeth. *Discipleship of Equals: A Critical Feminist Ekklesia-ology of Liberation*. New York: Crossroad, 1994.

———. *The Power of the Word: Scripture and the Rhetoric of Empire*. Minneapolis: Fortress, 2007.

Spellers, Stephanie. "Monocultural Church in a Hybrid World." In *The Hyphenateds: How Emergence Christianity is Re-Traditioning Mainline Practices,* edited by Phil Snider, 12–25. St. Louis: Chalice, 2011.

Afterword
A New Generation, A New Church?

Philip Clayton

The intrigue of this volume is precisely that it cannot have an "after" word. The trends covered here are unfolding even as the book is being written and published. We know that the face of religion in North America is changing as rapidly as any time in the history of the continent. The one thing we do not know, however, is what North American religion will look like when this tsunami has passed (if it passes).

The authors have walked a fine line between positive prospects and serious problems. In the literature one finds authors who defend the emerging church movement (ECM) and those who attack it; authors who frame the movement theologically and those who approach it as a manifestation of North American religiosity to be studied by sociologists and psychologists; authors who see in the ECM an important motor for change in church and society, and others who interpret the movement as merely an effect of outside causes. It is rare, more rare than readers may at first realize, to see so many of these interests covered in a single volume. No other volume, to our knowledge, includes the whole range of scholarship about emerging churches in their broader social, cultural, and religious context.

CONTEMPORARY AMERICAN RELIGION

Some readers will have loved, and others will have hated the picture of contemporary American religion that emerges in these pages. Reading the chapters, I think repeatedly of Nietzsche's "Parable of the Madman" who proclaims the death of God. Some feel liberated, Nietzsche notes, by the loss of old structures and mores, by this new age of rapid change. But the madman seeks to convince the townspeople that they are not prepared for the consequences: "Whither are we moving? Away from all suns? Are we not plunging continually? Backward, sideward, forward, in all directions? Is there still any up or down? Are we not straying, as through an infinite nothing? Do we not feel the breath of empty space?"

The recognition of the "death of God" that came as a radical shock in the late nineteenth century has now become the subject matter of scientific surveys and extensive data analysis. As Stephanie Yuhas writes, "Religion and spirituality are in a process of splitting, morphing and reintegrating into new forms that align with a postmodern reality that Millennials have grown up with and learned to navigate." The examination of the emerging church is, in our view, one of the most fascinating case studies of this "splitting, morphing and reintegrating."

(In this text we have capitalized the Emerging Church Movement as the title of a specific movement, like the Social Gospel Movement. But I fear that the capital-E, capital-C in "the Emerging Church" creates the impression of a distinct thing or event, like Labor Day or the Golden Gate Bridge. Scholars of American religion are often guilty of similar mistakes: the New Atheism, New Age, New Thought, the Black Church. If the research presented here tells us anything, it is that this movement is [these movements are?] immensely fluid and lack clear boundaries, which is one reason why they are so hard to define. It's all the more important, then, not to turn a chaos of new attitudes and forms of church into a thing. Our task is to name the whirlwind, not to tame it.)

Never before in history have humans been able to survey themselves so effectively. Will Herberg published an extremely influential book on American religion in 1955 and could entitle it simply *Protestant, Catholic, Jew*. Some sixty years later, despite the fact that influential religious and spiritual options are now numbered in the dozens and statistically significant trends can arise in fewer than five years, we can track each one as carefully as Herberg tracked his three. But, like the 24-hour news cycle, it has become difficult to separate the significant from the merely known. Several authors here therefore rely on case studies and qualitative, ethnographic research to clarify what quantitative data alone cannot. In a sense, the study of the emerging church may be more significant as a case study, a window onto contemporary American religion, than as data points on the transformation of American religious attitudes.

If this is true of the emerging church, it is no less true of the subset of the population that is most deeply involved in the movement: Millennials.

MILLENNIALS

As Shenandoah Nieuwsma notes, "There are 83 million Millennials in the United States; they make up 26% of the U.S. population, a greater portion than any other generation." The United States Census Bureau affirms the same number using birth dates that fall in years from 1982 to 2000. That means we are mostly studying the cohort of North Americans who in 2018 were between 18 and 36 years old.

People often express skepticism about generational cohorts: why end Generation X in 1982 and start Generation Z in 2000? And yet data about common values and behaviors usually establish rough boundaries, as they did effectively for the Silent Generation and Baby Boomers; similar data point to Millennials as a distinct demographic group. It's important to set aside one's skepticism about demographic polling and data analysis in the social sciences in order to consider the features of Millennials that have been presented in these chapters. Many of these features do indeed distinguish a significant number of people in this cohort from those coming before and after them.

That said, as I reread the chapters above, a very distinct impression arises: At the end of the day, *we still don't know who "Millennials" are*, at least not in the way that we comprehend the deep similarities among most Baby Boomers. It's not just the arbitrariness of the snip between babies born in 1981 versus 1982, or in 2000 versus 2001. Nor is it that 83 million people put their worlds together in 83 million different ways.

It's actually a more fundamental uncertainty: is the Millennial generation "Generation We" or "Generation Me," as Randy Reed puts it in "The Problem of Anti-Institutionalism in Millennials"? One studies the best attested data from surveyors and sociologists and is still unsure: are Millennials more altruistic or more cynical? More giving or more snarky? More centered on acquisition and the comforts of wealth, or more ready to sacrifice for the common good? Are Millennials ready to reform and rebuild important institutions such as the church, or would they prefer to deconstruct and destroy it?

And yet nothing is more important for comprehending the ECM, its present forms and its long-term significance, than knowing the answers to these questions. If we don't know what the largest demographic in the American population will do in five or ten years, then we don't know the fate of the American church as history has known it. Will Millennials return to existing churches in large numbers as they become parents and begin to raise children? Early data suggest that this is not happening. Will they work to reform religious institutions, to make them more open and less judgmental—perhaps by creating new forms of church—or will they reject organized religion altogether? Early data support both options. Sunday Assemblies, as Joel Daniels shows, are still religious institutions, just ones that are not limited to a creed (or to a God, for that matter); but even here we cannot tell whether they will continue to grow and thrive. Return, reform, or reject? We just don't know yet.

THE EMERGING CHURCH MOVEMENT IN MOTION

I have argued that the behaviors of Millennials are changing; it's difficult to define "Millennial"; therefore one cannot yet assess the long-term impact of this, the largest and most influential demographic in the American population today. If these uncertainties characterize the Millennial generation, they arise ten-fold in studies of the emergent church movement.

I remember a conversation with Phyllis Tickle, the kind but strict grandmother of the emerging church movement. Phyllis argued passionately that I shouldn't use the word "emerging" any longer, or even "emergent," but only the phrase "the emergence church." Indeed, every single defining moment that I can think of—Fresh Expressions in Britain or The Emergent Village—was no longer definitive within a few years. People are critical of Millennials' suspicion of labels and unwillingness to categorize. "Ism's" are out. But there are also advantages to this mindset: what counts as social reality is changing rapidly, and supposedly unchangeable frameworks from the past are changing as quickly as adolescent rock bands. In a world of shifting sands one needs to tread lightly.

Perhaps it's for this reason that many of us as religious studies scholars, theologians, and activists find the emerging church to be one of the most interesting movements in Western Christianity today. It's also one of the most challenging. It's amorphous; its boundaries are not clearly defined; and it is moving in unexpected directions year by year. Adam Sweatman offers an extremely helpful brief overview of the changes in his section, "Emergent Village: A History." In fact, I can't think of a time when the ECM *wasn't* undergoing radical change.

The succession of leaders, institutional affiliations, activities, and self-understandings in the ECM is enough to give one vertigo. As soon as a canonical text on the movement was written—whether by "neutral" scholars, insiders, or outside critics—it prompted intense discussions . . . and then was pushed aside by the next analysis. We debated the ideas of the all-star cast in *The Emerging Christian Way: Thoughts, Stories, and Wisdom for a Faith of Transformation*; then we were caught be Dwight Friesen's *Thy*

Kingdom Connected; and then it was Christian Piatt's *Post-Christian: What's Left? Can We Fix it? Do We Care?* Some works people kept coming back to—Gibbs and Bolger's *Emerging Churches*, John Caputo's *What Would Jesus Deconstruct*, and the publications of Tony Jones, Shane Claiborne, and Brian McLaren. Other authors had insights that went beyond, and would thus outlast, the ups and downs: Letty Russell's *Church in the Round*, say, or Rachel Held Evans' *Faith Unraveled: How a Girl Who Knew All the Answers Learned to Ask Questions*.

In general, however, the ECM has not been kind to canonical works. Organizations and institutions have come and gone even more rapidly—too quickly for me to even list them here. The coin of the realm in the ECM is, of course, the communities themselves. After visiting and getting to know a community, we talk and write about it. That is one of the reasons why Gibbs and Bolger's *Emerging Churches* has held such interest. And yet follow-up studies of the various communities in their book revealed that many of these paradigm communities were no longer in existence five or ten years later. Even proclamations of the death of the ECM have not held. Sweatman nicely summarizes some of these proclamations between 2010 and 2012. But what happened? Each proclamation itself became the focus of an intense discussion within the movement, until the next proclamation came along and the old one no longer seemed useful. Indeed, for many of us, discussions of "the death of emergence" have produced not depression but new energy in the search for new forms.

The same has been true of central concepts. Postmodernism offers a particularly good example, since several chapters in this volume stress the important role of postmodernism in Millennial thought and the ECM. Yet no one knows what "postmodern" means. (Some of us love it, and others hate it, for precisely that reason.) Teaching Millennials, I hear clear suspicion about sharp, clear, unchanging definitions of "postmodern," such as those by David Ray Griffin or Nancey Murphy. The most widespread, "orthodox" understanding of postmodernism that people cite is French deconstruction. And yet deconstruction is also contested. Jean-François Lyotard is often taken to have given the canonical definition of "postmodernism," which is (roughly) the death of meta-narratives. But Derrida's writing undercuts all attempts to build a movement on a specific idea, since each one becomes fuzzy as soon as you try to specify it. Remember the cover of Foucault's book with a picture of the pipe and the title *Ceci n'est pas une pipe* ("this is not a pipe"). Maybe attempts to define the emerging church movement should begin with the caveat, "This is not a movement."

Building a movement around something that is emerging but hasn't yet emerged only compounds the difficulties. The ambiguities are as frustrating to sociologists as they are to philosophers and theologians. But this analysis has the virtue of being descriptively accurate. It is about changing paradigms. And that's what ECM seeks to do above all else.

STRENGTHS AND WEAKNESSES OF THE ECM

The power of the verb "emerging" should not be underestimated. My professional field in the philosophy of science is called "emergent complexity"; we look at cases of emergence across evolutionary systems. Here in a nutshell is what biologists and social scientists mean by emergence: *The goal of science is reduction; physicists often reduce complex phenomena to underlying laws. But in evolution we encounter systems that* cannot *be reduced. You can look at a single-celled organism only in terms of chemistry if you want, but you won't learn about its relationship to its environment that way. You can try to reduce a chimpanzee to her genes, but you will never understand her particular style of play or the unique way she interacts with others in her group. And to think that neuroscience will someday predict Hamlet or Hogwarts is absurd.*

The first time I met Tony Jones, during the "Theology after Google" conference in Claremont, we recorded a debate on emergence in science and the church. The parallels are remarkable. Emergence in science is about unpredictable novelty; it's about newness and transformation in the natural world; it's about unexpected objects and actions. So is the emerging church movement. Herein lies its fascination for scholars of American religion, as well as for Millennials and others seeking radically new ways to practice and understand religion. As Adam Sweatman points out, the ECM debates between emerging, emergent, and emergence are extremely complex. But so are the phenomena they point to.

Some interpret the ECM it in terms of deconstruction and postmodernism, others use process theology (Tripp Fuller and HomebrewedChristianity.com), and yet others employ political categories. In the Canadian context, Studebaker and Beach write, it's "a movement from Christendom to community churches, a focus on the Incarnation and contextual theology, and holistic spirituality." Their interviews show that "among innovative and self-described 'missional churches,' the word 'incarnational' is pervasive." Many of the definitions of the emerging church are "fluid, open, and malleable," which means that they also tend to flow away.

This book is subtitled "Prospects and Problems," and the authors have not been shy about raising and discussing significant shortcomings of the ECM. Its white, male leadership (and often membership) is the most unsettling because it raises suspicions of racism and sexism, and supporting evidence is not hard to find. Other challenges are raised by the different forms that the ECM takes in vastly different contexts, including the American South (Randy Reed); Canada, especially Ontario (Studebaker and Beach); and South Africa (Rachel Schneider). Schneider asks whether the emergent church can be postcolonial, Reed whether it can be postcapitalist. "Activities are often determined by the energy/capacity/interest of participants," Schneider writes, "and when these shift, so do the activities."

An even greater concern is whether the ECM is not only flawed but doomed to failure from the start. That red thread of concern runs through these chapters; indeed, there are so many such threads that one is tempted to speak of a tapestry. Perhaps it is a tapestry that reveals the impossibility of reforming the inherited religious institutions of North America and, for that matter, the institutions in Britain and the British Commonwealth. To put it paradoxically, how can a non-movement movement succeed as a movement?

A NEW REFORMATION?

As scholars, we don't do full justice to what the ECM has been and is if we cover only the doubts and criticisms. Something rich, and significant, in American religious history is happening around us. For many, it is a hopeful sign.

Of the options provided in this volume, I am drawn in particular to Scot McKnight's definition of the emergent church as "a politically left-leaning, anti-institutional group of people focused upon a reorientation towards practice over belief for the sake of critiquing meta-narratives in keeping with postmodern tradition" (quoted by Sweatman). On this view, we are embodied persons always already living in systems of power, and "we must prioritize the practice of living unsettled lives." This focus gives preference to the organic over the institutional. To recognize the value in organic, authentic connections does not necessarily make one *anti*-institutional, but it does create a certain suspicion of institutions.

Alvizo and Martí's analysis of the central attributes of the ECM bears quoting in full:

> For our purposes, three recurring ECM themes stand out: 1) claims that the Emerging Church is more localized and fluid in form and expression, 2) attempts to put into practice more relational and participatory structures of participation and leadership, and 3) desire for greater inclusion of diversity, welcoming the questioning and change that is brought about by encounters

with difference within the church as well as engaging with diversity outside of it. These three overarching characteristics, which we label here as organic, relational, and inclusive, reflect ECM's inclination for deconstruction and echoes [its] commitments.

In an age when suspicion of institutionalized religion has grown, the commitment to developing organic, relational, and inclusive ways of living religiously stands out as an important reform movement. One does not have to accept the rigid "every 500 years" of Phyllis Tickle's schema to draw parallels with the early Protestant Reformation in its challenge to the institutional religion of its time.

The emergent church stress on being "missional" implies a similar set of priorities. In the South African context, given the history of apartheid, it is particularly clear that "being missional meant, in part, committing oneself to critical engagement with one's culture and society, rather than withdrawing." That is, Schneider notes, an emergent church must show "active commitment to a specific locale as well as deep commitment to a specific community of people (rather than to an institution)." Emerging churches in that context depend on a diverse spiritual community composed of individuals who are committed to a shared way of life. One looks to

> individual and collective practices, such as intentional reflection, communal meals, informal gatherings, hospitality to visitors, the sharing of resources, and seeking to be as self-sustainable as possible (sometimes through social entrepreneurship) so as not to detract money and resources from community development projects, sustained their visions of spiritual and social transformation.

But bucking the surrounding society and embracing people who are very different than oneself is exhausting. Like other cross-cultural people, one faces opposition in one's new culture as well as in one's home culture. We can admire missional living and recognize its tenuousness at the same time.

MILLENNIALS AND THE EMERGING CHURCH

We come, finally, to the paradox that underlies this book's title: the ECM is widely recognized to be a Millennial movement; and yet according to much of the data, Millennials are not joiners of *any* institution or clearly defined movement—including this one! The paradox runs through many of the chapters in this volume. Even in the Sunday Assembles, Joel Daniels shows, Millennial attendees don't want to think of themselves as belonging to an organization.

So are we facing the most altruistic generation in memory, or the most selfish one—in the end will it be Me, or We? Is it Dr. Jekyll or Mr. Hyde? On the one hand, some suggest that the reason that Millennials move between emerging churches and traditional churches is "to increase intensity" (Daniel-Hughes). On the other, the emergent church can be a place of authenticity, even sacrifice: "Christianity was not a religious product to be consumed or a quick emotional release, but rather an invitation to a life of adventure, service, and personal growth with high demands" (Schneider). Or, some would say, perhaps it doesn't really matter which it is. As Reed notes, given the relatively small number of emerging churches, it may be that "while [the ECM] may attract a millennial following, it will not actually move the needle on the broader millennial anti-institutionalism related to church."

In the end, I find it hard to be cynical. Whether or not it moves the needle, the ECM is a sincere effort to move churches out of their comfort zone, to align them more closely with a first-century homeless rabbi who preferred to eat with tax collectors and sinners than to dine with the religious elite. There is something transformative about Mark Scandrette doing Bible study at the "Jesus dojo" in San Francisco and then leading his young participants out onto the streets to talk to homeless people and prostitutes. And there is reform when organizers agree to diversify an all-male panel, "with some men stepping down from the stage and some women stepping in to take their place" (Alvizo and Martí). It is a step forward when emerging churches take on "judgmentalism" (Reed) and hypocrisy. And it is progress when churches stop vilifying the culture around them and fully engage it. As Studebaker and Beach conclude, "A positive view toward culture was almost unanimous among the emerging Christians we visited. They regard the world as neither something to be avoided, nor to be engaged only reluctantly. Traditional evangelical churches tend to have a dim or, at best, ambivalent view of world outside the church. They engage the world hesitantly."

CONCLUSION

The questions that the authors have wrestled with in these pages are as important for scholars of American religion as they are for religious and anti-religious practitioners alike. They bring an appreciation of the often haphazard dynamics of religious transitions. Like other parts of the world, North America is facing the largest and most rapid sea change in the history of American religion, and no one really knows what it all means. One wants to add: not even (or especially not) the Millennials who are at the center of the storm, returning, reforming, and rejecting.

Whether from a scholarly or a personal perspective, each of us has a stake in the outcome. If Millennials should turn out to be as selfish as the Baby Boomers, as willing to insist on their own comfort at the expense of future generations, then the planet is probably finished. I remember the concerns of fellow environmentalists when a study showed that Millennials, as they reach child-rearing years, are beginning to leave the city centers for the suburbs, trading buses and Zipcars for SUVs. We had thought — hoped—that this was a generation that would stay in poor neighborhoods, not own cars, consume less, and thus break out of the well-worn American mold. It's certainly possible that Millennial altruism will give way to selfishness and the unrelenting drive to acquire. If so, the intriguing reforms and the drive to authenticity of the emerging church movement will dry up, as will the movement itself.

But it's also possible that that this generation won't be just like the last one, that some of the reforms will stick even after the demise of youthful enthusiasm. Think of the data on aging hippies. Clearly, there is ample evidence of exchanging Birkenstocks for Oxfords, tie-died shirts and bell-bottomed jeans for business suits. But longitudinal surveys also show some attitudes and lifestyle choices that individuals have retained through the decades since the Haight-Ashbury district of San Francisco became a tourist destination.

At this point, the future is hard to predict. As Stephanie Yuhas writes, "In many ways, the Emerging Church echoes the characteristics of the Millennials," and we don't know how those characteristics will change over the long-term. Roland Martinson sees today's spiritual seekers as aligned with U2's song "I Still Haven't Found What I'm Looking For."

A new generation, a new church? I think of Brian McLaren's open-ended conclusion: "If we have a new world, we will need a new church. We have a new world."

Index

1960s, 86, 87, 146, 194, 239, 257
1970s, 87, 257
1980s, 215
1990s, 45, 51, 61, 63, 73, 146, 215, 216
2010s, 170

abortion, 99
Abo-Zena, Mona M., 148, 163
accepting, 6, 13, 92, 149, 203
activism, 61, 190, 215, 222, 225, 226, 228, 231, 264
adaptation, 13, 52, 85, 90, 96, 97, 104, 109, 121, 129, 134, 163, 215, 216, 227
adult, 104, 141–43
affirmative, 178, 181
affirmed, 242
affirming, 189
affirms, 84, 106, 199, 201, 248, 263
Africa, 145, 197, 212–33, 267, 268
Afrikaner, 216, 217, 219, 221, 224, 232
afterlife, 154, 159, 201
agents, 69, 78, 81, 117, 118, 120–22, 124, 216
agnosticism, 5, 8–10, 14, 143, 158, 195, 207
ambiguity, 5, 10, 33, 105, 134, 137, 233
America, 5, 14–17, 19, 28–30, 37, 38, 46, 48, 50–52, 61, 63, 65, 71, 73–75, 77, 78, 80, 82, 84, 85, 91, 98–100, 103, 105, 106, 135–37, 141–44, 146, 150, 151, 153–59, 163–65, 172–75, 180, 186, 187, 194–97, 205, 208–10, 213–15, 219, 220, 224, 245, 248, 249, 261–64, 266, 267, 269, 270
Ammerman, Nancy, 161–63, 195, 208
Anglican, 59, 83, 136, 215–17, 247
anthropology, 14, 46, 68, 73, 79, 83, 118, 121, 136, 137, 156, 213, 223, 225
anthropomorphic, 121, 122
anti-foundationalism, 37, 38
anti-globalism, 70, 71, 78, 82
anti-hierarchical, 156
anti-institutionalism, 57, 141, 151, 166–68, 183, 185, 263, 267, 269
anti-racism, 229, 233, 235
anti-religious, 269
apartheid, 215–19, 221, 223–25, 227, 229, 232, 235, 268
apophatic, 114, 130, 132, 133
Appiah, K. Anthony, 69, 70, 81
assembly, 188–93, 197, 199–201, 203, 205, 206, 208–10
Astin, Alexander, 149, 163
atheism, 5, 12, 58, 59, 63, 119, 124, 136, 141, 143, 158, 171, 189–97, 199, 207–11, 262
Australia, 197, 213, 215
authentic, 4, 8, 29, 39, 47, 64, 81, 85, 91, 92, 96, 100, 102, 104, 108, 117, 118, 123, 125, 126, 130, 161, 182, 192, 217, 224, 227, 232, 234, 267, 269, 270
authoritarianism, 33
authoritative, 8, 9, 11, 113

authority, 5, 6, 9, 10, 25–30, 33, 49, 58, 60, 71, 80, 146, 156, 169, 184, 222, 225, 231, 232
axiological, 108, 109, 115, 124, 126–29, 131, 132, 134–36

Baby Boomers, 51, 87, 143, 144, 150, 151, 153, 157, 164, 165, 168, 174, 179, 263, 270
Bailey, Sarah Pulliam, 63, 64
Bakker, Jay, 16, 25, 29, 244
Baptist, 62, 65, 215, 217
Barna, George, 159
Barna Group, 25, 189, 204, 207
Barrett, Justin L., 122, 135
Barrett, Nathaniel F., 127, 135
Bass-Butler, Diana, 159, 164
Beauvoir, Simone de, 240, 241, 258
Belfast, 38, 46, 47, 64, 65, 248
belief, 3, 6, 10, 11, 17, 21, 26, 39, 41, 42, 50, 57–60, 62, 63, 73, 74, 81–83, 85, 87, 89, 90, 92, 95, 96, 98–102, 104, 105, 107, 110–120, 133, 141, 143–46, 148, 151, 152, 154, 156, 157, 161, 162, 164, 177, 180, 184, 189, 191, 193, 195, 198–202, 205, 213, 220, 222, 223, 227, 231–34, 237, 240, 241, 245, 249, 256, 267
believers, 98, 111, 153, 154, 195, 217, 234, 244, 258
Bell, Rob, 16, 29–38, 40, 41, 63, 64, 171, 244
belonging, 63, 100, 116, 118, 141–43, 145, 147, 157, 162, 165, 201, 220, 222, 237, 269
Bender, Courtney, 155, 163
Berger, Peter, 157, 158
Beyer, Peter, 70, 81, 146, 163
Bibby, Reginald, 87, 88, 106, 107
Bible, 10, 15, 16, 25–31, 33–35, 37, 38, 51, 59, 83, 84, 90, 92, 101, 102, 104, 106, 136, 183, 197, 269
Bielo, James, 16, 29, 46, 47, 60–64, 73, 74, 81, 213, 214, 218, 226–28, 234
Biko, Steve, 229, 231, 234
Biology, 72, 81, 266

bisexual, 90, 146
blogs, 54–56, 59, 62, 64, 126, 149, 153, 159, 208–10, 214, 217–20, 224, 245–48, 251, 258
blood, 46, 95, 227
Blumer, Herbert, 86, 106
body, 5, 46, 59, 60, 162, 198, 254, 256
Bolger, Ryan K., 54, 55, 64, 214, 234, 265
Bolz-Weber, Nadia, 16, 160, 167, 245, 249, 250, 257
Bons-Strom, Riet, 252, 256, 257
Borges, Jorge Luis, 128, 135
born-again, 18, 19, 21, 25, 51, 87, 95, 121, 141, 143, 153, 205, 217, 252, 263
boundaries, 45, 69, 77, 82, 83, 114, 116–19, 122, 133, 144–47, 156, 162, 164, 215, 237, 257, 262–64
Bowen, John P., 86, 106
boycott, 90
Bramadat, Paul, 86, 106
breaking, 53, 58, 60, 143, 163, 197, 203, 223, 226, 232, 246, 256, 270
broken, 26, 70, 81, 94, 102, 114, 136, 178
Buddha, 58, 83
Buddhism, 58, 80, 122, 136, 146, 154, 155, 201
bureaucracies, 71
Burge, Ryan, 73, 81, 205, 208
Burstein, David D., 152, 164
business, 68, 89, 97, 98, 144, 169, 170, 173, 178, 184–86, 192, 202, 206, 209, 270
Butler Bass, Diana, 159, 160, 164

Campbell, Colin, 45, 61–64
Campbell, Keith, 45, 61, 62, 64, 104, 107, 174, 187
Canada, 84–92, 96, 98, 99, 105–7, 197, 266, 267
capitalism, 76, 175, 177, 178, 218, 222
Caputo, John D., 31, 33, 38, 41, 49, 64, 243, 265
caste, 241

Index

Catholicism, 18, 22, 23, 41, 73, 83, 88, 103, 123, 136, 143, 159, 169, 172, 195, 226, 239, 240, 262
Cecil, Brad, 51–53
celebration, 72, 75, 191, 205, 217
charismatic, 40, 73, 83, 136, 153, 159, 214, 216, 217
Charmaz, Kathy, 86, 106
chauvinism, 241
Christ, 42, 46, 93–97, 100–102, 105, 160, 184, 191, 220, 241
Christendom, 13, 49, 84–86, 88–92, 101, 107, 123, 266
Christian, 10, 14, 16, 17, 29, 30, 33, 36–39, 41, 46, 47, 49–51, 54, 55, 58, 59, 61, 63, 64, 73, 77, 80, 82–88, 90–98, 100, 102, 103, 105–9, 115, 123, 131, 136, 153, 161, 162, 171, 172, 175, 184–88, 191, 194, 198, 199, 203, 205, 206, 208–11, 214, 217–19, 222, 223, 226, 234, 237, 239–44, 250, 253, 255, 257, 258, 264, 265
Christianity, 9, 10, 15, 16, 26, 27, 30, 32, 39–41, 46–51, 55, 59, 60, 63–65, 67, 72–74, 76, 80, 83–86, 88, 90, 91, 93, 99, 102–6, 122, 136, 159–61, 185, 186, 188, 194, 198, 199, 205, 210, 212, 213, 216–18, 221, 222, 225, 232–41, 243, 245, 248–51, 253, 255, 257–59, 264, 269
Christians, 5, 12, 16, 37, 39–41, 48, 49, 51, 53, 54, 59, 64, 74, 75, 77, 82, 85–88, 90–96, 98–107, 125, 143, 159, 160, 172, 195, 213, 223, 232, 233, 235, 243, 247, 253–56, 269
church, 1, 3–5, 8–11, 13–17, 25–34, 37, 38, 40–43, 45, 47–58, 61–69, 72–109, 114–16, 118, 119, 121, 123, 125, 129–32, 134, 136, 139, 141, 143, 151–53, 155, 157–62, 164–72, 174, 178–85, 188–95, 197–99, 202, 204–21, 224, 225, 227–30, 232–51, 253–59, 261–70
church-like, 191–93
Ciochina, Raluca, 190, 208
civic-minded, 153
Claiborne, Shane, 59, 91, 102, 106, 167, 168, 265
Clawson, Julie, 235, 237, 246, 247, 250, 258, 259
Clawson, Mike, 56, 57, 64, 257
coalition, 108, 115–18, 120, 121, 124
Cochrane, James, 217, 234
college, 30, 85, 145, 147–49, 163, 165, 169, 173–75, 180, 186
college-educated, 237
colonial, 86, 88, 123, 154, 212, 214–19, 221–24, 229, 231, 234
Colorado, 51, 55, 164, 165
Comaroff, John and Jean, 217, 234
commitment, 28, 40, 47, 56, 69, 81, 88, 92, 93, 96, 110, 117, 118, 143, 144, 149, 150, 156, 160, 197, 199, 204–6, 218, 220, 221, 225, 226, 229, 230, 233, 234, 236–39, 244, 246, 251, 254, 256, 268
commodification, 103, 217, 218
commonsense, 112, 131, 135
communal, 29, 110, 111, 114, 119, 122, 133, 144, 195, 226, 268
communion, 46, 118
Communism, 63, 64
Communitas, 83
community, 28, 29, 36–38, 47, 55, 59, 64, 69, 74, 75, 77, 85, 88–90, 92–94, 96–102, 107, 109, 111–21, 125, 131, 135, 155, 159, 162, 173, 175, 182, 188–94, 197–207, 210, 213, 217, 218, 220, 222–30, 232–34, 242, 243, 247, 248, 251, 252, 254, 256, 258, 265, 266, 268
community-building, 141, 202
comparison, 18, 22, 36, 67, 86, 132, 256
compartmental, 102
computers, 8, 152
confession, 111, 201
conformity, 79, 104, 124, 125
conforms, 178
congregation, 9, 12, 27, 46, 47, 51, 52, 54, 55, 58, 82, 86, 92, 93, 95, 99–103, 107, 119, 141, 143, 150, 152, 153, 158–61, 165–67, 184,

congregation *(continued)*, 193, 197, 208, 209, 224, 234, 236–38, 243–46, 249, 250, 254, 256, 258
congress, 170
consciousness, 110, 155, 224, 231, 233, 234, 253
consensus, 70, 116
conservatism, 9, 16, 28, 37, 57, 61, 63, 64, 83, 86, 90, 112–15, 131, 134–36, 146, 160–63, 184, 212–14, 217, 220, 225, 229, 238, 245
constructivist, 28, 30, 36, 38, 40, 41, 61, 67, 82, 122, 123, 135, 146, 179, 235, 238, 252
consumerism, 8, 40, 69, 75, 102–5, 119, 123, 126, 176, 177, 218
contextually, 84
continental, 38
conversion, 12, 24, 28, 30, 94, 102, 103, 107, 134, 221, 227
Cooper, Betsy, 21, 29, 186
cooperation, 116–18, 120, 133, 136, 137
cosmology, 35, 42, 127, 136
cosmopolitanism, 69, 70, 78, 79, 83, 162
counter-cultural, 102, 146
Coupland, Douglas, 50, 51, 64
creed, 4, 60, 62, 119, 124, 125, 220, 264
cross-cultural, 137, 147, 268
cultic, 33, 45, 61–64
culture-war, 33, 92
cynical, 141, 144, 159, 177, 263, 269

Daly, Mary, 239–43, 253, 255, 258
Daniels, Joel D., 188, 264, 268
Darwinian, 116
Davenport, R. H., 217, 234
Davidson, Hillary, 175, 176, 187
Dawkins, Richard, 158
Dawson, Lorne, 87, 107
death, 34, 74, 77, 172, 205, 217, 261, 262, 265
decentering, 74, 225, 257
decision-making, 238, 251, 254, 255
decolonization, 222

deconstruction, 3, 13, 14, 26, 30, 31, 38–40, 45, 47–50, 58, 60, 61, 63, 65, 66, 75, 79, 83, 119, 130, 132, 134, 136, 159, 161, 164, 190, 206, 207, 213, 214, 218, 220, 223, 225, 229, 233, 234, 237, 238, 243–45, 251, 252, 254, 256–58, 265, 266, 268
deconversion, 50, 76, 82, 227, 234
democracy, 33, 133, 134, 178, 183, 216, 217, 234
demographics, 5, 153, 188, 189, 194, 196, 197
denominations, 17, 29, 33, 54, 60, 62, 73, 108, 119, 129, 133, 161, 166, 167, 207, 212, 213, 215, 216, 243, 244, 249
Denton, Melinda Lundquist, 171, 186
Derrida, Jacques, 38, 49, 52, 79, 243, 265
detournement, 3, 11–14
Dharmapala, 155
dialogue, 33, 37, 52, 57, 58, 74, 77, 82, 100, 147, 159, 206, 209, 220, 223, 224, 245
digital, 142, 145, 150, 152, 153, 161, 163, 186, 212, 214
disenchantment, 61, 228
disenfranchised, 51
disillusionment, 148, 189, 219, 225
dissatisfaction, 26, 28, 103, 126, 134, 216
diversity, 8, 47, 62, 72, 78, 88, 103, 104, 155, 214, 218, 224, 228, 237, 238, 244, 256, 258, 267, 268
divinity, 9, 85, 108, 122–25, 199, 240–242
divisiveness, 163, 177, 184
Djupe, Paul, 73, 81, 205, 208
doctrine, 36, 38, 58, 59, 70, 94, 97, 101, 110, 111, 134, 141, 143, 151, 181, 182, 184, 199, 206, 239, 240, 242, 243
dogmatism, 58, 60, 70, 153, 154, 156, 217
Dower, Nigel, 69, 82
Downey, Allen B., 196, 208
Dubuisson, Daniel, 67, 82

ecclesiology, 30, 41, 54, 73, 74, 79, 91, 92, 97, 120, 123, 124, 126, 214, 218, 222, 224, 239, 244, 258
eclecticism, 146, 154, 164
ECM-affiliated, 56, 244
ecology, 69, 76, 160, 206, 255, 258
economics, 10, 15, 16, 31, 40, 49, 51, 67, 69, 71, 72, 75, 76, 78, 80–82, 89, 92, 98, 127, 147, 149, 151, 157, 158, 163, 222, 226, 228, 230
ecumenical, 45, 47, 147, 210, 216
education, 5, 34, 37, 38, 89, 113, 123, 125, 133, 141, 144, 145, 147, 148, 151, 152, 157, 158, 163, 165, 176, 186, 187, 196, 197, 208, 216, 217, 222, 228, 258
egalitarianism, 54, 55, 163, 236–38, 247, 251, 256
election, 124, 179, 186, 187
elites, 73, 125, 147, 216, 224, 269
Ellingson, Stephen, 60, 64
Elphick, Richard, 217, 234
embedded, 93, 95, 128, 156, 158, 238, 239, 241, 246, 252, 254, 255, 257
embodiment, 35, 92, 94, 98, 101, 108, 111, 114, 132, 154, 155, 159, 163, 219, 225, 234, 237, 244, 252–54, 267
emergence, 30, 32, 33, 36, 48–50, 65, 66, 75, 83, 108, 116, 121, 224, 235, 251, 259, 264–66
emergent, 31–33, 37, 38, 40, 41, 45, 48–51, 53–57, 60, 62–65, 68, 74, 82, 83, 86, 88, 108, 109, 115, 116, 121, 131, 136, 156, 159, 163, 189, 205, 208, 209, 245–49, 251, 264, 266–69
Emerging Church, 1, 3–5, 9, 13–17, 25–32, 43, 45, 47–69, 72–109, 123, 131, 136, 139, 141, 143, 148, 149, 153, 158–68, 176, 177, 184, 185, 187–90, 202, 205, 208, 212–15, 217–20, 222–24, 227–29, 231–39, 243–51, 253–59, 261, 262, 264–70
Emmaus Way, 3, 9–11, 13, 14
empire, 91, 92, 102, 259

empiricism, 52, 114, 116, 125, 158, 162
Engelhart, Katie, 190–93, 197, 199, 208
Enlightenment, the, 52, 149, 157, 162
entitlement, 48, 56, 107, 142, 174, 175, 177, 187, 200, 222
environment, 25, 28, 45, 50, 52, 67, 72, 73, 76, 100, 105, 121, 126, 134, 144, 160, 217, 219, 222, 223, 227, 238, 249, 253, 255, 257, 266, 270
Episcopalians, 59, 60, 247
epistemology, 3, 6–8, 10, 35, 37, 52, 80, 125, 127, 163, 206, 219, 221, 235
Erasmus, Johannes, 215, 216, 234
eschatology, 34, 242
essentialism, 146, 147, 161
eternal, 121, 124, 199, 200
ethics, 7, 12, 36, 37, 58, 67, 71, 72, 79, 80, 142, 147, 163, 168, 213, 225, 229, 233
ethnic, 124, 145, 176, 218, 219, 224, 226, 228
ethnicity, 106
ethnography, 107, 244, 258, 262
Eucharist, 88, 89
Europe, 82, 86, 114, 157, 158, 163, 165, 190, 194, 195, 197, 209, 210, 213, 217, 219, 221, 224
evangelicalism, 5, 15–19, 25, 27, 29, 33, 37, 45, 47, 54, 57, 58, 60–64, 73–77, 81–83, 85, 86, 88, 89, 99, 102–5, 107, 115, 118, 119, 123, 124, 129, 130, 134, 136, 141, 143, 153, 158, 159, 180, 212–14, 217, 218, 220, 227–29, 234, 238, 245, 247, 249, 258, 259, 269
evangelism, 95, 99–101, 104, 107
evolution, 45, 62, 72, 83, 97, 109, 116, 117, 120–22, 124, 127, 130, 135–37, 159, 240, 242, 266
exclusion, 58, 130, 184, 201, 202, 226, 232, 241, 242, 246, 247
existence, 6, 8, 10, 14, 40, 59, 61, 62, 68, 113, 158, 196, 201, 265

existential, 4, 112–14, 120, 131, 133, 203
experience, 3–8, 14, 18, 19, 21, 25, 26, 36, 37, 48, 52, 61, 68, 72, 86, 94, 96, 102, 103, 105–7, 109, 126, 141, 142, 146, 147, 149–51, 153–56, 159, 163, 181, 188, 191, 193, 195, 197, 198, 205, 207, 219, 222, 223, 226–30, 233, 237–39, 241, 243, 244, 246, 247, 251–54, 256
experimentation, 9, 46, 53, 62, 108, 109, 111–16, 120, 121, 127, 129, 131–35, 147, 161, 212–14, 218, 222–24, 228, 248
explanation, 49, 119, 143, 180, 195
exploitation, 67, 78, 116, 117, 121
expressions, 8–11, 73, 74, 80, 85, 86, 95, 99, 100, 103, 126, 130, 188, 192, 197, 198, 204–6, 217, 226, 238, 244, 264, 267

Facebook, 8, 56, 149, 152
faith, 29, 30, 42, 46, 47, 55, 57, 59, 64, 67, 74, 77–79, 81–84, 86, 88, 91, 95–97, 100, 101, 105–7, 124, 150, 154, 158, 159, 171, 173, 186, 194, 199, 203, 208, 210, 217, 226, 234, 237, 242–44, 248, 249, 252, 256–58, 264, 265
Falk, Richard, 66–69, 71, 72, 75, 76, 78, 80–82
family, 63, 74, 75, 78, 96, 144, 145, 150, 151, 153, 164, 182, 208, 227, 228, 233, 242, 252
feminism, 162, 165, 168, 236–40, 244, 248, 251–59
fetishisms, 223
fideism, 125
fieldwork, 212–14, 222
Fiorenza, Elizabeth Schüssler, 252, 253, 255, 259
Fischer, Claude, 195, 209
Flatt, Kevin, 86, 107
football, 32, 36, 38, 39, 164
forgiveness, 96, 207

foundationalisms, 30, 36, 84, 89, 111, 113, 122, 133, 135, 177, 183, 187, 199, 203, 210, 240, 241, 243, 255
freedom, 26–28, 33, 35, 46, 74, 127, 136, 149, 156, 157, 162, 188, 189, 198–200, 205, 222, 226, 234
Friesen, Dwight J., 55, 264
Frisk, Liselotte, 161, 164
Fuller, Robert, 154, 155, 164
Fuller, Trip, 33, 41, 248, 249, 266
Fuller Seminary, 31, 34, 36, 38
fundamentalist, 12, 70, 83, 134, 136, 154, 158, 238
funding, 54, 75, 85, 187, 193, 230

Ganiel, Gladys, 26, 30, 46, 47, 57, 58, 60, 61, 63, 65, 75, 79, 83, 119, 130, 132, 136, 159, 164, 213, 214, 218, 234, 237, 238, 243–45, 248, 258
gatherings, 46, 54, 55, 58, 93, 97, 108, 109, 120, 126, 197, 199, 218, 220, 221, 226, 231, 244, 246, 247, 268
gender, 33, 77, 146, 154, 160, 173, 236, 237, 239, 241, 246, 249, 252–54, 256
generations, 3–6, 8, 14, 17, 27, 30, 45, 50–52, 61, 65, 87, 100, 105, 106, 112, 114, 119, 141–45, 150–53, 157–59, 162–65, 168, 170, 172–77, 179, 180, 184–87, 208, 209, 245, 261, 263, 264, 269, 270
Gibbs, Eddie, 54, 55, 64, 214, 234, 265
Giddens, Anthony, 33, 41
Giles and Deleuze, 52
globalization, 66–73, 75, 76, 78, 80–83, 141, 144–47, 149, 150, 154, 157, 161–63, 169, 185, 197, 206, 209, 210, 216, 220–223, 258
God, 8, 27, 34, 35, 84, 92, 94, 96, 98, 101, 103–6, 160, 205, 229, 240
goddess, 154
godless, 105, 191, 193
gods, 87, 106, 117, 119–22, 124, 136
goodness, 84, 106, 199
Google, 190, 266

gospel, 38, 76, 92, 94–96, 98, 99, 101, 102, 104, 105, 123, 160, 206, 246, 258, 262
governing, 110, 132
government, 71, 168–70, 174, 177, 178, 180, 183
Graeber, David, 80, 82
Greenbelt Festival, 167
Greenberg, Eric, 173, 186
Griffin, David Ray, 32, 36, 41, 265
Guder, Darrell, 94, 102, 107
Gutiérrez, Gustavo, 40

harmonies, 108, 127–32
Harris, Sam, 158
Harrold, Philip, 76, 82, 227, 234
hate, 12, 13, 265
Hauerwas, Stanley, 91, 107, 125
Hawtrey, Kim, 205, 209
healing, 96, 101, 201, 202, 226, 246, 251
heaven, 29, 34, 41, 98, 101, 103, 105, 160, 185, 241
hegemony, 50, 62, 67, 80, 223
Hendriks, Jurgen, 215, 216, 234
henotheists, 122
Herberg, Will, 262
hermeneutics, 32, 37, 38, 49, 123
heterodox, 59, 61, 63
heterosexism, 251, 252
heuristic, 63, 121, 254
hierarchy, 10, 54, 58, 60, 68, 71, 75, 104, 114, 123, 124, 130, 131, 164, 192, 216, 239, 241, 243, 254, 255
high-Church, 118
hipsters, 88, 193, 237
hispanic, 172
historians, 46, 59, 79, 144
history, 37, 45, 47, 49, 50, 54, 58, 60, 67–70, 78, 80, 83, 86, 87, 91, 94, 99, 107, 110, 114, 122, 132–34, 136, 142, 144, 145, 154, 156, 161, 188–90, 198, 210, 215, 216, 218, 219, 222, 223, 228, 231, 232, 234, 238, 240, 245, 252, 253, 255, 257, 261–64, 267–69
Hitchens, Christopher, 158
Hobbes, Thomas, 204, 209, 210

homogeneity, 128, 129, 131, 217
homosexuality, 25, 181, 184
Howe, Neal, 144, 165, 168–70, 172, 173, 186
humanitarian, 69, 72
humanity, 52, 58, 67, 69, 76, 78, 81, 96, 117, 119, 121, 124, 131, 156, 160, 205, 226, 241, 242, 253, 262
Hume, David, 122, 136
Huntington, Samuel, 71, 82
hypocrisy, 151, 162, 269

identification, 21–23, 25, 28, 91, 98, 142, 158, 216, 255
identity, 18, 28, 47, 56, 60–62, 69, 70, 75, 77, 78, 80–83, 89, 91, 97, 98, 108, 111, 114, 117, 119–22, 124, 125, 129, 131, 132, 136, 146, 147, 154, 156, 181, 190, 209, 218, 219, 221, 222, 224, 225, 231, 232, 235, 243, 258
ideology, 33, 48, 52, 82, 123, 144, 191, 201, 202, 208, 221
iKon, 39, 46, 47, 49, 59, 64, 65, 166, 167, 248
imagination, 198, 257
immigration, 85, 134, 145, 163
immutable, 27, 242
imperialism, 76
inauthentic, 132, 238
incarnation, 39, 83, 84, 89, 92–99, 101, 102, 106, 136, 224, 240, 242, 254, 266
inclusiveness, 11, 12, 15, 16, 72, 73, 77, 80, 81, 83, 141, 144, 159, 191, 205, 208, 219, 221, 224, 236–39, 244, 246, 251, 254–56, 268
individualism, 62, 102, 105, 147, 149, 156, 162, 174, 176, 177, 200, 221
inequality, 75, 76, 222, 256
injustice, 76, 80, 145, 184, 215, 223, 253
institutions, 25, 30, 54, 69, 70, 89, 94, 108, 109, 117, 122, 130, 131, 133, 134, 141, 143, 145, 148, 152–54, 156, 158–60, 162, 163, 166–72, 174, 175, 177, 178, 180, 183, 186, 191, 217, 222, 230, 233, 236, 237,

institutions *(continued)*, 239, 250, 252, 253, 263–65, 267, 268
insurrection, 38, 39, 42, 248
intellectual, 4, 10, 34, 36, 49, 50, 52, 59, 112, 124, 125, 127, 134, 154, 157
intentional, 13, 68, 85, 88, 94, 99, 112, 113, 121, 130, 176, 184, 218, 219, 226, 233, 243, 246, 251, 253, 268
interfaith, 45, 47, 147
interpretation, 27–29, 34–38, 86, 87, 113, 129, 136, 137, 147, 154, 198, 255
interpreting, 27, 35, 215, 216, 234
intersubjective, 86
Iraq, 77, 169
Ireland, 38, 46, 65
irreligious, 101, 191, 205
Isis, 158
Islam, 63, 64, 80, 194

Jenkins, K.E., 244, 258
Jerusalem, 98
Jesus, 10, 34–36, 40, 46, 49, 58, 61, 64, 65, 76, 83, 90–98, 100–102, 106, 153, 184, 199, 203, 205, 206, 218, 226, 227, 232, 240, 265, 269
Jews, 77, 146
Jones, Robert P., 16, 17, 25, 29–33, 36–38, 40, 41, 48–51, 53–56, 62–64, 68, 75, 77, 82, 83, 167, 172, 184, 186, 189–94, 196–200, 202, 203, 206, 209, 210, 217, 221, 234, 237, 244, 245, 248, 250, 265, 266
Jones, Tony, 16, 17, 25, 29–33, 36–38, 40, 41, 48–51, 53–56, 62–64, 68, 75, 77, 82, 83, 167, 172, 184, 186, 189–94, 196–200, 202, 203, 206, 209, 210, 217, 221, 234, 237, 244, 245, 248, 250, 265, 266
judgmentalism, 25, 32, 156, 181, 182, 184, 185, 264, 269
Juergensmeyer. Mark, 70, 82
justice, 32, 33, 37, 40, 75, 76, 90, 92, 102, 103, 105, 184, 185, 197, 206, 208, 212–14, 216, 217, 220, 221, 226, 228, 229, 231–33, 235, 246, 258, 267

Kant, Immanuel, 127, 198
Keane, Webb, 223, 234
Kenya, 197, 220
Keuss, Jeff, 205, 209
Keysar, Ariela, 28, 30
Kim, Jibum, 30, 187
Kimball, Dan, 9, 74, 75, 79, 82, 217, 245
kingdom, 34, 49, 55, 95, 98, 102, 103, 105, 212, 213, 215, 229, 265
Kinnaman, David, 25, 30, 98, 107, 182, 186
Kosmin, Barry, 28, 30
Kumar, Jessica, 150, 164
Kuperus, T., 216, 234
kyriarchy, 252, 253, 255–57

Labanow, Cory, 82, 229, 234
labor, 69, 72, 170, 178, 228, 233, 254, 262
Lacan, Jacques, 31, 39
Lakicevic, Dragan D., 190, 209
Lamm, Juile A., 198, 209
Lassander, Mika, 144, 164
late-modern, 109, 126, 134
Latour, Bruno, 6, 7, 14
Lawton, Kim, 58, 64, 159, 164
leadership, 45, 50–56, 64, 68, 93, 101, 103, 191–93, 195, 216, 225, 230, 233, 237–40, 244, 245, 251, 252, 254–57, 266, 267
leaving the Church/Religion, 18, 21, 23, 25, 28, 29, 56, 91, 94, 107, 141, 147, 168, 181, 182, 186, 204, 207, 215, 219, 221, 225, 229, 240, 244, 265
Leibniz, Gottfried, 127
Lenhart, Amanda, 8, 14
lesbian, 90, 146
letter, 77, 119
liberals, 13, 57, 73, 81, 83, 86, 134, 136, 137, 146, 155, 161, 196–98, 205, 208, 223, 229, 231
liberation, 10, 40, 76, 78, 223, 227, 236, 238–40, 252, 256–59

libertarian, 179
Lienesch, Rachel, 29, 186
Lim, Chaeyoon, 83, 194, 209
Lincoln, Bruce, 28, 30
Lipka, Michael, 8, 143, 164, 196, 209
listening, 199, 205, 206, 245, 254
liturgy, 33, 38, 74, 118, 123, 147, 162, 253, 254, 258
local, 62, 81, 89, 90, 92–99, 101, 102, 123, 126, 145, 166, 167, 170, 192, 218, 232, 244, 267
logos, 192
long-term, 150, 196, 203, 215, 224, 227–29, 231, 233, 263, 264, 270
Lorenz Dietz, Mary, 86, 107
love, 16, 29, 34–36, 40, 41, 74, 90, 91, 95, 96, 99, 101, 102, 160, 184, 200, 203, 206, 207, 250, 261, 265
loyalty, 69, 78, 108, 117–19, 125
Lugo, Luis, 194, 209
Lutheran, 53, 55, 64, 159, 160, 215, 249
Lyon, David, 61, 65
Lyons, Gabe, 25, 30, 182, 186
Lyotard, Jean-François, 265

Macgregor, Carol Ann, 83, 209
mainline, 17, 29, 37, 60, 64, 73, 88, 103, 107, 109, 118, 123, 124, 129, 130, 132–35, 141, 143, 158–60, 195, 207, 212, 213, 215–17, 237, 249, 259
mainstream, 51, 91, 102, 130, 131, 133–35, 153, 161, 228
Malaysia, 197
male-dominated, 241
Maranatha, 244, 258
marginalized, 80, 91, 92, 104, 226, 228, 230, 232, 238, 241, 246, 247, 254, 255
margins, 91, 92, 101, 102, 227, 235
market, 69, 71, 72, 76, 80, 149, 216
Markuly, Mark S., 153, 154, 165
marriage, 8, 14, 25, 27, 29, 55, 56, 90, 99, 151, 157, 164, 169, 181, 183, 185, 196
Marsden, Peter, 30, 187

Martí, Gerardo, 26, 30, 46, 47, 57, 58, 60, 61, 63, 65, 75, 79, 83, 119, 130, 132, 136, 159, 164, 213, 214, 218, 234, 236–38, 243–45, 258, 267, 269
Martinson, Roland, 148, 159, 164, 270
Marx, Karl, 38, 39
masculine, 241, 249
Masuzawa, Tomoko, 67, 82, 205, 209
materialism, 51, 117, 149, 174, 176, 177
Matthew, 25 House, 88, 94
McClendon, Jim, 36, 37, 125
McGlone, Teresa, 172, 173, 186
McKnight, Scot, 16, 26, 30, 49, 50, 57, 65, 217, 267
McLaren, Brian, 9, 16, 25–27, 29, 30, 50, 51, 53–56, 58, 65, 74, 76, 77, 83, 130, 136, 159, 168, 184–86, 205, 217, 220, 227, 235, 244, 245, 247, 259, 265, 270
McLeigh, Jill D., 144, 165
meaning, 5, 9, 10, 28, 48, 50, 86, 87, 100, 102, 107, 111, 117, 128, 129, 141, 147, 148, 156, 165, 167, 174, 194, 197–99, 201–3, 206, 207, 212, 213, 230, 231
meaningless, 4, 17, 30
media, 8, 14, 58, 62, 141, 143, 147, 149, 152, 161, 166, 167, 170, 186, 190, 193, 197, 209, 212, 214, 245, 249
meditation, 38, 114, 146, 154–56, 201
megachurch, 51, 60, 64, 120, 126, 153, 190, 193, 197, 199, 206, 208, 209, 216, 217
Mehta, Hermant, 190, 191, 193, 209
membership, 17, 69, 78, 117–20, 130, 166, 167, 266
memories, 223, 232, 233
mentoring, 16
Mercadante, Linda, 146, 151, 156, 164
message, 12, 15, 17, 28, 50, 95, 159, 178, 230, 247
Methodist, 215–17
middle-aged, 143
middle-class, 5, 9, 75, 93, 196, 212–15, 219, 220, 228, 237

millennials, 1, 3–5, 7–9, 13–18,
    20–23, 25–30, 87, 104, 106, 136,
    139, 141–47, 149–53, 158, 159,
    161–86, 189, 204, 207, 208, 210,
    262–66, 268–70
Miller, Jon, 17, 30, 51, 65
minister, 51, 53, 96, 159, 249
minority, 107, 152, 176, 191, 195, 210, 215
misogyny, 239, 241, 248, 251
mission, 16, 53, 92, 99, 101, 144, 164,
    168, 188–90, 200, 203, 205–7,
    209, 218, 234, 249
missional, 32, 83, 93–95, 97, 100, 101,
    105, 107, 136, 218, 221, 224, 225,
    228, 230, 235, 266, 268
mixed-income, 226
modernity, 29, 32, 33, 41, 47, 48, 60,
    64, 73, 79, 81, 96, 104, 123, 143,
    157, 162, 163, 185, 190, 196, 209,
    210, 212, 213, 219, 222, 223, 234
Mohammed, 58, 83
Mohler, Albert, 91, 107
Moltmann, Jürgen, 31, 37
monastic, 47, 85, 88
monotheism, 66, 72, 82, 122
Moore, Lee, 191, 210
moral, 9, 28, 75, 78, 80, 89, 90, 92,
    105, 107, 112, 120, 124, 158, 160,
    161, 176, 177, 202, 223, 242
Mormons, 115
Moses, 58, 83
multi-faith, 63, 77, 83
multi-generational, 41, 174
multiracial, 146, 164, 220, 233, 258
Murphy, Nancey, 36, 265
Murray, Stuart, 91, 107
Muslims, 77, 194, 244, 258
Muth, Darrell, 90, 91
mysticism, 45, 52, 59, 61–63, 83, 136,
    146, 155, 159, 162
myth, 59, 70, 82, 142, 145, 164, 228

narcissism, 104, 142, 174, 175, 177
nation, 23, 66, 67, 69–71, 77–81, 85,
    124, 152, 215, 217, 252
nationalism, 70, 71, 77, 222
naturalism, 108–15, 127, 132

nature, 70, 80, 86, 94, 100, 110, 114,
    130, 132, 133, 154, 155, 214, 238,
    241–43, 253, 254
neocolonialism, 71, 77, 220
neo-monastic, 33, 37, 41, 59, 218, 225
neo-pagans, 154
neo-traditionalists, 154
neuroscience, 35, 266
Neville, Robert Cummings, 114, 127,
    128, 131
New Testament, 63, 101
Nietzsche, Fredrich, 38, 39, 41, 261
Nieuwsma, Shenandoah, 3, 263
nomadism, 141, 145, 149, 150
non-affiliated, 142
nonbelief, 119, 157, 196, 208
nonbelonging, 196, 208
non-denominational, 18
nones, 4, 8, 13, 14, 17, 18, 21–25,
    141–43, 158, 161, 172, 182, 184,
    188–90, 192, 194–98, 202, 204–7
non-governmental, 170
non-judgmental, 160
North Carolina, 3, 5, 54, 166, 167
Nynas, Peter, 146, 156, 161, 164

obedience, 200
omnipresence, 105
ontologies, 35, 70, 80, 132
openness, 25–27, 29, 35, 38, 39, 141,
    144, 145, 155, 181, 182
opinion, 6–8, 13, 26, 27, 58, 59, 128,
    145, 170, 182
oppression, 38, 76, 102, 146, 162, 215,
    219, 221, 223, 224, 228, 230, 236,
    237, 240, 241, 253, 256
optimistic, 5, 172, 217, 242
ordination, 240, 247, 249
organically, 73, 97, 190, 192, 228, 238,
    244, 254, 255, 267, 268
orientation, 17, 35–38, 40, 47, 60, 90,
    92, 98, 102, 109, 111, 131, 133,
    146, 159, 213, 225, 243, 244, 257
orthodoxy, 39, 50, 54, 58–62, 74, 103,
    130, 132, 159, 195, 217, 265
orthopraxis, 60

Packard, Josh, 74, 214, 218, 228

Pagitt, Doug, 51–53, 55, 56, 58, 73, 74, 167, 168, 244, 245, 250
parable, 10, 46, 261
paradigm, 62, 68, 71, 75, 76, 80, 265, 266
pastor, 33, 34, 38, 51, 53, 56, 57, 73–75, 79, 90, 99, 126, 158, 159, 181, 217, 245, 249, 256
Patheos, 56
patriarchy, 33, 104, 236–40, 243, 248, 249, 251–57
patriotism, 67, 77, 78, 80
peace, 46, 82, 204, 216
Pentecostalism, 115, 153, 159, 217, 258
perennialism, 146
philosophers, 11, 52, 59, 109, 111, 127, 162, 229, 266
philosophy, 9–11, 14, 37, 38, 48, 52, 55, 71, 78–81, 110, 111, 113, 115, 127, 128, 147, 155, 198, 201, 202, 206, 207, 224, 239, 241, 266
pilgrim, 66–69, 72, 75, 76, 78, 80, 81
pilgrimages, 81, 223
Pinker, Steven, 133
Piper, John, 16, 56, 65
pluralism, 58–60, 62, 63, 73, 84, 106, 156, 157, 176, 177, 212–14, 217, 221
podcast, 33, 34, 41, 62, 248
poetry, 10, 11, 46, 99, 102
polarization, 87, 158
policing, 117, 118, 125
politics, 8, 9, 25, 31–33, 37, 39, 40, 45, 49, 57, 59, 60, 66, 69, 74, 76–79, 89, 90, 92, 123, 129, 132, 144, 151, 152, 156, 160, 162, 163, 170, 173, 176–79, 182–84, 189, 196, 197, 216, 217, 222, 224, 228, 229, 231, 232, 252, 256, 266, 267
polytheists, 122
post-apartheid, 215–17, 224, 232, 234
post-christendom, 84, 90–92, 107
post-christian, 51, 84–86, 90–92, 98, 104, 105, 217, 239, 265
Postcolonialism, 32, 162, 220–224, 233, 267
post-evangelical, 16, 37, 38, 57

post-feminist, 244, 258
postmodernism, 4, 7, 9, 12–16, 32, 33, 35–38, 40, 45, 48, 51–53, 57, 60, 61, 69, 79, 104, 123, 125, 159, 162, 190, 213, 219, 223, 224, 245, 262, 265–67
post-patriarchal, 33
Post-Secular, 144, 146, 156, 161
pragmatism, 110, 111, 113–15, 125, 132
praxis, 37, 45, 47, 57, 59, 69, 73, 75, 76, 78, 79, 252
prayer, 59, 114, 143, 162
pre-enlightenment, 59
prejudice, 133, 176, 239, 241, 242, 253, 256
Presbyterians, 54, 62
priest, 59, 247
pro-gay, 15, 16
progressive, 15, 16, 26, 33, 47, 54, 57, 63, 141, 143, 162, 212, 213, 223, 232, 249, 253, 257
prophetic, 49
pro-social, 116, 120, 124, 185
Protestantism, 5, 16, 18, 19, 22–25, 29, 41, 49, 59–61, 73, 88, 103, 118, 119, 123, 124, 129, 134, 143, 155, 158, 162, 172, 195, 212, 213, 226, 238, 262, 268
psychology, 59, 68, 120, 148, 154, 156, 200, 205, 226, 231, 240, 241, 261
psychopathology, 175
Pui-lan, Kwok, 162, 164

Quakers, 155
queer, 160
questioning, 9, 26, 28, 40, 54, 58, 68, 81, 112, 127, 128, 147, 148, 157, 159, 163, 183, 207, 217, 218, 220, 221, 238, 243, 244, 252, 254, 265, 267

Rabinow, Paul, 79, 83
race, 33, 77, 95, 123, 146, 154, 173, 176, 196, 203, 212–16, 218–34, 244, 247, 252, 254, 256, 258
racism, 77, 219, 220, 231, 232, 247, 252, 266

radical, 31, 33–36, 39, 55, 62, 70, 98, 104, 106, 113, 135, 161, 198, 200, 225, 227, 228, 233, 236–39, 251, 256–58, 262, 264, 266
Ramey, Steven, 17, 30
Rampell, Catharine, 151, 164
rational, 7, 8, 122, 125, 141, 149, 155, 158, 163, 183
reactionary, 3, 14, 33, 61, 73, 75
realism, 27
reality, 22, 56, 66, 69, 72, 76, 79, 90, 93, 94, 96, 98, 99, 101, 111, 123, 130, 145, 157, 160, 162, 175, 178, 199, 201, 226–28, 230, 241, 245, 247, 252–54, 262, 264
reason, 59, 113, 162, 183, 184, 198
rebellion, 13, 145, 151, 164, 225
receptivity, 15, 17, 25, 29, 185, 197, 217
reconciliation, 11, 221, 223, 231
Reed, Randall, 76, 263, 267, 269
reformation, 49, 66, 67, 123, 239, 240, 242, 267, 268, 270
reformed, 79, 215–17, 219
refugees, 88, 145
region, 15–25, 180, 181, 246
reinterpretation, 158, 165
rejectionists, 90, 91, 103, 108, 122, 123, 126, 130, 156, 181, 184, 185, 214, 233
relationality, 37, 48, 71, 100, 123, 125, 236–38, 244, 251, 254, 255, 267, 268
relationships, 89, 90, 92, 96, 97, 100, 102, 105, 109, 110, 122, 142, 150, 153, 157, 163, 175, 193, 200, 214, 220, 226, 231, 239, 266
relativism, 58, 59, 205, 207
relevant, 3, 6, 25, 84, 93, 96, 115, 134, 157, 162, 183, 216, 217, 232, 257
religion, 3–5, 25, 26, 29, 35, 49, 66, 67, 70–72, 77, 78, 80, 85–87, 105, 106, 108–10, 113, 115–17, 119, 121, 122, 124, 125, 127, 131–34, 141–44, 146–49, 151, 153–59, 161, 162, 171, 176, 179, 180, 183, 188, 189, 193–96, 198, 199, 201, 202, 204–6, 213, 214, 248, 261, 262, 264, 266, 268–70
religions, 58, 66, 67, 70–72, 77, 114, 117, 121, 132, 146, 147, 154–56, 192, 199, 205, 239, 240
religiosity, 67, 71, 74, 75, 110, 148, 261
renaissance, 87
renewal, 66, 103, 105, 212, 213, 239
repent, 239, 257
resistance, 9, 11, 13, 14, 47, 49, 50, 60, 63, 66, 70–72, 75, 80, 81, 113, 124, 131, 158, 168, 176, 178, 213, 223–25, 228, 230, 245, 253, 256
responsibility, 72, 78, 80, 172, 173, 176, 177, 185, 224, 230, 242, 253
resurrection, 25, 38, 39, 74, 181, 205
revelation, 115, 242
reverse-racism, 229
revisionists, 57
revolutionaries, 76, 196, 247
rich, 76, 133, 191, 227
right-leaning, 33
rituals, 59, 60, 63, 67, 113, 117–19, 141, 146, 155, 162
Robinson, Britney, 149, 150, 164
Robinson, John, 34
Rollins, Peter, 16, 31, 32, 38–41, 46, 59, 244, 248
romanticism, 198
Rorty, Richard, 52
routinization, 40, 81
rupture, 38, 39
Russell, Letty, 265
Rwanda, 220

sacraments, 160
sacred, 10, 11, 97, 99, 103, 104, 118, 123, 155, 157, 219
sacrifice, 116, 117, 128, 130, 203, 263, 269
salvation, 93, 124, 153, 200–202
Sanders, Bernie, 178, 183
Sanders, John, 125, 183
scandals, 141, 143, 169
Schleiermacher, Fredrich, 113, 131, 188, 189, 198, 199, 202–6
science, 6, 7, 35, 37, 50, 108, 109, 112, 113, 115–18, 121, 122, 124, 125,

Index

127, 133, 141, 143, 149, 153, 154, 158, 160, 163, 183, 184, 187, 209, 244, 258, 262, 266
secular, 28, 71, 73, 84, 87, 89, 102, 103, 105, 106, 109, 124, 126, 133, 134, 141, 148, 153, 154, 156–58, 162, 163, 195, 197, 217, 232
secularization, 61, 70, 84, 87, 103, 105, 106, 143, 148, 156–58
seekers, 45, 61–63, 95, 96, 119, 125, 141, 153, 154, 159, 162, 270
segregation, 215, 216, 225
self-conscious, 32, 109, 113, 115, 123, 125, 126, 131, 207
selfishness, 116, 117, 152, 173, 269, 270
selflessness, 173
Seligman, Martin E. P., 200
Selmanovic, Samir, 77, 83
service, 101, 168, 173, 174, 189, 190, 218, 231, 242, 250, 269
sexism, 238, 239, 246, 248, 251–53, 255, 256, 266
sexuality, 77, 146, 147, 162, 181, 182, 239, 241, 242, 252–54
simplicity, 127–30
sinners, 94, 160, 161, 184, 269
skepticism, 8, 142, 159, 195, 197, 247, 263
slavery, 145
society, 11, 69–73, 75, 90–92, 99, 100, 105, 133, 144, 146, 156–58, 161, 166, 167, 174, 175, 177, 179, 215, 216, 218, 220, 222, 224, 225, 231, 233, 238–41, 243, 252, 254, 261, 268
socio-economics, 196, 205, 209, 252
sociology, 28, 45, 49, 50, 61, 68, 85–87, 134, 146, 155, 162, 188, 189, 214, 244, 248, 261, 263, 266
Sojourners, 220, 235, 259
solidarity, 67, 69, 72, 76, 90, 96, 118, 228
soteriology, 72, 78
soul, 90, 184
spirituality, 8, 10, 28, 40, 47, 49, 52, 58, 62, 67, 71–73, 78, 80, 84, 85, 87–89, 102–6, 118, 137, 141–44,

146, 148, 149, 153–63, 195, 198, 202, 213, 216–18, 224–26, 230, 232, 233, 249, 262, 266, 268, 270
St. Ambrose, 241
St. Augustine, 52, 241
St. Jerome, 241
St. Paul, 34
strangers, 120, 193
Strauss, Anslem, 86
students, 5–10, 13, 14, 30, 88, 103, 147–49, 151–53, 163, 165, 168, 174, 175, 180, 187, 217, 219
subculture, 62, 153, 214
subjectivity, 6, 11, 190, 212, 213
subjugated, 7
subordination, 241
suburban, 51, 89, 93, 95, 212–14, 217, 225, 227, 230, 233
suicide, 160
Sunday Assembly, 188–93, 197, 199–201, 203, 264, 268
supernatural, 111, 115–17, 119, 121, 122
superstition, 158
survival, 114, 116, 117, 121, 216, 227
symbiotic, 109, 132, 134
symbolism, 60, 77, 86, 223, 225, 233, 239, 241, 253, 257
syncretism, 45, 61–63, 147, 159
system, 12, 16, 37, 51, 59, 67, 75, 76, 78–81, 112, 114, 122, 124, 125, 127–29, 141, 145, 163, 175–79, 183, 189, 192, 201–4, 215, 216, 238, 239, 241, 244, 247, 248, 252, 253, 257, 266, 267
systemically, 252, 253

talking, 26, 27, 34, 35, 58, 223
tattoos, 249
teachings, 122, 155, 218, 239, 240
technology, 3, 8, 59, 71, 80, 141–43, 145, 147, 152, 153, 157, 158, 160, 196
terrorists, 76
testimony, 46, 126
texts, 10–12, 52, 55, 114, 128, 255
theatrics, 166, 167
theisms, 34, 35, 119–22, 124, 132, 162

theologians, 31, 32, 34, 40, 49, 77, 125, 188, 198, 215, 219, 221, 224, 239, 240, 244, 251, 253, 255–57, 264, 266

theology, 9, 10, 13, 16, 31, 32, 34, 36–38, 40, 45, 49, 53–55, 57, 58, 60, 62, 68, 73, 74, 78, 79, 81, 84–86, 88–95, 99, 101, 106, 113, 114, 117, 120–26, 129–32, 134, 147, 153, 154, 156, 160, 164, 181, 182, 188, 189, 198, 201–5, 212, 213, 216, 217, 219, 220, 222, 224, 229, 232, 236–39, 241, 243, 244, 246, 248–57, 261, 266

theory, 28, 70, 71, 86, 111, 113–16, 126–29, 131, 147, 151, 157, 195, 196, 237, 242, 254, 256

Thiessen, Joel, 86, 87, 107

Thomas, 68, 83, 204, 209, 241

Thomas Aquinas, 241

Thoreau, Henry David, 155

Tickle, Phyllis, 49, 50, 66, 75, 224, 264, 268

Tillich, Paul, 34, 41, 113, 131, 188, 189, 198, 201–4

tithe, 192, 193

tolerance, 5, 7, 8, 13–15, 25, 59, 72, 129, 132, 133, 176, 177, 181, 185, 219, 233

tradition, 3, 4, 6, 9, 10, 13, 14, 17, 28, 33, 36–38, 40, 41, 47, 52, 57–61, 63, 67, 68, 73, 74, 85, 88–90, 95–100, 102–5, 112–14, 119, 124, 125, 129–31, 134, 135, 141–43, 145–47, 149–56, 162, 163, 181, 182, 188, 192–95, 198, 202, 207, 216, 217, 226, 238, 240, 241, 243, 244, 249, 255, 257, 267, 269

transcendent, 34, 155, 162, 229

Transcendentalism, 154, 155

transience, 129, 133, 166, 167

transnational, 47, 68–72, 78, 80, 124, 159, 213, 214, 218, 224

transubstantiation, 124

Uganda, 220
unbeliever, 206

uncertainty, 4, 9, 10, 14, 112, 141, 157, 182, 205, 263, 264

unchristian, 25, 182, 206, 237

uniformity, 71, 128, 205, 206

unions, 170, 178

universal, 59, 67, 72, 77, 78, 81, 126, 155, 199

universalism, 58, 146, 191

urban, 40, 84, 85, 88–90, 92, 93, 95, 96, 101, 106, 196, 197, 223, 225, 227

values, 7–9, 11–13, 15, 16, 29, 49, 73, 75, 77, 80, 81, 88, 89, 100, 104, 126–29, 131–33, 147, 149, 150, 154, 161, 174, 175, 178, 189, 190, 193, 198–200, 202, 204–6, 218, 220, 224, 227, 230, 231, 233, 238, 239, 244, 246, 253–55, 257, 263

Van Wyngaard, Geroge Jacobus (Cobus), 219–21, 223, 232, 235

Vatican Council II, 240

Vedanta, 155

victimization, 232

Vietnam, 168

violence, 76, 157, 158, 221

vision, 84, 88–90, 92, 93, 98, 100–102, 160, 174, 190–92, 200, 203, 224, 229, 238, 242, 256, 257

volunteerism, 54, 75, 145, 168, 169, 172, 173, 192

wealth, 72, 76, 91, 151, 196, 215, 218, 219, 222, 226, 263

Weber, Max, 40, 81, 173, 186, 251

Weise, Wolfram, 216, 235

Westphalia, 66, 70, 78, 79

white, 9, 17, 33, 40, 77, 93, 172, 196, 197, 212–34, 236, 237, 244–48, 251, 266

Whitehead, Alfred North, 32, 35, 42, 127

White Supremacy, 212, 214, 216, 221, 222, 224, 232–34

Whitman, Walt, 155

Wiccans, 154

Wild Goose, 54, 166–68, 180

Wildman, Wesley, 118, 121, 134, 137

Wilkinson, Michael, 86, 88, 107
Williams, John, 69, 82
Winston, Kimberly, 194, 211
witchcraft, 154
Wittgenstein, Lugwig, 52, 111
Wolfensbirger, James, 150
Wollschleger, Jason, 161, 165
Womanist Theology, 256, 258
women, 35, 51, 152, 160, 220, 237, 239–42, 244–53, 255–57, 269
worldview, 7, 8, 81, 99, 103, 123, 141, 143–49, 153, 155, 158, 162, 163
worship, 47, 54, 58, 59, 77, 130, 153–55, 159–61, 184, 244

Wuthnow, Robert, 151, 157

Yazykova, Ekaterina, 144, 165
yoga, 146, 147, 155, 156
Young Leadership Network, 45, 50–56, 64, 68, 93, 101, 103, 191–93, 195, 216, 225, 230, 233, 237–40, 244, 245, 251, 252, 254–57, 266, 267
youth, 51, 53, 55, 89, 149, 159, 168, 171–73, 176, 216, 218, 232, 245
Youtube, 56, 152

www.ingramcontent.com/pod-product-compliance
Lightning Source LLC
Chambersburg PA
CBHW032052220426
43664CB00008B/967